ULRICH WILCKEN (1862-1944) was educated at Tübingen and Leipzig and worked in Berlin under Theodor Mommsen. He taught at a number of leading German universities and subsequently was made University Professor at Berlin and became a member of the German Academy. Wilcken wrote widely in the fields of ancient history, legal studies, paleography, and epigraphy and was one of the founders of papyrology. His *Alexander the Great* was first published in 1931.

ALEXANDER THE GREAT

BY

ULRICH WILCKEN

Translated by G. C. Richards

*With Preface, An Introduction to Alexander Studies,
Notes, and Bibliography by Eugene N. Borza*

W · W · NORTON & COMPANY

New York · London

ISBN 978-0-393-00381-9

W.W. Norton & Company, Inc.
500 Fifth Avenue, New York, N.Y. 10110
www.wwnorton.com
W.W. Norton & Company, Ltd.
Castle House, 75/76 Wells Street London WIT 3QT

4 5 6 7 8 9 0

CONTENTS

70690

EDITOR'S PREFACE

THIS VOLUME is an unaltered reprint of Wilcken's work in the translation of G. C. Richards. The editor regards seriously his obligation not to rewrite Wilcken nor even to engage in extended argument on disputed points. From time to time, however, it has been thought best to comment on Wilcken's narrative in places where either new information or new techniques have substantially altered our interpretations (Wilcken would certainly take these into account were he preparing a second edition himself), or where a number of alternative views of some importance exist and are cited for the convenience of the reader who wishes to pursue them. It is not the editor's intention to call into question every point in Alexander's life which has been the subject of disagreement. A full commentary of this sort would make the volume too cumbersome and probably deny Wilcken's *Alexander* the wider audience it deserves.

The purpose of this edition is to appeal to two main groups of readers: the general reader and undergraduate for whom Wilcken may serve as a worthy introduction to Alexander the Great, and the advanced student who must welcome the return to print of such a classic and may appreciate the attempt to complement it with some notes on recent studies. It is hoped that students will find the editor's introduction on the background of Alexander studies of aid and interest in determining Wilcken's place in modern scholarship, and that others will find useful the collection of notes and bibliographical entries, although no attempt has been made to make these complete. Sources have been cited from time to time in the hope that the reader will turn to the pages of these ancient authors to read of Alexander's exploits, for only in the sources can the real nature of the evidence be seen. A number of small errors, some pointed out by the original reviewers, have also been corrected in the notes.

One can read Wilcken through without reference to the notes and still observe what is perhaps the most balanced characterization of Alexander yet to appear. Wilcken's interpretation, however, is only one among many. We may argue about interpretations so long as we recognize that a variety of views can be justified if they are based on an intelligent analysis of the evidence. There are other interpretations of Alexander which are as legitimate as Wilcken's; each lends some new dimension to Alexander's character which enables the student to come to a closer understanding of what was probably a very complex man. Wilcken's *Alexander* still stands on its original merits, the last thirty-five years of scholarship not having produced serious doubts about the value of his portrait.

The editor wishes to thank his friend and colleague, Professor Anthony J. Podlecki, for his helpful comments on the introduction, and the editors of W. W. Norton & Company for their service in bringing Wilcken back into print.

E.N.B.

AN INTRODUCTION TO ALEXANDER STUDIES

IN SEARCH OF ALEXANDER

EVER SINCE HE emerged from a somewhat backward Macedonian nation to claim much of Greece and Asia as his own, Alexander the Great has exercised a secure hold on the human imagination. The nature of this attraction is a complex phenomenon. It is enough to say that there are many Alexanders, perhaps as many as there are those who profess a serious interest in him. The multifarious nature of Alexander requires a brief inquiry into a dilemma in which the modern student frequently finds himself.

One soon comes to recognize that he is really dealing with three Alexanders or, rather, Alexander on three sometimes distinct, sometimes not clearly separable planes. The first of these is the mythological-romantic Alexander. He is an Alexander who is said to appear in the literature of eighty nations ranging from the British Isles to the Malay Peninsula. He is a hero in many religious and secular forms in European medieval romance, a quasi-holy man in Talmudic literature, a saint in the Coptic church of Egypt, and a new Achilles in Greek tradition. His Persian name, Iskander, still evokes quick and strange reactions in some of the peoples who inhabit the desolate regions stretching from the Caspian to the headwaters of the Indus. The bitter memory of Alexander as conqueror is occasionally still so strong in local folklore that at least one recent Western traveler attempting to follow his track across Asia was abused with scorn by certain Afghan villagers merely because he had asked if Alexander had passed that way. According to the many legends he was a king, a hero, a god, a conqueror, a philosopher, a scientist, a prophet, a statesman, and a visionary whose ideals of universal brotherhood are said to have laid the basis for Stoic thought and predated

Christianity by three centuries. He was also a drunkard, a parricide, a thief, and a butcher. He has been accused of depravities base enough to offend the sensibilities of all the ages. In short, he is a giant in literature and folk tradition, and his name and exploits, fanciful or true, are probably more widely known than those of anyone until modern times.

The second Alexander is the historical Alexander. We know that with his father, Philip of Macedon, he subdued and organized the quarrelsome lot of Greek cities now past the prime of their Golden Age. Succeeding Philip, he crossed from Europe to Asia, and on the field of battle brought to an end the ancient but tottering majesty of the Persian Empire. Having fulfilled his role as the leader of a holy war against the traditional enemy, Alexander took an army to the Indus, the edge of the known world, and returned to expire in Babylon in his thirty-third year. Of this incredible expedition we know only the bare outlines, with an imperfect chronology. That he changed a part of the world through which he marched is certain, having laid the basis for the eventual introduction of Greek civilization into a vast area of Western Asia. This process of Hellenization resulted partly in the development of institutions which produced, among other things, Roman harmony and the Christian religion. His legacy includes that important and fascinating city in Egypt which still bears his name, as well as some twenty other Alexandrias, most crumbled beyond recognition across central Asia. The descendants of his soldiers may have influenced the anthropomorphic form which Buddha eventually took. And in certain remote valleys of the Karakoram there are men living today who appear to be Caucasians, speak Indo-Aryan languages, and trace their ancestry to Alexander's army. He ranks historically among the most important men who ever lived purely on the basis of his accomplishments and the change which he wrought on the history of that part of the world.

The third Alexander is Alexander the man. What makes an understanding of the real man difficult is the constant conflict between the mythological and historical figures. For Alexander became a legend virtually in his own era, and that legend, extended and corrupted throughout antiquity, has made him an enigma, affecting as it did every piece of serious or foolish writing about him.

Thus each man who approaches the study of Alexander is confronted with the mythological and historical figures. What he makes out of these is for him the real Alexander, an interpretation which becomes personal. The problems confronting the biographer of Alexander, although not unique, are nevertheless compounded by the poor state of the evidence. The biographer of Winston Churchill or Franklin Roosevelt is faced with a superabundance of material that makes impossible a truly comprehensive study of all the evidence. He must, therefore, employ screening devices which will enable him somehow to reduce great quantities of data to what is useful and germane. The interpretation which results will depend not only upon how the writer reads the evidence he has selected but also upon the conditions of the initial selection itself, the standards of relevance and priority which the writer attaches to data. In the case of the ancients, however, there can be no such arbitrary selection of evidence. Time and tide have performed the initial screening, and the few data which remain must be read in their entirety. The startlingly dissimilar portraits of Alexander which issue from modern historians can be attributed at least as much to the psychological predilections of the scholar as to the state of the evidence itself.[1] Ulrich Wilcken clearly recognized that the problem was personal in his preface where he suggests that "every student has an Alexander of his own." One of the most perceptive scholars working on Alexander in recent years put the case more strongly when he wrote, "We all interpret the great drama of Alexander in terms of our experience and our

[1] That the problem may be psychological is a suggestion of C. B. Welles in a provocative review of Fritz Schachermeyr's *Alexander der Grosse, Ingenium und Macht,* in *American Journal of Archaeology,* LV (1951), 433-36. The reluctance of one Alexander biographer to accept this view in its entirety can be seen in C. A. Robinson, Jr., "The Extraordinary Ideas of Alexander the Great," *American Historical Review,* LXII (1957), 326-44.

dreams." [2] This recalls what Theodor Mommsen once wrote in an only slightly different context: "Those who have lived through historical events, as I have, begin to see that history is neither written nor made without love or hate." [3]

MODERN STUDIES

It may be said that modern Alexander scholarship began in 1833 with the initial publication of a biography by Johann Gustav Droysen.[4] Droysen was a product of a nineteenth-century school of German historiography which had developed the principles of modern critical historical method. But more important, Droysen was deeply moved by the historical events of his own era. He saw Prussia emerge as a powerful German state, and throughout his life he pressed for the unification of the German peoples under Prussian leadership. Droysen was especially optimistic in 1848, and entering politics (in an era in which historians were not reluctant to participate in making history), he became a member of Parliament. His hopes for German unity were soon crushed, and, except for another brief return to the political arena in 1859, he spent the remaining years of his life in retirement, reworking his material on ancient history, and writing vigorously on Prussia and German unity.

In the light of his own historical experience and political orientation as a Prussian nationalist and fervent monarchist, Droysen's conception of Alexander should come as no surprise. The intricate problems of the Greek city-states in the Classical period, with their almost constant strife and internecine conflicts, were of little interest to Droysen. The Greeks had managed to keep the Persian menace away from the Greek mainland but just barely, and had not yet begun to fulfill what Droysen later conceived as their historical mission. Eventually, however, Philip of Macedon appeared. For Droysen, Philip is

[2] E. Badian, *Studies in Greek and Roman History* (New York, 1964), p. 192.
[3] Quoted by G. P. Gooch, *History and the Historians of the Nineteenth Century* (2nd ed., London, 1952), p. 462.
[4] This was followed in 1836-42 by work on Alexander's successors. Eventually both studies were fused in *Geschichte Hellenismus* (Gotha, 1877-87).

the great unifier of Greece, and his son, Alexander, the agent of the diffusion of Greek civilization. Alexander is the world-figure, the historical hero who ended one era and began a new and more glorious one. Here the nation and the great national leader emerge as dominant historical themes. The roles of Philip and Alexander as unifier and innovator respectively reflect Droysen's own experience in mid-nineteenth-century Germany. Moreover, it was Droysen who vigorously expounded the notion of Hellenism, that is, the fusion of Greek and Oriental cultures which Alexander wrought and which influenced the course of Mediterranean civilization throughout the rest of antiquity. Droysen's conceptions were propounded so forcefully that they have conditioned virtually all subsequent scholarship on the subject. For most of Droysen's successors Alexander remained a world-mover, although opinions have varied widely on his personal motives and the exact extent of his achievement.[5]

Serious biographical investigations of Alexander were not a pronounced feature of classical studies of the late nineteenth and early twentieth centuries. This period saw the introduction of increasingly sophisticated techniques of historical study, and especially the development of a number of ancillary disciplines such as papyrology, paleography, numismatics, and epigraphy. It was, moreover, a period of classifying and cataloging various kinds of evidence. Tens of thousands of inscriptions were collected, edited, and published, the texts of most well-known Greek and Latin writers were revised according to the latest philological and paleographical techniques, great lexicons of the ancient languages were produced, and monumental encyclopedias and bibliographical surveys were assembled. The British and German universities, where the spirit of

[5] G. Walser, "Zur neueren Forschung über Alexander den Grossen," *Schweizer Beiträge zur allemeinen Geschichte*, XIV (1956), 180–81, has taken the position that, while the technical methodology used in the study of history has improved constantly, virtually all subsequent biographies of Alexander are based squarely on Droysen. Walser goes so far as to call Wilcken's *Alexander* little more than a new edition of Droysen. The Walser article provides a well-ordered account of recent historical studies on important aspects of Alexander's career.

classical studies was strong, managed to authenticate and or-
ganize a valuable mass of detail and to provide scholarship
with the tools by which a deeper understanding of antiquity
was now possible.[6]

In 1926 Helmut Berve published his *Das Alexanderreich
auf prosopographischer Grundlage*. The German tradition of
careful classification bore fruit in this valuable work in which
all references to proper names in the ancient sources on Alexander were collected and arranged in encyclopedic form.
Thus in order to secure information about Alexander's comrade, Hephaestion, for example, one only need turn to Hephaestion's name in Berve, and read the entry which includes
citations to all the sources and a critical commentary on the
nature of the evidence. Then in 1927 there appeared the first
of the volumes in the series *Die Fragmente der griechischen
Historiker* (ed. F. Jacoby) which presented newly-edited texts
and commentary on hundreds of fragments of lost Alexander
historians. As a result of this tremendous burst of activity there
was now available a large body of well-organized and docu-
mented material for fresh studies of Alexander.

Twentieth-century Alexander biography took a new turn
with the appearance of the sixth volume of the *Cambridge
Ancient History* in which W. W. Tarn contributed an extensive account of the young Macedonian monarch. Tarn, who
remains the great Hellenistic historian of this century, had produced some short studies on Alexander earlier in which he developed ideas that were destined to make his Alexander the
most debated, if not the most famous, of the modern era. In effect, Tarn took the basic Droysen conception of Alexander as
world-mover and added to it the dimension of a new social

[6] It should be noted that a number of biographies of Alexander were
produced as separate monographs during this period, of which David
George Hogarth's *Philip and Alexander of Macedon. Two Essays in
Biography* (London, 1897) is one of the better examples. Moreover, following the lead of the modern "father of Greek history," George Grote,
a number of comprehensive histories of Greece also appeared; inasmuch
as Alexander was an important part of Greek history he was given some
prominence. The names of the historians Beloch, Busolt, Meyer, and
Berve are notable.

philosophy. Aristotle had taught that Greeks were fit to rule and aliens only to be ruled. But

when [Alexander] prayed for a union of hearts and a joint common-wealth of Macedonians and Persians, he proclaimed for the first time, through a brotherhood of peoples, the brotherhood of man. . . . Alexander inspired Zeno's vision of a world in which all men should be members one of another, citizens of one State without distinction of race or institutions, subject only to and in harmony with the Common Law immanent in the Universe, and united in one social life not by compulsion but only by their own willing consent or (as he put it) by Love.[7]

When Tarn's critics attacked his Alexander as being too idealistic, he replied in a paper that Alexander was indeed the first to contemplate the unity of mankind. He described this unity (using the Greek term *homonoia*) as one of the great revolutions in human thought.[8] Tarn was a lawyer by training, and the extraordinary attention he paid to evidence in order to support his case shows an acute mind at work. Poor health forced him to retire from the Bar in 1905, and he was thus enabled to devote the rest of his life to historical pursuits. Tarn was a man of some means and did not find it necessary to seek a university position as a means of support. Ensconced on his Scottish estate, with occasional trips to London to gather material, he lived the "good" life of the British upper class. One critic has referred to "the gentlemanly and sporting Alexander of Tarn," credited "with the extreme views toward life and death and honor, and temperance in love and wine which are associated with the English gentry." [9] Tarn's idealistic Alexander became the dominant portrait; beside it Wilcken's more reasonable and accurate (though perhaps less interesting) conception paled to all but the more serious students of the subject.

[7] *Cambridge Ancient History*, VI (Cambridge, 1927), 437.
[8] "Alexander the Great and the Unity of Mankind," *Proceedings of the British Academy*, XIX (1933), 123-66. See Richard A. Todd, "W. W. Tarn and the Alexander Ideal," *The Historian*, XXVII (1964), 48-55, who gives some interesting information on Tarn's own life, and also shows how several others of Tarn's Hellenistic monarchs shared in this idealism.
[9] C. B. Welles, pp. 433 and 436 (the latter a reference to Tarn?)

Partly in response to the criticism leveled at him, and surely in defense of a commitment to his hero, Tarn published in 1948 his *Alexander the Great* in two volumes.[10] The first volume is a short biography of Alexander, substantially a little-revised version of his earlier chapters in the *Cambridge Ancient History* in which the main theses about Alexander's motives and conceptions were stated with great vigor. Volume II, subtitled *Sources and Studies,* is an inspired and highly technical series of studies on the main problems in Alexander scholarship as well as a detailed consideration of the source problem. Whatever disagreements scholars were later to have with Tarn's views and conclusions, it is generally agreed that this single work marks a large step forward in the progress of modern Alexander scholarship, manifesting as it does the careful work and erudition with which the author built his portrait.

In reaction to Tarn's idealizing portrait, A. R. Burn cast Alexander in a different mold.[11] An excellent general, a powerful ruler, a forceful personality, Burn's Alexander nonetheless made rather little impact outside the Greco-Roman world. His empire collapsed, and even the mythology surrounding his personality, which eventually came to form such a wide-ranging tradition in Asian folklore, was really only the product of the classical Romance of Pseudo-Callisthenes. For Burn, Alexander's only real achievement was in extending Greek influence into the East, but this put a strain on Hellenism which eventually exhausted it and prevented the Greeks from ever marshalling enough strength to ward off Roman domination. Perhaps no modern writer has argued so strongly against the standard interpretation of Alexander as a historical hero.[12]

10 (Cambridge, 1948). Volume I has been reprinted in paperback by Beacon Press (Boston, 1956).
11 *Alexander the Great and the Hellenistic Empire* (London, 1947), now in a paperback edition as *Alexander the Great and the Hellenistic World* (New York, 1962).
12 Burn's view has been echoed more recently in an essay by C. B. Welles, "Alexander's Historical Achievement," *Greece and Rome,* 2nd ser., XII (1965), 216-28.

In 1949, F. Schachermeyr published his *Alexander der Grosse, Ingenium und Macht*, and introduced an Alexander who, according to one reviewer, was a "conception which would have been impossible before Hitler and World War II." [13] Schachermeyr's Alexander was a brilliant, though ruthless, man of ambition who found the framework of Macedon too restrictive and so set out to expand his personal world as well as his kingdom. Possessed of an awesome ego and a seemingly limitless capacity to act decisively, this Alexander successfully threw off the strictures of the Macedonian feudal nobility and emerged in Asia as a Titan of the first rank. Ruthless, forceful and mystical, he destroyed an old order and established a new World-State centered on his own personality. Behaving "like a young Nazi let loose in the Alps," [14] he showed himself capable of dreaming the dream of world conquest and achieving it. Such is Schachermeyr's conception, conditioned in part by a tradition begun by Droysen, but certainly more recently intensified by the author's own experience in Germany. Schachermeyr finally pleads that the world has seen enough Titans, let us be spared another.

In recent years the work of Ernst Badian has contributed much to our understanding of Alexander by bringing to bear upon the work of Tarn and others a most perceptive kind of criticism. Badian has taken a portion of Schachermeyr's view that Alexander was seeking horizons larger than the kingdom of Macedon. Raised to the throne by nobles who expected to rule through him, Alexander soon recognized that he had to assert his independence from the various Macedonian factions for whom he was a puppet. As success piled upon success on the battlefields of Asia, Alexander began to replace the older Macedonians with his own men; he purged others from his court and in doing so emerged as a king in his own right. The price he paid for his freedom, however, was a barrier erected between himself and his European traditions, for as Alexander dissociated himself from his background he began to assume many of the trappings of an Oriental despot. He was never

---

[13] Welles' review in *American Journal of Archaeology*, LV (1951), 434.
[14] The comment is Burn's; see *Classical Review*, N.S. I (1951), 101.

able to return from the summit of power which was also a peak of loneliness. Badian has not produced a full biographical treatment (one eagerly hopes that he will), but the Alexander who has begun to emerge from a series of technical and popular articles is a man who reaches the pinnacle of success only to find himself alone, cut off from his own traditions, and made ruthless by insecurity.[15] Badian's Alexander is essentially a pragmatist, unpossessed of the philosophical world-view attributed to him by Tarn, but perfectly willing from time to time to exploit any convenient myth to reach his goal. This is an amoral Alexander, concerned almost entirely with the struggle to secure his position as absolute ruler. In the course of achieving this end, and abetted by his own enormous talents, he ended one era and began another. It is still the picture of the world-mover, albeit one whose motives are intimately connected with his own ambition and design for survival.

Georges Radet produced a mystical Alexander, convinced of his own divine origin, seeking his apotheosis in India, and acting out the *Iliad*.[16] Radet's fascinating story is a modern Romance, set in a religious and political framework, but it adds a dimension to Alexander's character which is attractive to the modern reader and which helps explain the charismatic hold the subject has always maintained on the audience. C. A. Robinson, Jr., following in the tradition of Tarn, accepted the idea of Alexander's dream of the Brotherhood of Man.[17] Robinson's portrait tends to cast Alexander in a favorable light, and avoids many of the traditions hostile to the king. And there are other Alexanders. A survey of the literature indicates that since Wilcken's biography (1931) alone, there have appeared over fifty serious biographical studies, two dozen works of fiction, including novels, poetry, and drama, and a number of translations and critical essays on older epics. There can be no question of the popularity of Alexander continuing unabated in the modern period.

[15] The best exposition of this view can be found in "Alexander the Great and the Loneliness of Power," in Badian's *Studies in Greek and Roman History*.
[16] *Alexandre le Grand* (Paris, 1931).
[17] In his *Alexander the Great. Meeting of East and West in World Government and Brotherhood* (New York, 1947).

ULRICH WILCKEN

Ulrich Emil Elias Friedrich Wilhelm Wilcken was born at Stettin (now Szczecin) on December 18, 1862. Wilcken began his formal training at Tübingen, moved to Leipzig where he studied Egyptology and Assyriology, and came ultimately to Berlin to work with Theodor Mommsen. A dissertation on the history of Roman Egypt enabled the young scholar to qualify as an assistant in Egyptian studies at the Berlin Museum, where by 1883 he was put in charge of a modest collection of papyrus documents. During the next three decades Wilcken taught successively at Breslau (where he was made University Professor in 1891), Würzburg, Halle, Leipzig, Bonn, and Munich before returning to Berlin as the successor to Otto Hirschfeld. In 1921 Wilcken became a member of the German Academy at Berlin. It was during this initial phase of his scholarly career that he established himself as one of the founders of papyrology. The sands of Egypt having only recently yielded up a number of precious papyrus documents, papyrology was still a fledgling in the closing decades of the nineteenth century. Wilcken traveled throughout Europe examining papyrus collections. Utilizing his excellent background in both Egyptian and classical studies, he became a self-taught expert of the first rank. Many years later, in recognition of his pioneering work in this exacting discipline, the international fraternity of scholars hailed him on his seventieth birthday as the *princeps papyrologorum*.

Wilcken's interests expanded rapidly. In 1899 he published two volumes on Greek ostraka in Egypt and Nubia, a work which was immediately recognized as an important essay in economic history. Very early this brilliant German had recognized that the study of papyri or ostraka was not an end in itself but rather a means to a clearer understanding of the larger historical scene. He became more involved in the study of Hellenistic Egypt and in 1917 and 1921 published materials on Alexander, the Hellenistic economic system, and Ptolemaic mercantilism. Wilcken's economic views will be apparent to the reader of *Alexander the Great*. The last chapter, especially, gives to Alexander and his successors probably the broadest economic orientation yet attempted. Wilcken was among that group of European historians who saw the importance of applying the new intellectual disciplines to the study of history. In 1924 Wilcken produced his *Griechische Geschichte in Rahmen der Altertumsgeschichte,* a textbook for students and teachers which has appeared in its eighth edition as late as 1958. The 1930's were for Wilcken a particularly productive period. History, papyrology, legal studies, paleography, and epigraphy all came into his province; it was during this decade that *Alexander der Grosse* appeared along with a number of shorter studies on the Macedonian king. The Second World War curbed Wilcken's activities as it did the efforts of many European scholars. We are told that the political events of that era angered and saddened him. Soon after celebrating his eightieth birthday in 1942, Wilcken left Berlin because of failing health and the increasing severity of Allied air raids. On December 10, 1944, he died in Baden-Baden.[18]

Alexander der Grosse was published in Leipzig in 1931 and within two years saw its English and French translations. Its reception was immediate and enthusiastic. Reviews of the time heralded it as an "amazingly complete and accurate picture," the "best biography of Alexander to date," and "a masterpiece of historical interpretation." There were some unfavorable comments from reviewers who noted errors in minor details or objected to the skimpy notes (a just criticism for serious students of the subject), or disagreed with particular interpreta-

18 Published biographical material about Wilcken is difficult to secure. He had the bad luck (this would fit his view of history) to spend his last years in the chaos of wartime Germany. During this period many European journals which would otherwise note his passing either suspended or reduced their publishing activities. In the immediate postwar period it was often difficult to reconstitute the scholarly societies and periodicals, especially in those nations which had suffered heavy devastation. Thus the death of an important scholar received far less attention than usual. A memorial notice by Matthias Gelzer can be found in the *Jahrbuch der Deutschen Akademie der Wissenschaften zu Berlin, 1946-49* (Berlin, 1950), pp. 244-51. A short summary of Wilcken's life by Wilhelm Schubart, emphasizing his contribution as a founding father of papyrology, appears in *Gnomon,* XXI (1949), 88-90.

tions of Alexander's personality and plans.[19] To suggest here exactly what Wilcken's Alexander is would anticipate his own narrative. Let it suffice to mention that Wilcken continued in the tradition established by Droysen. Wilcken's Alexander is an important historical figure; he does not, however, possess all of the idealism which Tarn attributed to him. For Wilcken, Alexander is essentially unmotivated by any large preconceived plan, but is one who, in most cases, reacts rationally to those historical circumstances which in time placed him in a position of great power.

THE SOURCE PROBLEM

Our literary evidence for Alexander's life is scanty, resting almost entirely on five biographical or historical accounts plus one Romance surviving from antiquity. In chronological order, these writers are Diodorus, a Sicilian Greek of the mid-first century B.C., who composed a universal history in forty books, fifteen of which survive and one of which (Book Seventeen) deals entirely with Alexander. Quintus Curtius was a Latin author of the mid-first century A.D. whose only known work was a *History of Alexander* in ten books, most of which survive. Possibly the most famous of the ancient writers on Alexander was the moral essayist and biographer, Plutarch, whose *Life of Alexander* was composed early in the second century. Also dating from the second century is an abbreviated account of Alexander in the works of Justin. Justin, however, is nothing more than an epitome of an earlier general history by Pompeius Trogus; it is unfortunate that Trogus is lost, for Justin must be a poor reflection of the original. Finally, there survives in complete form the *Anabasis of Alexander* by Arrian, written about the middle of the second century, the most

---

[19] Some of the English-speaking reviewers included C. A. Robinson, Jr., *American Journal of Philology*, LIII (1932), 383-85, and W. W. Tarn, *Classical Review*, XLVI (1932), 216, both of whom had fundamentally different interpretations of Alexander. Other conveniently available reviews are those of W. S. Ferguson, *American Historical Review*, XXXVII (1932), 528-29, and an excellent analysis by J. A. O. Larsen, *Classical Philology*, XXVII (1932), 97-98.

complete and reliable account we possess. One should note also a version of the popular Romance of Alexander which has come down to us in its early fourth-century form. While interesting as a reflection of the classical Romantic tradition about Alexander, little of the Romance can be considered as serious history.[20]

It should be noted that the earliest of our surviving accounts, that of Diodorus, was written nearly three centuries after Alexander's death, and the best version, Arrian, about two centuries later. The most immediate questions facing the modern student, therefore, relate to the sources and traditions which the surviving writers followed. The issue is complicated by the fact that most literature of the Hellenistic period is lost, including the many accounts known to have been written about Alexander in the period immediately after his death. We are, however, not entirely ignorant of the Hellenistic traditions about Alexander. Hundreds of fragments from dozens of lost Alexander historians exist in the works of later classical authors. For example, Plutarch (*Alexander* 54) says: "Chares of Mitylene relates that once during a banquet, Alexander, after drinking, gave the cup to one of his friends . . ." The beginning of this passage shows that Plutarch had either first- or second-hand knowledge of a statement of an earlier writer on Alexander whose name was Chares, whom he quoted for a banquet story, and whose work is lost except for about

[20] The reader interested in English translations of the sources might find the following useful: the only modern English version of Diodorus' Book 17 is that of C. Bradford Welles in the Loeb Classical Library (London and Cambridge, Mass., 1963) ; the sole modern English rendition of Curtius is John C. Rolfe's in the same series (2 vols.; London and Cambridge, Mass., 1946) ; the only English translation of Justin is by J. S. Watson, *Justin, Cornelius Nepos and Eutropius*, in Bohn's Library (London, 1853) , although this is rather difficult to come by; Plutarch's *Alexander* is widely available in a number of paperback translations, usually as a part of a collection of a number of his *Lives;* Arrian is in a version by E. Iliff Robson in the Loeb Classical Library (2 vols.; London and Cambridge, Mass., 1929-33), and more recently by Aubrey de Selincourt in Penguin Classics (1958). The classical Romance can be found in a translation by Elizabeth Hazelton Haight, *The Life of Alexander of Macedon* (New York, 1955).

twenty such fragments. Of some of these lost historians enough fragments have survived to enable the modern scholar to construct some kind of view of the writer's work, and in some cases even criticize our surviving writers on the basis of how dependable their sources seem.[21] Thus a picture, a blurred one, has evolved out of our attempts to reconstruct a three-century-long Hellenistic tradition about Alexander. We know, for example, that Alexander was a most popular figure in serious historical writing and in fiction, that he acquired the epithet "the Great," that famous Romans were compared (or compared themselves) to him, and that his final resting place in Alexandria became a pilgrimage stop for famous men. Alexander stories apparently were common, and, true or not, eventually formed a body of literature only a fraction of which survives.

The original account of Alexander's Asian expedition may have come from Callisthenes of Olynthus. Callisthenes bore the distinction of being the nephew of Aristotle, and may have been recommended to Alexander by his famous tutor. Callisthenes had already established himself as one of the foremost historians of fourth-century Greece, and may have eagerly anticipated becoming the chronicler for the ambitious young king. The task given him by Alexander was two-fold: to keep an official history of the Asian expedition, and to submit frequent accounts to be returned and published in Greece. Macedonian rule did not sit well with the Greeks; although they were perfectly willing to support Alexander in Asia where he would be little trouble to them, they did not really like him. So it became Callisthenes' responsibility to make Alexander more acceptable to the Greeks, to publish reports of the king's activities which would convince the Hellenes that their ruler was not a backwoods Macedonian boor.

[21] The texts and commentary on the fragments are in F. Jacoby, *Die Fragmente der griechischen Historiker*, IIB and IID (Berlin, 1927-30). Translations of the fragments have been collected by C. A. Robinson, Jr., *The History of Alexander the Great*, I (Providence, 1953). The most comprehensive analysis of the whole problem of the Hellenistic tradition is Lionel Pearson's *The Lost Histories of Alexander the Great*, American Philological Association Monographs, No. XX (New York, 1960).

In time, however, the relationship between the king and the historian degenerated over the issue of Alexander's adoption of certain Asiatic ceremonial customs, a feature of court life against which even the flatterer Callisthenes protested. Eventually Callisthenes was arrested and executed. The death of Callisthenes in 327 B.C. may have had a profound effect on the transmission of the Alexander story. First, it brought to a halt the "official" accounts, both the propaganda being sent to Greece, and the chronicle Callisthenes was keeping. Second, his death may have set in motion a reaction against Alexander among the members of Aristotle's school. It has been suggested that many of Aristotle's followers, which included some of the foremost writers and thinkers of the day, adopted a hostile attitude toward Alexander because of the execution of the great philosopher's nephew. The anti-Alexander bias may have come into the accounts which survive to this day. Thus much of the later tradition about Alexander may be based not only on the flattering accounts of Callisthenes himself, but also on this post-Callisthenean hostility.[22]

Another primary Hellenistic tradition was based on personal recollections. Alexander had failed to nominate a successor. Almost immediately after his death, the whole of the eastern Mediterranean and western Asia was caught up in a fierce war among his commanders. This struggle for succession continued for about two decades. By the beginning of the third century B.C., however, the issues had been resolved enough to bring about the division of Alexander's old empire into a number of Hellenistic kingdoms. Moreover, now that the war was over, some of the generals who had fought at Alexander's side began to write their memoirs (generals in every age have never refrained through modesty from putting pen to paper). The most important of these accounts was that of Ptolemy. Ptolemy,

---

[22] The exact nature of this hostile tradition has been widely debated in recent years: its origins and status in antiquity are still open to question. The staunchest defender of the existence of this hostile "Peripatetic" tradition is Tarn, *Alexander the Great*, II, 69, n. 1, 96-97, 131. The severest criticism has been that of Badian; see his "The Eunuch Bagoas," *Classical Quarterly*, N.S. VIII (1958), 153-57.

who had served under Alexander, managed to establish himself on the throne of Egypt, whence he founded that race of dynasts whose rule over the Land of the Nile ended three centuries later with the death of Cleopatra. Ptolemy's account of Alexander centered around military affairs, was generally favorable to the king, and may have been designed in part to justify the legitimacy of the author's grip on the rich prize of Egypt. Much of Ptolemy survives in the work of Arrian, our best extant source.

A number of other accounts appeared about the same time, some the personal experiences of those who had accompanied Alexander, others based on hearsay reports of what had happened, and still others concerned only with exotica and filled with the magical wonders of the mysterious East. In all there survive more than four hundred fragments from nearly thirty lost writers whose works were written between Alexander's death and our earliest account, that of Diodorus. Some of these works, as indicated, were serious history or biography, some were concerned only with Asian marvels, some were the products of the rhetorical schools of Alexandria. Our evaluation of the surviving sources depends in part, therefore, on what has been pieced together about the Hellenistic tradition.

It is agreed that Arrian provides the most reliable ancient evidence, even though he is furthest removed (some five centuries) from the events themselves. Arrian ranks first because he names his sources, he makes clear from time to time the critical method which he is employing, and he does not appear to possess any excessive prejudice about his subject. Moreover, Arrian depended on sources who were contemporaries of Alexander and presumably were in a position to know what had happened. Their proximity to the events, however, does not necessarily guarantee that they always spoke the truth, and Arrian himself exhibits an astonishing naiveté by telling us in his preface: "It seems to me that Ptolemy and Aristobulus are more trustworthy in their narratives, for Aristobulus took to the field with King Alexander; Ptolemy not only also campaigned with him, but being a king himself, to speak falsely would be more shameful to him than to another." We know that kings are not only capable of lying, but that they might have more than ordinary cause to lie if their accounts are in part designed to justify their crowns. This is not to say that Ptolemy did speak falsehoods (as a matter of fact his account, at least that part of it preserved in Arrian, appears to be rather straightforward), but that he, like ordinary men, was not incapable of it.[23]

Of the remaining four accounts, Justin may be dismissed, in Wilcken's words, as a "wretched excerpt" on Alexander although it may yet prove valuable in future attempts to reconstruct the history of his source, Pompeius Trogus. Plutarch's *Alexander* is fascinating and complex. It is especially valuable for a reconstruction of the intrigue at the Macedonian court which led to Philip's death and the succession of Alexander. On the whole, Plutarch's narrative is favorable to Alexander, touches on romance in places, and appears to be derived from a number of sources, some of whom he names. To judge from the number of other writers he quotes, Plutarch was one of the best-read men of antiquity. No one has yet succeeded in establishing the underlying tradition of his *Alexander*. It may be that his eclectic manner of composition makes this impossible.

Diodorus presents even greater problems. Nowhere in his book on Alexander does he name a source, although he shares much with both Plutarch and Arrian. Diodorus' account is generally colorless, frequently confused on questions of chronology and geography, and lacking in the recognition of any great theme or motive in Alexander's life beyond the role which Fortune (*Tychê*) plays in determining the course of men's affairs. This is an author who contains much good material, but who must be used with care and common sense until more can be said about his methods and the traditions he

---

[23] No one is certain about the purpose of Ptolemy's history. It may have been merely the exercise of an old man, secure on his throne and looking back on the excitement of an earlier era; it may have had some political purpose. E. Badian, *Gnomon*, XXXIII (1961), 666, thinks that Arrian's naiveté is not as great as usually suggested, but that he did fail to recognize that kings are more tempted to lie when it appears they cannot be detected.

followed.

Curtius provides us with the most colorful of the surviving historical accounts. His *History of Alexander* is highly rhetorical, riddled with impossible speeches, and contains a well-defined unflattering tradition. Its fullness also supplies information about a number of events hardly recorded elsewhere, although it is frequently difficult to determine to what extent such matters are credible. The nature of Curtius' *History* is such that it has led modern critics to suspect that his main source was Cleitarchus, an extremely popular author who probably wrote in the early third century B.C., and whose flamboyant account of Alexander's exploits may have been the most widely-known in the classical world.[24] Moreover, Curtius even mentions Cleitarchus' name on two occasions, and if Curtius did indeed rely heavily on Cleitarchus, about whom classical antiquity had a low opinion as a reliable historian, then Curtius' account is at least suspect.[25]

Such is the state of our literary evidence for the life of Alexander. The interpretations of his career which have emerged rest mainly on this small group of sources. Alexander's biographers differ depending upon which of the sources each chooses to trust: accept Curtius here, reject Arrian there, accept Diodorus here, reject Plutarch there, etc. Some modern writers reached the point in their investigations where a conception of Alexander became rather fixed, and they began to reject or accept evidence depending upon whether that evidence was consistent with their characterization.[26] There is no

[24] No less than nineteen different ancient writers mention Cleitarchus' name.

[25] The traditional view that Curtius depends heavily on Cleitarchus is dubious. That Curtius mentions Cleitarchus' name twice is in itself no proof that Curtius actually used him as a source; he may have relied on Cleitarchus through some intermediate account, or through a collection of rhetorical sayings which included some quotations from Cleitarchus. Moreover, not enough of Cleitarchus remains (thirty-six fragments) to establish anything beyond tenuous conjecture about the *content* of his work. We possess many opinions and criticisms of Cleitarchus from ancient writers, but unless we know more about Cleitarchus' writing itself, it is dangerous to make close comparisons with any surviving authors. Finally, the highly rhetorical style of Curtius may after all be due not to Cleitarchus, but to a fashion of Curtius' own day.

need to point out the danger here. Yet the trap is easily sprung when the evidence is so minute and frequently confusing; moreover, the modern student, perhaps influenced by behavioral studies, sometimes feels constrained to seek patterns of order in Alexander's character. But why must Alexander (or any other historical figure) be marked by consistent behavior? Must there necessarily be something systematic about Alexander's actions? [27] Might it not be true, for example, that Alexander was capable of brutality *and* kindness, depending upon his mood, or what suited his purposes at the moment? There also might be mixed in his nature more than a little mystical and non-rational behavior not in keeping with the normal portrait of a shrewd soldier and calculating statesman.

Wilcken's biography of Alexander has endured, for it recognizes the complexity of the man. It does not attempt to cast him into a particular mold. It portrays him as an individual of shifting moods and ambitions whose horizons were enlarged as success brought power and opportunity. Wilcken's Alexander is no ordinary man; no one who accomplished what he did in so short a time can be ordinary, yet for Wilcken he remains human. It was Alexander's lot that to act as a human being was to move on a vast stage, affecting the lives of countless persons in his own day and capturing the fancies of those who lived after.

EUGENE N. BORZA

[26] W. W. Tarn, especially, chose to evaluate sources according to his view of Alexander's character and motives. This became a problem for him when he came to evidence alluding to excessive drinking, murder, and homosexual behavior. See Tarn's *Alexander the Great*, II, 260-62 and 319-23, where he must prove his sources wrong by arguing historical characters out of existence in order to protect Alexander's reputation. For an excellent criticism of Tarn's methodology see Badian, *Classical Quarterly*, VIII (1958), 144-57.

[27] A. J. P. Taylor comments in another context: "In my opinion, statesmen are too absorbed by events to follow a preconceived plan. They take one step, and the next follows from it. The systems are created by historians . . ."; *The Origins of the Second World War* (London, 1961), p. 69.

PREFACE

It is no light task to write the story of Alexander's unique life in a continuous form, owing to the gaps and distortions of the traditional account: it is doubly difficult when the description is intended in the first instance for the general public of educated readers with their different interests and varied attitudes to the ancient world. Alexander is no easy personality to grasp. Since Droysen, in 1833, paved the way for future students by the brilliant work, in which he made his début, such different conceptions of the great monarch have been put forward that it is hardly an exaggeration to say that every student has an Alexander of his own.

How comes it that after a century of zealous study Alexander is still a problem and subject of controversy? In the first place the fragmentary character of our tradition is to be taken into account. The dominating influence of classicism in the Imperial Age brought about the loss of Hellenistic prose generally, and in particular the whole of the literary work on Alexander between his lifetime and the reign of Augustus. It is only because later writers made use of them that we can form approximate ideas of the older authors who wrote either in Alexander's lifetime or soon afterwards, such as Callisthenes, Onesicritus, Nearchus and others, or Cleitarchus, who about 310 B.C. created the—already in part legendary—Vulgate, or Aristo- * bulus and Ptolemy, son of Lagus, who as king of Egypt wrote, from personal recollection and with use of Alexander's official diaries, his memoirs, which are so important in military matters. The comprehensive narratives preserved to us start only with the age of Augustus. First we have Diodorus and Trogus Pompeius, the latter only in Justin's wretched excerpt of the second century: then comes Curtius Rufus in the reign of Vespasian, and finally Plutarch and Arrian in the second century. The three first-named in the main draw their information from Cleitarchus. We owe it to Arrian that we are so well informed about Alexander's military exploits; for these Ptolemy was his chief authority. As soon however as we attempt to estimate Alexander as statesman or economist, or try to grasp his inner life and his personality as a whole, we find that we are faced by what can only be described as a heap of ruins.

Secondly, in this ancient literature itself there are diametrically opposite conceptions and estimates of Alexander. On the one hand we have favourable, nay panegyrical pictures; on the other depreciatory, even hostile judgments which represent him as a despot made degenerate by the East or as an adventurer owing everything to luck. This twofold character of tradition has contributed to cause the wide divergences among modern writers in their treatment of the problem.

The greatest difficulty of all lies in Alexander's own personality. Not only was his character very complex and contained apparently irreconcilable opposites, but there was in him a superhuman quality; and genius is never quite capable of explanation, and must remain to us miraculous. The riddle of his life cannot be solved by resort to reason alone, for alongside of a clear and sober intellect he had in him much that was non-rational. To regard him simply as a coolly calculating politician is to overlook the romantic and mystical traits in his nature.

Lastly, a judgment of his achievements is rendered more puzzling by the fact that a premature death carried him off in the middle of his creative activity. We have before us only beginnings, and in no single instance was the last word spoken.

The study of history can offer no harder task than the attempt to get hold of the real personality of Alexander. No one will be presumptuous enough to imagine that he has taken his true portrait. But to approximate to it is a tempting enterprise, and one which carries with it its own reward. As it has attracted many inquirers in our own day, so it has been my pursuit from earliest youth. My object in this book is to represent the growth and development of Alexander's personality, which was in a constant process of evolution, and to show how ideas successively sprang up and ripened in his mind. It is in this sense that I have tried to give the reader a connected narrative of his life. I have introduced it with a sketch of the age into which he was born, and added at the end a survey of the effects on future ages of his life's work.

ULRICH WILCKEN

Berlin, *January* 1931.

THE CONQUESTS

R. Jaxartes Sr Doria)

Lake
Aral

SACAE

CHOR   MIA
                                    Alexandreschate
MASSA ETAE   (Chodjend)

Oxus (Amu Doria)

Marakanda
SOG   IANA
Nautaca

S E A

B A C
Zariaspa
(*Bactra*)

Drapsaca   Western
                            Himalayas

I A

OS (Hindu Kush)

adracarta   Aornos
Hecatompylos
ARDI   T   ila
PARTHIA   u
hagae   Artacoena   R H   Acesines
             Alexandria Arion   H rooted
I A   (*Herat*)   A R I A   Parepa   host   dras

(Salt Desert)   RAN   ANA   30

NA   lexandria A   ot   HOSIA
            CARMANIA   (Cand   R Pe
                                R Indus
PI
         Pasargadae   of Craterus
         Persepolis   Return of Craterus
                                       (*Shikarpore*)
S I S   GEDROSIA   R. Indus
         Alexandria   Old course of Indus   INDIA
         (*Gula.   rd*)   · Pura

IAN   GULF   Pattala

I N D I A N   O C E A N

R.C.

OF ALEXANDER

PART I

PROLOGUE

[Alexander represents the whole course of Greek life, for he has as much of Achilles as of Epaminondas; he has even something of the spirit of Pericles, political insight and love of beauty and truth. In him even more than in Alcibiades nature showed her power, and he did not waste her gifts like Alcibiades; fortified by a good education, which Alcibiades did not enjoy, he was able to devote these gifts to great tasks, and in his short life he did little harm, and much good.

A. HOLM

History and poetry seem to have taken Alexander as the type of an ambitious warrior. The phrase 'Macedonia's madman', and the circumstance of his weeping for worlds to conquer, hardly convey a correct idea of one whose views of glory were so intimately connected with the effects his conquests were to produce. From Alexandria to Candahar the unlettered do him more justice.

G. FINLAY]

INTRODUCTION

ALEXANDER THE GREAT opened a new era in the history of the world, and by his life's work determined its development for many centuries. He is conspicuous among the great men of history, because this work was accomplished in so short a span; when he died, he had not yet reached his thirty-third year. It was as a great conqueror that he impressed the popular imagination of every race. He subdued the East and penetrated into India, that land of wonders. The legend about him, equally current in East and West, took him to the limits of the earth and even to the gates of Paradise. The permanent result of his life, however, was not the empire which he won by hard fighting, but the development of Greek civilisation into a civilisation which was world-wide. It is in this way that his influence has affected the history of mankind even down to our own time. He had first to create his empire; the decision of the battle-field had, as usual, to produce the external conditions for the new civilisation.

In the disputed question, what are the forces which make and mould history, Alexander is the strongest instance in favour of the view which maintains the decisive importance of personality. One cannot comprehend a genius like Alexander from the surroundings in which he lived, or as a product of his age and country. He was of course like any other man affected by his period and birthplace, but his spirit took a course of its own, to which the natural development of his age and surroundings would never have led by itself. Like every great leader of men he threw himself into the currents of his epoch; but he did not allow himself to be merely lifted and carried forward on their waves—where they were in opposition to his own ideas, he vigorously struggled against them. No doubt we can trace before him in the fourth century phenomena and tendencies, which we may regard as forerunners of Hellenism—the name we apply to the later transformation of the classical Hellenic world that he inaugurated—and yet they are only forerunners, to which he first gave full effect; they show that in many respects he only fulfilled the aims of his own time. The preliminary work of his great father Philip was most important. From him he inherited not only the instrument of victory, the incomparable Macedonian army, but also the solution of the Greek question in the Corinthian League, and the idea of a Panhellenic campaign of *revanche* against Persia.

Doubtless, in pursuance of his own ideas, Alexander gradually modified this inheritance and diverged from his father's path; but without Philip, who is equally one of the great personalities of the world's history, Alexander cannot be understood. We shall therefore have first to present to ourselves the political, intellectual and economic tendencies in the Greek world of the fourth century, so far as they contribute to an estimate of the rise of Macedonia under Philip and to our appreciation of Alexander.

CHAPTER I

THE GREEK WORLD IN THE FOURTH CENTURY DOWN TO PHILIP

AFTER the collapse of Athens and the Athenian Empire in the Peloponnesian War, Sparta was left victor and proceeded with brutal violence to establish her supremacy over the Greeks and to introduce oligarchic institutions in place of the democracies previously favoured by Athens. The victory, however, had not been won by her own strength, but only through the scandalous alliance with Persia, which was purchased by the sacrifice to the Great King of their brethren of Asia Minor, the descendants of the old Aeolian, Ionian and Dorian colonists.

Irritated by the senseless attitude of the radical democrats of Athens, who, in spite of the renewal of the Peace of Callias by Darius II, had interfered with the internal affairs of the Persian Empire, the Great King had since 412 supported the Spartans with his inexhaustible purse. In return for this they were prepared, without any nationalistic qualms, to surrender to him the Greeks of Asia Minor, for whose liberation the Delian League organised by Athens had fought under Athenian leadership down to 448, when we may date the Peace of Callias. It was Persian gold that built the fleets with which the Spartans overcame the resistance of Athens and finally (404) starved it into surrender, and thus at one stroke the Persian Empire, in spite of internal weakness, had become the determining factor in Greek history. It is true that Sparta, who soon fell out with her ally, and had already compromised herself at Susa

by her secret support of prince Cyrus in his march with
the famous Ten Thousand against his brother Artaxerxes
Mnemon, drew the sword against Persia, according to the
official account, in order to protect the Asiatic Greeks, who
were about to be punished for their participation in that
expedition. But patriotic motives can hardly have been
the deciding factor with the Spartans, who had previously
in cold blood awarded those cities to the Persians; it was,
rather, the desire to retain the powerful position which
they had won in Asia Minor, chiefly through the great
Lysander, and perhaps also the wish, as lords of Greece, to
purge themselves of the stain of the Persian alliance.

But while Sparta's armies, first under other commanders
and finally under Agesilaus, were fighting the Persians overseas, at home the hatred evoked by the brutal reign of
force the Spartans had exercised there brought together
Thebes, Athens, Corinth and Argos in a coalition, which
compelled Agesilaus to break off the war with Persia and
to fight in Hellas against the allies. Then again Persian
gold played its part, this time on the side of the allies.
More decisive in its effects than the victory of Agesilaus at
Coroneia was the victory of the Persian fleet at Cnidus
under the command of the Athenian Conon (394); this
meant the collapse of Spartan power at sea, and Conon
was able to have the walls of his native city rebuilt, though
by Persian money. This melancholy civil war, however,
which shockingly exhibits the miserable and incurable
divisions of the Greek nation, continued with varying
success for many years.

After the rise of Athens had emboldened the Athenians
to support the revolt from Persia of the Cypriot prince
Euagoras and the rebellion of Egypt, and had by a
new grouping of powers brought Sparta into connexion
with Persia, the so-called King's Peace was concluded in
386, which was also called after the clever Spartan who
negotiated it the Peace of Antalcidas. As early as 392 this
Antalcidas, together with the satrap Tiribazus, had de-

bated terms of peace with the representatives of the allies at Sardis. Then the Athenians were still strong enough to be the only allied state which refused the Persian demand for the cession of the coast of Asia Minor, on the patriotic ground that they could not admit that the Greeks who lived in Asia belonged to the Great King. For this and other reasons the negotiations broke down. But now Antalcidas, who was also a skilful admiral, succeeded, with the additional support of ships from Dionysius I of Syracuse, in closing the Dardanelles to the Athenians, and bringing to bear on them the same compulsion as in 405. Resistance was no longer possible. The Greeks had obediently to receive the peace, which the Great King sent down to them from Susa to Sardis in the most humiliating form by the hand of Antalcidas, with whom he had settled its terms. The King's edict comprised two clauses and a sanction. The first clause laid down that all the Greek cities in Asia as well as the islands of Clazomenae and Cyprus should belong to the Great King, the second that all other Greek cities, great and small, should be free and independent, the only exceptions being the cleruchies of Lemnos, Imbros and Scyros which were left to Athens. The sanction stated that the King in conjunction with the states that were of the same mind would wage war by sea and land against anyone who did not accept the peace. On the basis of this edict the peace was confirmed at Sparta by the oaths of all present at the congress. Thus the Hellenic brethren on the other side of the sea were finally awarded to the Great King. The clause about autonomy corresponded not only to the interests of the Persian monarch, to whom it implied the permanent subdivision of Greece into countless sovereign communities, *Poleis*, but in particular to the interests of Sparta, inasmuch as all leagues of states which did not guarantee autonomy were thereby excluded. Accordingly the Theban League was immediately dissolved, while the Peloponnesian League, the members of which were nominally autonomous, remained in existence under the leadership of Sparta. In this respect the King's Peace was a triumph for Sparta, who had now to superintend the strict execution of its terms in the sorry rôle of Persian agent. No doubt many short-sighted particularists, who were incapable of learning by experience, were well content that the old ideal of freedom and independence was guaranteed to each individual *Polis*. But the better elements felt it to be a disgrace, that this peace, which, as Isocrates put it, was not a treaty but a dictation, had been forced on them by the Persian King, and that he now as official guarantor exercised a supreme control over Greek policy. The disgrace was all the more crying, as the military superiority of the Greeks was unquestionable after the expedition of the Ten Thousand, and might have made a conquest of Persia possible, if in place of their disunion a unification of Greek forces could have been carried out. It is of prime importance for the understanding of the fourth century to realise that this shameful peace of 386 was a fundamental law in Hellas for fully half a century, and a burden which was now more, now less galling. Philip first cut the ground from under it by uniting the nation in his Corinthian League, and Alexander completely abolished it by the destruction of the Persian Empire.

The conclusion of the King's Peace was followed by years of difficulty for Greece, during which Sparta used her new hegemony to extend her power still further. As a protection against Spartan encroachments, Athens succeeded in 377 in founding a new Attic naval league, in which according to the terms of the King's Peace it guaranteed freedom and autonomy to each member of the league. By care in avoiding the faults which had produced the dissolution of the first naval league in the fifth century, a new organisation was created, the chief point being that the members each sent a representative to a federal council (*Synhedrion*) sitting at Athens, which had to keep in touch with the assembly of the Athenian people.

While this league in the next following years was

extended in Northern and Central Greece and in the islands of the East and West by the successful operations of the Attic generals Chabrias and Timotheus, Thebes had in the meantime rapidly risen to power in the struggle with Sparta under the leadership of Epaminondas, on the recovery of the citadel, the Cadmeia, which the Spartans had seized in time of peace by a brutal violation of international law. Epaminondas' immediate aim was the formation of a united Boeotian state, and when at the peace congress at Sparta in 371 objection was raised to this on the ground of the King's Peace, he defied the congress and at Leuctra inflicted so severe a defeat on the Spartan king Cleombrotus that Sparta's military predominance was at an end for ever. This battle of Leuctra was also of the greatest significance for the development of the Macedonian military system; the so-called 'oblique battle-array', which Epaminondas, its inventor, and one of the greatest military geniuses of all time, first applied here, was later adopted and expanded by King Philip, and with it Alexander won the day in his three great pitched battles, as did Frederick the Great at Leuthen.

Sparta was prostrate and could not interfere in the following years, when Epaminondas by repeated expeditions into the Peloponnese rendered it completely impotent, by robbing it of Messenia, on whose harvests and supply of labour its economic and political position largely rested, and by the organisation of a federal Arcadian state with a newly created capital, Megalopolis.

But the aims of Epaminondas flew higher: he was working for the hegemony of all Greece. If, as was once erroneously assumed, his intention had been a Panhellenic national policy, he would, as the political situation then was, have been bound to attempt the unification of Hellas under the leadership of Thebes for a war against Persia and the destruction of the supremacy of the Great King. Instead of that he fell a victim to the curse of his age. In order to win domination over the other Greeks, he made overtures to the Persian King, to whom the rise of Attic sea-power was as much an eyesore as it was an obstacle in his own path, and caused his ambassadors, Pelopidas among them, to dance attendance at Susa, and humbly beg for the co-operation of the Great King. But in 362 when Epaminondas fell at Mantineia in a battle which he again had arranged with genius, the policy of Thebes as a great power collapsed, since it did not correspond to the actual strength of the state, and had only been maintained by his personality.

This episode of Theban hegemony was of no permanent value to the Greeks; it merely caused an aching void in the military strength of the nation by the annihilation of Sparta. Nor was the second Attic naval league destined to flourish long. In spite of the promises of 377, Athens began to slip back again into the policy of the first league in its dealings with the members, and in 357 Chios, Rhodes and Cos, incited by the intrigues of Maussollus of Caria, revolted and seceded. Nothing can throw a more lurid light on the impotent condition of Greece than the fact that after unsuccessful fighting Athens in 355 was forced, by the threat of a declaration of war by the Persian king, to let the seceders go: this was the new and vigorous king Artaxerxes III Ochus. Thus Athens too resigned the position of the sovereign great power, and the result was universal chaos in Greece. Opposed to the Greeks stood the Persian monarchy. Certainly at times it seemed to be approaching dissolution through the revolt of satraps and provinces, but by the help of Greek mercenaries it constantly maintained its existence; the unity of the empire was first and foremost, whereas in Greece there was a permanent division, out of which there seemed no way leading to unification of forces.

If this conflict of the Greek states with one another was discomforting, no less so were the internal conditions of the various *Poleis*. Whether democrats or oligarchs held sway, the oppositions of the hostile parties became everywhere embittered, and the domination of the victorious became ever more destructive to the defeated. The radical tendencies of democracies, such as Athens, which had begun in the fifth century grew ever more extreme. The rule of the proletariat under the leadership of its demagogues developed more and more into a class-domination, and the popular tribunals, which, since the raising of the payment of members, were overwhelmingly composed of the poorer citizens, dealt out a class justice, which was directed not merely against political opponents but specially against property-owners as such, with an eye to the confiscation of their property; it was at bottom a struggle of the poor against the rich, and in this process the most radical demands were raised, such as for a new division of land, the abolition of debts and so forth. In oligarchic states the war of classes was carried on with the same passion from the opposite point of view. Thus the exiles and bankrupts formed an ever-increasing proletariat without means or occupation, such as Isocrates describes in 380 and with greater emphasis in 346.

This became a danger to the whole of Hellas. There were then no great industrial concerns to supply work for these masses. Many turned to brigandage on the country roads, or as pirates rendered the sea unsafe, but most of them were driven by want to enlist as mercenaries in the service of the potentate who offered the highest pay. This mercenary system was a deep-seated evil which affected the whole nation. The gold of the Persian king was the chief attraction. After the shock of the expedition of the Ten Thousand he endeavoured more and more to prop up his power by armies of Greek mercenaries. But his efforts were partly defeated, because rebel satraps and countries like Egypt also enlisted Greek mercenaries to fight against him. Nor did Greece supply only soldiers: it also produced officers. Many of the most prominent generals of the day, if they were unemployed or disgusted by political conditions at home, entered foreign service, and often turned the scale in fighting for or against the Great King. What a waste of national vigour this was for the benefit of foreigners!

The ease with which mercenaries could be found had another mischievous consequence; in Greece too many civic communities began to enlist mercenaries, in order to escape more or less from the duty of bearing arms themselves. Even when the Athenian Iphicrates was organising a new body of light-armed peltasts, it appeared that citizens thought themselves too good to undergo the severe drill required by this new formation, and preferred to recruit mercenaries instead. The worst result was the decay of the old idea of the state which had once inspired citizens with the proud consciousness that it was their highest and noblest duty to defend their state with their property and their blood. The state came to be regarded more and more as an institution of maintenance, whose chief task was to assure the citizen of as easy and comfortable a life as possible and to organise for him many magnificent festivals. Thus at Athens, after the above-mentioned inglorious end of the Social War in the fifties, the inevitable result was a pacifism, which abandoned the policy of imperial power, provided that material interests were promoted.

But not only had the idea of the *Polis* been lowered in the hard struggle of actual life, it had also been shaken by the theories of the leading intellectuals. The individualism, preached by the Sophists in the far-reaching intellectual revolution of the fifth century, seriously threatened the feeling which had hitherto prevailed on the subject of the state. To the laws which had formed for the citizen of the *Polis* the supreme rule of life the Sophists opposed the natural rights of the individual, and declared the laws to be only the conventional ordinance of man. In proclaiming the right of the stronger, they struck at the roots of the *Polis*. How dangerous the translation of these doctrines into practice could be, appeared from the deliberate attempt of Alcibiades to play the super-man. Socrates certainly combated the aberrations of Sophistic, but even his requirements of professional training for the citizens and the formation of the government out of experts implied the complete transformation of the ancient *Polis*. The real downfall of the *Polis*, which took place in the fourth century, led only to the strengthening of individualism and the abandonment of the idea of a ruling state. The conception of the individual who is sufficient unto himself by knowledge and morality so that he has no need of the state, led the Socratic Antisthenes, the founder of the Cynic School, the son of a Thracian woman, who could not become a citizen of Athens, to the ideal of an all-embracing community of mankind; and thus arises the cosmopolitan idea, which was developed further by his pupil Diogenes of Sinope, who coined the word *cosmopolites*, 'citizen of the world', the fatal phrase, which has exercised its dangerous fascination down to the present day. However different the world-empire created by Alexander was from this *Cosmopolis*, there is no question that this idea of the Cynics was one of those elements in the fourth century, which prepared the Hellenic mind for his universal empire.

But there set in a reaction against this individualistic tendency. Numerous thinkers appeared, who, though disgusted with the state of the day, would not deny the idea of the state, but wanted to cure the maladies of the *Polis* by proposals of reform. The boldest and most radical is the wonderful fabric, which Plato, the greatest Athenian of the time, erected in his *Republic*, in which he drew the ideal state of justice. Later he was compelled to see that this construction was only suitable for gods, and at the end of his life he drew out a new ideal picture, taking more account of the actual world—that of the *Laws*, in which he put in the forefront the strict legal cohesion which he had rejected in the *Republic*.

Though the starting-points and conclusions of the theorists differed widely, many of them agreed in one point, in the idea that monarchy is the ideal form of government. This awakening of the monarchical idea is

one of the influences which paved the way in Greece for
the successes of Philip and Alexander. It may be traced
back to the individualism of the fifth century. In practice
it was promoted not only by the decline of the *Polis* but by
the appearance of strong rulers on the outskirts of the
Greek world, who defended or advanced Greek interests,
such as Dionysius I of Syracuse, who protected the western
Greeks against Carthage, or Jason of Pherae, the powerful
lord of Thessaly, on whom many hopes were based, or even
Euagoras of Cyprus. The first of the theorists to arrive at
the monarchical solution was the above-mentioned Cynic,
Antisthenes. It was a consequence of his cosmopolitan
views, that he saw in the Cynic model of the one perfect
wise man the ideal head of this world association of mankind. The fashion of the age was to look back into the past
to find a basis for requirements for the future, and so
Antisthenes presented Heracles as the mythical pattern,
who by his ceaseless services had been a benefactor of mankind; and from the history of the world he selected the great
Cyrus, the founder of the Achaemenid empire, and portrayed him as Persian legends knew him, the ideal monarch who cared for his subjects, as a father for his children
or a shepherd for his flock. Xenophon also in his *Cyropaedia* presented Cyrus to the future Greek conqueror of
Asia as the ideal of the world ruler, thus representing monarchy as the justest form of government, because it alone—
in contrast to the dreary mechanical levelling of democracies—knew how to estimate individual achievements on
the principle *suum cuique.* Plato in his *Politicus* found the
ideal in the absolute monarchy of the wise man, which was
difficult of realisation, but finally in his *Laws* he gave
the preference to the monarch bound by the laws and
ruling constitutionally; and what a strong interest he felt
in monarchy as actually existing, is shown by his repeated
visits to Syracuse and his zealous but ineffectual endeavours
to ennoble its government. At an advanced age Isocrates,
the great political pamphleteer, associated himself with

those who saw in monarchy a cure for the miseries of the day. In his writings addressed to the Cypriot prince Nicocles (in the seventies of the fourth century) he spoke quite plainly of the advantages of monarchy, but maintained that the Greeks themselves could not endure a king. It was precisely this monarchical idea which led him in the end to Philip.

Even in these politically dismal days of the fourth century Greek civilisation continued the great traditions of the fifth century and was in full flower; both in the intellectual and artistic spheres it produced wonderful achievements which are immortal. Athens in particular, notwithstanding its political collapse at the end of the Peloponnesian War, still maintained the leading central position, which it had won in the fifth century from Ionia. If Attic civilisation took on a Panhellenic character, the Attic empire of the fifth century in spite of its short duration contributed not a little to this result. From Athens, the head of an empire over hundreds of tributary cities, a broad stream of Attic civilisation had flowed in Hellas and throughout the islands and coasts of the Aegean Sea: Attic law and Attic institutions, Attic speech and customs had spread far, especially in Ionia. But this influence was not confined to the empire. As Athens, with its harbour the Piraeus, had become the economic centre not merely of the allies but of the Greek world, it had also, as the centre of civilisation, exercised a magnetic attraction on prominent intellectuals and artists from all parts. Sophistic found its centre in Athens, worked in Attic speech, and even helped to construct the artistic Attic prose-style, though scarcely a single sophist was a native of Athens.

All these influences had gone too deep to be removed by the collapse of the empire. Isocrates, the master of the new oratorical style, was able to boast in his *Panegyricus* (380) that his native city had so out-distanced other men in thinking and speaking—in philosophy and rhetoric—that her scholars had become the teachers of others, that she had caused the term Hellene to signify no longer racial descent but mode of thought, and that those called Hellenes were those who partook of Attic culture rather than those who had a common descent.[1] This means that Isocrates saw the true Hellene only in the Greek educated on the Attic model, and thus narrowed the concept of Hellene; but it does not mean, as is usually assumed, that he regarded barbarians of Attic education as Hellenes. This latter idea, which changes the race-contrast of Hellene and barbarian into a contrast of civilisations, was quite alien to him by reason of his hatred for Persia, the hereditary foe, to which he gives sharp expression in the same treatise; indeed it only manifested itself in the Hellenistic age after the establishment of Alexander's world-empire.

Yet when Isocrates wrote, there were already many barbarians more or less influenced by Greek civilisation; and in the next decades it penetrated further into non-Greek areas, in some parts very thoroughly. In so far as this phenomenon had its cause in a capacity and need of expansion possessed by Greek civilisation, it is of the greatest importance for the understanding of Alexander's work; he gave these forces undreamt-of possibilities of actualisation. But the phenomenon has other causes as well. One was the hopeless condition of the mother country, which drove out many vigorous elements to seek their fortune abroad. We have spoken already of the masses who went over sea to serve as mercenaries in Asia Minor or Egypt for or against the Great King. Grievous as their loss was to the mother country, these many thousands of mercenaries, who lived abroad for decades, were bound, consciously or unconsciously, to contribute to the spread of Greek customs and life in foreign lands. On the other hand these Greeks from the most different cantons of the mother country lived together in military units and so could not but prepare for

[1] U. Wilcken, *Griech. Geschichte im Rahmen der Altertumsgeschichte*, Munich, Oldenbourg, 2nd ed., 1926, p. 164; J. Jüthner, *Hellenen und Barbaren*, 1923, pp. 34 ff.

that levelling of local peculiarities, which was completed after Alexander. It was not merely mercenaries and traders, however, whom necessity sent abroad, but artists also who could find no commissions in their impoverished homes. In the Peloponnese, where the school of Sicyon was flourishing, we hear at the beginning of this period of works like the famous temple of Athena Alea at Tegea, built by Scopas and renowned for its size and beauty, and of fine new buildings at the Hieron of Epidaurus: but Athens was then so poor that only necessary buildings were in question, and thus we often meet with Attic artists abroad.

This supply from Hellas found a corresponding demand; for the satraps and dynasts of Asia Minor desired to adorn their cities with Greek art and to attract Greek poets, musicians and orators to their courts. The cause of this phenomenon, which has been rightly regarded as another 'precursor of Hellenism', is to be found in the fact that for centuries Greek civilisation, proceeding from Ionia, had deeply penetrated Lydia, Caria and Lycia, kindling the ambition of their self-conscious dynasts. The most powerful of them all was Maussollus of Caria. He enlarged his seat of government, Halicarnassus, by forcibly increasing its population (*Sunoikismos*), and had it adorned by Greek artists with fine palaces and temples. An admirer of Greek culture, he made his court a court of the Muses by summoning Greek artists and poets. When he died in 352, his widow Artemisia held a competition of Greek poets and rhetoricians at his funeral, and began the erection of the gigantic tomb, which he had perhaps himself planned. It was counted among the Seven Wonders of the World and called the Mausoleum, a term still applied to large tombs, as it was in the later days of antiquity. This wonderful building was the work of the foremost artists of the Greek world, the architecture being by Pytheus and Satyrus, and the sculptured decoration by Scopas and Leochares, Timotheus and Bryaxis. Another Eastern example of Greek art of this period is offered by the fine marble sarcophagi, made by Attic artists for the fourth century kings of Sidon. But probably the most striking instance of the introduction of Greek culture into these lands is afforded by an unimportant Persian vassal, Hermias of Atarneus (in the Troad), who lived on terms of intimacy with the Platonists Erastus and Coriscus and in gratitude assigned to them his town of Assos. After the death of Plato Aristotle settled there, and spent three important years of his life in research and teaching, in close friendship with Hermias.[1]

While we can observe the beginnings of a quiet and peaceful penetration of Greek culture in the East, as also in Italy and Carthage in the West, the idea of a national war of the united Greeks against Persia arose at the same time and was vigorously propagated. This Panhellenic idea, as we call the essential feature of the movement, is of fundamental importance for the understanding of Philip and Alexander: for it was they who, in the interest of their policy, finally adopted the conception and in their own manner put it into execution. The old thought of an opposition between Hellene and barbarian awoke to new life. In the great Persian War it had been the expression of that strong self-conscious national feeling which had largely contributed to the amazing advance of the nation in the fifth century.

This opposition was bound to be felt more keenly by those who were striving to avert the constant internecine wars of Greeks, when, after 412, Persia had again begun to interfere with the history of Greece. Nor were they led astray by the fact that in the meantime the Sophists, starting from the law of nature, had proclaimed the equality of all men and therefore of Hellenes and barbarians. It was the distress of the moment that drove men to adopt the Panhellenic idea. The first to proclaim it publicly was the eloquent Gorgias, who when the Greeks were assembled for the Olympic games—unfortunately we

[1] For Hermias of Atarneus see W. Jäger, *Aristoteles, Grundlegung einer Geschichte seiner Entwicklung*, 1923, pp. 113 ff.

do not know for certain in what year[1]—urged them to concord (*Homonoia*) and war against Persia, and called on them to choose not Greek cities but the territory of the barbarians as the prize for which they fought. It was a war of conquest against Persia which was demanded, a necessary preliminary being concord among the Greeks themselves. The Panhellenic program of Gorgias was frequently handled by rhetoricians after him,[2] and we are justified in the conclusion that it aroused the interest of the public. But it was first raised to historical significance by Isocrates, the pupil of Gorgias, whose extraordinary importance as a political writer has only recently been recognised, though his oratorical skill has never been questioned. In the year 380, six years after the King's Peace, he produced his *Panegyricus*, a masterpiece of epideictic oratory, which established his fame as the first political writer of the day.[3] In form it was a speech before the Olympic festal gathering, after the model of Gorgias; in reality it was a pamphlet which was circulated and read throughout Greece.

Starting from the Panhellenic program, the reconciliation of the Greeks with the object of a united national war against Persia, Isocrates answered the question, not yet treated by his predecessors, who was to lead this campaign, by the double answer, Athens and Sparta, who were first to be reconciled for the purpose. By depicting at length, however, the great services which Athens had rendered to Hellas, he sought finally to show that Athens had the higher claim to the sole leadership. To be sure, Athens must first of all once more control the seas, and with this in view he very cleverly threw out the idea of a new Attic naval league. But he justified the national war, which he,

---

[1] [Probably July 408 B.C.]

[2] [*E.g.* Lysias at Olympia 388 B.C. exhorted the Greeks to be reconciled and liberate Ionia from the Great King and Sicily from Dionysius.]

[3] [*Cambridge Ancient History*, vol. vi. p. 518 (E. Barker); *Classical Philology*, vii. 1912, p. 343, 'Recent Views of the Political Influence of Isocrates' (C. D. Adams).]

like Gorgias, regarded as a war of conquest, not only by the material consequences of the victory—the rich acquisition of territory in Asia would transfer the wealth of Asia to Greece, and the poverty of Greece, the root of all internecine disputes, would be abolished—but also, from the standpoint of national honour, by the demand that the shameful King's Peace should be cancelled and the Greeks of Asia Minor set free. The ultimate good of the war, however, was that by sharing the danger and gains the Greeks themselves would secure a permanent peace.

His propaganda was brilliantly successful so far as it concerned Athens' new sea-power; for three years later, and certainly in part owing to the influence he had exercised on public opinion, the second Attic naval league was founded. On the other hand, the idea of a reconciliation between Athens and Sparta and the sharing of the leadership on sea and land, which he had urged almost as zealously, was demonstrated to be Utopian. It was still more inconceivable that Sparta would resign the supreme command to Athens alone. In the following years, as the antagonisms of the leading states showed themselves even more acutely, Isocrates soon recognised that Hellas of herself would never arrive at internal peace and therefore fulfil the conditions for a general national war; the particularism represented by the ideal of the free and independent *Polis* was too deeply engrained in the Greeks. So he, like many others as we saw, turned to the monarchical solution, and looked round the fringes of the Greek world for a strong man, who was not tied to the laws and constitution of a *Polis* and had the power and inclination to realise the Panhellenic idea. He presented his program to several rulers successively, to Jason of Pherae, the forceful unifier of Thessaly, who was credited with aiming at a war with Persia, and afterwards to Dionysius I, the great ruler of the West. But the former was murdered soon afterwards (370), and the latter, for whom such plans were too remote, soon died (367).

Isocrates, however, could wait. In spite of his disappointments, in spite of his renunciation of Attic sea-power in the oration 'On the Peace' of 355, to which he was brought by the failure of the Social War, he adhered tenaciously to the Panhellenic idea. Meanwhile he lived to see the powerful expansion of Macedonia under King Philip, and perceived there in the north a great power arising. In 346, therefore, when after many years of war Athens concluded the Peace of Philocrates with this Philip on the basis of the *status quo*, the old man—he was then ninety—in great joy at the final restoration of peace, took up his pen and in his 'Philip' indited an open letter to the king, laying before him his Panhellenic program with the invitation to reconcile the Greeks and lead them against Persia, the traditional foe. Who was this Philip, that from him Isocrates could hope for the fulfilment of his desires?

CHAPTER II

PHILIP II OF MACEDONIA

THE beginnings of Macedonian history are shrouded in complete darkness. There is keen controversy on the ethnological problem, whether the Macedonians were Greeks or not. Linguistic science has at its disposal a very limited quantity of Macedonian words, and the archaeological exploration of Macedonia has hardly begun. And yet when we take into account the political conditions, religion and morals of the Macedonians, our conviction is strengthened that they were a Greek race and akin to the Dorians. Having stayed behind in the extreme north, they were unable to participate in the progressive civilisation of the tribes which went further south, and so, when in the time of the Persian Wars they emerged on the horizon of the other Greeks, they appeared to them as non-Greeks, as barbarians.[1]

When Alexander I of Macedon, who, though a vassal of Xerxes, had in the Persian War given many proofs of his sympathy with the Greek cause, desired to take part in the Olympic Games, to which only Hellenes had access, he was at first refused as a barbarian, and it was only when by a bold fiction he traced back the pedigree of his house, the Argeadae, to the Heraclid Temenus of Argos, that he was admitted as a competitor. Since then the kings of Macedonia passed with the Greeks as Hellenes, and as descendants of Heracles; but, as before, so afterwards, the people were regarded as barbarians—even by Isocrates in his 'Philip'—though in the meantime many kings had done much for the introduction of Greek culture into their country. Even in Philip's day the Greeks saw in the Mace-

[1] [See F. Geyer, *Makedonien bis zur Thronbesteigung Philipps II*, Oldenburg, 1930.]

donians a non-Greek foreign people, and we must remember this if we are to understand the history of Philip and Alexander, and especially the resistance and obstacles which met them from the Greeks. The point is much more important than our modern conviction that Greeks and Macedonians were brethren; this was equally unknown to both, and therefore could have no political effect.

Quite apart from the local separation of the two peoples, the barbaric impression which the Macedonians made on the Greeks is explained by the close relationship in which the Macedonians lived for centuries with their barbarian neighbours, the Illyrians (the ancestors of the Albanians of to-day) in the West, and the Thracians in the East. Even the level land of Lower Macedonia, north of Mt. Olympus, on the lower courses of the rivers Haliacmon and Axius, into which the Macedonians penetrated in their eastward advance from Mt. Bermius out of the mountainous country of Upper Macedonia, was then occupied in its western parts by Illyrians and in its eastern by Thracians. The Macedonians had to win it gradually from them by fighting. This is proved by the names of the two Macedonian capitals, Aegae and Pella, which are Macedonian translations of the original Illyrian names Edessa (water-city) and Bunomus. Though most of the ancient inhabitants were expelled, yet certainly, as generally happens, many stayed behind, and in course of time, at any rate in civilisation, were assimilated to the lower classes of the conquerors—the same thing happened with the Greeks who went farther south and the original Anatolian population they found there. A strong Illyrian and Thracian influence can thus be recognised in Macedonian speech and manners. These however are only trifles compared with the Greek character of the Macedonian nationality; for example, the names of the true full-blooded Macedonians, especially of the princes and nobles, are purely Greek in their formation and sounds.

Above all, the fundamental features of Macedonian political institutions are not only Greek but primitive Greek.

The old patriarchal monarchy over people and army lasted here down to the days of Philip and Alexander, a monarchy such as had once existed in all Greek tribes, until it had to give way to aristocratic forms of government under the dissolving influence of the *Polis*. One of the factors which explain the tenacious retention of the old monarchy is that the progressive idea of the *Polis* had not entered Macedonia. Another point is that the power of the king, who was supreme general, judge and priest, was tempered by the fact that the old Greek community in arms, in whose eyes the king was *primus inter pares*—which had once existed in primitive times among the Greeks—maintained itself down to Alexander's day, and beyond, in the assembly of the army, which was possessed of definite privileges.[1] This assembly of the army, though bound to the hereditary right of the Argead house, had the right and duty of electing the new king, that is of confirming him by acclamation. None was counted as lawful king but he whom the assembly of the army had recognised. A further right which it possessed was that trials for high-treason had to be conducted before it. It dealt with both sentence and execution.[2] In other respects the king was the representative of justice, and his subjects appealed to him with their affairs in personal audience, in truly patriarchal fashion.

But the Argeads were not at first lords of the whole Macedonian nation. Originally the tribes of Upper Macedonia, the Lyncestae, Orestae and Elimiotae had their own princes or kings. Tedious struggles were necessary to incorporate them into the Macedonian state, and it is likely that the mediatisation of these princely houses was only completed under Philip, by whose hand the unified Macedonian state was thus constituted.

The army consisted originally of the nobility attached to

[1] Friedrich Granier, *Die Makedonische Heeresversammlung*, Beck, Munich, 1931.

[2] [The nearest parallel is presented by the Lombards in Italy. Gibbon (Bury), v, c. 45, p. 20.]

the land, who were bound to serve their prince or king on horseback. Their personal relation to the king was expressed by the patriarchal title of *Hetairoi*, the king's followers, a title which again recalls the conditions of early Hellas: the 2500 Myrmidons of Achilles are called in the *Iliad* his *Hetairoi*. When the king formed a council of several of these *Hetairoi*, the members were called 'The *Hetairoi* of the royal entourage'. But this was not the origin of the title, as has recently been supposed: the old Homeric title of honour persisted in Macedonia for centuries, as applied to the noble following of the king. It is typical of the relationship of the king to the nobility, that he was not distinguished from them by dress. He had no special royal emblems, and the purple of the *chlamys* (mantle) and the *causia* (a broad-brimmed hat) were also worn by the nobility. Besides this noble cavalry, the free peasants and shepherds may have come in disorderly bodies from time to time to fight, but it is only in the fourth century that they appear to have been organised into a regular infantry, recruited and arranged, like the cavalry, according to districts. Thereafter the honourable title of *Hetairoi* was given to the infantry also, in the form *Pezhetairoi* (foot-companions). According to an ambiguous statement, this was done under Philip's elder brother Alexander; perhaps, however, it was completed only on Philip's reorganisation of the army. At any rate, the introduction of the title *Pezhetairoi* denoted that the infantry henceforth came into the same personal relation to the king which the noble cavalry had long enjoyed. In this one may trace a statesmanlike move of approximation to the lower classes of the people, such as could only secure and raise the power of the king. It was probably only after the grant of the title of *Pezhetairoi* that the infantry were allowed to participate in the assembly of the army and its privileges.

With the grant of rights and liberties the Macedonian monarchy was firmly based on the people. If at times there was friction between the king and the proud nobility, on the whole the Macedonians were loyal to their king and showed him due respect. It was customary for the soldier to take off his helmet, while he was speaking to his king, while on the other hand the king was on terms of comradeship with his officers. The Macedonians were a thoroughly healthy people, trained not by Greek athletics, but, like the Romans, by military service. But alongside much that was good, they had many rougher habits, retained from earlier times, such as excessive drinking, which tended to make them appear as barbarians in Greek eyes. The dislike was reciprocal, for the Macedonians had grown into a proud masterful nation, which with highly developed national consciousness looked down upon the Hellenes with contempt. This fact too is of prime importance for the understanding of later history.

The further advance of the eastern frontier of Macedonia, which under Alexander I had reached the river Strymon (Struma), had been stopped by the brilliant development of Athens at the head of the Delian League. Athens established itself on the north coast of the Aegean including the Macedonian coast, made subject the cities on the peninsula of Chalcidice, and finally founded the colony of Amphipolis near the mouth of the Strymon, which soon rose to great prosperity. But when the terrible disaster in Sicily (413) caused the collapse of Athens as a great power, and Macedonia like other states found fresh scope, Archelaus, who then ascended the throne, used the situation to give his state an enhanced military and political importance; he built fortresses and military roads and he fundamentally reorganised the army, paying special attention to the equipment of the cavalry. In Thucydides' judgment he did more than his eight predecessors put together.[1] His interference in the conflicts of the Thessalian nobility bore witness to the increased striking power of Macedonia. He also has the merit of having laboured to introduce Greek culture into his country, even more thoroughly than was attempted by Alexander I, the Phil-

[1] [Thucydides ii. 100.]

hellene. At his court in the new capital Pella he succeeded in developing a rich intellectual life, by inviting there the most famous poets and artists of his day. Euripides spent with him the last years of his life, and there wrote the *Bacchae*, and in honour of his royal patron the *Archelaus*. Timotheus also, who was then highly celebrated as musician and poet, was one of his guests; and he caused his palace at Pella to be decorated with paintings by Zeuxis. At Dion in Pieria under Mt. Olympus, where there was an old cult of the Muses, he established scenic contests in honour of Olympian Zeus and the Muses. We do not hear what attitude the Macedonian nobles adopted to this introduction of Greek culture by their king—which makes us think of the later courts of the Diadochi (the successors of Alexander). It is possible that it was not easy to reconcile them to it. But subsequent history shows that the seed was not sown in vain.

The position of prestige won by Archelaus was short-lived. After his murder (399) began a calamitous period of forty years. Severe fighting within and without, rival candidates for the throne, and incursions from Illyria and Thrace so weakened the Macedonian state that it finally became a dependent on the successive predominant powers of Greece, and under Amyntas a tributary to the Illyrians. The very existence of the state was at stake, when in 359 King Perdiccas, the son of Amyntas, was defeated by the Illyrians in a great battle, and slain with 4000 of his men. On all sides the enemy poured into the country, and no less than three pretenders, supported by foreign powers, rose against Philip, the youngest brother of Perdiccas, who as regent took the reins of government on behalf of his nephew Amyntas, the young son of Perdiccas. At this most critical moment of Macedonian history, Philip, who was then twenty-four, acted with astounding energy and skill. By brilliant feats of arms and by most subtle and cunning diplomatic skill, he promptly succeeded in removing perils from without and within, and was soon acclaimed king by the Macedonian army.

In the first year of his reign Philip has already reached the height of his powers. His extraordinary capabilities as general, statesman and diplomat, which made possible this rapid and thorough salvation of the state, explain to us also the extraordinary success of his career. Yet the greatness of this man was not understood till the nineteenth century.[1] Not merely was his fame obscured by the glittering achievements of his son Alexander. His memory has suffered from this disadvantage too: the greatest orator produced by Greece, Demosthenes, was his political opponent, passionately attacked him in his incomparable speeches, and, in the interest of his policy, presented to the Athenians a picture—distorted by hatred—of Philip 'the barbarian'. In the age of classicism especially, everyone was dazzled by the fine periods of Demosthenes, and accepting them literally, judged the life work of Philip purely from the Athenian standpoint—and that too from the standpoint of Demosthenes. This was accentuated by the political tendencies of the period. Barthold Georg Niebuhr had a passionate hatred for Philip, in whom, with his vivid conception of history, he saw a parallel to Napoleon, and before Austerlitz published a translation of the first *Philippic* of Demosthenes, to produce a political effect against the *Gallus rebellis*, as is shown by the motto he affixed to it. To reach a just estimate of Philip, historical science had first to be liberated from the Athenian-Demosthenic point of view. It is modern research alone that, following the lead of J. G. Droysen, has tended more and more to set out from the one correct point of view; the Macedonian King Philip must be judged by the standard of Macedonian interests only.

If we do this, Philip stands before us as one of the great rulers of the world's history, not only because he laid the foundations for the exploits of his still greater son Alexander, on which Alexander, in conformity with his own

[1] The author has developed this in: 'Philipp II von Makedonien und die panhellenische Idee', *Sitzber. Preuss. Akad.*, 1929, xviii.

genius, erected a new world, but also as a man in himself of far-seeing aims and achievements. There is no space here to explain in detail, how Philip, starting from the little country he found, made gradual advance in each quarter, how in the west he fought the Illyrians and won influence over Epirus, how in the east he fought against the Thracians, in the north reached the Danube, and in the south secured by fighting the coast so essential for Macedonia's development and the Chalcidic Peninsula as well, won Thessaly, and intervened ever more decisively in Greek affairs. All those undertakings, which show him in kaleidoscopic fashion active now here now there, are only reflections of one great idea, which possessed him quite early, perhaps from the start—to make his Macedonian people master of the whole Balkan peninsula. This imperialistic program was raised to a higher level by his policy of introducing Greek culture more thoroughly and so making Macedonia a really civilised state: it was this that gave his vigorous imperialism its deeper character. The example of Archelaus had been followed by Perdiccas, who at his court associated with the Platonist Euphraeus and learnt from him geometry and philosophy. Philip too attracted many prominent Greeks to his court. He had the very successful idea of inviting Aristotle to educate the successor to the throne, and took a step of the utmost moment in the adaptation of Hellenic culture in his own country: he introduced the language of Athens into his chancery, and both in administration and in the formation of his military system followed Greek models. Though only isolated features of these endeavours have come down to us, they point plainly to his principal intention, the intensified Hellenisation of his country.

This civilising policy had a consequence; if it was part of Philip's plan to dominate not merely the main mass of the Balkan peninsula but Hellas as well, he could not incorporate Greeks, as he did Illyrians and Thracians, into his Macedonian empire, he must look for some formula of association, which would save the face of the Greeks and make their position tolerable. He was certainly clear that the control of Greece would necessarily involve him in a conflict with the Persian empire: for by the King's Peace it was the Persian king to whom belonged the control and supremacy of Hellas. On the other hand, if Philip wanted to win Thrace and the north coasts of the Propontis and Bosphorus, it could not but appear to him desirable, nay even essential, in order to secure this important water-way, to extend and round off his empire on the coast of Asia Minor; and this could not be done without war with Persia. In view of the appeal of Isocrates, it may be stated with confidence that from early days, alongside of the immediate aim of securing the Balkan peninsula, he was also possessed by the idea, if only as a distant goal, of a Hellenic combination and a war against Persia.

It is a matter of course that Philip, a master of diplomacy, kept all these ideas and plans for the future locked up in his own breast. But if he was to execute them, he required an army which would be ready to strike. No doubt both with barbarians and even more with Greeks he often accomplished his objects by bribery, but in the main he owed his successes to his good sword. His reorganisation of the Macedonian army is a real work of genius; as he was the creator of the army-system which Alexander took over, some account must be given of it.

It is significant that Philip in his youth lived for three years in Thebes as a hostage, and thus became acquainted with the strategic methods of Epaminondas. When he came to the throne, he took over and made the starting-point of his reorganisation 'the oblique order of battle', an invention of Epaminondas which caused a revolution in tactics. Hitherto the Greeks had usually fought in parallel lines. Epaminondas divided his front into an offensive and a defensive wing in order to decide his battles. The former wing was unusually deep—as previously had sometimes been the case in Boeotia—and was formed of the best troops. Its task was to advance to a concentrated attack, break through and bring about a decision, while the weaker wing moved forward slowly and remained more on the defensive, so that at the moment of conflict the front of the battle line was in fact oblique, as the ancients called the formation. Epaminondas, who formed both wings out of the heavy infantry—his cavalry served only to protect the flanks—fixed on the left wing for the attack. As hitherto in parallel battle formations a decision had generally been attempted by both sides on the right wing, his attack with the left had all the more the effect of surprise. These tactics which gave Epaminondas the victory at Leuctra and Mantineia were now adopted by Philip, but modified in correspondence with the different constitution of his Macedonian army. He assigned the offensive to his excellent cavalry, the *Hetairoi*, and the defensive to the infantry phalanx which he created with this object. He did not confine the offensive to one wing, but launched his cavalry attacks sometimes on the right wing, and sometimes, as at Chaeronea, on the left, probably according to the peculiarities of the ground or the nature of the hostile position.

To carry out these tactics he had fundamentally to reorganise his army. The mounted squadrons which he took over he transformed into regular cavalry, dividing it into regiments (*Ilae*), tactical units, which were recruited according to districts. These *Hetairoi* were armed with helmet, corslet and sword, and fought with a thrusting spear of dog-wood. As stirrups were not yet invented, they could not, like the riders of the Middle Ages, by pressing the spear under the arm, increase the force of the thrust by pressure on the stirrups, but had to wield their spears with a free hand, as appears from the mosaic representing Alexander in battle. The reorganisation of the infantry was yet more thorough. Whether and how far before Philip there was any organised foot at all which could be called infantry, is debatable, as was stated above in discussion of the name *Pezhetairoi*. At any rate, Philip was the creator of the famous

Macedonian phalanx. In order to carry out the oblique formation, it was essential to create infantry suitable for the defensive wing. This explains the peculiar equipment and use of the Phalangites. On the pattern of the light-armed peltasts introduced by the Athenian Iphicrates, who were armed with long spears and only a small round shield (*pelta*), Philip gave his Phalangites as chief weapon, besides the sword, much longer and heavier spears, the *sarissae*, and also, in addition to a small *pelta* carried by a ring on the arm, a helmet, greaves and probably metal-protected jerkins of leather as well. They were accordingly a cross between heavy hoplites and peltasts, better suited for slow advance and the sustaining of attacks than for quick movements, though in case of necessity capable of executing the latter. Drawn up in thick formation of regiments (*taxeis*), in battle they had, on the defensive wing, to follow slowly the attack of the cavalry and detain the enemy. By their side Philip also had a light-armed infantry, the *Hypaspists*, whose battle-rôle was to hasten forward at quick march or the double and make connexion between the cavalry and the phalanx.[1] This was the Macedonian kernel of the army, but it was supplemented later by auxiliary troops from Thrace and other neighbouring barbarian countries.

Philip occupies a prominent place in the history of the art of war, by being the first to combine all classes of fighters into one tactical unit. He also marks a turning point in the development of strategy; for he was the first—if the intention is not to be ascribed to Epaminondas—who with a view to the total destruction of the enemy consciously carried out the 'strategy of defeat', as it is usually called, after the classical book of General von Clausewitz, *Vom Kriege*. Whereas earlier battles were usually regarded by the Greeks as competitions, the victor being he who kept the battle-field and erected a trophy, while the de-

[1] [One of the battalions of the Hypaspists, the *Agema*, was the king's bodyguard.]

feated side retired, Philip after winning a victory put himself at the head of his cavalry and pursued the fleeing enemy to the last breath of man and horse. What a wild chase that was, is shown by a statement that has recently come down to us, according to which, after a victorious battle with the Triballi, Philip in pressing the pursuit was accidentally wounded in the leg by the spear of one of his own followers.

Philip also marks an epoch in the art of besieging towns. The old method of starving the enemy out was not good enough for the introducer of the strategy of defeat. He was the first to employ in the East siege-engines, such as Dionysius I of Syracuse had had constructed by Greek and Carthaginian engineers. His sieges of Perinthus and Byzantium (340), though unsuccessful, were epoch-making in the science. On account of the impression caused by this revolution in the conduct of sieges, Athens and other cities began to convert their walls into stone in place of the brick that had hitherto sufficed.

It is obvious that all these innovations, especially the execution of the oblique battle-formation, required far greater training of the troops. So they were well drilled and exercised for fighting, marching and manœuvring. As Demosthenes recognised with admiration, summer or winter, day or night made no difference to Philip's operations. While in the Greek free states the citizens were generally above submitting to military exercises, and preferred to hire mercenaries, the Macedonians, noble and peasant alike, followed with enthusiasm their king, who led them from victory to victory, and as was shown by the scars which covered his body, himself shared in all their perils and fatigues. In particular Philip succeeded in attaching his officers to his person by the institution of the corps of 'royal pages'. By giving these noble youths who personally attended the monarch, a physical and intellectual training at court, he created a sort of cadet-corps for his officers. It was also a means of attaching permanently to the interests

of the court the Macedonian nobility, which in earlier days
had often been malcontent.

But in other respects than in the military sphere this
monarchy was superior to the Greek *Poleis* in striking
power. Not only was the supreme command in the King's
hands, but also the sole conduct of foreign policy. While in
the free states, torn by internal factions, questions of foreign
policy were decided now in this way, now in that, by
decisions of the majority after long contradictory speeches
of demagogues, in the Macedonian monarchy the king
alone had the decision. This too Demosthenes recognised
as a great advantage for his opponent. A steady uniform
far-sighted policy could be formed; plan and executive
were in the same hands, and statesman and general were
united in one man.

Such was the powerful position of the prince, to whom
Isocrates in 346, in his *Philip*, commended the execution
of his Panhellenic program. In the first part of the treatise
he deals with the reconciliation of the Greek states, which,
as Gorgias and he himself in his *Panegyricus* (380) had shown,
was a necessary preliminary to a common military enterprise. He made the practical proposal to Philip, that he   *
should first reconcile with one another the four leading states, Athens, Sparta, Thebes and Argos, who would
confer with him by their ambassadors; and then the small
states would of themselves follow the example set. For him
as a descendant of Heracles it would not be difficult, as
each of these great states had some connexion with his
ancestor Heracles. Their desperate condition would make
them inclined to a peaceful agreement and Philip would
win glory and goodwill throughout Greece. In the second
part of the treatise he discusses the war with Persia. The
moment was as favourable as possible, since the Persian
Empire was effectually weakened by the revolt of large
territories. Philip need only go over to Asia Minor and
proclaim liberty and many of the satraps would greet him
as their friend in need and throw off allegiance to the

Great King. Here too Isocrates points to his ancestor Heracles who once overcame Troy in a few days, and Philip might well rival him in philanthropy and goodwill to the Greeks. If practicable, he should destroy the whole Persian monarchy, but if this was not possible, he should cut off Hither Asia Minor from Cilicia to Sinope, settle in colonies the homeless wanderers who were a terror to Hellas, and thus secure Greece by erecting a bulwark against the East. If this also was impossible, he should at least liberate the Greeks of Asia Minor from the Persian yoke. He was sure of the greatest glory and gratitude of the Greeks. Isocrates ends with the warning, that Philip should be to Greeks a benefactor, to Macedonians a king not a tyrant, and that he should liberate the barbarians from barbaric despotism and admit them to Hellenic care and protection.

The modern reader will notice with surprise how full this treatise on practical politics is of arguments drawn from mythical history, and in particular from the legend of Heracles. But in order to understand the Greeks of this age, one must enter into this peculiarity of their mentality; as Jacob Burckhardt once formulated it, the myth was 'the ideal basis of their whole existence'. Even in the most sober political questions it was quite usual to refer to mythical parallels, or even, as Isocrates did here in part, to shape the myths in the interest of the present and to project into mythical times views of the present in order to give them more force. In Alexander's own life this practice played a great part. When Isocrates in this treatise makes so much of Heracles as Philip's ancestor, this was meant not merely for Philip but for the Greek public as well; for this open letter to the king, which was also circulated as a pamphlet throughout Greece, was intended to have a double effect, on Philip to influence him to be the leader in the national war, and on the Greeks to prepare public opinion for his leadership. The strong emphasis on Philip as a Heraclid and therefore a true Hellene, was to make easier for Greeks the idea of subordination to foreign leadership.

When Philip read the book, the insistence on his descent from Heracles must have been welcome to him; for in his policy he had to stress this mythical derivation, as the types of Heracles on his coins show. But on the other hand he must have smiled at the naïveté shown by Isocrates. What was according to Isocrates to be the result of this war waged by Philip against Persia with his Macedonians and the united Greeks? He was to serve exclusively Greek interests: the Greeks of Asia Minor were to be liberated; Asia Minor colonised with the homeless Greeks, in order to free Greece from its grave economic and social distress; it was the Greeks that the riches and plenty of the East were to benefit. Only faintly and in general terms was it indicated that Philip would also win power and riches, but solely in order to recommend to him, instead, as a higher aim, glory and the goodwill of the Greeks. Isocrates must have taken this strong realist for an idealist, such as he was himself, if he believed that Philip would draw his sword for the *beaux yeux* of the Greeks. He judged Philip as wrongly in the one direction as did Demosthenes in the other by thinking that Philip aimed at the total destruction of Athens. If Isocrates had known the secret plans of Philip's Macedonian policy, he could never have written his *Philip*.

And yet it is of the greatest historical importance, that he turned to Philip; for it is unmistakeable that he influenced Philip's subsequent procedure. Though these suggestions of a fulfilment of purely Greek desires may have appeared strange to Philip, whose policy was purely Macedonian, the *Philip* as a whole unquestionably made a deep impression on him. He certainly greeted it with joy: it was a great moral success, which might materially benefit his secret plans, that this distinguished publicist and professor, who had the greatest influence on the public opinion of the whole Greek world, should call on him to take the lead in the Panhellenic national war which many Hellenes had long desired. Philip no doubt at once recognised that ideas were proposed to him which had the closest contact with his secret plans and ideas; he needed but to modify these plans cleverly, in order to conceal his Macedonian aims with Panhellenic catch-words.

The chief difference between his own plans and the program of Isocrates was that he himself in the last resort contemplated the domination of Greece in effect if not in appearance, in order to lead a Macedonian war of conquest against Persia and so round off his empire, while Isocrates regarded the reconciliation of the Greek states merely as a presupposition of the national war. The *Philip* has often been interpreted in the sense that Isocrates recommended to the king a union of the Greek nation into one state, either a federal state or a league of states with Philip at its head, and it has consequently been held that Philip afterwards at Corinth carried out this idea of Isocrates; but actually there is no trace in the treatise of such a view. Isocrates never for an instant thought of a politically unified state under Philip's leadership. It is simply the internal unification of Hellas which he calls on Philip to bring about, the concord (*Homonoia*) of the Greek *poleis*, which is to be effected by the reconciliation (*Dialysis*) of existing antagonisms. It is equally an error to believe that the Panhellenic idea started with the object of the union of the nation into one state, and to compare Isocrates and the representatives of this idea to the men of 1848, who prepared the ground for German unity. In reality nothing more is implied either in Gorgias or in the *Panegyricus* of Isocrates (380) than the reconciliation and internal accord of the Greeks. Actually, both in the fourth century and previously, the Greek people had no conception of a national unified state. This conception, which is so familiar to us to-day, should not be imported into Greek history, and taken as a standard of judgment in estimating the political performances of the nation. As Hellenes, the Greeks felt themselves united

merely by their common civilisation, and on this their
national feeling rested.

While Isocrates considered as possible an internal reconciliation of all Greeks by Philip, the statesman Philip
could not fail to see at once that this was the dream of an
idealist; in fact, when one takes a retrospect of the passionate internal struggles of the previous decades, in which the
Greeks tore each other in pieces, one cannot conceive how
Isocrates arrived at this belief. By friendly persuasion, such
as he envisaged, nothing was to be done. Compulsion alone
could avail—but this course assumed that Philip should
first carry out his plan of dominating Greece: only then
could he attempt to attain peaceful conditions there. The
invitation of Isocrates, therefore, can merely have confirmed him in his old plan of Hegemony over Greece, far
off as it was. On the other hand, he could immediately
adopt the second point of Isocrates' program and take over
the leadership in the Panhellenic national war. This was
no doubt uncommonly desirable to him. He could cover
his long-contemplated Macedonian war of conquest in
Asia with the Panhellenic flag, and thus obtain a first-rate
method both of winning the sympathies of the Greeks,
which were extremely valuable to him because of his policy
of culture, and of gaining a moral justification for his intended domination of Greece.

How far Philip utilised for his policy the instigations of
Isocrates, was to appear in 338, when as victor of Chaeronea, he organised Greece anew at Corinth and urged the
Greeks to take up arms against Persia. Intervening events
can only be briefly sketched. Philip's prestige in Greece was
much enhanced by the successful termination, immediately
after the Peace of Philocrates and before the end of 346, of
the war with the Phocians, the so-called Sacred War,
which had devastated Central Greece for ten years. He
forced the Phocians to capitulate, was admitted in their
place into the Amphictyonic Council, and thus recognised
as a Hellenic power. Soon afterwards he won a dominant

position in Thessaly by becoming *Archon* of the Thessalian League. In the following years we see him fighting hard and pressing victoriously forward. After overcoming the Odrysian kingdom, securing his new territory by colonies such as Philippopolis and extending his power to the Black Sea, he was brought by his effort to win the Thracian south coast into fresh collision with Athens, which in the Thracian Chersonese had vital interests to maintain—the security of the supply of grain from the Black Sea.

The policy of Athens was then under the spell of the eloquence of Demosthenes, who, representing a specifically Athenian standpoint, had for many years seen in Philip the enemy of his native city, and finally did not hesitate to combine with Persia against him. Consequently, in Athens there was a violent clash of opinions; for the diametrically opposite view, the Panhellenic idea of a national war against Persia under the leadership of Philip, was gaining ground, especially in intellectual circles, like the Academy, now directed by Plato's nephew Speusippus. But the guidance of policy was in the hands of Demosthenes, and he urged Athens on to war. Though Philip in the interest of his latent plans earnestly endeavoured to avoid, if possible, a conflict with Athens, and in spite of all provocation was trying with inexhaustible patience to come to a peaceful understanding by diplomatic negotiations, albeit not without alarming Athens by his operations on the Chersonese and Bosphorus, yet finally war broke out, and it was Athenian troops that in 340 forced him to raise the siege of Byzantium. Immediately before, his siege of Perinthus on the north coast of the Sea of Marmora had been upset by the intervention of a new enemy, Persia. Some years previously, with a view to the war against Persia which he contemplated later, and as a preparation for crossing into Asia Minor, he had formed secret relations with Hermias of Atarneus on the other side of the Dardanelles, but then as a cunning diplomat concluded a treaty of amity with the Persian king, in order to lull the suspicions of his future enemy. In spite of that, the king caused his satraps to support the Perinthians against Philip, because he feared his establishment on the opposite Thracian coast.

Though Philip felt irritated by the relief of Byzantium by Athens, still he avoided direct action against her, and to secure his Macedonian kingdom went off to the Dobruja to fight the Scythians and Triballians (339). It was only when the Amphictyonic Council gave him the command of a new 'Sacred War' against Amphissa that he moved into Central Greece by way of Thermopylae (339). So finally in August 338, in the Boeotian plain of the Cephissus near Chaeronea, there was a great and decisive battle, and Philip completely defeated the combined forces of Athens and Thebes. Though, in view of the course which affairs had taken in Athens and all Greece for several decades, the policy of Demosthenes is open to the criticism that in his Athenian aspirations he did not take actual facts into account, yet he will always remain as a conspicuous pattern of ardent patriotism; and it is a glorious page in the history of Athens, that under his guidance it remembered its proud past and did not yield to superior force without a struggle. With emotion we still read in the state cemetery of the Cerameicus at Athens the lines inscribed on the grave of those who fell at Chaeronea:

> O Time, nought human can escape thy view:
> So tell to all, what fate befel us too,
> How, striving on Boeotia's storied plain
> To save our sacred Hellas, we were slain.

Once more Philip won the battle by the oblique formation. The offensive on the left wing and the command of the cavalry he entrusted to his son Alexander, then eighteen years old, while he himself led the defensive right wing. So at the head of the *Hetairoi* the young Alexander charged the 'Sacred Band' of the Thebans, while his father, facing the Athenians, kept back his phalanx and even at first retired for a short distance, to tempt them out of their advantageous position. After he had succeeded in this, he advanced victoriously, and, as Alexander in the meantime had routed the Thebans and wheeling to the right was rolling up the enemy's centre by a side attack, the victory was complete.

It was an unusual action on Philip's part not to pursue the enemy after Chaeronea, but to stay on the battle-field, allowing them to retreat southwards. In this we see the man to whom in the words of General von Clausewitz war was only the continuation of policy by other means. The hour had now arrived for him to introduce the long-designed reorganisation of Greece, the necessary condition of which was reconciliation with the Greeks. So to renounce the pursuit and annihilation of the enemy was a manifest gesture of his sincere desire for an accommodation. Here again most plainly we see the great advantage of the union of military command and political control in the person of the monarch, as compared with the *strategoi* of the *Poleis*, dependent on popular assemblies.

Thebes had to pay indeed for the disappointment it had given Philip by joining with Athens. It had to submit to the restoration of Plataea and Orchomenus, and to the reception of a Macedonian garrison in the Cadmeia. But to the Athenians Philip showed the greatest leniency: he restored to them their prisoners without ransom, caused the ashes of the dead to be taken to Athens in solemn procession by Antipater and Alexander, and offered friendship and alliance with the assurance that Athens should remain free and independent. They must however dissolve their naval league, and give up the Thracian Chersonese, for the loss of which the retrocession of Oropus was no compensation. The Athenians, before whose eyes Demosthenes had for years exhibited a caricature of Philip as the great brigand whose sole aim was the destruction of Athens, had prepared for a desperate resistance. This leniency so surprised them that they lost their heads in joy and gratitude. They granted Attic citizenship to Philip and his son

Alexander, and erected a statue of the King in their Agora.

Even during the course of these negotiations for a separate peace with Athens, Philip slightly lifted the veil from his plans, in the clause in which he invited the Athenians, if they would, to accede to the 'universal peace' and to join the 'League council' (*Synhedrion*) which he intended to institute. Moreover, to win Greek sympathies, he carefully circulated the rumour that he wished to lead Greece in a Panhellenic campaign against Persia. When he moved with his army from Athens into the Peloponnese, he was joyfully welcomed by the towns devoted to his cause, and separate peaces were concluded with those that had hitherto opposed him; only Sparta refused to yield, and had to submit to a devastation of Laconia by Philip in conjunction with her old enemies, the Argives and Messenians, whereupon a general Greek court of arbitration awarded to those hostile neighbours all the boundary districts which Sparta had acquired in the course of centuries.

Thus Philip had in fact become master of all Greece, and could now proceed to clothe his power with legal forms. With this object he called on all the sovereign Greek states of the mainland (up to the Macedonian frontier) and the islands as well to send envoys to Corinth, to consult with him as to a new order of things in Greece. The Spartans, in spite of their political impotence, were the only state which proudly refused. And so at the end of 338 opened the memorable Peace Conference of Corinth, the decisions of which represent the crown of Philip's life-work. We must consider them in detail, as they also formed the basis of Alexander's relation to Greece.

Philip opened proceedings by reading a *Diagramma*, a manifesto, in which he laid his proposals before the assembled envoys. No doubt in form this recalls the fact, that in the discussion of the King's Peace at Sardis a message of the Great King was laid before the Greek representatives; but whereas they were then constrained by threats to accept what was dictated to them, in this case Philip submitted his document only as a basis for the impending discussions. At any rate they lasted for months, perhaps into the spring of 337. That the *Diagramma* was couched in the most obliging forms is the more to be assumed, as Philip—so we are told—during the congress exhibited to the envoys the full charm of his amiability, which he could show, when he liked. He was most seriously anxious to win the sympathy of the Greeks, which was vital for the pursuance of his activities. The result of these negotiations was a treaty of alliance between Philip and the Greeks represented at Corinth, which was to be confirmed on oath by either side.

Its chief points are as follows. Philip concluded with the Greeks amity and an offensive and defensive alliance (*Symmachia*) for ever. It is not certain, but not improbable, that even then, as at a later renewal of this treaty of alliance in 302, the Greek states at the same time agreed to friendship and an offensive and defensive alliance with one another.[1] The League of Greeks formed by this alliance (styled 'The Hellenes') was represented in a general *Synhedrion* (federal council), to which the individual states had to send their deputies (*Synhedroi*) in number varying in proportion to their military strengths. This *Synhedrion* was to hold its ordinary sessions at the times and places of the four great Panhellenic festivals (at Olympia, Nemea, Delphi and the Isthmus), while for extraordinary meetings Corinth was probably chosen: and it was there also that the necessary permanent business committee of five presidents (*Prohedroi*) no doubt sat. In the very first paragraph freedom and autonomy, and probably also exemption from

[1] [The author has developed his views in the *Proceedings of the Prussian Academy*, 1929, vol. xviii. W. Schwahn (*Klio* xxi. Beiheft 1930) argued that the alliance simply referred to the contemplated war with Persia. The author in reply points to the fact that the punishment of Thebes after its rebellion is referred to the 'allies' (Arrian I, 9, 9-10). See p. 73.]

tribute and military occupation, were granted to each individual member of the League. If, notwithstanding, apart from Thebes, Macedonian garrisons were placed also in Acrocorinth, Chalcis and Ambracia, this was doubtless consequent on league interests and approved by the congress. As in the second Attic naval league the hegemony of Athens was outside the *Synhedrion* of the members, so here by the side of the *Synhedrion* Philip was the *Hegemon*, the federal general, elected for life by the congress. His kingdom of Macedonia naturally did not belong to the Hellenic League: rather, through Philip's position as *Hegemon*, this Hellenic league of states, to whose individual members freedom and autonomy were guaranteed by treaty, was permanently connected with the kingdom of Macedonia by personal union.

This then is the legal form which Philip finally found for his domination over Greece, so long pursued, a form, as one can see, which tried to deal as gently as possible with the Greek feeling of independence. What trouble he took to pay regard to Greek sensitiveness is shown by the description of him in the treaty, not as 'King', but as '*Hegemon*'. Functions were so divided between the *Synhedrion* and the *Hegemon* that the former had to take resolutions and the latter to carry them out. To the federal council, which also formed the federal tribunal, very important decisions were assigned, as for example on the question whether measures should be taken against a transgressor of the treaty, that is on peace and war. In the latter case the *Hegemon* had to fix the contingents to be supplied by the members and to conduct the war on behalf of the League. In accordance with the sense of the offensive and defensive alliance he had in such a case to support the League with his Macedonian army, and vice versa the Greeks, if he was attacked or an offensive war had to be carried on under his leadership, had to place their contingents under his command. With regard to the latter proviso the same authority states that no one doubted that, by this, war with Persia was intended. This shows that Philip for obvious military and political reasons carefully avoided speaking officially of the Persian King during the constitutive session. In order not prematurely to irritate the King, he wanted to perfect his Greek league and thus have firmly in hand the command of the Greek troops by land and sea, before he came out in public with the plan of a Persian War. Nevertheless, as it was necessary to fix the number of the representatives he began by fixing officially the fighting strength of the individual members. It follows from the relative powers of both sides that as *Hegemon* Philip was not only military leader of the league, but had also complete control of the foreign policy of the Greeks.

In this manner Philip united all the Greeks (with the single exception of Sparta) into a League of states, and so for the first time in history created a Greek unified state. Clearly, after what was said above about the Panhellenic idea, he was not, as has often been assumed, following the instigation of the *Philip* of Isocrates, which entertained no notion of a unification of Greece into one state. The creation of this 'Corinthian League' was not a product of the Panhellenic idea, but of Philip's policy of raising the power of Macedonia. To realise this helps to explain the fact that this solution by Philip of the Greco-Macedonian question, in spite of his efforts to give it a shape which offended Greek susceptibilities as little as possible, was coldly received in wider circles than he had expected. The Greeks regarded the hegemony of Philip as, after all, a foreign domination; they did not look upon the Macedonians as Greeks.

Though the League of states under Philip's guidance did not accord with the intentions of the Panhellenists, yet we may recognise the influence of Isocrates in the 'universal peace' proclaimed by Philip at the congress. If the internal concord of the Greeks, as desired by Isocrates, was unrealisable, within the frame of the League of states thus created measures could still be taken to secure tranquillity and peace in the Greek world. Accordingly, provisions for a 'universal peace' were included, as a vital and fundamental condition in the treaty of alliance. At first it was a peace between Philip and the League. Thus, to take an instance, each member had to swear that he would not try to overthrow the monarchy of Philip and his descendants. The addition of the 'descendants' shows that the treaty was 'eternal'; for if it had merely been with Philip, the Greeks could not take over obligations to his descendants. It was of greater political importance, however, that the Greeks bound themselves by oath to keep the peace perpetually among themselves. No one member might engage in hostilities against another by land or sea. Piracy was forbidden to league-members, and thus the freedom and security of the sea were placed under the protection of the League. Anyone who disobeyed was declared an enemy, and had to expect the punishment of his fellows. But peace was also to prevail within the states themselves. The *Synhedrion* in concert with representatives of the *Hegemon* had to see to it that no executions or sentences of exile were passed against the existing laws, and that there were no confiscations, distributions of land, cancellings of debts or manumissions of slaves for revolutionary purposes—all the usual fearful accompaniments of the constant revolutions of the immediate past. Each member had to swear that he would not subvert the constitutions which existed in the states at the time when the oaths were taken—many had been previously altered by Philip to suit his own views. We must not conclude that the object was to stifle all political life in the various cities: only revolution by violence was forbidden; there was nothing at all to exclude a peaceful development of constitutional life.

It was under this form of a 'universal peace' that Philip sought to realise Isocrates' idea of reconciliation. The external and internal peace of the allied states was guaranteed by severe sanctions contained in clauses of the treaty. To be sure, a real reconciliation of hearts would have been better. But this was Utopian, as we have already observed, and it must be admitted that Philip's substitute of a compulsory peace was the only possible one under existing conditions; it at least promised a relief to the nation, if only it were treated in the spirit of Corinth.

After the draft treaty had been unanimously adopted by the congress, the envoys returned to their homes, and it was adopted and confirmed by oath everywhere. Elections of representatives immediately took place, for at the conclusion of the congress Philip had invited the council to sit as soon as possible, in order that he might address it on the interests of the League. So the federal council held its first meeting at Corinth in the early summer of 337. The hour had come for Philip to strike the last great blow of his Macedonian policy of power; now that he had the Greek contingents in hand, he could appear publicly with his long-cherished design of a Persian War.

It was of great value to him that Isocrates in his *Philip* had prepared the public opinion of Greece for a Panhellenic national war under his leadership. He had now to utilise this Panhellenic idea, in order to conceal his purely Macedonian aims. By leading in the war he might hope to win the sympathies even of those Greeks who were opposed to him, and to acquire even in their eyes a moral title to the powerful status he had obtained at the congress. He had a great position, if he delivered the Greeks of Asia Minor from the Persian yoke, and therewith cancelled the first clause of the King's Peace which had weighed on Hellas for fifty years. The second clause of that Peace he had already cancelled by diplomacy, for, according to the federal constitution, it was now Philip, and not the Great King, who guaranteed the freedom and autonomy of the Greek states.

But what reason was he to allege for the war with Persia? The simple and purely Greek motives of Isocrates were useless, nor could he proclaim his own Macedonian plans of conquest. The clever idea occurred to him of representing the war as a war of *revanche*, in which vengeance was to be taken for the crimes once perpetrated by Xerxes on the temples of the Greek gods.[1] This idea emanates from Philip; not from Isocrates, as is generally assumed, for it was completely foreign to him. We see and admire the delicate insight with which this statesman could enter into the Greek mentality, and how shrewdly he took up his position as a true Heraclid, in elevating the national war into a religious war of vengeance. At the same time he drew a spiritual parallel between his own enterprise and the great age of the Persian Wars. Probably this parallel also occupied him at the congress, when he connected the alliance with the 'universal peace'; for at the coming of Xerxes too the allied Greeks had concluded a peace which applied to the whole country.

So Philip rose in the first session of the council, and proposed that he with his Macedonian army and the contingents of the Greek allies should wage war on Persia, to take vengeance for those crimes of Xerxes against the Greek sanctuaries. Thereupon the representatives voted the war, and, as it was not an ordinary punishment of a member of the League, they specially gave Philip the supreme command of the Persian War with the title of 'commander (*strategos*) with unlimited power'.

After these brilliant successes Philip returned to Macedonia. Next spring (336) he sent across the Dardanelles a vanguard of 10,000 men under Parmenio and Attalus, to prepare in the first instance for the liberation of the cities of Asia Minor. More than this Philip could not do; for a few months afterwards he was murdered.

The work he accomplished at Corinth has been here depicted as a compromise between his Macedonian policy of power and the Panhellenic program of Isocrates, a compromise in which the Macedonian interests were the most prominent. To some extent the wishes of Isocrates were fulfilled, but in forms which he did not contemplate; for

[1] [It was an idea of Pericles, according to Plutarch, *Pericles* 17.]

they were fulfilled on the basis of Philip's chief aim, the domination of Greece. Yet in estimating his work at Corinth we may say that if it had been granted him, instead of dying at forty-seven, to conduct a successful war against Persia and rule for some further decades, his re-organisation of Greece, and especially the completion of the 'universal peace' which was necessary for the prosperity of his Macedonian kingdom, would also have had beneficent effects for the Greek world. It was the gradually ripening plans of Alexander for world-domination, which were quite unknown to his father, that altered the conditions of life for the Corinthian League. What a powerful impression Philip made on his contemporaries is shown by the words of Theopompus the historian, who thus in the beginning of his *Philippica* introduces his subject: 'Taken all in all, Europe has never yet produced such a man as Philip, the son of Amyntas'.

PART II

ALEXANDER

CHAPTER III

THE YOUTH OF ALEXANDER

ALEXANDER's father Philip was the son of the Macedonian Amyntas, but his mother Eurydice was an Illyrian. Perhaps in later life, under the Hellenising influence of the Macedonian court, she learnt to read and write Greek, in order to give her children a higher education, but by blood she was a pure barbarian, a daughter of the Illyrian prince Irras. Alexander's father consequently was half a barbarian. His mother Olympias, whom Philip made his lawful wife in 357, was the daughter of Neoptolemus king of the Molossians, whose dynasty was traced back to the son of Achilles and was therefore looked on as Greek, though the Molossians themselves, a tribe in Epirus, seem to have been barbarians, and were probably related to the Illyrians. In 356 Olympias, who was about twenty years old, gave birth to Alexander, and next year to his sister Cleopatra: there was no further issue of this marriage. So Alexander was not a pure Macedonian but had a dash of barbarian blood in his veins.

Assuredly Alexander inherited many qualities of his parents, but this does not entirely explain his individuality. Of his grandparents, who often strongly influence the grandchildren, we know too little to be able to conjecture anything. Both Philip and Olympias were unusually strong and impulsive in temperament. Philip's acts bear witness to a tireless energy and strength of will, and to an indomitable pertinacity in following out his secret purposes. His body, covered with scars, showed his bravery and a delight in battle which almost amounted to foolhardiness. These are all qualities which, perhaps even to a higher power, manifest themselves in Alexander. If, on the other

hand, Philip is described to us in his private life as an un-
bridled voluptuary who gave himself up without restraint
to the satisfaction of his sensual temperament, those of
the contradictory authorities which represent Alexander
as of a cool nature in amatory affairs are probably right.
At any rate, the love of women never played a leading
part in Alexander's life, and he never allowed it to exert
any influence on the prosecution of his great ambitions; it
was simply to explain this that fictions were told of his love
of boys. When he appears as a man of demonic passion, *
we may to a large extent trace here the inheritance of his
mother Olympias, in whom this quality was intensified to
the highest degree. But it is part of the wonderful combinations of opposites in Alexander's nature, that by the
side of this passion he also exhibits a quite surprisingly cool
and calm discretion.

Since heredity alone cannot explain his character, the
question what influence education had on him is all the
more worthy of interest. Philip, who from the first saw his
successor in Alexander, the offspring of Olympias, beside
whom he had other wives, devoted himself to his boy's
education with great love and care. In the early years,
probably through his mother's influence, it was entrusted
to a relation of Olympias, Leonidas, who tried to master
by severity the uncontrollable and defiant lad; and under
him were the pedagogues and elementary teachers, who
had to instruct the young prince along with other youths
of the Macedonian nobility. When Philip saw that the
boy was not to be influenced by force but only by persuasion, in 343, when Alexander was thirteen, he summoned Aristotle to be his tutor. This was to have a profound effect on Alexander's development.

To understand this lucky choice of Philip, one must not
picture the Aristotle of that period as the famous master
of science that he has been regarded through the centuries
down to our own time. After the death of his master Plato
(347) Aristotle had taught with other Platonists at Assos

in the Troad, and had entered into close relations with Hermias prince of Atarneus, who, as mentioned already, was politically connected with Philip; by his marriage with the niece and adopted daughter of Hermias this connexion became still closer. After staying about three years at Assos he then moved to Mytilene in Lesbos and was just opening a school of his own there, when the invitation reached him to educate the heir-apparent of Macedonia. Material as these years at Assos were for the development of Aristotle, he was not yet one of the famous great men of the day. His father Nicomachus had once been court-physician to Amyntas of Macedonia, but this was too remote to have been of decisive weight in Philip's selection. The recent conjecture that the political relations of Philip with Hermias had something to do with his choice has much in its favour.[1] Conversely, it was no doubt tempting to Aristotle to have a hand in the intellectual evolution of the heir to the great Macedonian kingdom, which had become a factor of commanding influence on the fortunes of Greece, and to which belonged his native town Stagira, that had been conquered and destroyed by Philip. So at the age of rather more than forty Aristotle went to Pella. To prevent the instruction from being disturbed by the animated life of the court, Philip assigned to him as his residence the quiet little village of Mieza. Here it was that near a sanctuary of the Nymphs Aristotle taught Alexander for about three years. Perhaps Hephaestion, who was Alexander's dearest friend to his death, was one of those educated with him.

It is natural that there was much fiction told about this education and its subjects later, when Aristotle had become the ruler in the intellectual sphere and Alexander the lord of the actual world: but unfortunately we have little information deserving of credit. Details in Alexander's later character may be traced with probability to Aristotle's

[1] W. Jäger, *Aristoteles, Grundlegung einer Geschichte seiner Entwicklung,* 1923, pp. 113 ff.

influence. But the chief result is clear; it was Aristotle who inspired in him a passionate love of Greek culture and made him wholly Greek in intellect. This profoundly affected Alexander's life. Naturally in dealing with this boy, whose heart he soon won, Aristotle struck a different note from that of his learned treatises. He was capable of warm feeling, as we see in the deep religious and emotional tone of the hymn to *Arete* (manly virtue), which he wrote about this time in honour of his friend Hermias, who had been betrayed into the hands of the Persian king, had been tortured at Susa to make him reveal Philip's plans, but had steadily refused to disclose anything and had thereupon been crucified. Deeply moved and exasperated at this, Aristotle raised in his honour a splendid memorial in this dithyrambic hymn to the *Arete* for which the heroes had formerly laid down their lives—and now Hermias, whom the Muses would also name as an immortal. With this ideal of manly virtue, which, because of his typical dislike of barbarians, he finds only in Hellas, Aristotle certainly inspired the young prince, and doubtless held before him as patterns the heroes, to whose company was now added his friend Hermias. Two of the heroes he mentions actually lighted Alexander on his path of conquest, Heracles and Achilles, whom Alexander revered as his ancestors: on his father's side he was a descendant of Heracles, and on his mother's side an Aeacid, sprung from Achilles. If in Alexander's later years Heracles becomes more prominent, in his earlier days Alexander was inspired by the pattern of the youthful hero Achilles. This deeply-rooted and vivid conception of his personal affinity with these heroes is one of those non-rational and instinctive motives, without which we cannot understand him at all.

The effects of the Aristotelian training are most unmistakeable in Alexander's close connexion, even later in Asia, with Greek literature and art and in his keen interest in scientific problems. It was especially the golden stores of Greek poetry that Aristotle laid before his pupil and enabled him to appreciate. Among the books that formed Alexander's reading later in Asia, are mentioned the three great tragedians, of whom he knew Euripides best: but he also read the modern authors of the fourth century, like the dithyrambic poets Philoxenus and Telestes, and others as well. In the Theban catastrophe he showed what reverence he felt for Pindar, the great lyrical poet of the past. But the *Iliad* was to him the book of books. It certainly also formed the staple of his youthful education. Aristotle actually made a revised edition of it for the benefit of his pupil, which was his constant companion on his Asiatic campaign.

How far Aristotle talked to the lad about philosophy, we do not know, though later fictions profess exact information. But he unquestionably roused in him the feeling for philosophic thought. In attendance on Alexander in his camp were philosophers of various schools. Rhetoric can only have been of secondary importance in his education. But certainly Aristotle endeavoured to develop political thought in him, to prepare him for his later duties as a ruler, though we have no exact knowledge on the point and are reduced to conjecture. In the political sphere the two men later pursued completely different paths, and could not understand one another. Notably in the question, what attitude to take to subjected barbarians, Alexander did not follow Aristotle, who was in favour of despotic control. Here rather we see him in agreement with the advice with which Isocrates concludes his *Philip*, that Philip should free the barbarians from barbarian despotism and entrust them to Hellenic care and protection. We may assume as a matter of course that Alexander read this treatise; and it is not impossible that Isocrates—we possess a letter from him to the young prince, written about the time of his instruction by Aristotle—in this sense had an indirect influence on Alexander.

Most notably, Alexander was inspired by Aristotle with a keen interest in natural science. The consequence was that his Eastern campaign signalised an epoch-making scientific advance, owing to the investigations and descriptions of Asia, which he ordered from various experts and specialists. The picture of the earth's surface, which he derived from his teacher, he tested on the spot during his Asiatic expeditions, and enlarged and corrected by his new discoveries. This deliberate promotion of the various scientific branches of study was, however, of less significance in the subsequent history of the world than Alexander's constant desire to introduce into the East the Greek culture into which he had been initiated by Aristotle.

The idyll of Mieza came to an end, when in 340 Philip left the boy of sixteen as regent at Pella during his campaign against Byzantium. Probably the trusty Antipater was placed by his side, advised him, and introduced him into the practical side of the business of government. That Alexander was really regent, is established by the fact that it was he who bore his father's royal seal and sealed with it the required documents of state. Meanwhile, the Thracian Maidoi rose in rebellion, and it was doubtless a joy to Alexander to have the chance of commanding for the first time in a campaign, though small. He defeated the enemy, took their town, and, following the example of his father whose practice was to secure by colonies newly conquered districts, resettled the town, and named it—certainly with his father's permission—Alexandropolis, on the analogy of Philippopolis. This was the first Alexander city; it was to have many successors.

What great confidence Philip had come to repose in his son, was shown on the decisive day of Chaeronea, when he gave the prince, then aged eighteen, the command of the cavalry on the offensive wing, though tried generals, to be sure, were associated with him. It was an honourable commission too to join Antipater in carrying to Athens the ashes of the Athenians who fell in the battle. This was the only time that Alexander ever saw Athens, but the impression this unique city left upon him was indelible, and it was not policy alone that caused him in the earlier period of his reign to single it out for visible distinction.

These pleasant relations between father and son came to an end, when Philip, soon after his return from the Congress of Corinth (337), was seized by a passion for a fair Macedonian, Cleopatra, the niece of Attalus, and made her his lawful consort. This implied the repudiation of Olympias, and might even endanger Alexander's claim to the succession. At the marriage feast there was a terrible scene between Alexander and Attalus, when the latter wished Philip a true-born heir as issue of the new marriage, and a scene still worse between father and son. Alexander and his mother immediately quitted Macedonia. He accompanied her to her home in Epirus, and then went himself to the Illyrians, a surprising step, difficult to explain, but in any case showing how deep was the quarrel. After some time, however, through the mediation of Demaratus of Corinth, who visited Pella as Philip's guest, a reconciliation was effected between father and son, whereupon Alexander returned to Philip. This presupposes that Alexander's fears as to his right of succession were completely allayed: certainly Philip had never for an instant demurred to it.

Once more there was an estrangement between father and son, but it did not go deep and soon passed away. Pixodarus, a Carian ruler and vassal of the Great King, had offered Philip a defensive alliance and sought to obtain one of the sons of Philip as husband for his daughter and heiress. As Philip was rightly of opinion that it was unsuitable for his son and heir to marry the daughter of a Persian vassal, he offered his illegitimate son Arrhidaeus to be Pixodarus' son-in-law. Alexander, misunderstanding this, felt himself slighted, and yielding to the bad advice of his friends, offered himself as son-in-law to Pixodarus behind his father's back. When Philip learned this act of youthful folly, he explained his motives to his son, and generously pardoned him, but exiled from the court, as a punishment, those friends, to whom he attributed the chief fault, among them Nearchus, Harpalus and Ptolemy the son of Lagus. So father and son were again reconciled, and even Olympias made overtures to Philip, when he proposed to marry their daughter Cleopatra to Olympias' brother, Alexander, the Molossian king.

It was at the wedding at Aegae, in the midsummer of 336, when Philip was going into the theatre without a body-guard, that he was stabbed by a certain Pausanias, a young Macedonian noble. The tragic end of Philip is indirectly connected with his alliance with the niece of Attalus, which had already brought so much misfortune on his house; for Pausanias had previously been insulted by Attalus, and, being unable to get satisfaction from him, turned his anger against Philip, who in spite of repeated applications had left the insult unpunished. Though the motive of Pausanias was private revenge, there were others in the plot with him. After all that had passed between Philip and Olympias, the suspicion was bound to arise that she either was privy to the murder or had instigated it. Her complicity cannot be at all confirmed, natural as it might seem in the case of so vindictive a character. But we must decidedly reject the idea that Alexander was implicated. That is a mere calumny of his enemies.

CHAPTER IV

ALEXANDER'S REIGN DOWN TO THE WAR WITH PERSIA

IN the midst of the intense excitement, caused by the murder of Philip in the vast concourse at the magnificent marriage festival at Aegae, the change of monarchs was smoothly effected. The faithful Antipater is said to have helped to quieten the people by addressing them on Alexander's great qualities. The army, which Alexander had led to victory at Chaeronea, had not the slightest hesitation. And so by the assembly of the Macedonian army, which according to ancient privilege had the deciding voice, Alexander, who was then twenty, was at once acclaimed king, and thereby recognised as lawful king of Macedonia.

The young king's first thought was to punish the murderers of his father. There are two irreconcilable traditions concerning the fate of Pausanias: one that as he ran away he was immediately caught and killed; the other, which is perhaps to be preferred, that Alexander, who had immediately seated himself on the throne in the royal castle, caused Pausanias to be brought before him, and, as guilty of high treason, handed him over to the judgment of the Macedonian army—whose assembly caused him to be crucified. Later at the solemn funeral of Philip at Aegae, other persons, regarded as accomplices, were executed in atonement of the crime. Among them were two brothers of the Lyncestian princely house, Arrhabaeus and Heromenes, who were accused of promoting the murder of

Philip for the further reason that they wished to win the throne for themselves. It is in favour of this assumption that Alexander pardoned the third brother, the Lyncestian Alexander, because immediately after Philip's murder he did homage to himself as king and followed him into the palace. Respect for Antipater, to whom this Alexander was son-in-law, may have influenced the young king, but what decided him was that this homage proved that this Alexander had nothing to do with his brothers' plan of usurpation. His close personal relation to Antipater may have kept him loyal. So he escaped suspicion of complicity. Alexander would have granted no pardon for this crime, however much he respected Antipater. That such Lyncestian princes might be regarded as possible pretenders, is shown by the fact that later Darius promised the third brother Alexander the throne of Macedonia, if he would kill Alexander the Great.

The security of the throne required further sacrifices. Amyntas, the son of King Perdiccas, for whom Philip had undertaken the regency, and then put him aside, was still alive. As he was not without a following, and there were many who looked upon him as the lawful successor, he became, after the death of Philip, against whom he had never dared to assert his claim, a danger to the throne of the new king. He was therefore removed, and also Caranus, a half-brother of Alexander, probably by an earlier marriage of Philip, who also might become dangerous as a pretender.[1] Above all, Philip's impolitic union with Cleopatra, the niece of Attalus, had left in her high-born kinsfolk an opposition which might prove a cause for alarm to his son Alexander; accordingly before Alexander crossed into Asia, he removed all the male members of this family who could threaten his position. But he was annoyed, when Olympias, to satisfy her hatred for her rival, murdered the infant daughter, to which Cleopatra had recently given birth, in the arms of her mother, and forced the mother to

[1] For Caranus see Helmuth Berve, *Das Alexanderreich*, ii. 199.

commit suicide. The conflicts of the past, for which Alexander was not to blame, caused much bloodshed. His firmness, however, had this effect: as long as he lived, his throne and kingdom were not endangered from Macedonia.

The news of the murder of Philip attracted the attention of the whole world, but nowhere did it produce a greater effect than in Greece. It testifies to the diplomatic skill of the young king that after the murder, at the audience he gave to the Greek ambassadors who had come to Aegae for the wedding, he expressed the expectation that the Hellenes would preserve towards him 'the loyal feeling which had descended to him from his father', thus showing his knowledge, that the treaty of the League was perpetual and gave him a legal claim to be *Hegemon* of the League. But in Greece this interpretation of his rights, though it had been confirmed by oath, was absolutely disregarded, as soon as the news of Philip's death arrived. The clauses of the Corinthian treaty were too recent to have already brought about a change in the mentality of the Hellenes. At once in many parts Philip's old opponents rose, in the hope of being able to shake off the Macedonian hegemony. Athens showed the way, and, led by Demosthenes, refused to Alexander the hegemony of the League, in the hope of winning back its own old hegemony over Greece. Under the impression of the defeat at Chaeronea Athens had undertaken sensible reforms, designed to strengthen the state, not only in her financial administration, which was reformed by the excellent Lycurgus, but in military matters as well; as in Prussia universal service followed Jena, so at Athens after Chaeronea the institution of the Ephebic system put compulsory service by the citizens on a new footing. At the news of Philip's murder the people were swept by Demosthenes into an intoxication of liberty; he appeared in the council dressed in white with a wreath on his head, thank offerings were made to the gods for the joyful news, and honours were paid to the murderer Pausanias. And yet at the marriage festival at Aegae the

Athenians had presented a golden wreath and announced a decree, promising to surrender anyone who attempted the life of Philip, if ever he took refuge at Athens! The call to freedom rang out from Athens to the other Hellenes. The Aetolians decided to recall those exiled by Philip, the Ambraciots expelled their Macedonian garrison, the Thebans resolved to liberate their Cadmeia; there were disturbances in Peloponnese too, in Argos, Elis and Arcadia. Even over sea Demosthenes was in secret communication with Attalus, who along with Parmenio was commander in Asia, and, disappointed of his hopes by the accession of Alexander, had become his mortal foe. Subsequently Alexander had this Attalus put out of the way, when he had proofs of his high treason. Demosthenes also entered once more into relations with the Persian King.

On hearing of these inclinations to revolt in Greece, Alexander, although serious reports had been received about the barbaric peoples of the North, put himself immediately at the head of his army, and entered Hellas by forced marches, resolved, if need be, to fight for his right. Thus at the first we find in him that determination and rapidity of action, by which later he won his successes. His sudden appearance nipped the revolutionary movement in the bud. The Thessalians, whose country he came to first, not merely elected him *Archon* of their federal state in place of his father, but also declared themselves ready to recognise him as *Hegemon* of the Greek League, and, if necessary, to render him their assistance in punishing Athens on behalf of the League. In his negotiations with the Thessalians Alexander pointed to their common descent from Achilles and Heracles, and it is interesting to see how from the first this conception of his heroic descent was vivid in his mind, though we must at the same time remember that it is also an instance of the political significance of the myth (p. 35). He then pressed southwards, and, after winning to his cause the Aenianes, Malians and Dolopians, occupied Thermopylae, summoned there a meeting of the Amphictyonic Council, and there too received from the assembled representatives of the tribes his recognition as *Hegemon* of the League. Then in still quicker marches he entered Boeotia, and to the terror of the Thebans pitched his camp near the Cadmeia. The rejoicing in Athens died down, and with horror the Athenians realised what a false estimate Demosthenes had formed of the young king, whom he had contemptuously called a simpleton (Margites) who would only go walks in Pella. In righteous wrath Alexander delivered an ultimatum giving them the choice of war or his recognition as *Hegemon* of the League. The Athenians, who at the news of Alexander's march towards Attica had prepared for fighting, in relief caught at the second alternative, and through their ambassadors asked pardon for not having at once recognised his hegemony. Demosthenes, who was a member of the delegation, conscious of guilt, did not venture to face Alexander but turned back on Cithaeron. Nevertheless, Alexander was glad to pardon the Athenians; he had had his way, and, at least since his training under Aristotle, he had cherished a secret affection for Athens. The people of Athens thereupon overwhelmed him with honours, even more numerous than those which they had conferred on his father Philip.

Alexander then summoned all the members of the league—and especially the Peloponnesians, who had not yet recognised him as *Hegemon*—to send envoys to Corinth, and at the same time convoked a meeting there of the existing representatives. The sole exception to his recognition by the Peloponnese was that of the Spartans, who sent the proud answer, that since the days of their forefathers it had been their custom not to follow but themselves to lead others. Afterwards in the autumn of 336 there was a second constitutive congress at Corinth, at which Alexander renewed the league-treaty with the envoys of the states. This time no long discussions were required as had been the case two years before; for the treaty, with a few

formal changes, had only to be altered to the name of
Alexander. This treaty also was perpetual, and was extended to the descendants of the king.

After Alexander had thus been recognised as *Hegemon* of
the League for life, the old council met, and entrusted him,
like his father before him, with the office of 'General with unlimited powers' for the campaign of revenge against Persia.
We may assume that this result of the Congress made a
very different impression on the mind of Alexander from
that which it had made on his father. To the latter the designed campaign of vengeance was merely a pretext and
an instrument of policy for making Macedonia a great
power. But Alexander, into whom Aristotle had instilled a
love of Greek culture, was bound to take up the Panhellenic idea with the greatest enthusiasm as affording him an
opportunity to carry Greek culture into Asia; there was
also the personal motive, the example of his heroic ancestors and especially of Achilles. Accordingly he crossed
over to Asia, full of the romantic conception, that he as a
second Achilles was leading the Greeks against the barbarians; but at the same time he went forth as King of
Macedonia, to conquer new territory. Though we cannot
divine his intentions and though no one can say how far his
plans then reached, during the first years of his Asiatic
campaign, so long as he was occupied with the Panhellenic commission, we may yet attribute a two-fold aspect
to his aims regarding the war.

The more passionately Alexander must have yearned for
the beginning of his campaign of vengeance, the more
must we remark how, after his return from Corinth in the
winter of 336-5, he did not prepare to cross into Asia, but,
with the deliberation and cool reflection which were characteristic of him in strategic questions, thought it necessary
first to settle accounts with the northern barbarians, in
order to cover his rear, before he left his home. The main
trouble was with the Triballians, a Thracian tribe, living
between the Balkans and the Danube, whom Philip had

fought but not subjected. Here Alexander's power was, if possible, to be advanced to the Danube, so as to secure for his kingdom a fixed and natural northern frontier. It was this political object which impelled him northwards, not, as has been supposed, 'the insatiable impulse of a soul hungry for exploits', which would at that time much sooner have sent him to Asia.

In this his first campaign Alexander exhibits the forethought with which he always prepared his military operations. He sent ships of war from Byzantium by way of the Black Sea into the Danube and ordered them to sail up to a point indicated by him, to co-operate there with his land forces; and if he found them at the right spot, we may infer that he took care to get accurate information about the territory of the enemy. In other respects too we find in this Danube campaign, as in the following operations of 335 in Illyria and Greece, all the excellences of his strategy and tactics, which have made him one of the foremost commanders of all time. This deserves to be emphasised all the more, as Parmenio, the trusty old general of his father, to whom there has been a recent unsuccessful attempt to give all the credit of Alexander's successes, was then in Asia and took no part in the expedition.[1] Nor was Antipater, Philip's other great general, with him; for he had been left behind with a part of the army to secure order in the kingdom and in Hellas.

In the spring of 335 Alexander started from Amphipolis. He marched from the Strymon along the coast to the Nestos (Karasu), followed its course inland, turned off by way of Philippopolis, his father's foundation, and reached the Kotcha Balkans, where he found the Shipka Pass[2] occupied by the independent Thracians, who had secured their position behind a fort constructed of waggons. When they tried to break up the phalanx by rolling down waggons, Alexander ordered his men partly to form alleys,

---

[1] Beloch, *Griech. Geschichte*, iv. 2, p. 290.
[2] [The Shipka reaches a height of 7800 ft.]

through which the waggons hurtled down, and in part to lie down in close formation with their shields over their heads, so that the waggons passed over these roofs of shields without doing any mischief. In this moment of peril the manoeuvres were executed with the calmness and precision of drill on a parade-ground, so that not a single man was lost, and we are reminded by this very first encounter that it was the foremost army of the world which Alexander inherited from his father. When the Shipka had been   *
taken by storm and Alexander had descended into the northern plain, Syrmos, the Triballian king, with the wives and children of his people, sought safety on an island in the Danube, the position of which it is difficult to identify— perhaps it was near Nicopolis: the Triballian army, which withdrew southwards, had suffered an annihilating defeat. Three days later, when Alexander reached the Danube, he found his fleet, but the banks were so steep that he failed in his attempt to land troops on the island in which Syrmos had taken refuge.

The brilliant idea then occurred to Alexander, that by a surprising demonstration of force he would break the enemy's inclination to resist him. He determined suddenly to cross the Danube, put to flight the Getae, who lived on the opposite bank, and by this demonstration startle Syrmos into surrender. To these political and military motives, a purely personal one was added. Our best authority here uses for the first time an oft-recurring expression, 'He was seized by a longing to cross the Danube'. This was the non-rational longing for the unknown, the uninvestigated and mysterious, which in his later years took him irresistibly to the ends of the earth. Now in his young soul, to which any ideas of world conquest were still foreign, it was this which impelled him to cast a glance upon the unknown and strange world beyond the new frontier of his realm.   *

Quite silently he prepared for the crossing. The boats used for fishing by the natives were collected, and the canvas of the camp-tents filled with hay to support swimmers. By such primitive methods and with the help of his fleet he used the quietness of a dark night to put across the river as many of his troops as possible. Before dawn there were already 1500 cavalry and 4000 infantry on the opposite bank. In the early morning Alexander led his troops through fields of corn which masked their approach. Then he burst out with the cavalry, and dashed upon the Getae encamped in front of their town. Completely surprised by this almost inconceivably rash feat of Alexander, the Getae, though far superior in numbers, rushed back to the town, hastily snatched up wives and children on their horses, and disappeared into the steppes of the North. Alexander plundered and destroyed the town, offered sacrifice on the north bank to Zeus the Saviour, Heracles and the river-god, who had permitted his crossing, and the same day led his army back to the camp on the south bank, without having lost a single man.

This almost fabulous expedition had the intended result; Syrmos and his Triballians made their submission to Alexander. Other neighbouring tribes south of the Danube also sent envoys to the king and did him homage. The fame of his deeds reached even the Celts, who had then pushed eastwards from the Adriatic, and they sent an embassy to ask for his friendship.[1] The terror Alexander inspired had a long after-effect. It was almost fifty years before the Celts ventured to invade Macedonia and Greece.

Alexander's intention was to return to Macedonia by the western route through Paeonia, but near Sofia in the region of the Agrianes, a tribe faithful to him, he was surprised by the news that Cleitus, king of Illyria, the modern Albania, had revolted. Straightway he proceeded by forced marches (it was about August), probably by way of

---

[1] [The Celts swore: 'We will keep faith, unless the sky fall and crush us, or the earth open and swallow us, or the sea rise and overwhelm us'. They added that they only feared the sky falling (*C.A.H.* vi. 355. W. W. Tarn).]

Kustendil, up the Erigon (Cerna) to the important frontier fortress of Pellion, which commanded the pass from Upper Macedonia into Illyria; it was, however, already in the hands of the enemy. He probably succeeded in driving the Illyrians from the heights and shutting them into the town, but he was prevented from besieging it by the arrival of the Taulantian prince Glaucias, who had joined the rebellion. Alexander had to retreat, and only by a brilliant manoeuvre escaped being surrounded. Finally, the enemy was defeated by surprise in an open battle, retreated to Pellion, set the town on fire and escaped. And so, hazardous as the conflicts were, Alexander was again victorious. It was fortunate that he attained his object so quickly; hardly had he occupied Pellion, before the news reached him of a dangerous rising in Greece which required his immediate intervention.

It appears that while Alexander stayed in Macedonia, the Greeks kept quiet, though the parties hostile to him in the cities felt his hegemony as a grievous burden. But when he went northwards and remained a long time in unknown and remote lands, from which no news came, the Greek world was filled with unrest and excitement. Meanwhile the new king of Persia, Darius III, who had come to the throne in May 336, became aware of the danger threatening him from the west, for his troops had already come into collision with the Macedonian vanguard in Asia Minor. As he was certainly acquainted with the war-resolutions of 337 and 336, and was cognisant of the state of feeling in Greece, he thought he could most easily ward off Alexander's attack in the time-honoured fashion, by attracting the Greeks to his side with his gold. Accordingly envoys of the Great King invited the various states to revolt from Alexander and offered large sums as subsidies. Only Sparta, which was not a member of the league, accepted the gold. The states of the league, even Athens, took a correct attitude, adhered to the treaty lately concluded, and refused. Demosthenes however had no scruple in accepting 300 talents from the Great King for propaganda in the Persian cause, though his native city had elected Alexander commander-in-chief against Persia. It was a reckless game that he began on his own responsibility, and he bears a great part of the blame for the disaster that fell on Greece.

The excitement in Greece, which must have been increased by the Persian proposals, grew, the longer Alexander was absent, and reached its maximum, when the rumour was circulated that Alexander had fallen in battle with the Triballians. Demosthenes cleverly used this to promote the agitation, producing in the Athenian ecclesia a wounded man who declared he had been wounded in the same battle, in which Alexander fell. The belief in Alexander's death became widespread, and this is of importance in arriving at a legal judgment on the ensuing insurrection; for if Alexander was dead, the Corinthian treaty was null and void in default of any issue of Alexander, and the Greek states had recovered the freedom of action they enjoyed before Chaeronea. So the Thebans, to whom the Macedonian garrison of the Cadmeia was an ever present eyesore, rose, at the instigation of the exiles who had been secretly fetched from Athens. They slew some Macedonian officers and began the siege of the citadel, trusting to the support of Athens, which, through Demosthenes, sent them arms that he had acquired with the Persian gold. The Arcadians also rose and despatched an army to the Isthmus, and would not draw back in spite of a message from Antipater. Aetolia and Elis also began to move.

This bad news reached Alexander, just when he had finished the struggle for the possession of Pellion. At once he led his army southwards, although it had just been engaged in severe fighting, by forced marches of an average of nearly twenty miles a day. On the thirteenth day he who was believed to be dead was already at Onchestus in Boeotia. The Thebans thought it could only be Antipater who had moved against them from Macedonia, and when it was announced that it was Alexander they thought it could only be the Lyncestian Alexander; perhaps they reasoned that after the death of Alexander the Great the Lyncestian had won the crown of Macedonia. But the next day no doubt was possible: Alexander was before the town. For the correct view of this campaign of Alexander, it is important to notice what has often been overlooked, that he waged it in the capacity of *Hegemon* of the League to punish on behalf of the League its refractory members. This was also the Greek view; for he was hastily joined by small contingents of the neighbouring states, who, faithful to him but hostile to Thebes put themselves under his command in accordance with the treaty. Since Alexander must have learnt that he had been regarded as dead—which completely altered the legal position—he endeavoured at first to bring the rebel Thebans back into the league without bloodshed. When he proposed this to them, in case they had thought better of their attitude, they replied by a cavalry attack upon his outposts. Only with their recalcitrance to the living Alexander did the guilt of the Thebans begin. Next day the king marched round the city, and encamped on the south before the Electra gate, imposing remains of which still exist, where the road from Athens terminates. Here he was nearest to the besieged garrison of the Cadmeia, for its southern wall at this point coincided with that of the city. The Thebans had erected a double palisade before the gate, to cut off the garrison from all communication with the outside world. Still Alexander postponed the attack in the hope of the success of negotiations for peace. But when he promised the Thebans that they should be received back into the league, if they surrendered their ringleaders, they replied with the contemptuous demand that he should surrender to them Antipater and the commander of the Cadmeia, and caused a herald to proclaim from a high tower that anyone who wished, in company with them and the Great King, to free Greece from the tyranny of Alexander, should

forthwith join them. After this Alexander could not hesitate to draw the sword, and in angry mood ordered the
attack. But before he had given the signal, Perdiccas with
his regiment rushed forward against the stockade, and
began the fighting, which developed into a general engagement before the south wall of the city. When the
troops which had hurried forward under Perdiccas were
put to flight in a sunken road, Alexander with his best
troops came into action. In spite of a brave defence the
Thebans were routed, and the Macedonians pressing on
after them succeeded in entering the city by the Electra
gate along with the fugitives. Other divisions joined the
garrison of the Cadmeia, and rushed with them down into
the city, where the Thebans made one more fruitless stand
near the Amphion. There was a terrible massacre of the
population, due more to the old hatred of the Boeotians
and Phocians than to the anger of the Macedonians.

What was to be done with the conquered city? As *Hegemon* of the League, Alexander called an extraordinary
meeting of the federal council, and referred to it the decision of the question: for this decision belonged to the
Synhedrion, not to the *Hegemon*.[1] Only the neighbouring
allies, chiefly Boeotians and Phocians, can have hastily
sent their deputies, and so in the meeting the pent up
hatred of the oppressed, who for many generations had
suffered under the supremacy of Thebes, found irresistible
outlet. At this spectacle we are touched by the lamentable
disunion of the Greeks. As formerly after the collapse of
the Athenian empire (404) the Thebans and Corinthians
had called for the destruction of Athens, so the deputies
now demanded the destruction of Thebes, and no member
of the League was found to hinder the execution of the
sentence, as Sparta had then done, a fact which should be
remembered to her credit. It is true that whereas Sparta
had then been able to point to the imperishable merit
Athens had acquired in the wars of liberation from Persia,

[1] [See p. 43 note.]

this time the deputies pointed to the treason of which Thebes had been guilty then as now against Greece. Under this stimulus the resolution of the league was to level Thebes with the ground, to divide the territory (except that which was sacred) among the Boeotian members of the league, to leave a permanent Macedonian garrison in the Cadmeia, to sell the women and children into slavery, and to declare the Theban refugees outlawed from the whole territory of the league. Certainly if Alexander had wished, he could have tempered the severity of the decree; but in the interest of the Panhellenic idea and the campaign of vengeance against Persia an example had to be made of the rebels, who had deserted the league and played into the hands of the Persian King. So he did not hesitate, as *Hegemon*, to order the execution of the decree. Thus the sacred city, the city of Cadmus and Oedipus, the city of Epaminondas, was wiped off the face of the earth. Yet contemporaries felt that Alexander was troubled by remorse for his behaviour; later when he had opportunity of showing favour to individual Thebans, he always took it. His order to spare the house of Pindar, the great Theban poet, shows that he did not order the destruction of the city like 'a raving demon', but under the pressure of political considerations and with divided feelings in his Greek soul. It is also undeniable that he only determined to fight after serious attempts at conciliation. One consequence of this terrible example, which was clearly welcome to him, was that he could without risk pardon all the other rebels.

The most surprised by this were the Athenians. Conscious of their guilt as the intellectual authors of the Greek rising, when the startling news of the Theban catastrophe fell on them as a thunderbolt during the celebration of the Great Mysteries, they had every reason to expect punishment from the victor, though they had prudently kept back their promised aid and left the Thebans in the lurch. At once they sent an embassy and congratulated the king on his safe

return from the north and his punishment of the Theban
rising. This behaviour is so contemptible that it can hardly *
be excused by their deadly terror. It was not until they
saw his inclination to mercy that they ventured, on his demand for the surrender of the anti-Macedonian leaders
with Demosthenes at their head, to beg for the withdrawal
of the demand by a second embassy headed by Phocion.
Alexander, who, quite apart from his love for Athens, felt
it important not to drive into the arms of the Persian King
the strongest naval power in Greece, agreed, and was content with the banishment of the general Charidemus, one
of his most bitter opponents, who thereupon went off to
Persia, accompanied by other irreconcilables.

CHAPTER V

THE PERSIAN WAR
DOWN TO ECBATANA (330)

THUS peace in Greece was restored, and after his return to
Macedonia (October 335), Alexander could finally devote
himself to the preparations for his Asiatic expedition. But
it was only an enforced peace that prevailed in Hellas;
after the melancholy experiences of the last two years, no
one saw that more clearly than Alexander, and he drew
his conclusions accordingly as regards both his preparations and his plan of campaign. Being necessarily mistrust-
ful of a large section of the Greeks, he left the faithful Antipater in Macedonia with half his Macedonian levy, 12,000
phalangites and 1500 cavalry; Antipater was also charged
with the oversight of the league as representative of the
Hegemon, perhaps with the title of *Strategos*. The same mistrust caused him to limit the contingents he called for from
the league to no more than what a regard for the Panhellenic campaign seemed to require. Apart from the fleet
of 160 triremes supplied by the league and therefore called
the 'Greek Fleet', only 7000 infantry and 600 cavalry are
mentioned, and in addition 1500 Thessalian horse. The
latter, presumably attached to the king as their *Archon* and
enjoying his special confidence, played an important part
in the great battles in Asia. On the other hand, we look in
vain for the 7000 league infantry in the battle front. One
gets the impression that, apart from the Thessalians, Alexander took the Greek contingents rather as hostages, who
would help to keep Hellas quiet. The 'Greek Fleet' at first
was prudently kept out of action. This was anyhow inevitable owing to the great superiority, both in numbers and

quality, of the Persian fleet of 400 ships of war, with their first-rate Phoenician and Cypriot vessels.

The naval superiority of the enemy had a determining effect on Alexander's plan of campaign. As the Persian fleet controlled the sea, the greatest danger was the possibility that the Great King might transfer the war to Greece and by his immense treasures coerce the Greeks into fighting against him. As a decision at sea was out of the question owing to the small size and unreliable nature of the Greek fleet, Alexander formed the clever scheme of paralysing the maritime superiority of his opponent by first conquering with his land army the Mediterranean coast regions of the Persian empire, in order to occupy the recruiting grounds and stations of the Persian fleet and above all the Phoenician coast. He did not move into the interior of Asia, until with unwearying energy he had carried out this program to the last detail. As we cannot guess the scope of his plans of conquest when he crossed into Asia, we do not know how far this strategic plan was formed beforehand or took shape during his victorious advance.

Alexander's whole strength was in his land-army. On it, and especially on the incomparable Macedonian élite, which his father had bequeathed to him trained to perfection, and also on the self-confidence of military genius was based an absolute assurance of victory. This not only filled the soul of the young king, but he also succeeded in inspiring with it his Macedonians who were enthusiastically devoted to him. Without this assurance of victory and the invincible will to conquer, many of Alexander's actions and successes would be unintelligible. Numerically his army was far inferior to that opposed to it. Inclusive of those Greek contingents and about 5000 Greek mercenaries and of contingents of Thracians, Agrianians, and other Balkan races, the army of Alexander, when it crossed into Asia, amounted only to about 30,000 infantry and 5000 cavalry. Among the latter were 1500 Macedonian cavalry (*Hetairoi*), who, apart from the royal regiment, were recruited from the coastlands added by Philip to his kingdom; the levies of the nobility from the districts of Old Macedonia, however, were left behind with Antipater. The opposition of the men of Old Macedonia which was later directed against Alexander, when he went counter to Macedonian interests, came rather from the Macedonian infantry than from the *Hetairoi*.

The question, how many troops Darius had at his disposal, when so framed, admits of no answer. His empire, which extended to the frontiers of India, had theoretically incalculable possibilities, but in practice they were considerably limited by the immense distances and the consequent difficulties of a levy. We can only ask, how many troops the Great King actually put into the field against Alexander in individual battles. If we abandon the fantastically colossal numbers, which tradition gives us, as it did in the Persian wars of the fifth century, it is incontestable that Alexander won his three pitched battles—the Granicus, Issus and Gaugamela—against superior numbers which grew larger on each occasion. Besides his picked troops from Persia and Eastern Iran, the Great King, like his predecessors, relied especially on his Greek mercenaries, who, in spite of the decree of the Corinthian League that no Greeks might enlist as mercenaries under the Persians, served him to the number of many thousands, some of them loyally to the very end.

Still more marked was Alexander's inferiority in finance.[1] The Great King had the disposal of unlimited treasures of silver and gold, stored up in his capitals. At his accession Alexander not only found in the treasury barely 60 talents of ready money, but also took over a debt of 500 talents, to which he had to add 800 talents of personal debt. On the assumption that these figures are correct, it would be surprising if, according to another account which is equally

[1] For Alexander's finances see A. Andreades, *Les Finances de guerre d'Alexandre le Grand* (Annales d'histoire économique et sociale 1, No. 3, p. 21 ff), and Helmuth Berve, *Das Alexanderreich*, 1926, vol. i. p. 302.

incapable of being tested, Alexander owed only 200 talents when he left for Asia. In any case he was in debt when he crossed the Hellespont. He is said to have had then merely 70 talents in cash for the maintenance of his army, and provision for no more than thirty days. If he had not possessed that confidence of victory, he might be called an adventurer: but he calculated with absolute certainty that the enemies' country would feed his army, and his calculation proved correct.

His assurance of victory partially explains why he took with him from the start a historian, who was to write a history to inform the Greeks of his great deeds in Asia. This was Callisthenes of Olynthus, nephew and pupil of Aristotle, whom the latter had recommended to the king for this purpose: he was already well known by a Greek history, *Hellenica*, which had recently appeared. Through the agency of Callisthenes, who was to celebrate him as the realiser of the Panhellenic idea, Alexander intended first and foremost to influence Greek feeling; at the same time the marvels of the East which he hoped to behold were to be described for the benefit of the Greeks. The mental changes of the king led later to a tragic conflict with his historian. It was the first literary description of the Asiatic expedition, and up to then, under the eyes of Alexander himself Callisthenes adopted the language of panegyric. On account of his proximity to the king, what we learn of his work claims our special interest; he tells us how Alexander wished to be thought of by the Greeks, but, because the standpoint is so partial, we naturally have to use his statements critically. On the other hand the official description of the daily actions of Alexander in the Royal Gazette (*Ephemerides*) was not intended for publication. From the day of his accession it was composed by Eumenes of Cardia, the chief of his secretariat, and it had certainly been begun under Philip, whom Eumenes had served for several years in the same capacity. We owe our chief idea of the nature of this official journal to the fact that Ptolemy I King of

Egypt used it as the authority for his Memoirs; and as Ptolemy was one of Arrian's chief authorities, this explains why the latter's work reads like a diary. The Gazette was not intended to glorify the monarch, but to serve the practical requirements of government.

In the king's entourage we find besides Callisthenes other historians as well as philosophers and poets; but these generally joined the travelling court later. The surveying section (*Bematistae*), whose business it was to measure and enter in a journal the distances covered by Alexander's army, and who also added accounts of the peculiarities of the countries it traversed, no doubt accompanied the king from the start; but the specialists who had to investigate the flora, fauna and mineral wealth of the newly discovered countries of the Far East, were enlisted in some cases as time went on.

From the very first it was apparent to Alexander, the pupil of Aristotle, that this Asiatic campaign was to be not merely a military expedition but a great civilising event; for he aimed not only at introducing Greek culture into the East, but also at revealing to the Greeks the nature and culture of Asia. His campaign was at the same time an enterprise of research and discovery, which was to have new and fruitful results for Greek science. To be sure, he could as yet have had no conception to what extent he would ultimately succeed. No doubt it was only in the course of his victorious advance that these aims assumed a more definite and solid shape.

The Persian empire, against which Philip had opened the attack and Alexander now took the field, had lost the youthful vitality which it possessed under Darius I, but nevertheless it was no longer the depressed and internally unsound empire, which a few decades earlier had come near to dismemberment, owing to the insurrections of ambitious satraps and vassals, and the rebellion of important areas like Egypt and Cyprus; the energy of Artaxerxes III (Ochus), by overcoming these dangers and especially by the reconquest of Egypt, in which his success was chiefly due to the help of Greek officers and mercenaries, had once more firmly compacted the empire into a world empire, so that it now confronted the Macedonians as a strong and imposing colossus. In the spring of 336, when Philip sent his vanguard over the Dardanelles, Arses, who after the death of his father Ochus (338) had been raised to the throne by the all-powerful eunuch Bagoas, was still reigning. But soon afterwards, perhaps in May 336, Bagoas put Arses away, and placed on the throne Codomannus, a prince of a parallel branch of the Achaemenids, who promptly poisoned him to win greater freedom of action. This Darius III, as he called himself, was the unlucky monarch on whose shoulders fell the task of defending his realm against an Alexander. We are told of the great personal bravery which in youth he displayed in fighting the Cadusians, but in the decisive moments at Issus and Gaugamela, when he saw the superhuman figure of Alexander charging madly upon him, he was seized with panic on each occasion, turned his chariot to rapid flight, and left his brave men to fight and fall. He is to a great extent personally responsible for the downfall of his empire.

The troops which Philip had sent ahead to Asia Minor under Parmenio and Attalus, after a victorious advance at first, were pressed back again to the Dardanelles. Our inadequate authorities tell us merely that Parmenio, who had at first advanced by way of Ephesus to Magnesia on the Maeander, was there defeated by the Great King's excellent general Memnon, forced to retreat northwards and manœuvred back to the Dardanelles, so that at last the Macedonians held only Abydos and Rhoeteum on the Trojan coast. Though the murder of Philip and the tragic fall of Attalus had a paralysing and disturbing influence on the operations, one derives the impression that Memnon showed himself a better general than Parmenio. Alexander may have been well satisfied with the result, which secured him the bridgehead for his crossing into Asia and reserved to him himself the glorious overture of the liberation of the Greek cities. So he issued no orders for a second advance, but in the autumn of 335 summoned Parmenio to Pella to help him in the arming of the host.

Alexander thus gave Parmenio, who was then about sixty and had proved his efficiency in many of Philip's battles, a unique position above all his other commanders; he did not assign him the permanent command of a single division, but kept him by his side without any special command. Yet we must not describe Parmenio as 'the chief of Alexander's staff' or as 'his Moltke'. Sometimes before important decisions, for the purpose of deliberation, Alexander summoned a war-council of officers or the 'Comrades' personally attached to him, but he never had a regular general staff in the modern sense; he was his own Moltke. Nor did Alexander in strategic questions allow himself to be influenced by the generally divergent views of the cautious Parmenio. Nevertheless, he obviously had great confidence in him as a tactician, for in the three pitched battles in Asia he gave him the command of the defensive wing, while he reserved to himself that of the offensive. How loyal the old general was to the royal house, he had shown in Asia Minor, where in obedience to Alexander's command he gave Attalus up to justice— though he was his son-in-law—as soon as the latter's high treason was unmasked. It was also anxiety for the dynasty which made him and Antipater counsel Alexander not to cross over to Asia until he had married and begotten an heir to the throne. One can understand how Alexander, who passionately longed for the opening of the great war, rejected this idea. But the anxiety expressed in this advice was not without justification: for if at Alexander's death a son of his by a lawful Macedonian marriage had been forthcoming, the fate of his world-empire would perhaps have been different.

Finally all preparations were finished, and the march

was begun in the early spring of 334. Alexander led his army from Amphipolis along the Macedonian coast to the Hellespont, which he reached at Sestos in the Chersonese. It was lucky for him that the Persians had not thought of preventing his crossing with their vastly superior fleet—an omission which was a strange mistake. So by help of the 160 triremes and merchant ships requisitioned for the purpose the army was ferried over without fighting to Abydos on the opposite coast. While Alexander left this task to Parmenio, he was himself impelled by his romantic feelings to visit the sacred sites of the *Iliad*. Accompanied by friends and a small body of infantry, he went to the southern promontory of the Chersonese, where a tumulus passed for the grave of Protesilaus, who, according to the legend, was the first of Agamemnon's men to be killed in the landing. To him Alexander offered sacrifice, that he himself might succeed in making a more fortunate landing. So, when on his flag-ship he crossed to the Trojan coast, in the centre of the Dardanelles he sacrificed to the gods of the sea, Poseidon, Amphitrite and the Nereids; and when he had come near to the further shore, he hurled his spear on to the sandy beach, jumped down after it in full armour, and cried out that he received Asia from the gods as 'land won by the spear'. This symbolic annexation of the enemy's country is related by Cleitarchus alone, but it is so characteristic of Alexander's manner that we may regard it as historical. The wording, however, of his exclamation rests on authority too doubtful to justify conclusions as to the extent of his military plans at the time. Next he went up to Ilium and enthusiastically revelled in recollections of the Trojan War. He dedicated his armour to Athena, and in place of it took a sacred shield, supposed to date from the heroic age, and on the altar of Zeus Herkeios sacrificed to Priam, who according to the legend was slain by Neoptolemus, son of Achilles. Thus as descendant of Achilles, Alexander sought to allay the wrath of Priam. In the plain below he and his friend

Hephaestion laid wreaths on the mounds which were supposed to cover the remains of Achilles and Patroclus. This
excursion to Ilium gives us a profound insight into the
romantic soul of the young king.

After he had rejoined his army, which in the meantime
had been transported across by Parmenio, he advanced,
carefully reconnoitring the country as he went, to meet
the foe, who, as he had been informed, had concentrated
his forces not far off at Zeleia, south of the Sea of Marmora.
By order of the Great King, who had as yet no correct idea
of the danger which threatened him from Alexander, the
satraps and generals most immediately concerned had
assembled their forces from the countries on this side of
Mt. Taurus and joined Memnon and his troops. In the
war-council at Zeleia Memnon urgently dissuaded a
pitched battle, and proposed an alternative plan, to retire
into the interior and by devastating the settlements and
destroying the crops to reduce Alexander to extremities
and force him to retreat, meanwhile carrying the war over
into Europe by means of the fleet. This clever plan, which
shows profound insight into Alexander's precarious situation, and would have put him into a position similar to
that of Napoleon in Russia, was received, as coming from
a foreigner, with the most violent opposition from the
proud Persians, who refused to lay in ashes a single house.
Inspired by this feeling of superiority they determined
rather, at the gates of Asia, to force Alexander to a battle;
nevertheless, they were prudent enough not to meet him in
the open field, but to oppose an obstacle to his frontal
attack. So they marched westwards to the lower course of
the Granicus, a mountain stream, which descends from
Ida and empties itself into the Sea of Marmora, and posted
themselves on the right or southern bank. The river there
runs through flat country, but the southern banks rise
steeply in places to a height of as much as eight feet. By a
glaring error of tactics, they placed their excellent cavalry
(according to Arrian 20,000 strong) in front on the steep

banks, where they were unable to charge, and posted their infantry of Greek mercenaries (also 20,000 according to the same authority) some distance behind on a level elevation.[1]

When Alexander arrived from the north-west with his columns in marching order and surveyed a position which was favourable for him, he determined to make use of this mistake of the enemy by an immediate attack which would take them by surprise. The cautious Parmenio advised him to encamp for the night, and attack in the early morning, but Alexander rejected the advice, and ordered his troops who were experienced in manœuvring to form in battle line from column of route. For the first time he employed the 'oblique battle-array', which his father had borrowed and developed from an idea of Epaminondas. He divided his army into an offensive wing on the right commanded by himself, and a defensive wing on the left, the command of which he entrusted to Parmenio. In the next two great battles at Issus and Gaugamela he also used the same tactics, but each of the three battles exhibits peculiarities corresponding to the local conditions; for Alexander knew no fixed pattern. The fundamental idea of all three battles was, by an impetuous attack of the Macedonian cavalry on the right to pierce the enemy's left wing, and then turning to the left if possible to roll up the enemy's line, while the regiments of the phalanx—which were stationed in the centre, and, covered by cavalry on the left, followed more slowly en échelon—had in the meantime to make contact with the enemy and engage him with the support of their cavalry. The special feature of the battle of the Granicus was that Alexander did not charge the extreme left wing of the enemy, where Memnon was, and where, in expectation of Alexander, the Persians had posted their ranks in very close order; instead, he ordered light troops of foot and horse with a squadron of heavy cavalry to attack and hold

---

[1] ['The Persian leaders meant if possible to strangle the war at birth by killing Alexander.' W. W. Tarn (*C.A.H.* vi. 361).]

them, while he himself at the head of his *Hetairoi* looked for a point of attack further towards the centre on the left of them.

Amid the blare of trumpets and the battle-cry of his men Alexander rushed into the river—which was then swollen, as it was the month of May—and across up the steep bank, where there was a violent cavalry engagement on a broad front. Further to the left his other troops gradually reached the opposite bank and took up the fight. The battle raged most madly round Alexander himself, who was engaged at close quarters with several Persian nobles, among them Mithridates, son-in-law of Darius, to whom he gave his deathblow. While still engaged with Rhoesaces, he was himself in the greatest danger of his life, when Spithridates, the satrap of Lydia and Ionia, approached him from behind with uplifted scimitar to deal the *coup de grâce*. His life was saved by Cleitus, the son of Dropides, the commander of the royal regiment, who cut off Spithridates' uplifted arm, or, according to Plutarch, ran him through the body. It is a startling thought, how different would have been the course of the world's history, if Cleitus had not dealt his blow at the critical moment, and Alexander had fallen on the threshold of his glory. But they are wrong who have sought to deprive him of the title of one of the world's greatest generals, because on this occasion—and later too—he bravely joined in the actual fighting. In the oblique battle-order the commander's place was necessarily at the head of the offensive wing. It was at that point alone that a decisive change in the direction of the attack towards the centre might take place during the battle, and in those days there were no reserves, which in modern strategy compel the general to stay behind the battle-line, in order that he may launch them at the proper moment.[1]

When Alexander had victoriously broken through with

[1] ['If he charged himself, so did every general before Hannibal; the use of reserves was practically unknown, and the moral effect all-important.' W. W. Tarn, *C.A.H.*, vi. p. 425.]

his *Hetairoi*, and turning leftwards was pressing to the centre, the flight of the Persian cavalry began; and when, after crossing the river, Parmenio had successfully resisted the hostile attack, in which the Thessalian horse had especially distinguished themselves, the defeat of their left made the Persian ranks waver, and soon the flight became general. Starting with his whole line to pursue them—for like his father he aimed at the complete annihilation of the enemy—Alexander came upon the Greek mercenaries in the rear, who by the inconceivable tactics of the Persian nobles had been made witnesses of the cavalry fighting without taking any part themselves. He ordered his phalanx to attack them in front, while his cavalry took them on the flanks, and so this first-class body of Greek troops was destroyed, with the exception of about 2000 survivors. This, however, prevented any further pursuit on the part of the cavalry.

Thus in a few afternoon hours of a day in May 334 a great victory was won, above all by the genius of Alexander's generalship, but also owing to the superior arms of his troops; for, as the well-informed Arrian relates, in the decisive cavalry engagement the Macedonian thrusting-lance proved its superiority to the Persian throwing-spear. These thrusting-lances were all the more formidable, as the Macedonians by Alexander's orders aimed as much as possible at the faces of the enemy, and this superiority of weapons must have given his cavalry from the start a great confidence in victory. The losses of the *Hetairoi* were quite small; only 25 of the regiment sent against Memnon had fallen, while the rest of the cavalry had lost over 60, and the infantry about 30. Such small numbers have a suspicious sound, but we must add the wounded, of whom perhaps many more died.[1] Alexander ordered the sculptor Lysippus to make statues of those 25 *Hetairoi*, which were

---

[1] [In the siege of Sangala, Arrian (v. 24, 5) gives the number of the wounded as 1200, and those killed as under 100. So at the Granicus there may have been 1200 or more wounded.]

set up at Dion in Macedonia; their families were given exemption from taxation. The Persians must have suffered heavily, and in particular many of their leaders fell. The day after the battle Alexander gave solemn burial not only to his own men but to the Persians. He showed his humane disposition also in his kindly attention to the wounded. He made them individually display to him their wounds and relate how they had got them, and gave them a kindly ear, even when they were somewhat vainglorious. One can conceive how enthusiastically the army was devoted to such a leader.

With subtle diplomacy, which was suggested to him by his recent troubles in Greece, Alexander in the capacity of Generalissimo of the Panhellenic war of revenge published to the world this victory of the Granicus as a victory of the Corinthian League. This is the meaning of the dedicatory inscription he ordered for the 300 sets of Persian armour, which he sent to Athens to be offered to the goddess on the Acropolis: 'Alexander the son of Philip, and the Hellenes, all but the Lacedaemonians (dedicated this as booty) from the barbarians who inhabit Asia'. Not a word about his Macedonians! And out of the Greek contingents only the cavalry had been engaged. It is also noticeable that he does not describe himself as king, and that in the language of the Panhellenic propaganda he calls the Persians barbarians. In the same way it was with the intention of honouring the league and putting himself merely in the position of their elected Generalissimo that he sent the captured Greek mercenaries in chains to forced labour in Macedonia, giving as his reason, 'because, contrary to the resolution of the League of Hellenes, they had fought for the barbarians against Hellas'. The court historian Callisthenes certainly celebrated the Granicus as a Panhellenic victory; and when he said the battle was fought on the Adrastean fields, and, in explanation of the name, mentioned the old king Adrastus, who founded the cult of Nemesis in this region, he saw probably a divine dispensation in the fact that Alexander had here won the victory as the 'avenger' of Greece.[1]

And yet Alexander went not merely as the general of the league, but also as king, who aimed at conquering territory for himself. There is assuredly a correct idea conveyed in the story of Cleitarchus, how he threw his spear before him on landing. From the moment he trod on Asiatic soil he regarded it, as his further actions show, as 'land won by his spear', in the sense in which the Diadochi used the same expression to assert the lawfulness of their conquests. No doubt, as general of the league, Alexander undertook as his first duty the liberation of the Greek cities of Asia Minor from the Persian yoke, but what lay outside of these cities and their territories, he conquered from the first for himself. Yet he came not as a devastator, but as the future ruler who saw in the conquered peoples his subjects. He wished to reconcile them to the new rule, by taking account of their national characteristics, and by being prepared to secure to them their old traditions, as far as the security of his empire permitted, in order that under the new conditions they might settle down peaceably.

Scarcely had he entered the country, when he began to rule as its new king. Immediately after the battle of the Granicus, he organised the administration of the satrapy of Hellespontine Phrygia, whose satrap Arsites had escaped from the battle. He appointed in his stead a Macedonian noble called Calas. It was most significant—and perhaps very surprising to his Macedonians—that he gave Calas not a Macedonian title, but the old Persian title of 'satrap' (Kshatrapavân = protector of the country) to which the population had been accustomed for centuries past. With the title Calas received exactly the same functions as Arsites. Nor did Alexander make any change in his demands on his new subjects; the same tribute as they had hitherto paid to the Great King, they were now to pay

[1] F. Jacoby, *Fragmente griechischer Historiker, Callisthenes*, Fr. 28. [The author claims to be the first to draw the above conclusion.]

to their new master. He caused Parmenio forthwith to occupy the seat of government of this satrapy, Dascylium. So Alexander stepped immediately into the rights of the Great King, whose crown lands he further claimed for himself. These measures, by which he did not incorporate the new conquests into his Macedonian kingdom, but placed them independently beside it, show us that from the first, though we can form no accurate idea of his plans and hopes at that date, he did not contemplate a small rounding-off of his Macedonian kingdom.

The immediate effect of the victory of the Granicus was that the neighbouring parts of Western Asia Minor fell to Alexander without any fighting. When he reached Sardis, the seat of government of the Lydian satrapy, not merely the city but also the citadel, which was supposed to be impregnable, together with its rich treasures, were surrendered to him, and he placed over them a Macedonian as commandant. Here too Alexander showed that he came not to enslave but to liberate, and was minded to pay respect to national characteristics. To the Lydians, who were a people of ancient civilisation, and had once, particularly in religion and music, greatly stimulated Greek culture, he gave back their old Lydian laws, which they had had before the Persian conquest. He showed also that he had come to introduce Greek culture into the East; for on the summit of the citadel of Sardis he erected a temple and altar to Olympian Zeus, the Panhellenic god.

After having appointed a Macedonian, Asander, as satrap of Lydia—on this occasion Alexander gave the control of finance to an officer of his own—he reached the coast at Ephesus, and began, according to his Panhellenic commission, to liberate the Greek cities. From Ephesus he detached a large body of troops to occupy the Aeolian and northern Ionian cities; and in the south Magnesia and Tralles on the Maeander declared their adhesion to him. Everywhere he caused the oligarchies to be overthrown and the democracies reinstated with their former laws. This was done here and elsewhere as a counter-measure against the Persian government, which had always favoured oligarchies. Naturally the payment of tribute to Persia by the Greek cities was abolished. Everywhere the liberation from Persian rule was greeted with enthusiasm, and Alexander celebrated as the liberator. Though the assignment of the Greeks of Asia Minor by the King's Peace to the Persian empire had conferred many economic advantages on them through the unrestricted intercourse they enjoyed with the interior, with the result that they were in a better material position than the free Greeks of the motherland with their internecine quarrels, yet the history of the Ionians shows that they had always felt the yoke of the foreigner as a sore burden, and that they too, as should not have been disputed, regarded freedom as the greatest blessing. A third century inscription from Priene gives noble expression to this idea, when it says: 'There is nothing greater for Greek men than freedom'. *

The question how Alexander organised the liberated Greeks of Asia Minor is hard to answer in the almost complete silence of our tradition. But lately some arguments have been adduced which seem to indicate that, as previously the islands off the coast belonged to the Corinthian League, so now the cities of the mainland were made members of the league by Alexander, who doubtless followed the intention of his father Philip. The particular measures taken by Alexander agree with this assumption. The only special feature is that the Asiatic members of the league were not bound to furnish contingents for the army and fleet, like the states of the motherland, but to pay contributions in money (*Syntaxeis*). That the Ionic federal system, which had revived before the coming of Alexander about the middle of the century, was still in existence, is no argument against this view; for in Greece leagues had been admitted as members. In any case the other view that, instead of introducing the Greeks of Asia Minor into the Corinthian League, Alexander organised them in several local leagues which he made dependent on himself, is incapable of proof. Proofs are equally lacking for the widespread theory, that immediately after their liberation the Greeks of Asia Minor paid divine honours to Alexander. The instances quoted for this belong to a later date.

It was only at two points on the west coast that Alexander encountered opposition, and that where Greek mercenaries were to be found in large numbers, at Miletus and Halicarnassus. The Persian commandant of Miletus, who had at first been willing to surrender the town, later on resisted, relying upon the arrival of the Persian fleet. This had to anchor outside off Mt. Mycale, since Alexander's fleet had previously succeeded in taking up a position by the island of Lade immediately in front of the town's harbour. With the siege artillery, which he here used for the first occasion, a breach was made in the walls, and the town stormed, while simultaneously the Greek fleet entered the harbour and closed its mouth. Alexander pardoned the Milesians, who had evidently been coerced by the Persian garrison, and granted them freedom, and thus they too joined the Corinthian League. They thanked him by electing him *Stephanephorus* of their city for the next year (334-3). In the list of these eponymous officials which has come down to us, he is called simply 'Alexander son of Philip'— without the title of king, which at this time he did not use, being *Hegemon* of the League; where the dedicatory inscription of the temple of Athena at Priene describes him as king, the meaning is that he did not found it out of league moneys. Though the fleet had done him good service at Miletus, he disbanded the greater part of it, retaining only the twenty Athenian ships as hostages. This resolution, which at first sight is surprising, was rendered necessary by scarcity of money. Perhaps also he hesitated to expose his ships to the possibility of a defeat by the far superior Persian fleet then stationed at Samos.[1]

[1] [Köhler, *Das Verhältniss Alexanders des Grossen zu seinem Vater Philipp* (*Pr. Akad. Ber.*, 1892, p. 493) gives the reason that the fleet was the creation of Philip. Alexander was incapable of such paltry jealousy.]

At Halicarnassus, the capital of Caria, Alexander met with a much stronger resistance; for his greatest antagonist, Memnon the Rhodian, to whom Darius had just given supreme command of the Asiatic coast and the fleet, undertook the defence in person. Here a long siege was necessary, since the city was strongly fortified both by nature and art. A division of the Persian fleet lay at anchor in the harbour. But the city could not hold out indefinitely against the superior siege-craft of Alexander. After engagements in which both sides were alternately successful and several futile sallies of the brave garrison, Memnon was obliged to evacuate the city and leave it to the conqueror. Only the two citadels continued in Persian occupation. Alexander could not stay for them, but left a corps behind, which after some time effected a capitulation (p. 98). Memnon himself, who had conducted the defence with brilliant skill, escaped to the island of Cos.

How far Alexander was from following any rule of thumb in arranging the satrapies, he showed by entrusting Caria to the old princess Ada of the Carian dynastic house, who had formerly ruled as widow of her brother and husband Idrieus. She had met him with homage when he entered Caria, handed over to him the town of Alinda, which belonged to her, and proposed to adopt him as her son. Alexander restored the town to her and accepted the adoption. He was therefore to the Carians the son of their ruler, and all sting of foreign domination was removed. The sort of fiction which the Alexander romance subsequently fabricated in the case of Egypt and Persia—that he was the son of an Egyptian or a Persian king—was here anticipated by historical fact. By this attitude to Ada Alexander showed that he understood the special characteristics of the subjected peoples; we may consider strange the statements about the part this woman played, but they are explained by the fact that in Caria there were survivals of the so-called matriarchy which had once prevailed widely in the pre-Greek Mediterranean world. Since

Alexander in this case conferred the satrapy on a woman and a native to boot, he naturally separated from it the military command and gave that to a Macedonian officer. Ada received merely the civil functions. This separation of civil and military posts, which Alexander carried out in this instance for the first time, he afterwards adopted as a principle, when he appointed Orientals to satrapies.

The young Macedonians who had married shortly before the war were now sent home on leave for the winter, a measure as politic as it was humane, which called forth warm gratitude; Parmenio was despatched with the league troops to occupy Phrygia; and Alexander himself started during the winter months to traverse the southern coast of Asia Minor, in accordance with his strategic plan of paralysing the enemy's fleet by occupying the sea-board. He marched along the coast of Lydia and Pamphylia as far as Side, without encountering any serious resistance. Only when he turned off northwards through Pisidia, did he have severe fighting with the wild mountaineers. By way of Celaenae he arrived at his winter quarters at Gordium, the Phrygian capital on the river Sangarius, celebrated in legend. There Parmenio and his army met him, and in spring came the men who had been on furlough and the new levies from home. Gordium had been specially chosen as the rendezvous, because its position was convenient for reinforcements from Macedonia.

The first year of the war had produced striking successes. By the victory of the Granicus all Asia Minor up to the Sangarius had fallen into Alexander's hands; the Persian fleet had no port to put in at on the coasts as far as Cilicia; there was no Persian army any longer in Asia Minor, and the first point of the Panhellenic program had been quickly achieved: the Greek cities of Asia Minor were freed from the Persian yoke and incorporated in the Corinthian League. These cities, as the study of the buildings of many of them proves, now entered on a new period of great development; the wide regions outside them were occupied by Alexander as crown-lands and administered by his satraps.

In view of the rapid victorious advance of the young hero, how could it be doubted that he was under the special protection of the gods? They often sent lucky omens, which were interpreted either by the seers of his camp, the chief of whom was then Aristander of Telmessus, or at times by the king himself. Apart from the usual daily sacrifices, he did not neglect to give visible expression of his reverence and gratitude to the gods on special occasions. At Ephesus, for example, where he entered for the first time a liberated Ionian city, he led a solemn procession in honour of Artemis with his whole army equipped as for battle. He honoured the goddess further by ordering that the Ephesians should henceforth pay to her for the erection of her temple the tribute which they had previously paid to the Great King. The relation of Alexander to the gods being so close, it was natural to attribute lucky happenings to the immediate intervention of the gods. When Alexander was on the Pamphylian coast, he wanted to go along a narrow shore road, which was passable solely when the north winds blew back the tide; and at that moment, the south wind which had been blowing hitherto, suddenly changed to a north wind, so that he was able to get through. According to Arrian, not only his followers but Alexander himself saw in this a divine dispensation. This is not presumption, but rather a recognition that as man he would have been powerless without divine aid. Later his court historian Callisthenes made something quite different of it; in his panegyric on Alexander he related how the sea had retired from him, and bowed before him as its lord, thus performing its prostration of reverence (*Proskynesis*). Alexander is made out to be a superhuman divine being, to whom the elements do homage. But this narrative is influenced by the elevation of Alexander to the position of a son of Ammon (331), and the metaphor of *Proskynesis* points to the time when he began to receive this

Oriental homage from his Persian subjects (330). On the contrary, at the time of the experience on the Pamphylian coast such ideas were completely foreign to Alexander and his followers. The incident simply made him appear as a favourite and protégé of the gods.

We are reminded of another great problem of Alexander's history—the gradual appearance of the idea of world-sovereignty—by an event which now took place at Gordium. The natives of this place had an old oracle, according to which the man who unfastened the famous knot that tied the yoke to the ancient chariot of King Gordius in the citadel, would become lord of Asia. When Alexander heard of this in Gordium, he was again seized by that 'longing' for the mysterious, of which mention has been made before (p. 68), and so inspected the chariot. After vain endeavours to find the ends of the strap, by a quick resolution he drew his sword and cut the knot. In the night thunder and lightning followed, which he took as a divine intimation that his method of loosing the knot had been accepted by the gods. He had complete belief in oracles, and this promise from the ancient East of the sovereignty over Asia must have influenced him deeply henceforward.

Meantime in the West after his departure from Halicarnassus events had occurred which might imperil all that he had won by his successful advance. His gifted opponent Memnon, after the loss of Halicarnassus, had proceeded to try the plan, which he had proposed at Zeleia, of carrying the war over to Macedonia and Greece by means of the fleet. First the island of Chios was betrayed to him, and then he turned to Lesbos, where he gained possession of all the cities except Mytilene. So he blockaded Mytilene by sea and land, and began the siege. The news caused great excitement in the Cyclades and in Hellas: men talked of an attack by Memnon on Euboea, and not only in Sparta but elsewhere there were great hopes of a change in the fortunes of war. But suddenly Memnon fell ill and died before Mytilene. His death at this moment was the greatest stroke of luck in Alexander's life, and no one recognised this more fully than Alexander. At the first news of the siege of Mytilene, he had been full of anxiety, and ordered Amphoterus and Hegelochus to collect a new fleet on the Hellespont. Both to them and to Antipater he forwarded large sums of money for military equipment. Then, probably before he left Gordium, the news of Memnon's death reached him, and he felt as it were relieved from a nightmare. It was also fortunate for him that Darius on the news of Memnon's death strangely abandoned Memnon's plan of an attack on Macedonia and Greece, ordered the mercenary troops of Pharnabazus, whom he made commander of the fleet, to return to him, and determined under his personal command to offer battle on land to Alexander. Though the Persians had made further advances in the West after Memnon's death, had occupied Mytilene and Tenedos, and had compelled both to revoke their treaties with Alexander and on the basis of the King's Peace to enter into alliance again with the Great King, Alexander could now without anxiety leave the recovery of the islands and the pacification of the West to his admirals and to Antipater.

In the spring of 333 he left Gordium for Cappadocia by way of Ancyra (the present capital of Turkey), intending to turn southwards and with the greatest possible speed occupy the passes of the Taurus. He traversed merely a small portion of Cappadocia, and as he appointed here not a Macedonian but a native, Sabictas, as satrap, the inference is that he had not the power to introduce a Macedonian régime as he had done in the West. He had not time to conquer the whole country. It was only Southern Cappadocia by Taurus that he nominally made a satrapy; Northern Cappadocia by Pontus under its prince Ariarathes did not become subject to Alexander. It remained a gap in his Asiatic kingdom, and Armenia also remained independent.

His advance was so rapid that Arsames, the satrap of Cilicia, was completely taken by surprise. The extremely difficult pass which leads over the Taurus range was occupied without a blow, the guards running away, when on a dark night he climbed up with a few light-armed troops. Subsequently on reaching the plain below, Alexander learnt that the inhabitants of Tarsus, the capital, were afraid that Arsames would sack their city before abandoning it to him. He galloped ahead with his cavalry, and Arsames at once fled without doing the city any damage.

At Tarsus the heroic career of Alexander well-nigh came to a tragic end. On a hot summer's day he jumped into the icy waters of the Cydnus, which flows from the mountains through the town. He contracted a dangerous illness and wrestled long with death in fevers and convulsions, encountering almost the same fate as the old emperor Barbarossa, who met his end not far away in the Calycadnus. Probably Alexander was saved more by his youth and iron constitution than by the medicines of his faithful doctor Philip. But his expedition was long delayed by this illness, which was to have important after-effects.

When he recovered, he despatched Parmenio with a part of the army eastwards, to forestall the occupation of the coast-passes which lead from Cilicia into Syria, and started off westwards himself to reduce the mountainous district of Cilicia Tracheia, so as to complete the subjection of the coast as far as Lycia and to cover his rear completely, before setting out to meet the Great King. The rapid performance of this task in a few days showed that he had regained his former elasticity. On his way back at the old Greek coast town of Soloi he received the news that his generals, whom he had left investing the citadels of Halicarnassus, had won a great victory. In honour of this victory he celebrated a festival, and also in gratitude to the god Asclepius for his recovery. Beside a procession and a torch-race there were also gymnastic and musical competitions, mentioned here for the first time, and often afterwards. These were gymnastic exhibitions by the soldiers, and artistic contests, in which singers, musicians and actors took part, who had perhaps been fetched from head-quarters at Tarsus.

After this the main army began its march from Tarsus east-wards. When Alexander reached Mallus, he offered sacri-fice to the hero-prophet Amphilochus of Argos, who had here a famous oracle and was revered as founder of the town. At Mallus too he heard from Parmenio, who had in the meantime occupied the passes, that Darius with his army was encamped at Sochoi (a place unknown to us) in the plains of North Syria, two days' journey from the pass now called Bailan. After Memnon's death the Great King, who had decided to take over the command in person and meet Alexander in a decisive battle, had collected a large army at Babylon. In the late summer of 333, being in-formed that Alexander was in Cilicia, he had gone up the Euphrates accompanied by a huge baggage-train, and then passed into the plain east of Mt. Amanus, to be ready, when Alexander emerged from the Bailan Pass, to offer battle at Sochoi in a plain favourable to the deploying of his numerous army. Because of his numerical superiority he was confident of victory. Yet he had learned to estimate Alexander highly as an antagonist, as we can deduce from the fact that some time before, like a true Sultan, he had instigated the Lyncestian Alexander to murder him. As soon as the news about Sochoi reached Alexander at Mallus, he summoned a council of war to discuss what was to be done and with their approval set out to oppose the Great King.

But the battle was fought not on the other side of Mt. Amanus at Sochoi, but on this side in the north-west corner of Syria south of Issus. How came this about? It is one of the most interesting and thrilling chapters in the whole history of the war. Alexander's road, which he had previously caused Parmenio to reconnoitre and occupy, led him through the Cilician Gates along the Syrian coast, which soon bends round southwards, past Issus, over the river Pinarus (Deli-Tchai) and the smaller Payas to the Syrian coast-pass, and over the mountain-pass by the pillar of Jonah down to Myriandrus (near the modern Alexandretta-Iskanderun). From here the road led south-eastwards over the Amanus by the Bailan Pass to the Syrian plain. It was the road the younger Cyrus had once travelled over, and it was known to the Greeks from Xenophon's narrative. After leaving his sick and wounded at Issus, marching southwards Alexander reached Myriandrus, where, on account of the violent autumn storms and the rainfall which had taken place in the night, he kept his troops in camp on the following day, probably also to give them a rest before the impending battle. There in the evening to his great surprise he was informed by deserters that Darius and his army were north of him on the Pinarus. He would scarcely believe it, and sent some officers by sea northwards to find out; they confirmed the news.

How did this change of position occur? Darius had encamped for some weeks at Sochoi and there awaited his enemy's onward march from Cilicia. But Alexander's start was long delayed by his tedious illness and further events in Cilicia. Then as day after day passed idly by, the Great King lost all patience, and believing with his followers that Alexander was afraid and did not dare to advance, he determined to look for him in Cilicia. His contempt for the little army of Alexander, which he thought he could simply ride down with his masses of cavalry, together with regard for the approach of winter and difficulties of commissariat upheld him in this plan. In order to make his gigantic army more mobile, he sent to Damascus the treasure and the main part of the baggage-train, and with his army, still accompanied by a large train and his family, he marched east of Mt. Amanus northwards to the Lion Pass (Arslan-Boghas), then south-west over the mountain through the Gates of Amanus (Toprak Kalessi) into the coast-plain of Issus, to advance from there into Cilicia. If one compares the distances covered by the two armies and their different mobility, we may assume that Darius' start took place several days before Alexander left Mallus. About the same time that Darius arrived at the Gates of Amanus, Alexander reached Myriandrus. Thus the two armies, separated by the range of Amanus, unsuspectingly marched past one another over different passes of the same mountain, with the result that Darius was now north and Alexander south. Darius was first apprised of this strange accident by coming on Alexander's wounded at Issus, who received shocking treatment from his troops, and he learnt there that Alexander had just passed through, going southwards. He soon resolved to follow him and first encamped on the Pinarus, evidently with the intention of following Alexander through the Bailan Pass and thus finally, according to the original plan, offering battle in the wide Syrian plains which were so favourable to him.

It was fated to be otherwise. The moment that Alexander was informed of Darius' position on the Pinarus, with the lightning intuition of genius he perceived the great advantage given to him by this unexpected situation, and drew the necessary conclusions. He was cut off from his base of operations, and a defeat on the Pinarus would have been catastrophic. But the absolute confidence of victory, which had hitherto led him on from one success to another, was no idle fancy, but was well founded on consciousness of his army's superior quality and of his own talents for generalship. The only danger that could possibly threaten him from the vastly greater numbers of the enemy was that of being surrounded; but now this was, though not removed, yet greatly lessened, if he met the enemy, not in the broad Syrian plain, but in the plain of the Pinarus, shut in by the mountains and the sea. Quick action was necessary. So with the circumspection and calm, which characterised him at the supreme moments of decision, he took all measures towards meeting the enemy on the following day. At once some cavalry and archers were despatched to reconnoitre northwards as far as the top of the pass, the occupation of which was essential to his plan. After giving a quiet time to his troops to prepare a meal before moving off, he set out with the whole army, reached the summit of the pass by midnight and having placed outposts made his men rest among the rocks. With the first rays of morning, he descended into the plain, first in a long narrow column, the infantry at the head, till the gradual expansion of the plain permitted the deployment of column of route into line of battle. Here again, as at the Granicus, the march to the field of battle was executed with as much calm and precision as if it had been on the parade ground and not in front of the enemy.

Thus the Pinarus was the scene of one of the most memorable of battles, a duel with reversed fronts. We have good descriptions of it, for we can extract from later authors the accounts of two independent and primary sources: that of Ptolemy, who was himself one of the combatants, and that of Callisthenes, who as a civilian can have watched it only from a distance.

The Pinarus, which in its upper and middle course had steep banks, was utilised by the Persians, like the Granicus, as an obstacle to defend their front. The mistakes of the satraps at the Granicus, moreover, were avoided on this occasion, the best troops, the Greek mercenaries, being placed in front of the centre of the battle-line. Right and left of them stood the Oriental hoplites (Kardakes), whose right wing was behind the cavalry, which Darius had thrown over the river to mask his operations, and afterwards withdrawn across it. The bulk of his cavalry was then posted on the right of the Greek mercenaries on the lower course of the river, where the banks were flat and the stream hardly formed an obstacle, on ground suitable for a cavalry engagement and reaching right down to the sea. The remaining troops were drawn up in deep formation behind this front and arrayed according to nationalities. On the left wing by the slopes of Amanus Darius had thrown forward a corps, which was, if possible, to take Alexander in the rear. He himself in his magnificent chariot was in the centre behind the Greek mercenaries.

Before the battle Alexander secretly moved the Thessalian cavalry from the right wing behind the front to the left, making essentially the same disposition as at the Granicus. The only difference was that to meet the corps on the slopes he placed some troops at right angles to his right wing, but, as the corps fled to the hills before a rain of arrows, these troops were soon free to be brought back into the front. As at the Granicus, Alexander commanded the right, and Parmenio the left wing. The latter was given strict orders on no account to break contact with the sea. The importance of this position on the sea had been clear to Alexander the evening before at Myriandrus when he first planned the battle; he had accordingly sacrificed to the gods of the sea, and in particular had driven a quadriga into the waves and offered it to Poseidon. He thus relied on the favour of the gods and his excellent cavalry under Parmenio. We must again reject the fantastic accounts of the Persian numbers, which have been stated to be as high as 600,000; but we cannot doubt that Alexander's army, though through accessions it was somewhat larger than his command at the Granicus, must have been faced by a large preponderance of force.

Alexander opened the battle in accordance with the tactics of the oblique formation, by leading his heavy cavalry over the Pinarus and charging the left wing of the enemy. Here by his terrible onset he soon made them waver, receiving himself a slight wound in the leg. In the meantime, however, the advancing regiments of his phalangites in climbing the steep bank of the river had become dislocated and had broken line. No sooner did the first-rate Greek mercenaries opposed to them notice this than they threw themselves into the gap, and a severe struggle began on the edge of the river. The fighting was all the more passionate, in that both Greeks and Macedonians were filled with the ambition of showing their superiority to their respective opponents; the strong antipathy then existing between the two peoples found expression in this engagement. But the hard-pressed Macedonians received assistance not only from the neighbouring phalangites, but also from Alexander, who after overcoming the left wing of the Persians had executed the decisive turn and was vehemently attacking the centre. This decided the battle. As soon as Darius saw Alexander's impetuous onset, he turned his chariot and rushed northwards in wild flight. It is this moment that is represented after the dramatic exaggeration of Cleitarchus in the famous Pompeian mosaic from the *Casa del Fauno.*

However much Alexander's heart was set on securing the person of the Great King, he could not think of pursuing him; first the battle against the Greek mercenaries and above all the cavalry engagement on the left wing had to be decided. On the left at the outset the numerically superior Persian cavalry had crossed the Pinarus and fiercely attacked the Thessalian and Peloponnesian horse under Parmenio, who were soon in serious difficulties. It was all-important that there should be no breach in the line here, because in that case Alexander's position might have been turned; the events of the battle both in the centre and by the sea show how much more dangerous to Alexander the battle of Issus was than that of the Granicus. The cavalry engagement was conducted on both sides with the greatest fury, till the Persian cavalry heard that their king had fled and left them in the lurch. Then they wheeled round their horses in flight, and, pursued by the Thessalians, became entangled in the rout which was becoming universal throughout the whole Persian army.

As soon as the Persians turned to flee, Alexander took up the pursuit in the hope of still catching Darius. But the latter had quickly exchanged his chariot for a horse, had thrown off his royal cloak, and escaped leaving his shield and bow behind. The pursuit must have inflicted huge losses on the Persians; for north of the battle-field Amanus soon approaches the sea, and leaves only a narrow passage, through which the fleeing masses had to press. Ptolemy, who rode beside Alexander, tells us that in the pursuit they rode over a ravine, which was filled to the top with the corpses of the enemy. When darkness fell, Alexander broke off the pursuit and returned to the Pinarus. Here the royal camp with all its Oriental luxury fell into the hands of the victor. His most valuable booty was the royal family—the mother and wife of Darius with her three children—who as hostages might be of the greatest use. That same night, when they were lamenting over Darius as dead, Alexander caused them to be informed that he was alive. It was not mere diplomatic calculation, which made him treat these women with the honours due to queens, for after the death of Darius he behaved in the same manner to the mother who survived him, when such conduct could no longer serve any purpose; rather we observe here the chivalry which was a typical trait of Alexander's character. He went so far in his respectful treatment that he did not even see the royal consort Stateira, who was counted as the most beautiful woman of Asia.

Thus at the beginning of November 333 the gigantic army of the Great King was beaten and disintegrated, and he himself a fugitive. Only 8000 Greek mercenaries had escaped in good order over the mountains. The sensation caused by the news through the whole Greek world was immense. There the decision had been awaited with feverish excitement. All the hostile and turbulent elements hoped for a Persian victory, and no one more than Demosthenes, who on receipt of letters from the East went triumphantly round Athens, proclaiming that Alexander was cut off in Cilicia and would soon be trodden down by the Persian cavalry. Those who were friendly to the Macedonians were in the deepest anxiety. Then the news of Alexander's brilliant victory came like a thunderbolt, causing rejoicing here and dejection there. The feelings of the deputies at the Synhedrion of the Corinthian League must have been very mixed, when at the next regular meeting for the Isthmian Games of 332 they resolved to send Alexander a golden wreath by an embassy, to congratulate him on his victory, and to thank him for what he had done for the salvation and freedom of Hellas. The news of the victory was crushing to the Persian admirals in the Aegean; all prospect of co-operation with the Greeks was gone for ever. They had just entered into conference with Agis, the Spartan king, at the island of Siphnos, when the tidings arrived, and they broke up at once, Pharnabazus hurrying to Chios to prevent it going over to the victor on hearing the news. Agis, nevertheless, did not relinquish his plan of carrying on the war, but borrowed thirty talents and ten triremes from the Persians in order to win Crete for his cause.

The victory at Issus produced a great change in Alexander himself. While after the battle of the Granicus he had strongly emphasised his hegemony of the Hellenic League, he now publicly appeared for the first time as claimant to the lordship over the whole Persian empire. We cannot know whether this great ambition was not present to his mind before; we can only guess that possibly the oracle of Gordium, which had promised him the sovereignty of Asia, made the thought more definite, and probably the intention did not become fully clear, until at Issus he had defeated the Great King in person. Alexander was not slow to give it expression. He did so in a letter, which he wrote to Darius soon after the battle, in reply to Darius' request for the surrender of his family and to his offer of friendship and alliance. This letter, which Arrian gives us in an essentially authentic form, is one of the most interesting documents bearing on Alexander's life. In the *
opening he declares that, having been appointed *Hegemon* of the Greeks, he has invaded Asia, to take vengeance for the evil wrought by Darius' forefathers to Macedonia and the rest of Greece. He then recounts to him the hostile acts

which Ochus and then Darius had committed against Philip and himself. As now after the victories of Granicus and Issus by the grace of the gods he possesses the land and is lord of all Asia, let Darius come to him and receive his family. In future Darius must write to him as King of Asia, not as his equal. If he objects, let him fight and not flee; he will catch him wherever he is.

The history of the following years demonstrates that it was as a matter of fact premature for Alexander already to regard himself as lord of all Asia; he had to fight another dangerous battle for its possession. But to comprehend his gifted nature it is significant to learn that already under the impression of the victory of Issus and in full confidence that he would conquer, wherever it might be, he now claimed all Asia, that is the Persian world-empire, and at any rate for the Great King's correspondence demanded the title of King of Asia. In spite of this, afterwards as before, he regarded himself as *Hegemon* of the League, as the history of the following years shows, a title which he expressly asserted in the opening of the letter. The double nature of his aims is clearly indicated.

In itself it must have appeared tempting to Alexander after the victory to pursue the fleeing king and so take possession of the Asiatic empire. But the Persian fleet still controlled the sea, and the further Alexander penetrated from the coast, the greater would have been the peril of this fleet rousing Greece once more to revolt; King Agis of Sparta had by no means abandoned his design. Again one must admire the prudence of the young king, who resisted the enticing prospect of entering without much trouble the royal palaces of the Achaemenids, and adhered to his old strategic plan, first to subdue the Mediterranean coasts of the Persian empire, to deprive the fleet of its bases, and so completely to secure his rear against Greece. From this point of view it was a military necessity, first to occupy the Syrian coast.

Accordingly, from Issus he marched south with the main

army to occupy the cities of the coast, while he sent Parmenio to Damascus, to seize the town and take possession of the treasure sent there by Darius. At Damascus, which was surrendered by treachery, the military chest of the Persian King fell into the hands of the victor. This was an event of the greatest importance; the financial anxieties, which had hitherto sorely oppressed him, now ceased. Along with many other captives, ambassadors from Athens, Sparta and Thebes, who had reached the Great King just before the battle of Issus, and therefore had been despatched during the Panhellenic campaign, also fell into his hands. Instead of treating them as traitors, Alexander displayed surprising leniency and generosity to them.

In Asia Minor, apart from the Greek colonists, he had had to do only with peoples of the old indigenous races or with Indo-Germanic tribes of later arrival like the Phrygians; now he entered for the first time the Semitic world. In Syria were settled the most varied stocks, who had come in from Arabia centuries before, partly in the Canaanite and partly in the later Aramaic migration, and had developed distinct mixed cultures, influenced in the north by Babylonia and the Hittites, in the south by Egypt. There were no Greek colonies here, for at the period of Greek colonisation the Assyrian empire had made it impossible for Greeks to settle on this coast. Alexander's first object was to occupy the Phoenician towns, since the Phoenician ships with their first-rate crews, along with the Cyprians, constituted the best part of the Persian fleet. These prosperous commercial cities of the Phoenicians, each under a king, formed little independent states, among which Sidon and Tyre for ages had struggled with varying success for the hegemony. Some years before under the lead of Sidon Phoenicia had rebelled: but King Ochus had finally reduced them to obedience, and Sidon had been destroyed (350) but had soon recovered again. At this time Tyre was the leading city.

The northern towns, Aradus, Byblus and Sidon, opened

their gates immediately to Alexander, but at Tyre he was to meet with stubborn resistance. The local god of Tyre was Melkarth, identified by the Greeks long before, as Herodotus tells us, with their Heracles. Nothing was more natural than that Alexander should wish to sacrifice to Heracles, the ancestor of his house, in Tyre as elsewhere. But he did not suspect what it meant to the Tyrians, when he expressed to their ambassadors the desire to sacrifice in person in the old temple of Heracles in the island-city of Tyre. He did not know that according to Oriental ideas the Tyrians would have acknowledged him as king of their city by granting this request; for only the king was allowed to offer sacrifice. When the Tyrians without explaining this replied that they would grant him anything else but not this sacrifice, and, probably trusting to the often proved impregnability of their city, declared that they would receive neither Persians nor Macedonians within their walls and also desired to remain neutral, Alexander could see nothing but contumaciousness in their answer, and determined to take the city by storm, for he could not possibly in his march to Egypt leave this capital of the Phoenician world unsubdued in his rear. About January 332 he began the siege.

The conquest on which he had set his heart was more difficult than he supposed. Tyre was on an island, separated from Old Tyre by a narrow arm of the sea, defended on all sides by strong walls and also by the fleet. Alexander saw immediately that this insular position must be abolished by the construction of a mole from Old Tyre to the island, in order that his siege-engines might be brought up to the walls. In spite of extraordinary exertions, it was a slow business to push the causeway forward in face of the clever counter-manœuvres of the enemy. The Tyrians destroyed the first fortifications on the causeway by a fire-ship, but Alexander began at once to construct a fresh mole of greater breadth. Experience showed him that he was opposed to the traditional Oriental engineering, from which his father's siege-craft, taken over from Dionysius, was the latest off-shoot; for the engineers of Dionysius had been taught by the Carthaginians, who had derived their skill from the Phoenician motherland. In these arts of siege and defence the early Oriental peoples were, as the Assyrian reliefs make plain, far superior to the Greeks; indeed, they were their teachers.

When the fleets of the northern Phoenician towns left the Persian fleet and returned at the news of the occupation of their homes, and when soon afterwards the Cypriot contingent did the same, Alexander went to Sidon, united the two fleets that had hitherto been operating against him, and took them to Tyre, in order to invest the city from the sea. His strategic idea of cutting the Persian fleet off from the coast had brilliantly justified itself. He now posted the Cypriot fleet before the northern or 'Sidonian' harbour of Tyre, and the Phoenician ships before the southern or 'Egyptian' harbour. All hope of relief to the besieged was thus cut off. But in spite of that they continued to defend themselves with great bravery. A sally of the Tyrian fleet northwards against the Cypriots ended in their total defeat. On the completion of the mole it appeared that Alexander's engines had not the desired effect on the strong eastern walls, but the ships that were armed with siege-engines after repeated attempts finally succeeded in making a breach in the southern wall and laid the city open to storm. Simultaneously the fleets pressed into the harbours. After a short bloody struggle the city was in Alexander's hands. Quarter was given only to those who, like King Azemilkos and the Carthaginian ambassadors, had taken refuge in the temple of Melkarth. About 8000 Tyrians fell, and about 30,000 were sold as slaves according to the custom of Greek warfare. The city was spared and resettled, and placed under a Macedonian commandant to become the chief stronghold of Macedonian power on this coast.

Alexander could now make his sacrifice to Heracles. It

was combined with a solemn procession of the army in full equipment, as at Ephesus: but on this occasion the personnel of the fleet joined in the parade, and a gymnastic competition and a torch-race were held in the temple precincts. The engine which had made the breach was dedicated to the god in the temple.

Tyre fell in August 332. The population, which had held out so long in a desperate case, deserve admiration and sympathy. But the victor claims our admiration too. Alexander had been seven months before the city. He did not leave it till he had carried out what he regarded as absolutely essential.

While Alexander was besieging Tyre, a second and last letter reached him from Darius; in it he offered, along with a large ransom for his family (10,000 talents), the hand of his daughter, a treaty of friendship and alliance and the surrender of his empire west of the Euphrates. It was a fateful moment for the ancient world. If Alexander had been satisfied with this empire up to the Euphrates, the whole subsequent evolution of ancient civilisation would have been totally different; the after-effects of his decision, indeed, stretch through the Middle Ages down to our own day, in the East as in the West. For Alexander, who at least since Issus claimed the whole Asiatic empire, to refuse was a matter of course. Our authorities tell us that in the council of the *Hetairoi*, before whom Alexander laid the letter, Parmenio said that if he were Alexander, he would be satisfied with it and end the war, whereupon Alexander answered: 'And I too, if I were Parmenio'.   *

There is a deep meaning in this pointed anecdote. Two different generations face each other in the old general and the young king, and one might quite well replace the general by his master Philip—for herein lies the contrast between the policies of Philip and Alexander. We may state with confidence that if Philip had ever advanced so far, he would certainly have accepted the offer of the Euphrates frontier. Philip always remained a Macedonian, and would have done so, if he had incorporated parts of the Persian empire in his Macedonian Empire. Alexander, who already felt himself 'King of Asia', was in a course of development which was bound to lead him far beyond Macedonian interests. That for the Macedonian people Philip's more limited policy would have been the better, can scarcely be doubted. Nor can one dispute the fact that by being limited to the Euphrates frontier Greek culture in the nearer East might have been diffused in a more intensive and permanent fashion. But there never could have been that world-wide culture, whose effects can be traced to India and even to China. Would not too a strong Persian power beyond the Euphrates have been a permanent danger to the Hellenised nearer East? It is scarcely possible to weigh what might have happened against what actually did happen. At any rate, we see here most clearly what a decisive effect the will of Alexander had on the subsequent history of the world.

When Alexander marched southwards from Tyre, he met with resistance at one place only, the old Philistine city of Gaza, the last great coast-town before the Egyptian frontier, a strong fortress on an eminence, which was bravely and skilfully defended by the eunuch Batis with the help of Nabatean mercenaries. Not until the heavy siege-engines had been fetched from Tyre and placed upon an artificial rampart and the walls had been undermined, did he succeed in taking the city after a two months' siege. In the course of it he was wounded by a shot in the shoulder. As a clean sweep had been made of the population partly by death and partly by enslavement, Alexander fetched in new settlers from the neighbourhood, and converted the town into a Macedonian fortress.

From Gaza he marched along the coast, and in seven days reached Pelusium, the frontier fortress of Egypt, where he found his fleet. It was a necessary part of his strategic plan to occupy Egypt, before he penetrated into the interior of Asia. Though the principal danger, which had threatened him from the Persian fleet, was now removed, King Agis of Sparta was still active in stirring up war against him. An unoccupied Persian Egypt in his rear might also have been a rallying point or an asylum for all turbulent and hostile elements, and just before his arrival Amyntas, son of Antiochus, who had escaped from the battle-field of Issus with those 8000 Greek mercenaries, had attempted, though without success, to establish himself there.

Egypt fell to Alexander without fighting. Mazaces the satrap surrendered to him the citadel of Memphis with the garrison and the treasury (800 talents), and the Egyptian people hailed him with joy as their deliverer from the Persian yoke. For more than sixty years they had succeeded, by prudently taking advantage of the disorders in the Persian empire, and by the help of large Greek mercenary armies and prominent Greek commanders such as Chabrias, Agesilaus and others, in maintaining under their national Pharaohs their freedom from the Persian rule which had begun with Cambyses. But ten years previously Ochus had reconquered Egypt, expelled the last native king Nectanebo II, and dealt a deadly blow to the Egyptian people, in nothing so sensitive as in their religious life, by inaugurating the new Persian rule with the plundering of Egyptian temples. Hence the hatred of Persian government, and the joy and hope with which Alexander was received. Nor were they destined to be disappointed by him.

Alexander was a true Hellene in his complete toleration for the gods of the foreign peoples whom he encountered. Very early the Greeks began to identify foreign divinities with corresponding Greek gods. In Egypt in particular the principal gods of the Egyptians had been equated with Greek gods by the Greek residents, Ammon with Zeus, Osiris with Dionysus, Isis with Demeter, Horus with Apollo, and so forth. To Alexander it was quite natural to testify his reverence towards the Egyptian gods. But it became his special duty and obligation, when, probably soon after his entry into Memphis, he was recognised by the

Egyptian priesthood as king of Egypt, and therewith acquired the right of offering the royal sacrifices which
played so great a part in that country. This extremely important event is not mentioned in our historical sources.
But the Alexander romance states that at Memphis Alexander was placed on a throne in the temple of Ptah and
invested as king of Egypt. Suspicious as this authority is in
itself, the idea at least might be accepted as historical; for
the adoption of the royal state must have found expression
in some official act. However that may be, hieroglyphic
texts at any rate testify that Alexander bore the traditional
royal titles, like his Persian and Egyptian predecessors. Of
the five titles customary from the middle of the third
millennium B.C., the first, fourth and fifth, we learn from
inscriptions, were given to Alexander. As 'Horus' (I) he
was called 'the strong prince', also with the addition 'he
who hath laid hands on the lands of the foreigners' or 'the
protection of Egypt'. As 'King of Upper Egypt and king
of Lower Egypt' (IV) he was called 'beloved of Ammon
and selected of Ra'; and finally as 'Son of Ra' (V) he was
called 'Alexandros'. Here the Horus title 'he who hath laid
hands on the lands of the foreigners' seems to have been
invented for Alexander, whereas the other terms are frequently found before his time. These titles prove two things
of Alexander, his special sovereignty over Egypt, and his
consequent deification.

Probably the new Horus title points to his power outside
Egypt or according to Egyptian notions to his world-wide
sovereignty, but the emphasis lies on 'King of Upper and
Lower Egypt', by which he is specially claimed as king of
the Egyptian country. These inscriptions establish that
Alexander accepted the throne offered to him by the
priests, perhaps the high priest of Memphis. His whole behaviour in Egypt is therefore to be judged from this point
of view. To the Egyptians Alexander was thus their special
king, who by personal union joined Egypt to his other
realms, as Charlemagne brought the Lombards into his

empire by becoming their king. Previously he had neither in Lydia nor anywhere else thought of assuming a separate position, and later we shall find this happening only once again, at Babylon. These two states of ancient civilisation on the Nile and Euphrates, which for millennia had been the spiritual leaders of the East, had thus a special standing conceded to them in the Empire of Alexander; it was primeval traditions that demanded this solution.

From the earliest times divinity had been bound up with Egyptian sovereignty, for the Pharaoh was regarded as the incarnation of the greatest god. In the above titles divinity is expressly ascribed to Alexander, and in three grades: as Horus he was god; as son of Ra he was son of god, a title used from the fifth dynasty onwards, signifying that the holder was mystically begotten by Ra with the queen-mother; finally he was a favourite of the gods, as 'beloved of Ammon, selected of Ra', both high-flown phrases, applied already to earlier kings. Egypt was at that time the only country in the East in which monarchy and divinity were inseparable, and so to a people of about seven millions Alexander became the recipient of divine honours. But to Alexander this Egyptian apotheosis had a purely local significance; outside Egypt no effects of it can be traced.

It is stated that Alexander sacrificed to the other gods and also to Apis, who was not a god but a sacred animal, belonging to the cult of Ptah. We do not know whether he did this before or after the assumption of the state of a Pharaoh; perhaps this sacrifice to Apis was the first royal sacrifice which followed his enthronement in the temple of Ptah. The sacrifice to Apis was bound to make a profound impression on the Egyptians. Nothing had enraged them so much as the slaying of the sacred bull, first by Cambyses and then by Ochus; from the earliest times the cult of Apis had been not merely local, but one of those that were celebrated everywhere. In taking this step Alexander therefore had the political object of setting himself in diametrical opposition to these wicked Persians. Scanty and casual as is the Egyptian information that has come to us from the time of Alexander, we have evidence that he performed his religious obligations to the country as Pharaoh. He ordered the rebuilding both of the sanctuary in the temple of Thothmes III at Karnak and that of the temple of Amenhotep III at Luxor.

But Alexander had not come merely to promote the continuance of Egyptian culture; his desire was here, as in the case of his previous conquests, to pave the way for Greek culture. Egypt was no unknown land to the Greeks. Since the seventh century numerous Greeks had entered as mercenaries the service of Egyptian rulers, and some of them had settled in the country. From the reign of Psammetichus I also there had been on the Canopic arm of the Nile in the Delta a real Greek *Polis*, Naucratis (rediscovered near the present Nebireh),[1] in which, more particularly after the reorganisation of the kingdom by Amasis, Greco-Egyptian trade had been concentrated. Even in the capital city of Memphis there was a Greek community (Politeuma), the so-called Hellenomemphites, the descendants of those Ionian mercenaries, who had helped Psammetichus to found his dynasty. While the Naucratites were legally debarred from marrying native wives and had kept their race pure, in this community of Memphis, where the prohibition obviously did not exist, mixed marriages had taken place; and yet there, as at Naucratis, these Greeks were united in a 'Hellenion' for common Greek worship and life. Evidence has come down to us of their cultural life, in the two oldest papyri we possess, which are approximately of Alexander's time; the one, the 'Persae' of the poet and musician Timotheus, testifies to the cultivation of Greek literature, while 'the Cursing of Artemisia' before Oserapis, the god of the Serapeum, reveals a blend of Greek and Egyptian culture.

    [1] [The site was identified by Flinders Petrie, *Seventy Years in Archaeology*, p. 38, and excavated by Hogarth and others in 1899 and 1903. *Journal of Hellenic Studies*, xxv., 1905, pp. 105-36.]

How these Hellenomemphites must have rejoiced, when Alexander entered the city! They might well hope that a new era of Greek influence in Egypt was to begin. They were to be as little disappointed in their hopes as the Egyptians in theirs; Alexander knew precisely how both to satisfy the Egyptians, especially in their religious requirements, and to strengthen Greek influence in Egypt. At his first entry into Memphis, he expressed this double program in symbolic fashion; after the sacrifice to Apis he held there, in the centre of Egypt, for the first time since the erection of the Pyramids, a gymnastic and musical competition, to which the most famous artistes from Greece were summoned. One must not conclude that Alexander wanted to introduce these Greek games into the cult of the Egyptian gods or even into that of the Apis-bull, and in this manner inaugurate a policy of blending the two separate civilisations. He never aimed at a mixture of Greek and Egyptian culture. On the contrary he placed by the side of the Egyptian cult, the Greek games, as something different in kind and purely Greek, in order to affirm his program from the very first, that, without prejudice to the Egyptian cult, Greek ways of life, Greek gymnastics, Greek arts and literature in honour of Greek gods should in future have a home in Egypt.

The greatest contribution Alexander made towards the inclusion of Egypt in the Greek world was the foundation of Alexandria. As 332 was ending and 331 beginning, he started from Memphis, attended only by a small division of troops, the light Hypaspists, the archers and Agrianians, and the royal squadron of *Hetairoi*. Proceeding down the western arm of the Nile as far as Canopus, he turned to the left, and on the strip of ground between the inland lake Mareotis and the island of Pharos laid out the town which to this day bears his name. It was the first new foundation that Alexander established on his march, for the assumption that he had previously founded Alexandria by Issus (Alexandretta) is a disputed point. Not till the

interior of Asia was reached shall we find further foundations of cities; there he founded many. The object of this
foundation on the Egyptian coast cannot be doubtful. It
can hardly have been a military one, since, to keep Egypt
under control, forces should be concentrated not on the
coast, but in or near Memphis. It is expressly stated that
Alexander transferred to Alexandria the 'Emporium' of
the neighbouring Canopus; Alexandria was to be a staple
and trade centre, and for such no better site could have
been found on the whole coast. Whether Alexander himself or one of his followers made the choice, it was a stroke
of genius. The determining factor may have lain in these
circumstances: the island of Pharos in front provided a
sheltered harbour from the sea, while Lake Mareotis behind afforded an inner harbour, in particular the only one
on the coast unthreatened by the masses of silt brought down
by the Nile. The sea-current which here sets from west to
east has in the course of time silted up all the harbours on
the Egyptian and South Syrian coast; Alexandria is the
only exception because it lies west of the westernmost arm.
It is possible that one of the scientific men who attended
Alexander knew of this current. Thus it was Alexander who
first gave to Egypt a port with a future, though the history
of the country reaches back for millennia before him.

Naucratis had hitherto been the centre of trade between
Egypt and the Aegean. But it lay in the interior of the
Delta, and could not be as effective as a great Greek commercial city on the coast, such as Alexander now planned.
No doubt he was all the more eager in this project because
during his stay in Egypt he was impressed by the rich pro-
ductivity of the country and the enormous potentialities of
its export trade. His design of occupying first the Mediterranean coasts of the Persian Empire, however exclusively
dictated by strategic considerations, had succeeded, and
by the foundation of Alexandria, he showed his intention
of turning the military result to an economic use. The commercial area of the Levant with its coasts and islands was

under his control, but the finishing touch was still lacking in the south; he now supplied it. Later on under the Ptolemies the commercial importance of Alexandria was carried to a far higher pitch, but it is not improbable, as we shall see, that Alexander's final plans also connected Alexandria with even more ample schemes. At any rate down to the foundation of Constantinople, no city was founded which had such world-wide importance as Alexandria in Egypt.

The new city, like its later developments, had side by side with it an already existing settlement, a little fishing village called Rhacotis. The plans for the city, which adjoined Rhacotis on the east, were drawn up by Deinocrates of Rhodes, on the lines of the pattern then in fashion, which had been introduced in the fifth century by Hippodamus of Miletus. Two broad streets intersecting each other at right angles were laid out, and the remaining narrower streets drawn parallel to them, so that the whole consisted of square or rectangular blocks of houses. Alexander was passionately interested in the work. He was again seized by a 'longing', and himself indicated where the market-place and temples were to be, and decided what gods should have their temples in the new foundation. In accordance with his tolerant policy, and as a gracious Pharaoh, he also granted the Egyptians in Rhacotis an Egyptian temple, dedicated to Isis and certainly also to Osiris and Horus. The new city was, as usual, surrounded by a wall. It is described thus in a hieroglyphic document of 311: 'The fortress of the King of Upper and Lower Egypt, beloved of Ammon, and selected of Ra, son of Ra, Alexandros, on the shore of the great sea of the Ionians; Rhacotis was its earlier name'. One can imagine how many Greek architects, craftsmen and artists of the most different kinds were attracted to Egypt by the opportunities afforded in the building of Alexandria. This will explain the evident influence, even in Alexander's lifetime, of Greek art on Egyptian (p. 258).

The course of history caused Alexandria to take on more

and more of an international character; besides the Egyptians of Rhacotis at the beginning, many non-Greeks, Jews and other foreigners were attracted by the tempting profits and pleasures of the great city. But we must not fail to recognise that Alexander founded the city which he placed by the side of Rhacotis, as a purely Greek *Polis*, with its council (*Boule*) and popular assembly.

While Alexander was still on the coast, his admiral Hegelochus· arrived with the joyful news that his fleet once more controlled the Aegean, and that after the break-up of the Persian fleet Tenedos, Lesbos, Chios and Cos had all been recaptured. He now took a decision, which may give us an insight into his relation at the time to the Corinthian League. About a year before in a document preserved to us he had determined, according to the arrangements in force with regard to Chios then under siege, that the traitors when captured should be brought before the *Synhedrion* as the regular tribunal of the League—as it was to the *Synhedrion* that he had formerly referred the punishment of the Thebans. Notwithstanding, when Hegelochus brought before him the captive traitors of Chios, he did not send them to the *Synhedrion*, but in the exercise of his own authority commanded that by way of punishment they should be transferred to Elephantine, the most southerly city of Egypt above the First Cataract. This justifies the conclusion that in the interval he had won a more independent position with reference to the Hellenic League, so that he now denied to the *Synhedrion* a right which he had expressly recognised to it a year before. If we enquire into the psychological basis of such a change, the conjecture suggests itself that his great successes in the interval—the occupation of Syria and Egypt, the dissolution of the Persian fleet and recovery of the control of the sea—must have largely increased his feeling of power. Perhaps too it did not fail to impress the king, who was only twenty-four years old, that to these many millions of Egyptians he had become a god.

In this state of intense feeling, which drew his thoughts to the future, he was seized, while still on the coast, with the idea of consulting the oracle in the oasis of Ammon. This mysterious excursion to the oracle of Ammon in the oasis of Siwah is one of the most remarkable episodes in Alexander's life. In its varied panorama hardly anything has so much appealed to the imagination of contemporaries, later generations and moderns, as this romantic march through the desert. When one considers that it was Alexander's interest as soon as possible to meet Darius, of whose fresh and gigantic military preparations he was doubtless fully apprised, it is clear that it must have been a strong motive that induced him to undertake this digression to the west, a digression, completely useless, and rather dangerous from the military standpoint, which removed him for six weeks from his Egyptian base. It is one of those actions of Alexander's which are only intelligible if we take into account his religious inner life and the non-rational and unaccountable elements in his character. Arrian again employs the same expression: the 'longing' seized him to consult the oracle of Ammon. It was, in fact, a need which he felt in his inmost soul to hear the oracle about his future before the decisive encounter with Darius. To understand this, one must remember that Alexander was a son of his age, and attached the greatest importance to oracles and divine omens generally, whether they were manifested in dreams, in the flight of birds, or otherwise in the processes of nature.

But why did he go to Ammon in particular? It has nothing to do with his position as Pharaoh; no Pharaoh had ever made a pilgrimage to the oasis. He was not paying any regard to his Egyptian subjects when he did this. If he merely wanted to hear an Egyptian oracle, there were many oracular gods in Egypt that he might have consulted. His pilgrimage to Ammon may have produced a specially favourable impression upon the Egyptians, because thereby, as in the case of the offering to Apis, he appeared as the reverse of the evil Cambyses; the story was told how Cambyses once sent out an expedition to destroy the oracle, but it was annihilated by sand-storms. Yet Alexander would never have undertaken the journey simply to make an anti-Persian demonstration. It was as a Greek that he visited the god, because his oracle was then regarded as infallible in the Greek world. The Greek colonists of the neighbouring town of Cyrene had at an early period formed trade relations with this oasis, which was exceptionally rich in date-palms. They were the first to equate with their own Zeus this Ammon, who was an offshoot of the Ammon of Thebes in Upper Egypt, and the first to place on their coins the type of Zeus with the ramhorns of Ammon curved about the ears. From Cyrene the knowledge of the oracle spread throughout the Greek world. Pindar wrote a hymn to the god, and later evidence of the growing estimation of the oracle becomes abundant. It was consulted by Cimon, Lysander and others; it is named in the *Birds* of Aristophanes along with Delphi and Dodona, and constantly it takes a higher rank. Shortly before Alexander's visit also the Athenians had constructed in Athens a sanctuary of Ammon, who had been worshipped by them for decades already. So we understand how Alexander, if he felt the need of an infallible answer, used the opportunity of his stay on the coast of Egypt, where he was comparatively near to the god, to consult his oracle. It is possible that alongside of this leading motive, which is stated in our authorities, he contemplated with satisfaction the effect of a favourable oracle on the Greeks. In view of the great importance then attached by them to the oracle, a religious sanction might certainly be given in their eyes to his great enterprise.

Callisthenes, his court historian, who accompanied him on the journey into the desert, and gave an excellent description of it, tells us that Alexander went to Ammon, not only on account of the reputed infallibility of his oracle, but also because he had the ambition to rival Perseus and Heracles, who had likewise formerly consulted the god. If

one considers how vividly Alexander conceived his relations to the heroic ancestors of his race, this statement is
quite credible and suits the picture we have to form of him.
He may have given out this motive in an official proclamation to his friends and the troops accompanying him, in
order to kindle their zeal to endure the impending fatigues
of the desert march.

As he marched westwards from Rhacotis along the coast,
he was met by ambassadors from Cyrene, who conveyed to
him the homage of their city. They brought costly presents,
and invited him to visit Cyrene and its dependent towns.
Our authorities merely state briefly that Alexander made
alliance and friendship with the Cyreneans. We can
imagine how pleased he was with this unexpected recognition of his power, and how the eye of the conqueror in-
voluntarily turned westwards, where, with the Cyrenaic
district added, his sphere of interest extended to the Syrtes
and to the frontiers of the Carthaginian empire.

On reaching Paraetonium, he turned south-west on to
the old caravan road, which at present brings one to the
oasis after a march of about twelve days. Here his Macedonians were to become acquainted for the first time with
the toils and dangers of travelling in the desert. As formerly
on the Pamphylian coast the retirement of the sea had been
attributed to the direct intervention of the godhead, so now
divine protection was credited with the rain which suddenly fell when the provision of water, carried in skins on
camels' backs, had given out. Some days later a southern
sand-storm, a simoom, obliterated the road with masses of
sand, and the guides announced that two ravens were
cawing and flying ahead of the party. Alexander gave
orders that the ravens were to be followed, relying on the
god, who had sent the birds to show them the way in token
of his gracious reception of the visit. These tales have been
regarded as literary embellishments or inventions of Callisthenes; yet one sees in them only the heightened religious
feeling of the pilgrims, roused by the unwonted terrors

of the desert and the imminent danger of death, which thus transformed natural occurrences into supernatural miracles.

When Alexander and his party at last reached the oasis of Siwah, they were astonished at the wonderful forests of date-palms and olives, and the wealth of water in numerous springs and lakes. The oracular temple, to which he repaired, was on the citadel now called Aghurmi. The remains of the temple to-day are so built over by modern houses that its plan cannot be restored with certainty. What is preserved is the portal of the front colonnade, crowned by an Egyptian chamfer, which led into the priests' temple behind the courtyard; and also parts of the innermost sanctuary, the walls of which were decorated with reliefs and hieroglyphic inscriptions.

Callisthenes prefaces his narrative of Alexander's visit with a description of the usual ritual in the giving of oracular responses. This is thoroughly confirmed by the agreement of essential features with the ritual of the Ammon temple at Thebes, of which the temple in the oasis was a branch. According to Callisthenes, the answer was not given in words, as at Delphi and Branchidae. But the god, whose idol in the form of an *omphalos* was for the purpose carried round the temple courtyard in his boat on the shoulders of the priests in solemn procession and to the accompaniment of the singing of maidens and matrons, indicated his will through the idol, which directed the priestly bearers where to turn their steps, by 'nods and signs', which were the interpretation of the shakings and movements caused by carrying; and the chief priest as the 'prophet' explained these signs as consent or refusal, for which no doubt there were primitive traditions, shaped the oracle in accordance with them, and then announced it to the consultant. One can imagine that the excitement of the priests was like that of a disturbed ant-hill, when from the height of Aghurmi they saw in the distance the great caravan advancing with glistening weapons, and the news went round that the new king of Egypt was arriving in person; for never before, as was stated, had a Pharaoh visited the oasis. Preparations for a solemn reception had to be made in all haste. Some priests were forthwith despatched to receive the king and his escort outside the gate, and to acquaint them with the traditional ceremonial, before they entered the temple. In view of the constant intercourse with Greek pilgrims it may be assumed for certain that in this great body of priests there were people enough who could speak Greek. Accordingly the announcement was made to the visitors that only Alexander as Pharaoh might enter, and without change of clothes, the temple of the priests, which enclosed the portico and Holy of Holies, whereas his followers might enter only the court in front, the 'temple of the lay folk', after making certain changes of clothing prescribed by ceremonial. Meanwhile, it appears, the prophet, a venerable old man, had arranged that the idol in his boat should be carried by the priests out of the Holy of Holies into the temple-court to greet the king of Egypt as early as possible, and he himself awaited the king's arrival there.

When Alexander with his suite, conducted by the priests sent out to meet him, entered the temple-court, the prophet went to receive him, and, addressing him according to Egyptian ceremonial but certainly in the Greek language, greeted him as 'son of Ammon' in the name of the god. He then led the king alone into the temple of the priests, where Alexander put his question to the oracle in the Holy of Holies. Thereupon the procession with the idol was enacted as described above, and the prophet announced the answer of the god to the king in the Holy of Holies. When Alexander returned into the temple-court, and his friends eagerly asked what had happened, he said nothing more than that 'he had heard what was according to his wish'. Some of his friends also used the opportunity to put questions to the god on their own behalf. They too received answers, according to the rite described, by the mediation of the prophet, but outside in the temple-court like ordinary pilgrims. This was what happened in public.

As the answer of Alexander to his friends shows, he kept the oracle to himself and treated it as secret. He might have had his own reasons for doing so. But it might also have been indicated to him by the prophet that the answer was to be kept secret, according to Egyptian ideas, because the god had spoken to his son. At any rate, Alexander kept the secret; for he wrote to his mother Olympias soon afterwards that he had received secret directions, which he would impart to her alone after his return to Macedonia. As this never happened, Alexander took the secret with him to the grave. So we shall never know what question he asked. The existing military and political situation makes it more than probable that the question referred in some way to his future. But how he formulated it, and how far forward it extended, whether it concerned only the impending struggle with Darius, or the actual winning of the sovereignty over Asia, which he had claimed after Issus, or whether ideas going far beyond that, of actual world-wide rule, were already in his mind, as they appeared without disguise in the later years of his life, Ammon alone knew, and we shall never know.

By those words of Alexander to his friends the public doubtless learned that he had received a favourable answer from the god, and the Greek world, which believed in the infallibility of Zeus Ammon, might now perhaps acknowledge that what Alexander did henceforth was done with the consent and blessing of the god. But even if this was the effect, it fell far short of the impression that the previous salutation of Alexander as son of Zeus Ammon was bound to make. To the prophet this salutation had been a matter of course, because he had before him the king of Egypt; from the Egyptian point of view, it was simply a consequence of the recognition that Alexander was also king of the oasis. Alexander may already have been saluted, in the temple of Ptah at Memphis or in other Egyptian temples which he entered, as son of the particular god in question; but whether these salutations made any profound impression on Alexander, whether, indeed, his attention was specially called to these titles, which were wrapped up in traditional phrases and certainly given in Egyptian, whether their meaning was explained to him, is more than doubtful. Here in the oasis, however, the salutation of him as son of the god, which came to him as a complete surprise, could not but make the deepest impression upon him. The god he regarded as Zeus, the great Greek oracular god, and in Greek language, equally intelligible to him and his escort, the prophet had in addressing him described him as son of the god. This meant that he was saluted as son of Zeus! It must have entered his soul like a flash of lightning and caused the deepest emotion. In form the utterance was not an oracle—he consulted the oracle later—but the prophet had saluted him in the sacred spot and in the name of the god. Alexander beheld in this a revelation of the god, a revelation which he took on trust as a confirmation of the special divine protection under which he had long felt himself, and as a recognition of the divine power working in him, which had led him to his unprecedented successes. He could believe in this all the more, since according to Greek conceptions superhuman deeds raised a man into the divine sphere.

All his life long Alexander clung to this mystic faith that he was the son of Zeus Ammon. Thereby he disowned his natural father Philip as little as any Pharaoh had disowned his father, because he was simultaneously son of Ra, and also of other gods besides. Mysticism and reality ran thus on parallel lines. To the end of his life Alexander dutifully recognised Philip as his father, however much his policy might diverge from that of Philip. On the other hand, how deeply he was moved by his divine sonship, is shown by the fact that he decided later that he would be buried in the oasis near his father Ammon.

Yet he never thought of introducing a political cult of

himself as son of Zeus. Nor do we hear in our certainly very incomplete tradition that he took any steps to propagate or even to proclaim his divine sonship. Actually, the news of this startling event soon spread far and wide. Before he left Egypt, ambassadors came from Miletus, who reported that the sacred spring in the temple of Didyma, which had dried up since the time of Xerxes, had begun to flow again, and that the oracle had confirmed Alexander as son of Zeus, while the Sibyl of Erythrae also recognised him as such. It is possible and not improbable that Alexander was interested in the rapid spread of the news, but proofs of any official measures taken are not to be found. Nor can the work of Callisthenes, in which the event was explicitly described, explain the rapidity with which the news was spread; for it was not published till 330. It is conceivable enough, however, that the friends and companions who were witnesses of the salutation sent word of it home as soon as possible, as Alexander himself no doubt related it in that letter to his mother. That the first echo of the news came from Ionia, is not accidental; in Ionia Alexander as liberator from the Persian yoke was more popular than in Hellas, and the Ionians had formerly paid divine honours to Lysander in his lifetime. It must be emphasised that outside Egypt this idea of Alexander's divine sonship produced effect only in the Greek world, which in Zeus Ammon revered the supreme oracular god, but, on the contrary, not among the Macedonians, who were quite alien and hostile to such ideas—apart from the closest friends in Alexander's suite—nor among the Asiatics, who knew nothing about Ammon. But even within the Greek world, it appears that it was left to everyone to decide what attitude he should take up to the divine sonship.

Though the oracle was kept secret by Alexander, yet when some time had elapsed, Cleitarchus had the impudence to tell his readers minutely what questions Alexander put to the oracle. First he asked whether the god would give him world-wide dominion, and next whether he had

punished all of Philip's murderers. Later authors eagerly
seized on these obvious inventions, and some people believe them to this very day. They are recorded by Plutarch.
In other respects too fancy laid hold of the events at the
oasis. Since among the Greeks the divine sonship attracted
more attention than the favourable oracle, of whose contents nothing had been heard, the idea arose that Alexander had gone to Ammon to obtain recognition as his son.
Again it was Cleitarchus who introduced into literature this
falsification of history, and so what was merely an unfore-
seen accident became the goal of the journey. Stories were
even invented that Alexander sent on messengers ahead to
demand of the priests recognition as son of Ammon! The
explanation of the journey by Alexander's claim of divine
sonship not only had the widest circulation in antiquity,
but dominates modern students too. From this premise the
most varied conclusions are drawn. It is concluded that
even in his earlier years Alexander aimed at receiving
divine honours, or political motives are ascribed to him,
and it is thought he went to the oasis to secure another
basis for his relation to Greeks and Macedonians. This falls
with the premise. On the other hand, the effort of the
Greeks to analyse the idea of divine sonship in a rational-
istic way led to the tale that Ammon himself in the form
of his sacred serpent had had intercourse with Olympias.
Others again knew that Olympias had confessed this intercourse to her husband Philip, whereupon he repudiated
her as an adulteress. Thus in the course of time a luxuriant
growth of legends, myths and fantastic inventions gathered
round the march of Alexander to the oasis, and concealed
the real facts.

On his return journey Alexander made directly for
Memphis, following the desert route by Gara and Moghara,
which takes eighteen days to cover. At Memphis many *
embassies from Greece awaited him, and he was in the
mood to receive them graciously. From Antipater came
400 newly enlisted Greek mercenaries and 500 Thracian

cavalry. Alexander then offered sacrifice to Zeus the King, and again made a solemn procession with his army under arms, and held a gymnastic and musical competition. It is a mistake to see in this god either the god of the oasis or the Oserapis of Memphis; this 'Zeus the King' is nothing but the pure Greek Zeus. It is significant that the young son of Zeus offers his first sacrifice to the Greek Zeus, not to some Egyptian god. By his elevation to the position of son of Zeus his Greek character is evidently enhanced, and under the influence of those feelings he prepares this magnificent festival for Zeus in the capital of Egypt.

While there Alexander showed himself a true Greek by sending a scientifiç expedition to the Soudan. The question how to explain the Nile inundation which begins in summer, had long given rise to lively discussion among Greek scientists, and it was Aristotle who had instigated his pupil to get the question settled by eye-witnesses. Accordingly Alexander despatched an expedition of scholars up the Nile, to study the cause of its inundations. How far they went, we do not know. At any rate, they returned with the correct answer, that the swelling of the Nile is produced by summer rains in the Abyssinian mountains. When Aristotle heard the result of this scientific expedition, he wrote triumphantly on the question: 'This is no longer a problem'. Here for the first time we see Alexander as his docile pupil, who with enthusiasm places himself and his enterprise at the disposal of science.

In the organisation of Egypt, which Alexander arranged before his departure, it is noticeable that he did not concentrate the administration in the person of one satrap. He preferred instead decentralisation, probably because he did not wish to entrust to one individual a country of such economic importance, and so easy to hold from the military point of view owing to its natural frontiers. In another respect too Alexander's arrangement presents a special feature. Previously in Caria he had shown by the appointment of Ada that he was ready to pay regard to the national feelings of the subjected people. Similarly in Egypt he placed two natives at the head of the civil administration of Upper and Lower Egypt, while he assigned the western and eastern frontier districts of the Delta, Libya and Arabia (near Heroonpolis), to the Greek Apollonius and the Naucratite Cleomenes. The two Egyptians were coupled with two Macedonian military governors, and the fortresses of Memphis and Pelusium received their special commandants. In contrast to this decentralisation the whole administration of finance was placed in the hands of Cleomenes of Naucratis; the heads of districts had to pay the taxes to him after they had raised them in their own districts in the fashion previously adopted. No doubt the population were heartily glad that the collection of taxes was not in foreign but in native hands. When Alexander departed, he was accompanied by the affection of the Egyptians who felt themselves free of the load which had rested on them since the reconquest by Ochus. The legend might well arise that Alexander was in reality the son of the last native king Nectanebo II.

At the beginning of spring 331 he started from Memphis and proceeded to Phoenicia, where he spent some time at Tyre. Here he made many more changes in the government of the territories conquered up to that date. It is worth mentioning that he created two important offices of finance, one for Asia Minor west of Taurus, and another for Cilicia, Phoenicia and Syria. When he finally granted to an Athenian embassy the surrender, which he had previously refused, of the Athenians captured at the Granicus, it was because he wanted just then to influence popular opinion at Athens, while in Hellas Agis was busy in beating up recruits for an alliance against him. Agis had won a victory over a Macedonian force in the past winter, and in the spring he had succeeded in attracting to his side Elis, the Achaeans (all but Pellene) and the Arcadians (all but Megalopolis). If the Persian fleet had still been in existence, this situation would scarcely have permitted Alexander to march away into the heart of Asia. But as he now controlled the sea, he could rely on Antipater and be satisfied with sending his fleet—to be reinforced by 100 more ships —from Cyprus and Phoenicia—in order to protect the Peloponnesians who remained faithful.

The Great King, after Alexander abruptly declined his second offer, had begun vigorously to collect a great army at Babylon. This time, as the West was lost, it was the eastern peoples of the empire, who supplied the chief troops; besides the Persians and Medes there were the fine races of East Iran, the Bactrians and Sogdians under Bessus the satrap of Bactria, the Arachosians and Areians, the Parthyaeans, Hyrcanians and others. The Scythian Sacae, not as subjects but as allies, sent a contingent, and the Indians who dwelt this side of the Indus sent fifteen elephants. Again we must reject the usual fantastic numbers—most writers mention a million infantry and 40,000 cavalry—but the counter-measures of Alexander make it unquestionable that he had to face a very great preponderance of force. The statement that this Persian army was far larger than that which fought at Issus, is unquestionably correct. Moreover, obviously because of his experience at Issus, Darius had to some extent improved the arming of his troops. He set great store by his 200 scythed cars (with scythes on the wheels and long spears at the tip of the pole), which, like the tanks of to-day, were to spread death and destruction in the enemies' lines. One must recognise that he made thorough preparation for the decisive battle. The choice of the battle-field is also to be commended. Realising that he had suffered most at Issus from limitations of space, this time Darius chose a wide plain, as he had endeavoured to do at Sochoi. It was on the left bank of the Tigris, north of the old 'city of the four gods' Arbela (to-day Erbil), and thither he led his army from Babylon, as soon as he heard that Alexander had started from Phoenicia.

From Tyre Alexander marched northwards to the Euphrates, in order to cross the river at Thapsacus. His pioneers had already begun to build two big bridges over the Euphrates, but had not completed them; for on the other side was Mazaeus, the satrap of Syria and Mesopotamia, with several thousand men, stationed there less to prevent the crossing than to spy out the approach of Alexander, since it was in Darius' interest to draw Alexander over the Euphrates and Tigris to the battle-field which he had himself selected. Accordingly, as soon as Alexander appeared before Thapsacus, Mazaeus vanished, the bridges were completed, and Alexander led his army over unmolested. From here he turned northwards into northern Mesopotamia, probably by the old caravan road to Charrān and Edessa, and then proceeded south of the Armenian foot-hills eastwards by way of Nisibis to the Tigris. On approaching it he received from captured Persian spies the false report that Darius was awaiting him on the other side of the Tigris, to prevent his passage. But when by forced marches he reached the river, he found neither Darius nor even any watching force of Persians, and was able to cross the Tigris without opposition, but not without some difficulty; for this rapid river here justifies its name, 'swift as an arrow'. While his army was resting on the eastern bank, there was a partial eclipse of the moon; our astronomers calculate that it occurred on the evening of Sept. 20, 331. Alexander then sacrificed to *Selene, Helios* and *Ge* (Moon, Sun and Earth), whose work, as Arrian correctly adds, the eclipse was supposed to be. As Alexander selected these gods, it may be assumed that he understood the cause of an eclipse of the moon, though, to allay the excitement in his army caused by the phenomenon, he had recourse to the seers.

Marching in a south-easterly direction between the Tigris and the Kurdish mountains, in search of Darius, he passed near the ruins of ancient Nineveh, probably without having the least idea of the historical importance of the country. Just as the Assyrian empire was once broken by the destruction of Nineveh (612), so now the Persian empire was to receive its death-blow in the battle at the village of Gaugamela not far away to the east.

Here Darius had found a battle-field suited to his purpose. His dispositions have been exactly recorded, for after the victory the battle-order was found in the royal camp. In the centre, where again according to ancient precedent was the king himself in his chariot, was arrayed his mounted guard, the so-called 'Kinsmen', and the Persian infantry of the guard, the so-called 'Apple-bearers' (with golden pomegranates on their spears), covered right and left by the Greek mercenaries, who as at Issus were specially designed to engage the Macedonian phalanx. Left and right the two wings spread out, of combined cavalry and infantry, on the extreme left the Bactrian cavalry, the Dahae, Arachosians and others, on the right wing the Medes, Parthyaeans, and so on. In front of the two wings Scythian and more Bactrian cavalry were on the left, on the right Armenian and Cappadocian cavalry; before the centre the fifteen elephants, led by their Indian mahouts. The 200 scythed cars were distributed in front of the whole line, 100 of them opposite Alexander's right wing. Over the entire battle-field Darius had removed all unevennesses of ground, so as to give a smooth path of attack for his cavalry and chariots.

Alexander's intention was to use the 'oblique' formation in this battle as he had previously done. So his line was again divided into an offensive right wing, which he commanded in person, and a defensive left under Parmenio. Once more the position of the *Hetairoi* was on the right, of the Thessalian cavalry on the left, and of the Macedonian phalanx in the centre. But as Alexander, on account of the great numerical superiority of his opponent, was afraid of being outflanked or even surrounded, he set a second battle-line behind his front, with orders, in case there was a risk of being encircled, to turn round and face the enemy's attack in the rear. If this happened, the troops arranged left and right of his front, who in the other circumstances

were to prolong the line, would wheel and unite together
the two lines of battle and fight facing the flanks. Thus, in
the event of being encircled, Alexander's army would have
formed a square. But the contingency was not realised. In
this idea—produced by the necessity of the situation—of
an elastic double front which in case of need might develop into a square, we see the genius he possessed for
tactics. It was quite an original idea.

At the news of Alexander's arrival, Darius had arrayed
his army in line of battle on Sept. 30. Acting on the advice *
of Parmenio Alexander did not accept the challenge, but
pitched his camp at a distance of about four miles, and,
as pit-traps or similar obstacles were suspected, he rode
over the battle-field with a few attendants to reconnoitre.
In the evening he made his men prepare their food and
then take a thorough night's rest. His army thus was perfectly fresh to meet the enemy on the morning of Oct. 1st,
331, while the unfortunate Persians had been obliged to
spend the whole night in full armour ready for battle, as
Darius feared a night-attack. Parmenio advised a surprise
by night, but Alexander rejected his advice, saying that it
was disgraceful to steal the victory.

As Alexander approached from the north, he found himself, since his line was far shorter than the Persian, with his
right wing exactly opposite Darius and the Persian centre.
Accordingly, he inclined his advance more and more to the
right, so that, as in the earlier battles, he might charge the
left wing. The consequence was that the Persians, who also
advanced, moved in the same direction. Darius, however,
fearing that in this way they would get on to ground not
previously levelled, ordered his Scythian and Bactrian
horse, who were in front of his left wing, to take Alexander
in the flank. Alexander sent to meet them the light cavalry,
whom he had posted before the extreme right to deal with
such an emergency. While a vigorous cavalry engagement
was taking place, the scythed chariots were launched against
Alexander's right, but this attack, on which Darius had

rested his chief hopes, was a complete failure. Partly the drivers were shot down or pulled out of their cars by the Agrianians and archers stationed for the purpose, and partly, by quick withdrawal, Alexander's troops formed lanes, through which the chariots drove without doing much damage, till finally they were overpowered by Alexander's grooms—a manœuvre brilliantly executed, which recalls the events at the Shipka Pass (p. 67).

The two lines of battle were drawing close, when Alexander observed that opposite to him a gap had occurred in the Persian left, through the detachment by Darius of more troops of horse to support the Scythians and Bactrians. His eagle eye saw that the moment was come for the offensive blow. At the head of his *Hetairoi* he rushed into the gap, and began, wheeling to the left, to roll up the enemy's line towards the centre, while soon the Macedonian phalanx with their long pikes opened a fierce attack from the front. When Darius, alarmed by this lightning-like change in the situation, perceived the fierce attack of Alexander, as at Issus he turned his chariot round, and was the first to flee. The guards who were nearest formed a body round him, and soon the remaining troops of the centre and left wing followed suit.

On this occasion too Alexander was unable to take up the pursuit at once and win a complete victory with the capture of Darius. His left wing under Parmenio was still engaged in a very dangerous struggle with the Persian right under Mazaeus, who had succeeded in outflanking his adversary. The senseless flight of Darius was the more unpardonable, since the battle as a whole had not yet been decided. Moreover, the Indian and Persian cavalry of the right wing had succeeded in penetrating a gap, caused by the rapid advance of the phalanx, and in piercing Alexander's second line. But instead of wheeling round and attacking this from behind, the undisciplined Orientals rushed on to plunder Alexander's camp. The well-led second line then, according to Alexander's tactical plan, in

its turn wheeled round and took them in the rear, compelling them to retire hastily after severe loss. It was these
retreating masses of cavalry that Alexander encountered,
when at Parmenio's urgent request he was hurrying to his
aid. The cavalry engagement which ensued was the more
bloody, as the Indians and Persians now fought desper-
ately for their lives. Alexander lost in this affray no less than
sixty of his *Hetairoi*, and Hephaestion his favourite friend was
wounded. When the Oriental cavalry had forced their way
through and escaped, and Alexander could hasten on to
Parmenio, it appeared that his help was no longer necessary; the Thessalian cavalry had in the meantime proved
victorious. The victory was complete along the whole line.

At length Alexander was able to take up the pursuit of
Darius. As long as light lasted he hurried after him. After
giving his cavalry a rest on the other side of the Lycus (the
upper Zab), he started again at midnight, and arrived the
next day at Arbela, where he found Darius' treasure and
baggage. But the chief prize of victory was lost. The king
could not be caught up; he had too great a start. With only
a few attendants he escaped over the Kurdish mountains
into Media.

At Arbela Alexander abandoned the chase. Instead of
following the fugitive into the unknown, he rightly regarded it as more important, first to harvest the fruits of
victory, and occupy the central lands of the Achaemenids
with their chief palaces and treasure-houses. In sure expectation of these results he now officially adopted the title
of King of Asia, which the oracle of Gordium had promised
him, and which he had claimed in his first letter to Darius.
When we are told that after the battle he was publicly proclaimed King of Asia, this act of recognition can only have
proceeded from the assembly of the Macedonian army, although hitherto it had merely had the right and opportunity to acclaim kings of Macedonia. Alexander no doubt
gave them the idea and the formula. The proclamation of
sovereignty, which marked the climax of the celebration

of the victory of Arbela, was accompanied by magnificent sacrifices to the gods and rich presents to his friends.

It is especially interesting to notice that Alexander not only presented himself to them in the light of the conqueror of Asia, but also ostentatiously marked his position as *Hegemon* of the Corinthian League. After the victory he ordered that in the territory of the Greek allies all tyrannies should be put down and that all cities concerned should receive back their autonomy. He must have known that in the interval Antipater had favoured tyrannies in some instances and that this had caused much bad blood in Greece. His anxiety concerning the result of the conflict with King Agis, of which he then knew nothing, must have suggested this edict as a means of preventing further adhesions to the side of Agis. If, as appears, he issued the order without the co-operation of the *Synhedrion*, he could count on the gratitude and approval of the whole Greek world, though probably he had exceeded his powers as *Hegemon*. In this connexion, it is credibly stated that after the victory he reassured the Plataeans as to the rebuilding of their city, which Philip had promised them after Chaeronea; his reason, he declared, was that their forefathers had given their territory in the struggle of the Greeks for freedom from the Persians (479). Furthermore, he sent presents of booty to Croton in Lower Italy, because their citizen Phayllus had been the only Italian Greek to fight on the side of the Hellenes at Salamis. Alexander thus connected his own victory with the ancient victories of Plataea and Salamis, and again emphasised the national Panhellenic character of the war. Before the battle too he had already given proof of his special relation to the allied Greeks of his army. As he rode along the front, he came to the Thessalian and other cavalry of the Greek League, and when they cried out to him that he should lead them against the barbarians, he took his spear in his left hand, and lifting his right to heaven, prayed that if he was really the son of Zeus, the gods would assist the Hellenes. At this moment of intense excitement, when perhaps the recollection of the favourable oracle of Ammon strengthened his confidence of victory, the confession of his divine sonship came to his lips, and as son of Zeus he prayed the gods to help the Hellenes of his army. What he had previously said to his Macedonians on the right wing and in the centre, we are not told; but we may be perfectly certain that to them he said nothing of his divine sonship, for he was only son of Zeus to the Greeks.

From Arbela Alexander led his army southwards to Babylon. Expecting resistance, he approached in battle-array. But Mazaeus, who had hurried from Gaugamela to Babylon and taken over the command, came out with his sons in suppliant's dress to meet him, and surrendered the city. He was followed in solemn procession by the leading men of the city, among them Bagophanes, the command-ant of the fortress, and the Persian and Babylonian priests; and the whole population, as far as it had not already taken up its post on the city walls, thronged out, in great curio-sity to see their 'new king'. It was a memorable spectacle full of meaning for the history of the world, when at the head of his troops in glittering armour, through streets decorated with flowers and wreaths, and between altars from which clouds of incense were rising, Alexander en-tered this ancient metropolis of the Orient, which since the days of Hammurabi had been the soul of the East, and now for the first time received within its walls a western conqueror. Alexander occupied the royal castle, and after its severe fighting his army enjoyed itself in their luxurious quarters in the sinful Babel.

Alexander by his victory of Gaugamela having abolished Persian rule over Babylon, the Babylonians, like the Egypt-ians, saw in him their new king, and through their priests offered him a separate sovereignty, which he accepted. Thus by personal union he connected Babylon, like Egypt, with the rest of his Asiatic empire. It was a peculiarity of this Babylonian monarchy, that since the days of Hammurabi (about 2000), who made Babylon the capital of Babylonia, it had included the claim to 'world sovereignty', a conception which in the third millennium had already played a part in the history of Mesopotamia. From the time of Hammurabi it had been Marduk, the chief god of Babylon (in Semitic Bēl), who along with the throne of Babylon conferred also the rule over 'the four quarters of the globe', and he alone was counted lawful king, who at the new year festival had clasped the hands of Marduk in his temple. This prescription had been observed by successive dynasties and by Cyrus, the founder of the Achaemenid line. Darius I also, whose sovereignty had been given him by Ahuramazda according to his own documents, was to the Babylonians 'King of Babylon, King of the Countries', as the Babylonian texts state. But after putting down the rebellion of Tarzia (479), his son Xerxes had broken with this ritual. He destroyed the temple of Marduk (Esagila), carried away the image, and put an end to the separate kingdom of Babylon; and the Achaemenids never afterwards styled themselves kings of Babylon. The separate position of Babylon was first restored by Alexander. In order to meet the religious feelings of his new subjects as far as possible, as he had done in Egypt, and especially to set himself right with the priests, erroneously called Chaldaeans by the Greeks and Romans, he gave orders soon after his entry for the rebuilding of the temples destroyed by Xerxes and in particular the temple of Marduk. In other ways he endeavoured to carry out the wishes of the priests, and, as Arrian tells us, offered sacrifice to Marduk according to their directions. This was the royal sacrifice, which the Tyrians refused to let him offer in their city.

The old traditions, which Alexander had now taken over, connecting with world dominion the sovereignty of Babylon must have been very welcome to him, but they scarcely gave him anything new. This Babylonian world dominion had in practice been simply the claim to lordship over Asia (possibly including Egypt); it meant simply the sovereignty over Asia, promised him at Gordium, and officially confirmed to him by the assembly of the army at Arbela, before he reached Babylon. It would therefore not be correct to derive from the Babylonian traditions these claims to rule over Asia. Nevertheless, it might be valuable to Alexander to find in the old metropolis of the Orient respectful confirmation for that which he had acquired by his own right hand; for the proclamation at Arbela was really only a consequence of his gigantic exploits.

As in Egypt Alexander had placed natives at the head of the civil government, so henceforth on the conquest of country after country he bestowed, as King of Asia, these functions on Persians with the title of satrap. This was done for the first time in Babylon, and Alexander's special position as King of Babylon may have contributed to the result. To Mazaeus he assigned the satrapy in gratitude for his surrender of the strong fortress. Beside Mazaeus as civil governor he placed to keep him in check a Macedonian general with command over the troops. Finance and taxation were also severed from the satrapy and entrusted to a Macedonian. On this principle Alexander regulated the administration of the other satrapies of the East, till again changes proved necessary. As an exceptional measure—which was soon cancelled—Mazaeus as satrap was entrusted with the coining of money.

From Babylon, where he stopped about a month, Alexander marched eastwards and arrived in twenty days at Susa, the old capital of Elam, which had been the chief seat of government under the Achaemenids. In cooler Ecbatana they stayed for the hot summer months only, and also in winter or spring spent some time in Babylon. What a part Susa had played in the Greek world since Aeschylus, and particularly since the shameful peace of Antialcidas! How many embassies of opposing Greek states had waited in the Great King's ante-chamber! Alexander and his Macedonians now marched in without striking a blow. How anxious he was to secure this city and the treasures it contained is shown by his sending Philoxenus on ahead, straight from the battle-field of Gaugamela, to take possession of them. A message from Philoxenus reached him on the way, announcing that the inhabitants of Susa had surrendered the town and that the treasure was intact.   *

For the first time Alexander got possession of one of the great treasure depots of the Persian kings. They were of a peculiar nature. Darius I had introduced the coining of money into the empire, which had hitherto been administered on the basis of an exchange of natural products, and had imposed on the satraps money tribute beside tribute in kind. But the old system prevailed afterwards as before; instead of putting into circulation the cash received, he and his successors amassed it in their chief palaces, and in the primitive manner related by Herodotus melted it down into ingots of gold and silver, from which in case of need bars were cut off and made into coined money. Though Darius Codomannus had spent vast sums on the war, and also taken much into the field and lost it, Alexander found still colossal treasures in his palaces. When it is stated that at Susa apart from the precious stones 40,000 silver talents and 9000 coined darics of gold fell into Alexander's hands, the first figure alone implies a valuation, in Persian silver talents, of uncoined gold and silver bullion amounting to about £14,000,000. He was accordingly enabled to give Menes, whom he sent from Susa to the sea, as the new director of finance for Cilicia, Phoenicia and Syria, 3000 talents, with the order to pay Antipater as much as he required for the war with Agis; for no news had yet been received of the conclusion of this conflict.

The occupation of Susa was performed with great solemnity. Alexander sacrificed to the Macedonian gods according to ancestral ritual, and ordered a torch-race and gymnastic contests to follow. He left as satrap the Persian Abulites, who had surrendered the city to him, but placed at his side two Macedonians as commander of the troops and citadel commandant. While at Susa he was reinforced by several thousand fresh troops from Macedonia. In incorporating the mounted men into the *Hetairoi*, he created a new organisation, by dividing the regiments (*ilae*) for the first time into two squadrons (*lochoi*) and giving each squadron a commander of its own (*lochagos*). This was the first of a great number of reforms which were gradually introduced into the organisation of his army.

Alexander's next goal was Persepolis. After crossing the Pasitigris he reached the land of the Uxii. While the inhabitants of the plain submitted to him, the untamed mountaineers demanded that he should purchase by presents leave to cross their territory, as the Persian kings had previously done. Alexander refused to yield to this demand, as he was not willing to recognise the independence of any tribe in his empire, and by a stratagem succeeded in turning their position and overcoming them. Thereupon he imposed on them an annual tribute of horses, draught animals and sheep, for this mountain tribe knew no money, and depended upon stock-breeding.

While he made Parmenio march with the Greek troops along the high road, which had been made for the Persian court from Susa to Persepolis, he himself with his Macedonians hurried through the mountains by a shorter route to the Persian Gates. Here he met with serious resistance; the satrap of Persia, Ariobarzanes, had drawn a wall across the pass, and was awaiting him with a superior force. Only after heavy fighting and by help of a bold turning manœuvre did he succeed in putting the enemy to flight. He then sped down into the plain, over the Araxes (Kurr), which had been bridged in the interval, and on to Persepolis, in order to reach the town before its garrison had time to plunder the treasures. He was in time to secure them.

Alexander now set foot in the native land of the Achaemenids. The great Cyrus, founder of the empire and the dynasty, had erected his capital with palace and sepulchre at Pasargadae (near the modern Meshedi-Murghāb) close to the battle-field on which he overcame Astyages the Median. Later Darius I built south-east of this the strong citadel of Persepolis, within the walls of which he and his successors erected their residences and their open audience halls (*Apādana*) supported by columns, on a high terrace to which a double staircase led, richly decorated with reliefs. The ruins of the royal buildings at Persepolis (Takt i Dshemshīd) even to-day produce an overwhelming impression. The huge columns rising to heaven, the great bulls at the portal, the reliefs and inscriptions bear witness to the power and splendour of a world empire, which believed itself secure for all time by the grace of Ahuramazda. On the wall of the staircase leading up to the terrace are these proud words in cuneiform: 'Thus saith King Darius: this land of Persia, which Ahuramazda has granted me, which is fair, rich in men and rich in horses, according to the will of Ahuramazda and of me King Darius trembles before no enemy'. Now it lay defenceless at the feet of Alexander.

At Persepolis Alexander not only felt himself to be the new master, who by the conquest of this hallowed home of Persian tradition had laid the axe to the root of the Achaemenid power, but also appeared once more in the rôle of Generalissimo of the Corinthian League, who had taken over from the *Synhedrion* the task of conducting the Panhellenic war with Persia, to take vengeance for the crimes that Xerxes had formerly committed against the gods and temples of the Hellenes. Beyond all human expectation he had carried his victorious arms into the land from which the Persians took their origin. Yet his victories over the present ruler Darius did not count as vengeance on the dead Xerxes. Here where Xerxes had erected his palace, his magnificent hall of audience and the great portal in the sacred precincts of Persepolis, here should his memory be blotted out for all time and retribution be exacted. At

Alexander's orders torches were hurled into the buildings of King Xerxes, and in the process the others were partially destroyed. It was a symbolical act, by which to the listening world and especially to the Greeks it was intended to proclaim in an unparalleled *coup de théâtre* that the campaign of vengeance had fulfilled its object. One of the fables of Cleitarchus related subsequently that after a wild orgy of intoxication Alexander, incited by the fair Athenian *hetaera* Thaïs, fired the palace. Naturally this was eagerly repeated by later writers, and finds credence even to-day.

It was at Persepolis that Alexander finally received the news of Antipater's victory, which relieved him of a great anxiety. He had sent him money from Susa for the struggle with Agis, who, as we have already said, had formed a Peloponnesian coalition against Alexander in the spring of 331. Antipater had not been able to march against him at once, since he was detained by a rising in Thrace. After he had ended that war as quickly as possible, he hurried southwards, levied, in the sense of the treaty obligations of the League of Corinth, contingents from the Greek allies on the way, as it was a case of punishing the allies of the Spartans, if not the Spartans themselves, and entered Peloponnesus with an army which totalled 40,000. Here Agis with his allies had assembled 20,000 infantry and 2000 cavalry, and was besieging Megalopolis in Arcadia which had remained faithful to Alexander. Before the walls of this city, about the same time that Alexander was winning the victory of Gaugamela, there was a great battle in which, notwithstanding the most valiant resistance of his enemy, Antipater won a decisive victory. King Agis, the heart and soul of the struggle for freedom, after receiving many wounds, fell in the battle, and the vanquished, even Sparta, had to beg for peace. Antipater took as hostages fifty of the noblest Spartans, and referred the decision to the *Synhedrion*, as Alexander had done after the conquest of Thebes. But the *Synhedrion*, which met for an extraordinary session at Corinth, was weak enough to devolve the decision on Alexander. So later, when the Spartan hostages arrived, Alexander held the trial, punishing some and forgiving others, and forced the Spartans to join the League of Corinth.

Alexander rested his army at Persepolis during the winter months, though small raids were launched upon insubordinate tribes in Persis. The satrap of Carmania, the next province to the East, fortunately made his submission and was accordingly left in office. The treasures that Alexander found in Persepolis were three times as great as those of Susa; they were calculated at 120,000 Persian talents (about £42,000,000). Besides that, at Pasargadae, which was surrendered to him without fighting, he obtained from the treasure house of Cyrus 6000 Persian talents (£2,100,000). During his visit to Pasargadae, he paid significant respect to the memory of Cyrus, by ordering Aristobulus to decorate the interior of the sepulchral chamber in Cyrus' tomb; the tomb is still preserved. It is the first token we have of Alexander's great veneration for the founder of the Achaemenid empire, and it is noteworthy that he showed it before the death of Darius, before he felt himself to be the heir of Cyrus. It has been conjectured that the reading of Xenophon's *Cyropaedia* roused his admiration for Cyrus at an early age.

With the beginning of the spring of 330 Alexander set out to occupy the last of the Persian capitals, Ecbatana (Hamadan) in Media. It was reported that Darius was to be found there. After the defeat of Gaugamela he had escaped over the Kurdish mountains with a few troops to Ecbatana. Presently, as further units from the wreck of the army came in, he began to build up fresh forces. He hoped that Alexander and his troops would stay long in the luxurious quarters of his western palaces, or that he would not proceed further than Susa and would be contented with Asia west of the Kurdish mountains, which form a huge rampart barring off the Iranian countries from the

West. Should Alexander march against him, he planned to retreat to Bactria in the Far East, and make the road thither impassable for him by devastating the country as he went. At any rate, he sent on the harem and the baggage-train to the Caspian Gates, and waited the course of events at Ecbatana. As Alexander was marching northwestwards in the direction of Ecbatana, having subdued the Paraetacenians on the way, it was reported to him that Darius, trusting to Scythian and Cadusian reinforcements, meant to offer him battle. Immediately he left his baggage-train behind and hurried forward in battle-order. Soon he heard that the reinforcements had not come and that Darius had resolved to flee, and though he pressed on by forced marches, he reached Ecbatana too late. A week before Darius had escaped eastwards with 3000 cavalry and 6000 infantry, taking with him the 7000 talents stored there. It was a great disappointment. In all haste Alexander took only the most necessary steps in arranging for the West, and began the pursuit.

If by the conflagration at Persepolis he had shown the Greeks that he regarded the war of revenge as finished, he now carried this idea to its logical end by dismissing and sending home with rich rewards the Thessalian cavalry and the contingents of the other Greek allies. Thanks to the victory of Megalopolis he had Greece under his thumb, and no longer needed to take about with him these allied troops as security or as hostages. Not a few of them preferred, with his permission, to continue in his service; but as mercenaries, and no longer as allies. His special command as 'unlimited strategos' of the campaign of revenge, with which he was entrusted in 336 by the *Synhedrion* at Corinth, Alexander regarded as having expired. *Hegemon* of the League he remained as before; it was a life appointment, and up to his last days he acted officially in that capacity. But the Panhellenic campaign was now a thing of the past. The enthusiasm with which at the age of twenty he had taken up this idea six years before, must

long ago have been chilled by the sad experiences he had
had in the meantime with the Greeks of the motherland.
Yet he had never renounced it, even though from his first
crossing over into Asia the idea of conquest had stood with
it side by side. He had succeeded in connecting the two by
the ambition, which still continued to inspire him, to pave
the way for Greek culture in the East. But now he had no
longer two separate aims in the war, and could devote
himself to the idea of conquest without let or hindrance.

It speaks for Alexander's importance as a statesman that
before he plunged into the Far East, he centralised the
whole finance administration. He caused Parmenio, who
had brought from Persepolis the treasures of Susa and
Persepolis, totalling 180,000 Persian talents (about
£63,000,000), to deposit them in the citadel of Ecbatana
and hand them over to Harpalus, who had hitherto directed
the military chest, and was now appointed Imperial
treasurer. Alexander was determined to break with the
hoarding policy of the Persian kings, and ordered the incep-
tion of a gold and silver currency; the effects of this act
were momentous. To Parmenio he entrusted the safe-
guarding of the Imperial treasure, and left him with a
division at Ecbatana, also with the all-important duty of
securing the communications in the rear. It was a very
honourable and extremely responsible command which
was conferred on the meritorious old general; yet he himself
may have felt it as a slight, and very likely he was not wrong.
Not only his seventy years, which seemed to unfit him for
the great exertions that were impending, but still more the
contrast, which had been exhibited so often, between his
point of view and Alexander's probably appeared to Alexander as impediments, in prospect of the great changes that
were imminent. Thus freed from all restraints, from the
Panhellenic idea and from one who was so often an inconvenient mentor, Alexander could turn to the Far East.

CHAPTER VI

THE CONQUEST OF IRAN

THE first object was to secure the person of the runaway monarch. He had a long start on the Royal Road, which led from Ecbatana to Iran by way of Rhagae (not far from Teheran) and the Caspian Gates. The pursuit was one of the greatest efforts and maddest chases that Alexander ever undertook. In forced marches, reckless of the terrible exertions imposed on man and horse, Alexander followed on Darius' heels, and caught up with him finally beyond the Caspian Gates (not far from Hecatompylos) after a wild ride, in which only a small band of cavalry accompanied him. But it was only a corpse that he secured. The satraps of the Iranian provinces, especially Bessus, satrap of Bactria, saw that this broken man had no longer the energy to take up the struggle against Alexander in Eastern Iran. First they put him in chains and took him with them as a prisoner; then when Alexander approached, they gave him his death-blow, and themselves escaped eastwards.

The moment when Alexander stood before the corpse of Darius was one of the great turning-points of his life. Even after Issus he had claimed the Persian empire by right of the sword, and at Arbela he had been acclaimed by the assembled army as King of Asia, but now that the last Achaemenid had passed away, he regarded himself as his heir and lawful successor on the Persian throne. Whether by official proclamation he communicated to his Persian subjects his succession to the throne we do not know. But he exhibited himself as the new king immediately, and ordered the burial of Darius with all royal honours alongside of his ancestors at Persepolis. Just as formerly he had accounted vengeance for the murder of his father Philip as his first duty as ruler, so now he appeared in the rôle of avenger on behalf of the murdered Darius. The rebels who had murdered their royal master, were to be duly punished, while those who had been faithful to him were held in high honour. Nevertheless, it was not merely the necessity of vengeance which took him to the Far East against Bessus and his accomplices; in the proud consciousness of being the lawful successor of the Great King, he considered it his task to take possession in person of the eastern portion of his gigantic empire.

Very different was the impression which the death of Darius made on his Greek and Macedonian entourage and on his army. These hoped and believed that the war was now at an end, and that they might at last return home. Alexander's first duty was to summon an assembly of the army and make clear to them the necessity of a further advance. It was quite easy for his fascinating personality to carry the troops away with him; but the fact that an address to them in solemn assembly was necessary at all, was the first sign that a rift was beginning to open between the king and his Greco-Macedonian followers, which was destined in the ensuing years to become broader and deeper. They were separated not merely by different ideas of the object for which they were fighting, but above all by Alexander's conception that he was the successor of Darius on the Persian throne. To be sure, he was still King of Macedonia and also *Hegemon* of the Corinthian League; his Asiatic monarchy, however, involved consequences that were bound in the end to lead to conflict with the Macedonians, who could not endure to see their king an Asiatic Sultan. Externally the new era revealed itself in the fact that Alexander gradually began, though at first only in the presence of his Oriental subjects, occasionally to wear Persian royal attire and adopt Persian court ceremonial. It is hard to tell how far he was guided in this by love of pomp and display, which is generally put in the foreground or regarded as his only motive. The determining factor anyhow was the new position in which he felt himself towards the Persians and the other peoples of the Asiatic empire. As their lawful king he saw in them no longer his enemies but his subjects. Anyone who fought against him was a rebel against his master. For these subjects, and especially for the Persians, the hitherto dominant nation, their old traditions, monarchic as well as religious, were to be as far as possible preserved; but, in return for that, they were to look up to him, as they had done to the Achaemenids, and show their reverence in the same forms. It was the same statesmanlike idea, which had already induced him, in Egypt and Babylonia, where he had accepted independent thrones, to take over old-established traditions and ceremonies. The hearts of the new subjects were thus to be won for the new government, and they were to become a strong support of the new empire.

This new attitude to the Persians led gradually to their further employment in the imperial service as time went on. He had already begun to put Persians into the civil posts as satraps. But it was a novelty when after a time he began to draft Persians and later Iranians into his army, a measure which was suggested by the obvious fact that he could not execute his gigantic plans with the Macedonians alone, since drafts from home became more difficult, the further he went eastwards. These inevitable military changes led later to serious conflicts with his Macedonians.

It was in July 330 that Darius, at the age of about fifty, met with his tragic end. After recruiting his army and giving it some rest, Alexander had as his first task to occupy Hyrcania, the country south of the Caspian Sea. He crossed the lofty range of Elburz, and moved into the seaboard plain. It took severe fighting to subject the mountain tribes of the Tapurians and Mardians, the latter of whom had never yet been subject to Persian rule. But on the other hand many Persian magnates hurried to pay their homage to the new king. The Greek mercenaries too, about 1500 strong, who had remained faithful to Darius to the last,

asked pardon from Alexander. He at first required uncon-
ditional surrender, because they had transgressed the resolution of the Hellenes, that no Hellene should take the
Persian pay; and when he received their surrender he
made a distinction. Those who had entered the Persian
service before the foundation of the Corinthian League,
were free to go home; but while he pardoned those who had
entered later, he compelled them to continue serving in his
army under the same conditions. This proceeding shows
that while for the East Alexander was Great King, to the
Greek League he was *Hegemon* as before. He behaved also
as *Hegemon* of the League to the Greek ambassadors at the
Persian court, who were then brought before him. He set
free the ambassadors of Sinope, because that city did not
belong to the Corinthian League and therefore had had the
right to send ambassadors to the king. Conversely, he detained the Athenian ambassador, because he was despatched after the founding of the league. He also had the
Spartan envoys imprisoned, but this was because the decision about the vanquished Spartans, which the *Synhedrion* referred to Alexander, had not yet been taken.

If Alexander's stay at the south end of the Caspian Sea
reminds us of his position as *Hegemon*, it also displays his
tendencies to scientific investigation, which we saw before
in Egypt; apparently he was already occupied with the
problem, whether the Caspian was a gulf of the ocean or an
island sea, a problem which he took up later just before his
death. Geographical problems in overwhelming quantity
were forced on Alexander and his suite, when advancing
from Zadracarta, the capital of Hyrcania, he moved into
Eastern Iran. There he came into regions, of which the
Greeks had hitherto had either no information at all or at
least very vague ideas. For Greek geography this Iranian
campaign, like the Indian later, was also a voyage of discovery of the highest moment. The territory which Alexander conquered by several years of fighting, embraces
Bokhara in the north, Western Turkestan up to the Syr-

Darya, and in the south Afghanistan and the northern fringe of Beluchistan. This corresponded in the north to the satrapies of Bactria and Sogdiana, in the south to those of Areia and Drangiana, Arachosia and the Paropami-sadae on the Hindu-Kush. How erroneously these new regions were linked up with the map of the world as previously known is strikingly expressed in these two particulars: the Syr-Darya (by the natives called Jaxartes) was supposed to be the upper course of the Tanais (the Don!), the boundary river between Asia and Europe which flows into the Sea of Azoff; and the Hindu-Kush and its spurs were thought to be a continuation of Caucasus and were styled Caucasus. The Macedonians never heard of the Sea of Aral, into which flow the Oxus and Jaxartes. A consultation of the map will show how completely wrong was the Macedonian idea of the earth's surface. According to Strabo, they identified the Jaxartes with the Tanais, because fir-trees occurred on its further bank, and that tree, they thought, was only to be found in Europe, not in Asia. Perhaps, however, it was Aristotle who led them to this wrong identification; he had associated with the Tanais the Araxes, as he called the great river, that is either the Oxus or Jaxartes, which flows northwards from 'Parnassus' (the Hindu-Kush). At any rate, Alexander and his people, while they were in Eastern Iran, had no conception in what part of the earth they were. Nevertheless, by constant crossing and diagonal marching, which were necessitated by military operations, they acquired a thorough knowledge of the terrain itself with its lofty mountains and rich plains, its salt-deserts and steppes. In the histories of Alexander are very vivid descriptions of landscape; for example, of the sandy steppe between Bactra and the Oxus, or the snowy district between Kandahar and Kabul. The surveyors here were certainly equal to their task, and by their measurings of the road used by the army and their other observations laid a foundation for complete information about these regions.

The fighting in Eastern Iran which now faced Alexander was the most severe that he ever had to engage in. It lasted almost three years, from the autumn of 330 till well into 327, and not until then could he regard the conquest of these countries as secured. This is astonishing, when one considers that his unparalleled career of victory from the Hellespont to Media needed only four years to win the throne of Persia. The difference is due to the different quality and mode of fighting of his antagonists. The Aryan peoples of Eastern Iran, especially the Bactrians and Sogdians, had a very highly developed, proud national feeling, and a tenacious enthusiasm for freedom and independence, such as Alexander had found nowhere in the Persian empire, with the exception of Tyre and a few brave mountain tribes. This national feeling welded them together the more inseparably, because it was inspired by their common Zoroastrian religion. They would hear nothing of submission to this foreign Macedonian, however much he might proclaim that he was marching against Bessus as the avenger and successor of Darius. On the contrary, they saw in Bessus their leader in the national struggle, when he, a kinsman of the Achaemenid house, on his return to Bactria, set the tiara erect upon his head, a right possessed by the king alone, and proclaimed himself as Great King under the name of Artaxerxes. He soon perished, but they then found in the Sogdian Spitamenes an excellent leader. For more than a year he was the mainspring of the national struggle for freedom, and it was only with his death that their capacity for resistance collapsed.

Not only was the quality of the enemy different from before, but their mode of fighting differed. Here in Eastern Iran no great battles were offered to Alexander, such as he had hitherto won—principally by the same method of the 'oblique' battle-formation in which the army he had inherited from Philip was particularly well drilled; it was a genuine people's war which awaited him. The enemy was difficult to get hold of; they never opposed him in large numbers, but as soon as he advanced, they appeared in his rear, if possible in several places simultaneously; they made a fresh rising; they entrenched themselves in inaccessible rocky recesses, or, if in danger, vanished into the Turkoman steppes, only to break out again suddenly and make a surprise attack upon him. How dangerous and exhausting such a guerilla-war may be, is shown by the fighting of Napoleon in Spain, in which he was unable to get the upper hand.

The great importance of Alexander as strategist and tactician, which has, without justification, occasionally been contested of late, meets us more strikingly in this guerilla-warfare in Eastern Iran than in the great pitched battles of the previous years; here he was faced by quite new tasks which presented new difficulties to his generalship. Let us remind those who would like to give Parmenio all the military credit (p. 67), that during this fighting he was at Ecbatana. Unfortunately, reliable information about Alexander's arrangements is so incomplete that no clear idea can be formed of them. If the army led by Alexander to India was completely different, in numbers and in composition, from that of the first four years, the changes must have been partly introduced during the fighting in Eastern Iran. Besides the considerable accession of mercenaries from Greece and Asia Minor, which we have recorded, one may probably infer from his new attitude to the Persians that he drafted into his army a large number of Persian troops. The great losses of these years demanded extensive recruiting, and the peculiar features of a guerilla-war required a special expansion of light troops and cavalry, since the Bactrians and Sogdians were admirable horsemen. The heavy-armed Macedonian phalanx could not be utilised at all as a close formation, but only in divisions, and the same applied to the heavy cavalry, who no longer operated as a separate corps. In crossing the snowy Hindu-Kush Alexander's cavalry lost many horses; these were replaced in 329 by the first-rate Sogdian mounts, which made his cavalry more like that of the enemy. The chief object of the changes thus made was speed and greater mobility. To this end new tactical units were created. In place of the organisation, initiated in 331, of the cavalry regiments into two squadrons apiece (*lochoi*), in 329 he formed hipparchies, which fell into several subdivisions, and embraced riders armed differently, and soon of different nationality. New classes of men-at-arms, borrowed from the Persians, were introduced, such as the mounted javelin-men (*Hippakontistai*), who appear in his army soon after Darius' death, and the mounted archers (*Hippotoxotai*). These are but trifles; yet they give us a glimpse of the gradual transformation of the army.

One consequence of the scattered mode of fighting practised by the enemy was that Alexander was driven to new tactics. He had often to cause his army to advance in separate columns; different fighting units were grouped under one commander, and the columns thus made capable of independent action at a moment's notice; in case of need, however, the columns could by a clever manoeuvre be reunited again. As new as the mode of fighting were the measures Alexander took to secure the conquered districts in Eastern Iran. On the basis of doubtful statements it was earlier assumed that he had already founded new cities in Hither Asia, but recent investigation has made it probable that his city foundations in Eastern Iran were his first foundations on Asiatic soil (p. 117). At any rate, they are the first authentically attested foundations of Alexander in Asia, and are not to be confused with previous re-settlements of old towns, such as Tyre and Gaza. They were preceded only by one new foundation on African soil, in Egypt. While we excluded a military motive for that, in the case of Eastern Iran it is obvious that the necessity of securing in a military sense this hard-won territory was the occasion and leading motive of the innovation. Of the importance of these foundations in promoting trade and culture we shall have to treat later.

After this general estimate of the campaign in Eastern Iran, it is necessary to give a sketch, at any rate in broad outline, of the course of the military operations. In the summer of 330 Alexander moved eastwards from Hyrcania through Parthia, and had reached the northern extremity of Areia, when he received the news that Bessus, as has been mentioned, had been recognised in Bactria as King of Asia under the name of Artaxerxes. Satibarzanes, satrap of Areia, had just done him homage, and Alexander was about to hurry by the nearest and direct route to Bactra (Balkh), but he was obliged instead to push southwards into Areia, as Satibarzanes on hearing the news had taken the field for Bessus and had raised an insurrection there. Again Alexander gained his object by the amazing rapidity of his operations. By forced marches with part of his army he reached Artacoana, the capital of Areia, in two days. Satibarzanes escaped and the insurrection collapsed. To secure the unruly country—whether then or later is uncertain—Alexander determined to found a Greek city there, 'Alexandria in Areia' (Herāt). Instead of returning northwards to the road that led directly to Bactria, he next went further south, without meeting with any substantial resistance, into Drangiana, then eastwards to Arachosia, and finally to Paropamisadae at the southern end of the Hindu-Kush; his march seems to have followed the line of the Persian Royal Road. This great detour southwards to the Hilmend gave Alexander no time this winter (330–29) for prolonged winter-quarters. His strategic plan no doubt was, after the unpleasant experiences he had had in Areia, to occupy the regions south of the Hindu-Kush, and so prevent their defection to Bessus in his rear. He secured these regions too by founding several cities, as 'Alexandria in Arachosia' (Kandahar) and 'Alexandria at the Caucasus'. Here a breathing-space was granted to the troops, though a column had to be detailed to crush yet another rising in Areia.

In the spring of 329 after a short rest he led his army

with great labour over the snowy Hindu-Kush, and, in spite of the devastation of the territory at its northern end, by which Bessus sought to detain him, made a victorious entry into Bactria. Before his impetuous onset Bessus escaped over the Oxus (Amu-Darya), burnt his boats, and retired to Nautaca in Sogdiana. Meanwhile Alexander occupied Bactria, including the capital Bactra, and advanced to the Oxus, which he crossed near Kilif. On account of the lack of wood it was impossible to build bridges, and it took him five days to get his army across. They swam across, supported by inflated leather skins sewn together out of tent coverings, and holding their swimming horses by the bridles. This was, in antiquity, as it is to-day, a well-known method of crossing a river in the East, and Alexander had already employed it on the Danube. Bessus had lost prestige by retiring without fighting, and soon fell into Alexander's hands. Gradually deserted and betrayed by his troops, and abandoned by his followers, among them Spitamenes the Sogdian, he was easily caught by Ptolemy —later King of Egypt—who was detached with a flying column for this raid. Alexander, who met him as the Great King exacting punishment for high treason, had him later condemned to death at Bactra. In the Persian fashion, in which Darius I had formerly punished his rivals, his nose and ears were cut off, and he was then sent to Ecbatana, where he was cruelly executed by his equals, by crucifixion or dismemberment.[1] In Spitamenes, however, who now took Bessus' place as leader of the national resistance, Alexander found a much more dangerous antagonist.

Alexander now penetrated by way of Maracanda (Samarkand) to the Jaxartes (Syr-Darya), and thus reached the extreme north-east limit of the Persian empire. Beyond the river, which the Macedonians, as we saw, identified with the Tanais, in the broad steppes lived the nomad Dahae,

[1] In the Behistun inscription Darius mentions these mutilations. Arrian iv. 7. 3 shows Bessus was condemned to death by a Persian tribunal.

Sacae and Massagetae, who had always been a danger to the empire on this side. As a bulwark against them, Alexander founded on this side of the Jaxartes a Greek city, 'Alexandria Eschate' (Khojend), which was to keep watch on the frontier river. By reason of the endless steppes on the other side, Alexander had no more idea of moving the frontier further north than he had before at the Danube: he had here reached the limit of the 'inhabited world' (*oikoumene*), which is bounded not merely by the ocean but also by deserts. Nevertheless, as at the Danube, he now made a single victorious advance over the Jaxartes, to inspire these barbarians with respect for his arms.

While Alexander was occupied with preparations for the founding of the city, Spitamenes had roused to revolt a number of localities in his rear. A severe punishment was meted out to these, when the insurrection had been crushed with much bloodshed; the townships were destroyed and the inhabitants executed, for Alexander regarded them as rebels against their master. Soon afterwards the indefatigable Spitamenes succeeded in fomenting a rising on a greater scale in Sogdiana, a rising which was all the more dangerous because he was supported by the northern nomads. When he began to besiege the Macedonian garrison of Maracanda, Alexander sent an expedition against him, but remained behind to supervise the foundation of his city. Maracanda was relieved, but after retiring into the northern steppe and obtaining 600 cavalry from the allied nomads, Spitamenes completely defeated and destroyed the expeditionary corps on the Polytimetus, and was able to besiege Maracanda again. Thereupon Alexander left the Jaxartes and in person hurried by forced marches to Maracanda with a contingent of light troops. He covered the 180 miles from Khojend to Samarkand in three days and a few hours! At the news of Alexander's approach, Spitamenes escaped into the steppe. Alexander followed him to the Polytimetus, subdued the northern frontier, and severely punished the rebels; he then led his army back southwards into Bactria, and made his winter-camp (329–28) in the capital Bactra.

The following year too (328) was occupied by vigorous fighting against insurrections in Bactria and Sogdiana. Part of the army, commanded by Craterus, stayed behind in Bactria; the other part, with which Alexander moved again into Sogdiana, had to be divided into five columns, to catch the widely dispersed rebels, most of whom had taken refuge in fortresses. After their resistance was broken, the columns united again at Maracanda. While Alexander was still coercing the remnant of the rebels, he caused Hephaestion to plan out several cities in Sogdiana. In the same year, Pharasmanes, King of the Chorasmians living in the far north, did homage to Alexander, who concluded alliance and friendship with him. In the meantime Spitamenes, supported by his friends the Massagetae, had made an inroad into Bactria, and driven off rich booty from the neighbourhood of Bactra. The garrison of the city set out in pursuit after him, but was enticed by Spitamenes into an ambush, and defeated with severe loss. Craterus then hurried up, and inflicted a severe defeat on him before he could reach the desert. But he made good his escape into the desert again, and before long led a fresh raid into Sogdiana, this time accompanied by 3000 Massagetae. Meanwhile, Alexander had gone into winter-quarters (328–27) at Nautaca, and had handed over to Coenus the command in Sogdiana. At his hands Spitamenes suffered a severe defeat, but what sealed his fate was the action of the Massagetae. On the rumour that Alexander himself intended to invade the desert, they betrayed their ally; they cut off his head and sent it to Alexander.

With this tragic end of the great hero of Iranian independence resistance was practically over. Only a last fragment of brave rebels held out in some inaccessible rocky citadels in the south-eastern mountains of Sogdiana. In the spring of 327 Alexander marched from Nautaca against the fortress of Ariamazes on the 'Sogdian Rock', which seemed so proof against attack that many of the rebels had deposited their wives and children there, among them the Bactrian prince Oxyartes, once a companion of Bessus. When Alexander summoned them to surrender, they called down to him from above in mockery that he should get 'flyers' for soldiers: for no others could get up to them. Alexander thereupon offered high rewards for the scaling of the highest peak, which overhung the fortress. As it happened, there were 300 bold mountaineers among his Macedonians, who undertook the dangerous feat by night. Thirty fell on the ascent, but the rest got up successfully, by the help of ropes and iron tent-pegs, which they drove into the ice or hard frozen rock. When in the early morning the besieged saw to their astonishment these Macedonians high above them, they capitulated and surrendered the fortress to Alexander. The fairest prize that fell to him was Roxane, the daughter of Oxyartes, in the first bloom of youth, and in the judgment of Alexander's companions, next to Statcira the wife of Darius, the most beautiful woman that they had seen in Asia. Alexander fell passionately in love with her and determined to raise her to the position of his consort.

From here he marched eastwards into the district of Paraetacene against the citadel of Chorienes, which, placed high on a steep rock and surrounded by deep ravines, was regarded as impregnable. Alexander however set himself undauntedly to the task, in the conviction that nothing was impossible to him and his army. Out of the big pines, which grew on the mountains, he constructed ladders to descend into the ravine, and then by clever engineering succeeded in erecting from below a causeway over the ravine.[1] As soon as Alexander, with his Macedonians protected by pent-houses from the enemy's artillery, opened a bombardment from the causeway upon the citadel, Chorienes too surrendered. He was pardoned and left in possession of his principality. Alexander then returned to

[1] [See Arrian, *Anabasis*, tr. Robson (Loeb 1929), Appendix, p. 449.]

Bactra. The difficult task of the conquest of Eastern Iran
was at an end. The persistence and tenacity of Alexander,
which we admired at the siege of Tyre, comes out even
more strongly in Eastern Iran. He did not leave the
country, till he had so completely subdued it that he
could now safely enlist in his army Bactrians and Sogdians,
whose excellent military qualities he had experienced to
his cost. This victorious struggle also made such an impression on the peoples of the northern steppes that in
future we find Dahae and Sacae in his army too.

Before his return to Bactra Alexander celebrated his
marriage with Roxane up in the castle of Chorienes. As
we have so very little reliable information upon the sexual
side of the king's nature, it is interesting to learn from our
best authority, Arrian, that it was love of this fair Bactrian woman which moved him not to treat her as a
captive of war, but to make her his lawful wife. In a
famous painting the contemporary artist Aëtion represented the marriage of Roxane as a love scene with many
Cupids, and we can still get an idea of the famous picture,
for it went to Italy, where Lucian saw and described it,
and it was from this description that Sodoma made his
charming fresco in the Villa Farnesina. The glimpse into
Alexander's inner life, which the testimony of Arrian
gives us, is all the more valuable, as it is obvious that this
marriage had and was meant to have great political importance. The wedding of Alexander to a daughter of
Bactria was a gesture of reconciliation with his previous
enemies; of a convincing force, which even the keenest
nationalists among the Iranians could not fail to acknowledge. It was also bound to flatter their national pride, that *
the marriage was performed according to the Iranian
ritual. Alexander and Roxane ate of one loaf, which he
severed in two with his sword—a custom which prevails to
this very day among the natives of Turkestan, with the
exception of the sword, which was probably Alexander's
spontaneous addition and is just like him. But this mar-

riage with Roxane meant far more than merely reconciliation with the Eastern Iranians. It also indicates that
Alexander's idea of the equality of the Persians and other
Iranians with the Macedonians, which had first imposed
itself on him as a military necessity, had in these last years
of war developed into the thought of a fusion of these two
peoples, a thought which in the following years influenced
ever more strongly the secret policy which he adopted for
his empire.

It is only too conceivable that the Macedonians with
steadily growing surprise and dislike resisted the change in
their king, which became more prominent after the death
of Darius, for from that time he regarded himself as the
latter's lawful successor. Had they incurred these unspeakable toils and battles, merely in the end to look on and see
how the despised Orientals were made their equals? Consequently there soon arose a secret discontent, which on
occasion led to violent collisions between the king and his
entourage.

In the lack of authentic information it is not quite certain whether the first of the three catastrophes which happened during these years of war in Eastern Iran is attribut-
able to the relations just described, or merely to personal
motives; but the former has all the probabilities on its side.
It is only certain that in the autumn of 330, while Alexander was still in the capital of Drangiana, there was for
the first time a conspiracy against his life. Of its deeper
reasons and extent we hear nothing. The whole interest of
the writers who allude to it was absorbed in the fact that
Philotas, the eldest son of Parmenio and the most brilliant
officer in the army, whom Alexander had made commander of his *Hetairoi*, was implicated in the trial. Being
accused of having taken part in the conspiracy, he was
brought before the assembly of the Macedonian army,
which was alone competent to judge Macedonians in cases
of high treason. When Alexander in person had conducted
the prosecution in vehement language, and Philotas had

defended himself, the military court condemned Philotas to death, and the execution was immediately carried out in Macedonian fashion, by shooting with javelins. We learn nothing further of the reasons that led to the sentence than that Philotas, though communications had been made to him about the conspiracy, had, in spite of his daily close intercourse with Alexander, given him no warning. The motives of his behaviour are not known. If this extraordinarily proud and ambitious officer expressed himself sharply in criticism of Alexander then and, as it is said, sometimes even in Egypt, that is not enough to prove his participation in the conspiracy, though it might as an indication influence the judgment of the court. Whether the sentence was just or not, we cannot tell. We must content ourselves with the fact that the military court, which functioned in the regular way, was convinced of his guilt, while Amyntas, son of Andromenes, and his brothers, who because of their friendly relations with Philotas were accused before the same court, were able to prove their innocence and were acquitted. If the condemnation of Philotas was a judicial murder, it is not the fault of Alexander but of the assembly of the Macedonian army.

On the other hand Alexander has the sole responsibility for the sequel in the cruel execution of Parmenio, the father of Philotas. Later sources which state that he too was condemned by the military court, falsify history for the benefit of Alexander; and though the conjecture has recently been made that Alexander's action was covered by the special full powers given him by the army to restore his position of security, it lacks all foundation. It is rather the case that Alexander on his own responsibility, immediately after the condemnation of Philotas, sent orders to Parmenio's subordinates in Media to put him to death, and these orders were immediately carried out. It is the darkest spot in Alexander's life. Here more than ever, we lament the unsatisfactoriness of our authorities, which give us nothing authentic but simply conjectures as to the motives of the act, and yet it would be very important for the judgment of Alexander's character to have clear information on the point. He was firmly convinced of the guilt of Philotas: had he any occasion to assume that the father also was a participator in the conspiracy? This is as a matter of fact scarcely credible, when one considers with what loyalty Parmenio served him as the first in his army—just as he had served his father Philip—in spite of the differences of opinion which occurred between them from time to time. Moreover, if Alexander had believed in his guilt, he might have arrested him and had him tried by the army like his son. It is more credible that he was afraid that Parmenio on the news of his son's execution, which he would naturally regard as unjust, might use the great position, which he had entrusted to him in Ecbatana a few months before, to take vengeance, relying on his troops and the imperial treasury, by rising in rebellion and attempting to raise against him the western part of Hither Asia. Was it not in fact a dangerous situation, that the father of the executed man controlled the communications in Alexander's rear? Does not this explain the immense haste with which Alexander sent his messengers, with the secret order of execution, on hunting dromedaries to Ecbatana, in order to anticipate the news of the condemnation of Philotas? There was indeed no other way but death to prevent this news reaching Parmenio. So it was probably, as Arrian also indicates, such reasons of state policy which compelled Alexander, as he might rightly or wrongly believe, in the interest of self-preservation and the security of his realm, to put Parmenio to death.

Alexander was not deterred from this act by the consequence, which it was easy to foresee, that it would evoke horror and disgust in the whole Greek world, and especially in his army, where Parmenio had been greatly respected, more particularly among the old Macedonians of the school of Philip. On the contrary he took severe measures, when after the deed was done the displeasure of his

Macedonians voiced itself. He picked out the persons in question and formed them into a special company, separated as a punishment from the rest of the army; but this arrangement does not seem to have lasted long. Irritated by the discovery of the conspiracy and by his observation of the signs of discontent in his Macedonian companions, he showed in other ways too that he did not mean to brook opposition. In connexion with the conspiracy case, Alexander the Lyncestian, who had done him homage at his accession but had been for the last three years a prisoner under suspicion of high treason, was brought before the military court and by it condemned and executed.

Two years passed, during which Alexander modelled his life more and more after the fashion of a Great King. About the autumn of 328 he was in Maracanda after that year's victorious fighting in Sogdiana, and there was again an alarming fracas. Later accounts have coloured the facts to suit theories, so that they are difficult to establish in detail. Probably the most trustworthy account is that of Plutarch, which seems to go back to some good and ancient authority in which the facts were plainly stated. According to this account, Alexander, one evening after receiving some fruit from the coast, invited his friends to a symposium. Feeling was already high owing to the heady wine of Turkestan, when, immediately after the singing of a topical song in derision of some Macedonian officers recently defeated, there arose a discussion on Macedonian bravery between Alexander and his friend Cleitus, who had formerly saved his life at the Granicus. In the course of it, Cleitus, annoyed by a personal observation of Alexander's, made a contemptuous allusion to him as son of Ammon, and under the influence of the sweet wine gave sudden vent to his long-restrained indignation, and fiercely cast in the king's teeth all that had been weighing on the hearts of his noble companions and himself, the preference shown to the Persians and the adoption of Persian dress. When he finally called out to him that he had better invite barbarians and slaves,

Alexander, who also was far gone in liquor, was seized with fury: he threw an apple at Cleitus' head and put out his hand for his dagger. But the body-guard had carefully placed it out of the way. It appears that Alexander misunderstood this and suspected treason. He shouted in Macedonian for his hypaspists, and ordered the trumpeter to sound the alarm; and when the man had the courage and prudence to disobey, hit him in the face with his fist. To his anger with Cleitus was added rage and excitement at the supposed plot. At this moment Cleitus, whom his friends had succeeded in pushing out of the room, rushed back again by another door, to hurl another insult in the king's face. Alexander lost all self-control; he seized a pike from a bodyguard, and ran his friend through. Scarcely was the terrible deed done, when he collapsed, and spent three days in the deepest remorse without food or drink.

Who, in the face of this sudden eruption of human passion like to that of natural forces, can judge, which side is the more to blame? The two friends who contended with each other, were really not the two men—rather they were two different views of the world, which exploded with elemental violence. The horrible scene illuminates for us as with a lightning-flash the state of feeling which had been silently produced among the Macedonian followers of Alexander by the change in his conception of his royal position. By the unrestrained recriminations of Cleitus Alexander too must have been for the first time enlightened on the psychological effects of his policy upon the Macedonians. But this did not result in his altering his views. He never thought of concession or even of compromise. His aims and the means and ways which led to them were for him fixed and immoveable. He must now have seen more clearly than ever, that he could not climb the steep road to world sovereignty without conflicts with his Macedonians, and all the more he must have felt it essential to rely on the Persians and the other Iranians. In spite of Alexander's passionate remorse, which had no reference to the underlying causes of the collision, the catastrophe of Cleitus had rather the opposite effect: Alexander adhered the more stubbornly to a policy of which the Macedonians disapproved, and immersed himself still deeper in the ideas of an assimilation between victors and vanquished. The idea of a fusion of the nations, which had perhaps suggested itself to him before, developed in his mind, and a few months afterwards, in the spring of 327, found for the first time its visible expression in his marriage with Roxane.

As a corollary of this, immediately after his return to Bactra he attempted to introduce the Persian *proskynesis* among his Macedonians and Greeks. Since primeval times it had been an Oriental practice for the subjects of a king to greet him by throwing themselves on the ground. It probably did not imply a recognition of the king as god; it was merely a sign of the most complete subjection to an absolute ruler. This custom of *proskynesis* as the Greeks called it, which was introduced by Cyrus, the founder of the empire, and applied to the Persians as well as to his other subjects, was always regarded by the Greeks, as soon as they came in contact with it, as something particularly contemptible and quite specially Oriental. The free Greek could abase himself before his god, but never before a man, and thus the observation of the custom may have contributed to the error, which appears as early as Aeschylus, that the Persians worshipped their kings as gods in their lifetime. Alexander certainly knew from his Persian courtiers that the Persians regarded the *proskynesis* simply as an expression of the deepest reverence for their lord. But as he was naturally familiar with the Greek conception, it was a dangerous undertaking to promote the levelling of his subjects by an attempt to establish among Macedonians and Greeks a custom which the Persians followed in his case as a matter of course.

We must decidedly reject the view that he meant indirectly to force his recognition as a god, for later on he required the obeisance only of the Greeks and not of the

Macedonians. His purpose rather was to express the equal position of the Persians with the Macedonians and Greeks by means of this common court ceremonial. It was a step which went far beyond anything he had previously done in this direction. Perhaps he would not have undertaken it, had there not been at his court in his immediate circle individuals who were ready in this matter to go with him through thick and thin. In particular his closest friend, Hephaestion, seems to have been the stage-manager. How conscious they were of the danger of the experiment is shown by the caution with which it was presented. It was agreed that at a symposium the king should drink out of a cup to the friends who were in the plot one after the other, and that each should drain the cup, fall down before him, and then exchange with him the kiss of friendship, also a Persian custom. At first all went according to plan. But when it came to Callisthenes' turn, he, surprised by the suggestion of making the *proskynesis*, omitted it. Alexander had turned to Hephastion: when his attention was drawn to the omission, he refused to kiss Callisthenes, who thereupon defiantly called out to him: 'Well, I go away the poorer by a kiss.' The evening thus ended with an unpleasant incident. But what finally induced Alexander to give up his design was not so much the refusal of Callisthenes as the realisation that on this point his old Macedonians would stubbornly resist him. We do not hear that in later years he again required the *proskynesis* from them. It is to the king's credit that he saw he had been too hasty in his attempt, and did not hesitate to give way. The West was to be spared this Eastern ceremony for many years. It was not till Diocletian that it was introduced along with other Oriental court customs.   *

It was the more surprising that Callisthenes opposed the king in this matter, as in his book he was unbounded in his glorification of him, and had even most vigorously supported his divine sonship. Nor had the change of his Panhellenic hero into a Great King apparently disturbed his

personal relations with Alexander; after the murder of
Cleitus he was one of those who sought to comfort the dis-
tracted monarch. His resistance to the *proskynesis* did not
so much imply a protest against the deification of Alexander, such as is formulated in the language ascribed to
him, but is probably to be explained on the ground that he
saw in it a barbaric and ridiculous mode of reverence, by
which the free Greek was depressed to the level of the
barbarians he despised. His tie with Alexander was ir-
remediably broken, and the king hated him, since now he
was regarded as head of the opposition.

Soon afterwards a new conspiracy was detected, among
the royal pages. This time the reason was not political but
purely personal, the wounded honour of young Hermolaus,
whom Alexander had caused to be chastised in front of
the other pages, because he had shot a wild boar before
him at a hunting party. Though the conspiracy was in
itself more harmless than the first, it was yet more dangerous; for these pages waited on the king's person and intended to kill him at night when sleeping. If on the night
agreed upon Alexander had not stayed till morning in a
symposium,—as was said, by the warning of a Syrian pro-
phetess—he would have been lost. The conspiracy was
discovered the next day: the pages, as sons of Macedonian
nobles, were brought before the military court, and on their
confession condemned to death and executed by stoning.

Callisthenes had been tutor to many of them and in
close relations with them; in Alexander's mood towards
him, the suspicion was natural that he had known of the
conspiracy or even instigated it. Alexander had him
arrested and an enquiry instituted. As Callisthenes was a
Greek, there was no question of trying him by the Macedonian army. Alexander's first thought was to send him
before the court of the *Synhedrion* at Corinth. This information is valuable, because it again shows that Alexander
still looked on himself as being for the Greeks *Hegemon* of
the Hellenic League. But subsequently he abandoned the

idea, and after taking Callisthenes with him for months as a prisoner, he had him condemned and executed by a private court in India. It is beyond doubt that Alexander believed in his guilt, for Ptolemy and Aristobulus both maintain that he was the instigator of the plot. Yet his guilt was not judicially proved and is difficult to accept. In the Greek world, which regarded his execution as a judicial murder, Alexander was sorely compromised by his condemnation. The excitement in the Peripatetic School, which counted Callisthenes as one of its adherents, was particularly acute. Theophrastus gave vent to his grief for the tragic end of his friend in a treatise, *Callisthenes*, or *On Mourning*, in which he stated that Alexander did not understand how to make a right use of his good fortune. The Peripatetics thus initiated the unfavourable estimate of Alexander as a tyrant intoxicated by his power and dazzled by his luck, an estimate which was developed ever more incisively in succeeding histories. On the other hand the relation between Alexander and Aristotle, who as uncle and teacher of Callisthenes must have been very closely affected, was in spite of this incident, only temporarily, if at all, disturbed. They continued to correspond and exchange ideas.

A consecutive treatment of the catastrophes that took place in Eastern Iran, from the trial of Philotas to the trial of Callisthenes, such as has been given to bring out the principles that connect them, might easily display too gloomy a picture of the relation of Alexander to his army. If one envisages the military events of 330 to 327, which ended in the extremely difficult suppression of the national resistance of Eastern Iran, one sees that in the teeth of everything Alexander succeeded in keeping a tight hand on his army, officers and men alike. On the march and in battle he was just the same as ever, he was the king of the Macedonian nation, who shared with them the unspeakable fatigues, and the hunger and thirst of this guerilla warfare. Moreover we have anecdotes from these years, which perhaps cannot be taken as historical but which obviously illustrate correct impressions, and they show us with what humanity Alexander cared for his people amid personal sacrifices and privations. That was why they followed him with enthusiasm.

CHAPTER VII

THE INDIAN CAMPAIGN

SCARCELY had Alexander completed the conquest of Eastern Iran, before he began a vast new undertaking, a march to India. It had given him much thought during the Iranian campaign. When in the winter of 330–29 he was in Arachosia south of the Hindu-Kush, he had come into contact with the so-called Mountain Indians who bordered on this province. It is related that in 328 in his negotiations with Pharasmanes, prince of the Chorasmians, who challenged him to fight the peoples of the northern steppes, Alexander refused the contest on the ground that he was contemplating India as his next goal. Actually he had had dealings with the prince of Taxila (Punjab) in 329–8 when in Sogdiana. The addition of strong reinforcements from the West, and the extraordinary increase in the size of his army point to these new military projects. We may perhaps connect with the special nature of his Indian schemes the fact that in 329–8 he fetched to the camp Nearchus, the friend of his youth, who afterwards played so prominent a part in the maritime enterprises in India.

How are we to place this resolve to go to India in perspective with Alexander's life-work as a whole? Those scholars, who hold the view that he never aimed at world empire at all, see in this resolve nothing but the intention of personally taking possession of the Persian empire in its fullest extent, or of restoring the frontiers of the empire, as they had been under Darius I. But Alexander's proceedings in India are not thereby explained; for he went far beyond these frontiers. Darius I had conquered the north-west corner only up to the Indus, and had himself been unable

to maintain his sovereignty later. In the battle of Gaugamela Indians were fighting on the Persian side, but they
were merely the frontier tribes of the Mountain Indians,
who belonged to the satrapy of Arachosia, and the Indians
who bordered on Bactria. The fundamental idea which
impelled Alexander to India was not the winning or restoration of the Achaemenid power. It went much further: by
marching to India he intended to reach the Eastern end of
the world. If we are to understand this, we must make
clear to ourselves the geographical beliefs in which he had
been brought up. To the Greeks India was the easternmost
country of the inhabited world, to Hecataeus as well as to
Herodotus and Ctesias, none of whom had seen India: its
east coast was washed by the waves of Ocean that engirdled
the earth. How narrow their conception of the size of India
was, is revealed by the dictum of Aristotle, that when
one crosses Parnassus (*i.e.* Hindu-Kush), the outer sea (the
Ocean) appears in view.[1] Alexander had grown up in the
belief that India was the eastern edge of the world. This
comes out in his answer to Pharasmanes, when he said he
wanted to subject the Indians, 'because he would then have
Asia entirely in his hands'. It also plainly expresses his
motive: he wanted not merely, like the Achaemenids, to
bear the title of a world sovereign, but to become in reality
a world sovereign who extended his empire to the limits
fixed by nature to the inhabited world. This idea of world
sovereignty, which had been in vague outline in his mind
for years, he would now begin to realise, by penetrating
beyond the former eastern frontier of the Persian empire. *

But he was not impelled purely by the desire of conquest.
If anywhere, here again his inclination to research and
science combined with the will to power; he wanted at the
same time to clear up the geographical position and extent

---

[1] Aristotle, *Meteor.* i. 13, 15, p. 350 a 21 f. Wilhelm Reese, *Die
griechischen Nachrichten über Indien bis zum Feldzuge Alexanders*, 1914.
H. Endres, *Geographischer Horizont und Politik bei Alexander in den
Jahren* 330-323, 1924.

of India. No doubt in the previous negotiations with Taxiles, conducted in Eastern Iran, he received information about India which did not fit in with his previous views and opened out problems for him. But even the fantastic statements about India as the land of wonder and romance which were circulated among the Greeks—deriving from Hecataeus and Herodotus and especially from the fabulous accounts of Ctesias—must have tempted him to examine them in the light of actuality. The staff of scholars who accompanied him worked in no country so zealously and successfully as in India. His Indian campaign was in fact a voyage of discovery as well, which brought the richest gain to Greek science, pre-eminently to geography, botany and zoology.

It was a memorable moment in the history of the world, when Alexander invaded India with his army. For the first time Greek and Indian came into contact. India was a separate world. It was connected with western Asia in the north-west alone, by the Kabul valley, the road which had seen the invasion of the forefathers of the Aryan Hindus, and along which Alexander now arrived. By the same road vague information about India had from time to time reached Persia and finally the Greeks. Through this gate also went Indian wares by caravan routes to the Caspian, to be transported further to the Black Sea. Occasionally to the Persian court too had come rare products of the country, and examples of its strange fauna, like the parrots, of which Ctesias, who had seen them there, relates so charmingly that they spoke Indian but could also learn Greek. Through that gate there were already trade relations with the Far East; for Nearchus recounted that he saw in India Serian, that is Chinese, silk. But these scanty connexions with the outer world did not alter the complete intellectual isolation of India.

As Alexander did not get beyond the Punjab (the land of the five rivers) and the valley of the Indus, and so never trod the sacred soil of India proper, the Ganges valley, he did not come into contact with the doctrine of Buddha, which was proclaimed on the Ganges almost two hundred years earlier, for at this time it had not yet reached the Punjab. He encountered the intellectual and religious life of the Indians only in the Brahmins, and those monkish hermits and penitents, called by the Greeks 'Gymnoso-phists'.[1] The former met him, especially in the south, with the hostility of religious fanaticism, but he attempted friendly intercourse with the latter. One can scarcely imagine greater contrasts than the unparalleled energy of Alexander, the representative of the active life, and these meditative and enquiring Indians, representatives of the contemplative life in its extreme form. In them two com-pletely different worlds were to touch. From the beginning it was therefore questionable whether Alexander would succeed in paving the way for a spread of Greek culture in India by the foundation of Greek cities. A profound con-noisseur of the Indian character has said,[2] 'Alexander came too late for India: when he appeared, the Indian nation in its introspectiveness had long become a peculiar people, dominated by forms of life and customs of thought, which were incommensurable with the standards of the out-side world'. Yet without Alexander Indian and Greek art would not have been fused later, as we shall see, into a composite art, the reflections of which we can follow to-day through Central Asia to China and Japan.

The summer of 327 had begun when Alexander started from Bactra. The young queen Roxane accompanied him to India, and next year bore him a son there, who however soon died. To secure the important satrapy of Bactria, he appointed not a Persian, but Amyntas a Macedonian, with whom he left behind no less than 10,000 infantry and 3500 cavalry. His own field army was considerably larger than that with which he had crossed the Hellespont seven years before, and was totally different in personnel and organisa-

[1] *Berl. Akad. Abh.* 1923, xxxiii. p. 160.
[2] H. Oldenburg, *Buddha,* 1903, p. 2.

tion: it included many thousands of Persians, Bactrians, Sogdians, not to speak of Dahae and Sacae, along with the Macedonians and Greek mercenaries. It was a strange medley of nations, and it was also accompanied by women and children and a big baggage-train. We have no reliable figures. In the autumn of 326 the army, including the Indian troops added in the interval, is said to have totalled 120,000.

All Alexander's campaigns were preceded by most careful diplomatic preparations; this one was no exception. He knew by the enquiries he had instituted, that in India he would not meet the united resistance of a great kingdom, but that there were several large or small principalities side by side, which were generally at feud with one another. This favourable situation he had exploited by making previous agreements with some of these rajahs, Taxiles and a certain Sisicottus.

From Bactra he led his army back over the Hindu-Kush, this time by a shorter road over a more westerly pass, to Alexandria in Paropamisadae. In the autumn of 327 he started to make his way to the Indus by the Kabul valley, which connects India with the West. The subjugation of the mountainous district north of Kabul (Kophēn) in the Indian 'North-West Frontier Province' of to-day required severe fighting, as its brave and warlike tribes were very populous, and the mountainous country presented many difficulties to an advance. After officially opening the war by a sacrifice to Athena at Nicaea—the site is not exactly known—he divided his army into two columns, sending Hephaestion and Perdiccas with the lesser half along the Kabul with orders to build a bridge over the Indus, while he with the main army undertook the conquest of the mountainous region. The very first fighting with the Aspasians showed that he had to do with strong antagonists. In one battle Alexander himself as well as Ptolemy son of Lagus and Leonnatus were wounded. On another occasion there was a duel between Ptolemy and an Indian prince: Ptolemy laid him low and took off his armour, whereupon there was vigorous fighting over the corpse. One fancies oneself back in the Homeric age. After the crossing of the Swat, fighting began with the powerful tribe of the Assacenes, who were all the more formidable through being allied with Abisares, the prince of Kashmir. Their chief fortress Massaga was only won after hard fighting.[1]

After further losses the enemy forsook their towns, and fled eastwards to the fortress of Aornos situate on a ridge overlooking the right bank of the Indus. This Aornos, the position of which was long disputed, has been successfully identified by Sir Aurel Stein with the huge massif of Pir-sar (about 5000 ft. high) situated in a bend of the Indus.[2] It was a correct strategic idea of Alexander not to pursue the fleeing enemy immediately over the impassable mountains, but rather to march south to the Kabul, and thus make a safe journey up the Indus. So he went down into the valley of Peshawar (Peukelaotis), and then proceeded from the south up the right bank of the river against Aornos. Only now that we have identified Aornos with Pir-sar, do we clearly understand the detailed account of this fighting by Arrian; and only now do we see what huge difficulties Alexander and his army had to overcome. We admire again the tenacity with which he stuck to his object, though several times driven back. It was obvious to him that he could not enter the Punjab, until he had broken the concentrated resistance of the Assacenes at Aornos. So he constantly invented new methods of attack, till finally he began by a dam to bridge over a ravine, which separated his position from the isolated rock. As soon as this was so far advanced that his siege-engines could get the range of the enemy, their resistance broke, and Alexander was enabled

---

[1] [According to Diodorus (xvii. 84) Alexander was guilty of gross treachery on this occasion. Arrian says nothing of the kind, and this no doubt is an invention of the hostile tradition, like the treatment of the Branchidae (*Classical Review*, 1922, p. 63, W. W. Tarn).]

[2] Sir Aurel Stein, *On Alexander's Track to the Indus*, 1929.

to rush the plateau. He himself was the first to reach the top. With the conquest of Aornos, which is one of Alexander's most brilliant feats of strategy and tactics, the campaign was over, and the door to the Punjab lay open. The whole region was put under a satrap, Nicanor; and the Indian Sisicottus, who had previously joined Alexander, was placed in command of the fort erected by Alexander on the summit of Aornos, which had previously had no artificial fortifications.

*

As the universal flight of the population to Aornos shows that they regarded this natural fortress as impregnable, the Macedonians must have been proud in the consciousness of having performed a superhuman feat in the storming of it. One can understand how they began both in Alexander's retinue and in the camp to relate how Heracles, the divine ancestor of their royal family, had once tried to conquer Aornos, but had failed. The thought of Heracles had previously occupied the Macedonians when they were crossing the Hindu-Kush; as they identified it with Caucasus, they supposed they had found the spot where Heracles had formerly delivered Prometheus. On the march to the oasis of Siwah, Alexander had himself told his troops that Heracles and Perseus had been there before him, and had in this way set the example for such mythical parallels. Here in the East the development of the myth of Heracles seems rather to have proceeded from the army; but it was certainly very welcome to the king and was no doubt promoted by him. Cleitarchus afterwards invented the theory that Alexander wanted to storm Aornos, in order to outdo Heracles. We have, however, already observed that the conquest of Aornos was a strategic necessity. In this case too, as in his narratives of Gordium and the oracle of Ammon, Cleitarchus made a motive of the final result. *

The Heracles legend is not the only one that was amplified by this campaign; the same is true of the Dionysus legend also. When the Macedonians found on a mountain in the highlands vines and ivy, which they had not seen since leaving Macedonia, they rejoiced to think they were on the tracks of the god. So the city in the valley they called Nysa, and thus the story was evolved that Dionysus, whose great conquests in Asia—though not yet in India—were already known to men, had come here and founded the city of Nysa. This simple and psychologically quite intelligible occurrence was fantastically embroidered by later writers. It provided the basis of the legend of Dionysus' victorious Indian campaign, a legend which owed its life to Alexander's campaign in India and later gave much employment to poets and plastic artists.

From Aornos Alexander next marched to the spot, where Hephaestion had according to his instructions thrown a pontoon-bridge over the river. When he had given his army a rest of thirty days after the severe fighting, in the spring of 326 he crossed the Indus into the land of his ally Taxiles, whose rule extended from the Indus to the Hydaspes, the next Punjab river. Taxiles received him with valuable presents, and welcomed him in Taxila, his capital. He was confirmed in his principality by Alexander, but was treated as a vassal prince; for on his departure from Taxila[1] Alexander left a garrison behind.

Here they became acquainted with the actual wonders of India, and its strange manners and customs, and here Alexander's scientists began to examine the Indian flora. In Taxila they first made the acquaintance of those monkish Gymnosophists described above. One of them, Calanus, attached himself to the king's camp, and accompanied it to Persia, where he fell ill and to the astonishment of the army ended his life with philosophic calm by ascending a funeral pyre. We still possess fragments of a book on Alexander by Onesicritus, one of his attendants, in which, after the style of a romance of a philosophical and historical nature, he reports a conversation which he carried

[1] [For the excavation of Taxila see Sir J. Marshall, *Archaeological Survey of India, Annual Reports* from *1912-13* onwards, and *A Guide to Taxila*, Calcutta, 1918.]

on with some Gymnosophists at Taxila by means of interpreters. Dubious as is the setting of the narrative, the fact
of a conversation between Onesicritus and Gymnosophists need not be doubted, and it is interesting to see how
this Cynic and pupil of Diogenes thought he found the
Cynic doctrine in the general view of these Indian penitents with their simple and ascetic life, and represented
the Gymnosophists as true Cynics with the Cynic ideas of
monarchy and citizenship of the world. On the other hand,
the fragments we have of a later conversation between
Gymnosophists and Alexander himself are the deliberate
invention of a subsequent age, and are doubtless traceable
to members of the Cynic circle, who had none of Onesicritus' personal veneration for Alexander.

Taxiles had sent his ambassadors to Alexander in Sogdiana, because he hoped he would protect him from his
hostile neighbours, Abisares king of Kashmir, and Porus,
as the Greeks called the Paurâva king, whose great kingdom east of the Hydaspes adjoined his own. While Abisares
sought to deceive Alexander as to his real intentions and
his alliance with Porus by an embassy with valuable presents, Porus collected a strong army on the opposite bank
of the Hydaspes to prevent him from crossing. There, about
the summer solstice of 326, another pitched battle took
place, the last that Alexander fought.

As regards both the history of warfare and our judgment on Alexander's generalship, this battle is full of interest. It is quite different from the three earlier big battles.
In those he adhered to the fundamental principle of the
oblique battle-array, but here he carried out a quite new
tactical idea, and without adopting any fixed scheme took
his decisions according to the special circumstances of the
case. His task was to force a crossing and defeat the enemy.
Opposite, on the left bank, was Porus with 200 elephants
and 300 war-chariots, and a large force of infantry and
cavalry. Besides, the river was swollen with the tropical
rains which had just set in. As Alexander could not think

of crossing directly from the camp he had pitched on the right bank, if only because of the elephants, he devised a stratagem. When by repeated night-manœuvres he had wearied the enemy, till they gave up believing in the serious intention of an immediate attack, one night without attracting attention he went upstream to a favourable place, and there succeeded in crossing the river with 5000 cavalry and 6000 infantry, Craterus remaining behind with the rest of the army. On reaching the other side Alexander began next morning his march against Porus. He himself hurried forward with the cavalry, and ordered the infantry to follow. At the news of what had happened, Porus first sent a small division to meet him under the command of his son, who was defeated and fell. Meanwhile he brought his main force up and placed them in battle-array in a suitable spot. In the centre were the 200 elephants, between and behind the infantry numbering from 20,000 to 30,000, so that the elephants stood up like the towers in a city wall, and on the wings were the cavalry which numbered from 2000 to 4000, and the 300 fighting chariots.[1]

When Alexander approached and saw their strong position in front of him, he went straight from the march to the attack, as he had done at the Granicus. With a total of about 11,000 men he was facing very superior numbers, but his 5000 cavalry were more than a match for the Indians. Accordingly he attempted by a brilliantly conceived attack to bring about a cavalry engagement first, before his infantry came up. The plan succeeded to perfection. He held back the left wing of his cavalry under Coenus, while he himself with the right charged the opposite left wing of the Indian cavalry, and thus, as he had hoped, enticed the cavalry on the enemy's right to come to their aid. No sooner had this happened than Coenus,

[1] [Arrian, v. 15. 7 describes the chariots as placed before the cavalry on both wings, but makes no mention of them in the battle: probably their drivers were all successfully shot down.]

as had been arranged, making a wheel to the left rode forward, and executing a turn fell on the rear of the combined Indian cavalry, so that it had to face both ways.[1] The result was that the Indian horsemen were hurled back on the elephants in wild flight. At this moment Alexander's infantry, which had marched up in the meantime, attacked the Indian centre, which had been thrown into the greatest confusion by their fleeing cavalry. The confusion became more terrible, when the elephants, whose mahouts were soon shot down by Alexander's archers, became frantic and trod down more Indians than enemies. In spite of the Indians' brave resistance the end of the dreadful struggle was their complete defeat. Finally surrounded, and beset too by Craterus, who had in the meantime crossed over, and now joined in the pursuit, they sustained losses that were colossal. Alexander's genius as a general is scarcely ever so convincingly impressed on us as in this battle of the Hydaspes.

King Porus, a giant of manly beauty, fought to the last with the greatest bravery, till wounded and exhausted he had to surrender to the victor. He approved himself as general too, by his arrangements before and during the battle, but he was certainly not equal to the genius of an Alexander. The story goes that when Alexander met him after the battle, and admiring his fine appearance asked him how he would like to be treated, Porus replied, 'Like a king'. Even if this is fictitious, which is improbable, at any rate Alexander, himself the most chivalrous of men, who valued nothing in an enemy more than chivalry, did treat him like a king. He confirmed him as king in his dominions,

---

[1] [It is agreed that Alexander opened operations by sending forward the mounted archers, and that he caused Porus to bring his cavalry from his right to support those that he had posted on his left. Some think Alexander drew the Indian cavalry into an attack on him, so that Coenus might unnoticed catch them in the rear. See A. Bauer, *Festgabe für Max Büdinger*, Innsbruck, 1898, p. 71. See also J. B. Bury, *History of Greece,* p. 804, Fig. 201.]

without subordinating him to a satrap, and later extended his kingdom to the Hyphasis. King Porus repaid him by fidelity to death. Politically it was of the greatest importance to Alexander to have gained in this powerful ruler a secure support for his own rule in the Punjab. The situation was further stabilised by his success in reconciling the old enemies, Porus and Taxiles. To preserve what he had fought for, Alexander founded on the Hydaspes two Greek cities, one Nicaea (victory town), where he had succeeded in crossing, and the other, where the battle was fought, Bucephala, named after his famous riding horse, which is said to have died there of old age. A gymnastic competition and a cavalry race were organised on the bank of the Hydaspes to celebrate the victory.

After a long rest Alexander started eastwards and first reached the Acesines, which farther south receives the Hydaspes, and finally falls into the Indus. Here he made an observation, which led him to a bold geographical hypothesis. The crocodiles of the Indus had reminded him of Egypt. When on the Acesines he saw also Egyptian beans, he thought from these two observations—in combination with the information that the Acesines flowed into the Indus—that he could conclude that he was in the land where the Nile took its rise. In his joy of discovery he mentioned it at once in a letter to his mother, and already planned an expedition to Egypt down the Indus. From this one sees that he and his suite knew nothing of the voyage on the Indus, which, according to Herodotus, Scylax of Caryanda had carried out by order of Darius I. Still more by this conclusion is a vivid light thrown on Alexander's complete ignorance of the southern boundary of Asia, especially of the Indian Ocean. It can only be a later mistake on the part of Cleitarchus to assert that Alexander even on the Hydaspes, immediately after the battle with Porus, ordered a fleet to be built to sail into the 'Great Sea', that is the Indian Ocean; for Alexander did not hear of the 'Great Sea' until shortly after forming the Indus-

Nile hypothesis he learnt by further enquiry of the natives that the Indus discharged its waters southwards into this 'Great Sea'. Then, to test his information, Alexander did order a fleet to be built, with the intention of sailing to the Great Sea in it. These orders he sent to the Hydaspes, because he had left Craterus behind there with a division of the army to found the two cities.

Perhaps the fresh news of the southern ocean aroused in Alexander doubts of the correctness of his previous idea, that by advancing through the Punjab he must soon come to the Eastern Ocean. That Aristotle was wrong in thinking that one could see the Ocean from the Hindu-Kush, he had found out by proceeding through the Kabul valley. He must have been all the more eager to be clear about this problem of the Eastern Ocean, and as the building of the fleet would necessarily take a long time, he set out eastwards in the interval.

He was quickly to receive new and surprising information, which entailed very serious decisions. In his advance he had subdued the tribes of the eastern Punjab, often without serious resistance—he had to fight hard with the Cathaeans for their town Sangala—and after crossing the Hydraotes was approaching the Hyphasis, the last great river of the Punjab, when he learned from Phegeus, the king of this district, that beyond the Hyphasis there was first a desert of twelve days march, and then a great river, Ganges by name, the greatest of all the Indian rivers, on whose banks dwelt warlike and rich people, the Prasians and Gangarids, who had thousands of elephants. Porus, his faithful vassal, confirmed the accuracy of this statement. It was the first time a European heard of the Ganges. In a moment Alexander's previous idea of the world was completely changed. The Eastern Ocean into which the Ganges must fall was moved away to an indefinite distance. Should he then give up his aim of reaching the eastern edge of the world? Lately it has been supposed that he never had this aim; for his command to build a fleet on the Hydaspes showed that in the first instance he thought only of a voyage on the Indus, and doubts are raised whether he ever received the above-mentioned information about the Ganges.[1] The latter point, however, is vouched for on the most excellent authority, and apart from that, the theory overlooks the fact that Alexander knew nothing of the Ganges when he issued the order for the building of the fleet. It has also been supposed that on receiving the news Alexander from political and military insight turned back at the Hyphasis of his own accord.[2] But this is a view which contradicts reliable sources. According to these there can be no question, that at the news he really wanted to invade the Ganges country, and this determination, however judged, must be included in the picture of Alexander: otherwise a characteristic trait will be wanting.

But when Alexander, on reaching the Hyphasis, revealed his gigantic plans to the army, he met with a refusal. It was not a mutiny in which the Macedonians gave vent to their opposition to the king's policy of conquering the world; it was a refusal based on the deepest physical and intellectual exhaustion. Hitherto Alexander by the charm of his personality had swept them along with him to unparalleled achievements. The troops which had originally followed him from home, according to the calculations of Count Yorck von Wartenburg[3] in the eight and a half years had marched between Amphipolis and the Hyphasis, about 11,250 miles, 'in any case a remarkable feat of endurance'. Now Alexander was face to face with the impossibility of beginning a new great undertaking with his quite exhausted soldiery. The forlorn condition and mood of the army at the Hyphasis are chiefly to be explained by the tropical rains, which for seventy days since they left Taxila had poured down upon them without cessation.

[1] By Tarn, Wilcken, *Berl. Akad.*, 1922, xvi. p. 114. Ernst Meyer, *Klio*, 21, 183.   [2] Endres, *op. cit.* p. 14.
[3] Maximilian Graf Yorck von Wartenburg, *Kurze Übersicht der Feldzüge Alexanders des Grossen*, 1897, p. 64.

Hard as Alexander found it—he retired into his tent and sulked for two days—he could not avoid seeing the hopelessness of his plan. When he had ordered the usual sacrifice for crossing the river and this had proved unfavourable, he proclaimed his will to turn round, for which he was thanked by the immoderate rejoicing of his army. By his self-conquest he got his troops in hand again. But the refusal of his Macedonians left a sting in his soul, and it is perhaps to be referred to this thrilling incident, that later—we do not know exactly, when—he gave orders that 30,000 young Persians of special strength and beauty should be selected and trained with Macedonian weapons, to form a counterpart to the Macedonian phalanx. These are the so-called 'Epigoni', who in 324 were paraded before the king at Susa.

In commemoration of his advance to the Hyphasis and in gratitude to the gods who had led him victoriously so far, as his ancestor Heracles had erected his pillars in the far West, so Alexander built twelve great tower-like altars on the nearer side of the river. We have been informed by those who refer everything to Babylonia, that this was for the twelve signs of the zodiac. In reality it was the twelve gods of Macedonia to whom these altars were raised.

The march back to the Hydaspes now began. No obstacles met Alexander in the pacified country, which had been added to the kingdom of the faithful Porus. On the Acesines he came to the city named after him, which Hephaestion by his order had been engaged in founding, and settled in it natives and discharged mercenaries. Here he was met by envoys from Abisares of Kashmir, who sent him a present of thirty elephants, and was now recognised by Alexander as a vassal prince of his country, independent of Taxiles, with title of satrap. This arrangement seems to have lasted; for after the death of Abisares (325) Alexander confirmed in his succession a son who bore the same name.

Meanwhile the two new cities on the Hydaspes, Nicaea and Bucephala, had suffered severely from the persistent rains—which suggests buildings of unburnt bricks. Alexander had them repaired by his troops. The most pressing business next was to finish the building of the fleet, which he had entrusted to Craterus. Men were thereupon sent up the Hydaspes to the fir-growing region of the Himalayas to float down timber for the construction of ships. The king, denied the goal of the Eastern Ocean, was now fired with the desire of sailing down the Indus, which, according to the inhabitants, flowed into the Ocean of the south. Great exertions were made to finish the fleet, and it was a very strong one, when the voyage began. There were 80 boats of thirty oars, fitted out as warships, and hundreds of horse-transports, grain-ships and other lighter craft for holding men or cargo, requisitioned from the neighbourhood, in all at least 800 vessels. To defray the expense, Alexander selected thirty of the richest of his attendants, among them the seven body-guards, and on the Athenian model gave them each a trierarchy. He probably did this not so much for economy, to save the imperial treasury the expense, as to give a personal interest in the enterprise to his immediate followers. The crews of the ships were formed of the most maritime peoples of the East, Phoenicians, Cyprians, Carians, and Egyptians, who had followed in the baggage-train, and of the Greeks most accustomed to the sea, from the islands, Ionia and the Hellespont, who were picked out of the army for the purpose. Alexander could not take over the chief command in person, as in case of need he would have to command by land. So he conferred it on one of the most intimate friends of his youth, Nearchus, and made him admiral (*Nauarch*).

After he had taken final measures for the administration of the Punjab districts and in particular had placed Philip as satrap over the vassal king Taxiles, the memorable voyage was begun at the commencement of November 326. It was inaugurated in the most solemn fashion. While the crews went on board at sunrise, the king on the bank offered not only the usual sacrifices, but by direction of the soothsayers sacrificed also to the gods on whose favour he was now particularly to depend, Poseidon, Amphitrite, the Nereids, Oceanus the goal of the journey, and the river-gods of the Hydaspes, Acesines, and the Indus which received them both. Musical and gymnastic contests followed. When Alexander had gone on board his own ship, he poured from the bows a drink-offering out of a golden cup to the same gods of sea and rivers; his 'forefather' Heracles and his 'father' Ammon were similarly honoured. A blast of trumpets then gave the signal to start. On the fleet with Alexander went the hypaspists, the archers and the *Hetairoi*; the main army was divided into two columns, that on the right bank commanded by Craterus, that on the left by Hephaestion, who also had 200 elephants. It was a wonderful sight for the Indians, when this great fleet with its gay sails passed majestically down the river, with the splash of the oars, the word of command of the pilots and the hurrahs of the rowers echoing in the ravines of both banks. With astonishment the Indians saw the army on board ship and especially the horses. At the noise they came out of their forests in troops, and escorted the fleet part of the way, singing their Indian songs—'for no people loves singing and dancing so much as the Indians', says Arrian, to whom we owe the fine description of this voyage. When in explanation he refers to the Indian triumph of Dionysus, he refers to a legend which grew up only in consequence of Alexander's campaign (p. 180).

The voyage was not to be peaceful for long. Before Alexander reached the Acesines, he heard that the Malli and the Oxydracae, the largest and most warlike of the Indian tribes, were preparing to fight him. He therefore insisted on pushing forward more rapidly, in order to pass the point where the Hydaspes enters the Acesines; in this process owing to the violent whirlpools and rapids, produced by the meeting of the two rivers, his fleet suffered severe damage, and had to be hastily repaired. The plan of campaign which he then drew up for engaging the enemy, displays him again to us as a consummate strategist. The territory of the enemy stretched along the Hydraotes, which farther south enters the Acesines, and seemed to be protected against Alexander's camp on the Acesines by a waterless desert. The Malli therefore expected that he would attack them from the mouth of the Hydraotes. But he determined to surprise them by advancing with part of the army through the desert into the heart of their country, and to drive them down the Hydraotes into the arms of another column under Hephaestion, who was to occupy the lower course of the river, while the fleet and Craterus with the elephants, stationed on the right bank of the Acesines opposite the mouth of the Hydraotes, were to prevent them from escaping westwards. The surprise was a signal success, and the contemplated junction of the Malli with the Oxydracae was frustrated. Nevertheless, the fighting for the towns and strongholds of the Malli was severe and bloody, since they fought with the courage of despair. Several towns had to be stormed, among them a town of the Brahmins, and lastly the chief town of the tribe. Here Alexander's victorious career might have come to a tragic end. To spur on his wavering troops, he climbed a ladder and was the first to mount the castle wall. Thence he jumped down alone into the interior of the castle, and with his back to the wall and exposed to the enemy, who recognised him by his glittering armour, was hit by an arrow in the breast, and collapsed in a swoon. Peucestas and Leonnatus, who had jumped down after him, covered him with their shields, Peucestas with the sacred shield of Ilium, till finally the storming party scaled the wall and laid the enemy low. While the troops, believing their king to be slain, vented their fury on the garrison and the women and children as well, Alexander was carried out for dead on his shield. But his youthful vigour prevailed, and after the arrow was extracted from the wound, he slowly recovered.

The news that the king had fallen had already reached the camp at the mouth of the Hydraotes, and had caused

the deepest grief, and also terror and dismay at their desperate position without Alexander. Fearing that disturbances might break out, Alexander had himself taken on
board ship down the Hydraotes to the camp, as soon as
his condition rendered it possible. The sight of the sick-
tent on deck at first confirmed the troops in the belief that
the vessel was bringing the king's corpse. But when he had
the tent opened and beckoned with his arm, and when on
shore he actually mounted a horse to show himself to all,
and then walked on foot to his tent, their rejoicing knew
no bounds, and with tears in their eyes they broke into
a triumphal shout, so that the wooded ravines re-echoed.
From all sides they thronged to touch the hands or knees
or clothes of their beloved king, or at least to gaze into his
face and utter words of affection, overwhelming him with
flowers and gay ribbons. One cannot without emotion
read the description which Arrian gives of this scene. It
brings home to us the fascination of Alexander's personality. The deep affection the army felt for him broke out
with elemental vehemence. Everything that had ever come
between him and his Macedonians was forgotten.

Theoretically his friends were probably quite correct to
reproach the king for behaving not as a general but as
a soldier, in leaping down into the castle. But the old
Boeotian was right, who when he heard that Alexander
was angry about this, said in his dialect to him 'a man's
duty is to act', adding a verse from Sophocles 'he who acts
must also suffer'. For it was not the capture of the town
itself, but this unprecedented act of Alexander's which
spread so great a terror among the enemy that not merely
the Malli but also the Oxydracae humbly submitted themselves. By this spontaneous act, conceived and carried out
in the wild excitement of combat, he both rendered superfluous the whole second part of his carefully thought out
plan of campaign—the driving of the Malli into the trap set
at the mouth of the Hydraotes—and also brought about the
submission of the Oxydracae without the striking of a blow.

After Alexander had completely recovered, the fleet, which during this involuntary interval had been strengthened by fresh construction, sailed past the mouth of the Hyphasis to the point where the Acesines joins the Indus. Here Alexander fixed the southern limit of his North Indian satrapy, left the satrap Philip with some troops, and ordered him to found an Alexander city at the confluence of the two rivers.

Approximately half of his river voyage was now completed. About February of 325 began the voyage down the Indus, the banks of which down to the sea were finally united in the satrapy of Lower India under Peithon. Much fighting was needed before this region was conquered; for the population, who are described as swarthy in contrast with the Aryan tribes of Northern India and were obviously Dravidian, were under the influence of the Brahmins, who from religious motives urged them with the hatred of fanaticism to a desperate resistance against the foreigner. The Sogdians, however, whom Alexander reached first, had been impressed by the subjugation of the Malli and entered into friendly relations, with the result that he was enabled to enlarge their capital and rename it 'Sogdian Alexandria'. Farther south in the countries of Sambos and Musicanos, who ruled on the west bank opposite to the great desert of the east bank, there was much hard fighting, for though the kings fled, the peoples, incited by the Brahmins, rose in arms. Alexander punished the Brahmins with great severity as the real culprits and hanged some of them. To secure his rule he had several fortresses in Lower India strengthened and garrisoned, and also founded some new cities. Here again we see the combination of military and economic considerations.

Finally in July 325, in the ninth month after his departure from Nicaea, he reached the town of Pattala at the apex of the Indus Delta. The king of the town, who had previously done homage, ran away. On account of the commercial importance of its situation sheds were here built for ships, and a station created for a large portion of the Indus fleet.

Alexander's campaign in India was finished. The whole of the country watered by the Indus from Kashmir to the sea, including the entire Punjab, was subject to him. A great, rich and extremely fruitful country had been added to his Asiatic empire, under the rule of Macedonian satraps, to whom the native vassal princes (all but King Porus) were subordinated. The wonders of India, previously known only through literature or from hearsay, had now been seen by the Macedonians and Greeks, and the reality had not fallen short of the fantastic descriptions of a fabulous world. If there were no such monstrosities—Cyclopes and Umbrella-footed men—as had been invented by Scylax, who applied to India the marvels of epic poetry, or monstrosities again which were based on Indian ideas, they saw quite enough that was novel and astounding in the way of plants and animals; the natives also with their system of caste and their strange customs had impressions to give that were utterly new. Alexander's staff of scientists had a great opportunity to collect information and specimens. Some extracts from their works on the flora of India can be seen in Theophrastus' treatise on plants, as, for example, the treatment of the air-roots of the Indian fig-tree (*Ficus Bengalensis*), and they give us an idea of the care and keen interest with which these scientists explored this new world in all directions. Alexander even ordered an investigation of the mineral riches of the country. Thus Gorgus, a mining expert in his following (*metalleutes*), examined the salt mines in the country of Sopeithes, in the north between the Hydraotes and the Hyphasis, and the gold and silver mines in the neighbouring mountains, and described them in a treatise used by Strabo. He stated, among other things, that these salt mines would suffice for the whole of India, and that the Indians did not know the art of the technical extraction of gold and silver and the assay of metals by smelting, but worked them in quite a primitive fashion. In this way Greek technology and Greek science were employed on Indian soil, while Alexander was subduing the country.

Beside all this the king was now particularly occupied with the great geographical problem which, along with his will to conquer, had impelled him to his voyage down the Indus. That the Indus fell into the ocean which he yearned to find, he had learnt from the natives, as we saw, after his first crossing of the Acesines (326); and as this completely changed his notions of geography (p. 185), he had ordered a fleet to be built. Probably, if not at once, yet soon his inquiring spirit grasped the idea that if the Indus flowed into the ocean, then supposing the ocean enclosed the southern verge of Asia, from the mouth of the Indus a sea passage might be found to the mouths of the Tigris and the Euphrates. It was not at Pattala, not when he stood on the actual shore of the Indian Ocean, that he first conceived the project of sending an expedition by sea from the mouth of the Indus. We can deduce this from the fact that before reaching Pattala, and while still in the territory of Musicanus, he despatched Craterus with part of the army to Arachosia and Drangiana, where disturbances were reported to have arisen, with orders to march from there to Carmania, to join forces with him in that province. The inevitable assumption is that at least by that time the whole scheme of the expedition by sea and land, as afterwards carried out, was already complete in Alexander's mind. So, during the journey, and perhaps beforehand, he kept in view the great plan of finding a way by sea from the Indus to the Tigris and Euphrates, and if he succeeded, of forming a connexion between his western empire and his new colonial empire in India; not only would military security and administrative control be facilitated in his Indian possessions but the trade of India would be connected with that of Hither Asia, and wide perspectives opened to world-commerce throughout his Empire.

It is surprising that no historian of Alexander and no

later authority in dealing with the Indus voyage or this sea expedition or Alexander's later Arabian plans refers to Scylax of Caryanda [1] as at least his partial forerunner. By order of Darius I Scylax set out from Kabul down the Indus, sailed along the coast of the Indian Ocean to Ormuz, and from there, instead of entering the Persian Gulf, circumnavigated Arabia and landed in the gulf of Suez. As far as Ormuz, but only so far, he performed what Alexander's fleet was now to do, and after Ormuz, what Alexander at the end of his life wanted to do. Some people have doubted the historicity of this voyage, but they are wrong, for there are monuments on the Suez Canal to confirm Darius' undertaking. The silence of the authorities about Scylax shows only that the knowledge of his intrepid voyage, in spite of the narrative of Herodotus, was forgotten in Alexander's day, as the discovery of America by the Vikings had been at the time of Columbus.

After the construction of a station for the fleet and of ship-houses at Pattala had been put in hand, Alexander proceeded to examine the two chief arms into which the Indus divided at that time—to-day the Delta has taken a very different shape—in order to see which was better suited for the passage of his fleet. In these trial trips he took the command himself, as now at least he had before him the satisfaction of his greatest wish, to see with his own eyes the boundless Ocean. With the swiftest ships of his fleet, at first without pilot, he sailed down the western arm to the sea, while Leonnatus with 9000 men marched alongside on the island formed by the Delta. The very second day a great storm from the south arose, and Alexander obtained Indians who knew the country and could act as pilots on the river as it became wider. For protection from the strong ocean winds they had just diverted the fleet into a side-channel, when forthwith, to the surprise and terror of the Macedonians, the swollen waters sank, and the ships were left high and dry. It was the ebb-tide of the ocean, which

[1] For Scylax see Wilh. Reese, *op. cit.* p. 48.

became known to these Europeans for the first time. They were still more astonished, when the incoming tide floated the ships again, damaging many of them. As the king approached the river-mouth, he left most of his ships behind at an island, and proceeded with the best to a second island, which was further on. After offering sacrifices there, as at the first, by Ammon's direction,[1] he sailed out into the open to spy, as he said, whether there were some land standing up in the sea. But when he saw only the unlimited ocean before him, then in the proud and happy consciousness that he had reached a limit of the world, he offered to Poseidon, lord of the sea, a great sacrifice of gratitude for the past, and prayer for the future. Bulls were slaughtered on the ship and thrown into the sea; and then he hurled into the waves the golden cup out of which he had made the drink-offering, and the golden mixing-vessels in which the wine for the sacrifice had been contained, and as he did so, he prayed that the god would graciously conduct him to the mouths of the Tigris and the Euphrates. This must have been one of the greatest and most elevating days of Alexander's life.

On his return to Pattala, he next explored the eastern arm, and came to the conclusion that this, which then flowed through a great lake, was more convenient and less dangerous than the western. Probably the voyage was easier, because the south-west monsoons blew into the western but not into the eastern arm. On arriving at the mouth, he walked with a few attendants for three days along the shore, to examine the nature of the country and have wells dug for seafarers, and then returned to Pattala.

It was a hard thing for Alexander to put Nearchus, who was very dear to him, as admiral at the head of the expedition, since he feared great dangers for the voyage. Only at the pressing request of Nearchus did Alexander reluctantly give way. But the crews, who at first contemplated the future with anxiety, were much encouraged by

[1] [Arrian, vi. 19, 4, as Alexander himself stated.]

this appointment, concluding that the king counted on a successful result. How far-seeing were the plans which Alexander coupled with this voyage, is disclosed by his commission to Nearchus to obtain information about country and people as he sailed along the coast, to look out for appropriate anchorages and the supply of drinking water, the arrangements of the natives, and the fertility of the various districts. Obviously he designed to fix stations for future trade voyages at suitable spots between the two ends of the passage, and if possible, to found colonies.

But communication by sea was not enough: on the mainland too between India and Persia no people was to remain independent, which might in future break the connexion by hostilities. Therefore Gedrosia (Beluchistan) must be incorporated in the empire, particularly as its coasts were very important not only for the present expedition but for future trade voyages as affording places of provisioning. As the commission of Craterus to meet him in Carmania shows, Alexander recognised the necessity of journeying himself with the main body of the army through Gedrosia to Carmania, going as close as possible to the coast, in order to provision the fleet by sinking wells and making depots of grain. He was naturally also influenced by the desire to have his share in the discovery of the southern limit of Asia.

Nearchus expressly assures us that Alexander knew beforehand all about the terrible hardships which he would have to inflict on his army by marching through the waterless sandy desert of Gedrosia. When Nearchus places beside this practical motive of providing for the needs of the fleet Alexander's ambition to outdo by this march Semiramis and Cyrus the Great, his intimate relations to Alexander forbid us to reject the statement: and indeed it is not in itself improbable, when one remembers how on the desert march to the oracle of Ammon Alexander adduced the parallel of Perseus and Heracles to fire the ambition of his troops, and how in India the examples of Heracles and

Dionysus had been effective. For the march through Gedrosia he appealed not to Greek mythical figures but to those of Oriental history who had become legendary, and in whom he might also see prototypes of Oriental world-rulers. We pointed above to his close connexions with Cyrus. When Semiramis appears by the side of Cyrus, one can trace the effect of the East upon Alexander.

CHAPTER VIII

RETURN AND END

ABOUT the end of August 325 Alexander left Pattala on his return westwards, to make preparations beforehand for the provisioning of the fleet when it arrived, while Nearchus was to wait for the setting in of the north-east monsoons in October. At first he traversed the country of the Arabitae and Oreitae, who were subdued after much fighting. A satrap, Apollophanes, was appointed, and Hephaestion was left behind with orders to found an Alexander city in connexion with Rhambalia, the chief village of the Oreitae. Leonnatus, who was to await the fleet on the coast, was to found a second Alexandria there. Alexander now plunged into the Gedrosian desert, and the further he went the greater were the privations and sufferings of the army. The complete barrenness and absence of water on the coast made it necessary to go further inland, so that the intention of establishing depots for the fleet could not be carried out. The burning heat rendered it impossible to march except by night. Scouts who were sent to the sea described the wretched *Ichthyophagi* (fish-eaters) who subsisted on mussels and lived in huts.

On went the army suffering from hunger and thirst, and the maintenance of discipline became more and more difficult, but Alexander was indulgent, having humane regard to the plight of his men. By thousands they lay down by the roadside, and horses and mules were killed and eaten. Very rarely could food be procured from villages further inland. Finally they were able to follow the coast again, when good water and food could be depended upon, and then they passed through more fruitful regions into the interior. They reached Pura, the capital of Gedrosia, sixty days after leaving the country of the Oreitae. If here and there the descriptions of the sufferings of the troops are rhetorically embroidered, on the whole they do not seem to be exaggerated. Alexander marched on foot with them and, by his example and by sharing all privations as their comrade, did his utmost to keep up the courage and perseverance of his men. When some soldiers, who had been lucky enough to find water, offered it to him in a helmet, he praised them but poured the water into the sand. This invigorated the whole army, says Arrian, as much as if they had all drunk the water he had poured away. How great were his losses in men and animals, cannot be calculated, as it is not known how many he started with from Pattala. But they must have been appallingly large.[1] It is stated that the women and children who accompanied the army suffered most. Even here in the sandy desert of Beluchistan Alexander caused his scientists to observe the flora of the desert; and we possess many of their observations. It is also interesting to read that the Phoenician merchants, who were in the baggage-train, used the opportunity to collect the resin from the myrrh-bushes and the scented roots of the spikenards, whose value they knew from the home market.

In the plenty of Pura the survivors of the army were able to get thorough refreshment and rest. The subjection of Further Asia was thus completed by the conquest of Gedrosia, and this country was placed under a satrap, Sibyrtius, and united in one satrapy with Arachosia, which bounded it on the north. About the beginning of December 325 Alexander started to march westwards to Carmania, which had given him its submission in 330, when he was in Persis, but on which he had not yet set foot. In Carmania,

---

[1] [W. W. Tarn defends Alexander against the charge of foolhardiness. He says, 'Apollophanes was to collect and forward supplies; but the Oreitae rose and killed him, which upset Alexander's arrangements'. This assumes that Arrian vi. 22, 2 states correctly that Apollophanes was killed, but that in vi. 27, 1 'Apollophanes', who was deposed, is a mistake for Astaspes of Carmania.]

according to arrangement, Craterus met him. With his division of the army and all the elephants, he had left India by the Mulla and Bolān passes, gone by way of Arachosian Alexandria (Kandahar) and Drangiana, subdued rebels, among them Ordanes, whom he now had with him in chains, and had then proceeded into Carmania to keep his rendezvous with Alexander. So, except for those who had perished in Gedrosia and the troops left behind in India, the whole field army was reunited. After the great losses in Gedrosia, the large numbers of camels and beasts of burden, brought by Stasanor, the satrap of Areia and Drangiana, were very welcome. After joining Craterus Alexander held a festival of thanksgiving for the conquest of India and their preservation from the deserts of Gedrosia. Sacrifices were offered to the gods, and a musical and gymnastic contest held. Peucestas, who had saved the king's life in the citadel of the Malli, was enrolled as the eighth of the royal body-guard. These festivities and the joyous mood of the army after its recent preservation gave rise to the legend, which we may trace back to the fertile imagination of Cleitarchus, that Alexander and his troops marched through Carmania in a Bacchanalian revel of seven days in imitation of the triumphal procession of Dionysus.

While in Carmania Alexander was relieved of his great anxiety for the fleet, of whose fate he had not yet heard. Nearchus had had to leave a month earlier than was arranged with Alexander, because of the threatening attitude of the Indian population after the king's departure; he sailed about 20 September 325, before the setting in of the north-eastern monsoons. The consequence was that shortly afterwards on the coast of the Arabitae he was becalmed for twenty-four days amid great privations, until the hoped-for winds arrived. On the basis of the log which he kept, he subsequently wrote an account of his voyage of discovery, of which we have in Arrian's *Indike* a much abbreviated but very valuable extract. We have in particular the notes of the various points at which the fleet put in, so that we can follow the voyage from day to day with its chief experiences. On the other hand we have lost most of the descriptions, which by Alexander's orders Nearchus gave of the flora and fauna, the customs of the natives, the formation of the coast, and much besides; but we hear, for example, of a people which was unacquainted with iron and used sharp stones, and thus was still in the Stone Age. It is to Nearchus that we owe the valuable passage about the mangroves of the Persian Gulf in Theophrastus' *On Plants*. On the whole the voyage was successful, without much loss of ships, and only once was armed resistance encountered. Nevertheless, from want of food and especially of drinking water the crews often suffered severely. They soon became accustomed to the alternation of the tides. But at the first sight of whales there was terror and consternation. When they saw the great columns of water which seemed to them to be hurled forth as if from machines, they asked the native pilots what it meant, and when they were told that these were blown up by large animals, the oars fell from their hands for fright. At Nearchus' command they charged at the whales with their prows 'as if for a sea fight', and by their war-cries, with which, as Nearchus later wrote, they gave themselves courage, and by their trumpet blasts, they scared the creatures into diving down to the depths.

After this and other exciting experiences they reached the strait of Harmozeia (*Ormuz*), and, when opposite the Carmanian coast, saw the Arabian promontory Maketa (*Ras Mussendam*). Onesicritus, who as on the Indus fleet was steersman of the admiral's ship, wanted to follow the coast of Arabia, instead of entering the Persian Gulf. But Nearchus as his superior officer abruptly refused this, pointing to Alexander's instructions. A few days later his dutiful behaviour was rewarded; near Ormuz, when he reached the mouth of the Anamis, he heard that Alexander was only five days' march away in the interior. Nearchus' tale of the manner in which he met his king is very touching in its simplicity and is one of the gems of the literature about Alexander. Some of his people had encountered a Greek, who had repaired from Alexander's camp to the shore. Deep emotion seized them, when they saw a Greek once more and heard him speak Greek. With joy they led him to Nearchus, who thereupon agreed with the commander of the coast that the man should take him to Alexander. But while Nearchus was drawing his vessels on shore and surrounding them with a rampart, the Greek in the hope of a reward hurried on by the shortest way to give the king the joyful news of the arrival of the fleet.

Alexander at first was highly delighted, but as days went by without the coming of Nearchus, he became ever more impatient, till finally believing the man had deceived him, he had him arrested. Meanwhile some messengers sent out by Alexander met Nearchus, who with Archias, the second in command of the fleet, and five others had started off without a guide into the interior to look for Alexander's camp. But Nearchus and his companions were so changed by the fatigues of the expedition—pale and emaciated, with long hair and ragged clothes—that the messengers did not recognise them. They were about to pass by, when at Archias' advice Nearchus asked them where they were going, and when they said they were looking for Nearchus and the fleet, Nearchus said to them: 'I am Nearchus, and this is Archias. Be our guides: we want to tell Alexander about the voyage.' Thereupon the messengers took them in their chariots and drove them to the camp, and announced to the king that Nearchus and Archias with five men had come; but they were unable to answer Alexander's question about the fleet. Then the king believed that the whole fleet was destroyed, and when Nearchus and his companions came before him, hardly recognising them, he gave his right hand to his friend Nearchus, took him aside, and wept for a long time. At last he said, 'You and Archias at any rate are saved; that is a comfort in my disaster. But how did the ships and crews perish?' When

Nearchus replied that the fleet and men were safe, Alexander wept more, and swore by Zeus of the Hellenes and Ammon of the Libyans that he rejoiced more over this message than over the conquest of all Asia. We must thank Nearchus for lifting the veil from this touching scene, which took place in private, and for thus giving us a deep insight into the human side of Alexander.

A great festival was held. Thank-offerings for the preservation of the fleet were made to Zeus the Saviour, to Heracles, to Apollo Averter of Evil, Poseidon and all the gods of the sea; and musical and gymnastic competitions were again held. When a procession followed, Nearchus was at its head, and the rejoicing army covered him with flowers and gay ribbons. He was the hero of the day.

Only at the urgent request of Nearchus did Alexander leave him in command of the fleet to take it to its destination at Susa; for he was very loth to expose his friend again to the dangers of a sea-voyage. So Nearchus continued the voyage. Hephaestion was commissioned to march to Persia by the southerly road, where good provision was to be obtained, with the bulk of the army and the elephants. Alexander himself with the light troops and the *Hetairoi* set out by a more northerly road direct to Pasargadae, where he arrived at the beginning of the year 324.

More than five years had elapsed, since he first visited Pasargadae, then still as the commander-in-chief of the Corinthian League, who was about to declare the Panhellenic campaign at an end. He returned as the paramount Great King of Asia, who, far beyond the limits of the Achaemenid Empire, had conquered India, and at the mouth of the Indus had reached the limit of the inhabited world. Not only battle and victory lay behind him but many a severe collision with men who had been his closest friends. The bitter experience, that only few in his suite understood and approved the policy of comprehension which became ever more dominant in his mind, was bound to weigh heavily on him and make him severe and reserved. He must have felt as a relief the rain of tears that his impulsive nature drew from him when he met Nearchus, one of those few. Severe and hard had been his attitude in Carmania, when the first news reached him of insubordination among some imperial officials.

The further west he came, the more numerous were the reports, that because of his long absence several of his satraps, in the belief that he would not return, or on false rumours that he had perished, had been guilty of the plundering of temples or the oppression of his subjects. It was high time that he got back and reduced them to order. He proceeded against the miscreants with iron severity, so that by stern punishment he might warn others against following the bad example. The Mede Baryaxes, who was brought to him at Pasargadae in chains by the Median satrap Atropates, was executed with his whole following, because he had put the tiara upright on his head in royal fashion and usurped the title of Great King of the Medes and Persians. Alexander also was extremely indignant, when he revisited the tomb of Cyrus the Great, to find the sepulchral chamber plundered and laid waste and the corpse torn out of its coffin. He tortured the Magians who were in charge, but as they could not be convicted, he let them go free, and commissioned Aristobulus to restore the damage. He, in his history of Alexander, expressly reports on this incident, and has left us a very valuable description of the still extant building and its condition at the time.[1]

When Alexander left Pasargadae for the neighbouring Persepolis, he had Orxines hanged. After the death of Phrasaortes this man had usurped the satrapy of Persis, and was now convicted of having plundered the royal graves and sanctuaries, and of having put to death many Persians without trial. Peucestas was appointed satrap in his place; he seemed to be specially appropriate for the

[1] [The tomb is illustrated in *Cambridge Ancient History, Volume of Plates I*, p. 312 b.]

cradle of the Persian nation, because he alone of the Macedonians had assumed Median dress and Persian customs and had learned the Persian language.

We are told by Arrian that as Alexander gazed on the ruins of the palaces of Persepolis which he had formerly set on fire, he 'did not praise' their destruction. Then he had not shrunk from sacrificing these wonderful buildings to the Panhellenic idea, in order to take vengeance for the crimes of Xerxes. How distant from him now were such thoughts. What did he care for the Panhellenic idea, which he had once accepted with enthusiasm, himself carried out, and then discarded for ever? Since then he had followed his second aim only, the winning of Asia for himself and for Greek civilisation, and one can conceive how regret seized him, that he had not left standing these proud monuments of his predecessors, witnesses to the high culture attained by the old Achaemenid Empire.

From Persepolis Alexander marched to Susa. Shortly before he reached the city (about February 324) he met Nearchus and his fleet at the bridge of boats by which his army was to cross the Pasitigris. Nearchus had successfully sailed along the Persian Gulf to the mouth of the Euphrates, and then at the news of Alexander's approach had gone up the Pasitigris to the bridge. There was great rejoicing on the reunion of the army and crews, who had not seen each other since they left India. Sacrifices were offered to the gods in thanksgiving for the preservation of the fleet, and games celebrated. Nearchus, who was again covered by the army with flowers and ribbons, received from Alexander the highest distinction of a golden crown, and Leonnatus the same for his victory over the Oreitae. After Hephaestion had also joined them, the victorious army was granted a long rest at Susa. There, if not before, under the title of Chiliarch, which he also bore as colonel of the first hipparchy of the *Hetairoi*, Hephaestion was given the position of a Persian Grand Vizier, so that officially he had precedence after the King.

At Susa also bad news came in concerning disorders in the Empire. Not only had the Oriental satraps of the Eastern parts taken advantage of the King's long absence, but his Macedonian satraps as well in the West had somewhat exceeded their authority by enlisting large bodies of mercenaries. Alexander immediately ordered the mercenaries to be dismissed, and by taking other measures of the greatest severity, quickly restored order.

Only one of these offenders succeeded in escaping his tribunal of punishment, the old friend of his youth, Harpalus, who had been left at Ecbatana in 330 as imperial treasurer, and had later removed to Babylon taking the treasure with him. The longer Alexander stayed away, the more impudently did he employ Alexander's treasure for his own extravagant life. He lived riotously with the Athenian courtesan Pythionice; and when she died, he built a temple and altar to her as 'Pythionice Aphrodite', a frivolous precursor of the Hellenistic apotheosis; and not only in Babylon, but also near Athens, on the Sacred Way to Eleusis, paid many talents for costly tombs to be erected to her. Subsequently he lived for a time in the royal castle at Tarsus with another Athenian, Glycera, and made the people do *proskynesis* to her as 'queen'. These shameless pranks were brought to an abrupt end by Alexander's return. As Harpalus could not hope for pardon, his only safety was in flight. He hit on the mad idea of staging a rebellion of Athens against Alexander by the use of Alexander's own money, and with thirty ships of war, an army of 6000 mercenaries which he had enlisted in the course of years, and a capital of 5000 talents from the treasury, he made his way to Greece. All this was destined to entail far-reaching consequences.

During this stay at Susa which lasted many months, and in the spring and summer of 324, are to be placed certain actions of Alexander, by which he gave clear expression to the thoughts which had ripened in his mind about his policy in Asia and about his relations to Greece. On the one hand we have the so-called 'Mass marriage at Susa', and on the other the demand he made of the Greeks for his 'apotheosis' and the decree on the 'restoration of the exiles'.

In connexion with his marriage to Roxane it was pointed out that it was the first indication that out of the military necessity of drafting Persians and other Iranians into his army, and under the influence of his maturing plans for world-dominion, the idea had grown up in him that these nations should be combined with his Macedonians into a dominant people, to whom he could entrust the defence of his Asiatic Empire, for which his Macedonians alone were not sufficient. After his successes in India, the more he was occupied with schemes of world domination, the more he seems to have become absorbed in this project of an amalgamation of the nations. Here it is to be noticed, though it is often overlooked, that Alexander did not aim at a universal world fraternity, but exclusively at an intermingling of his Macedonians with the Persians, heretofore the ruling nation, and with the Medes their kinsmen and the other Iranians, but not with Semites, Anatolians, Egyptians and other races.[1] At Susa he expressed this idea with unmistakeable plainness in an act of symbolic meaning before all the world, by arranging, for himself and eighty Macedonians who were nearest to his person, marriages with Persian and Iranian princesses and daughters of magnates. With unprecedented pomp a gigantic royal tent, in which Alexander was wont to hold his audiences, was erected on the model of the Persian *Apādana*, and the marriage ceremonies performed in it after the Persian rite, just as in the case of Roxane the Bactrian rite had been used. Chares, the court marshal, has left us valuable information both about this structure and the solemnities of the day. Alexander himself married Stateira, a daughter of Darius, certainly with the added motive of legitimising his sovereignty over Asia in the eyes of the Orientals by alliance with the

[1] [But see p. 311. That was the mixture that did take place.]

former ruling house; and his dearest friend Hephaestion married her sister Drypetis, because Alexander wanted their children to be cousins. Alexander himself provided the dowry for each of the young bridegrooms. In addition he gave wedding presents to the ordinary Macedonians, who then or previously had taken Asiatic wives. We are told that enquiry established their number as exceeding 10,000.

But in spite of all their king's generosity his Macedonians grumbled, when those young Persians named *Epigoni*, who had in the meantime been trained in Macedonian fashion, were paraded before him at Susa to the number of 30,000, and incorporated as a separate unit in the army. What specially annoyed them was that in the reorganisation of the army, which was a necessity after the return from India, Alexander, first in the case of the cavalry, proceeded from a system of parallel Macedonian and Persian formations to a mixture of both races in one, and went so far as to receive Persians and Iranians into the proud *Agema* Guard. The temperature became sultry and ominous, and anger gained strength among the Macedonians against their commander, who seemed to them ever more and more like an Asiatic Great King. To remedy this discontent, Alexander announced that he wished to pay back the debts which they had contracted in camp life during the campaign, but it became evident that their confidence in him had been shaken. For when he ordered that the debtors should declare in writing their names and the amount of their debts, many were afraid to do this. They feared he only wanted to find out which of them had not found their pay sufficient. The mistrust of his troops wounded him most deeply, and he told them that a king might only speak the truth to his subjects, and the subjects might only expect truth from their king. He then commanded that the money should be paid out to them, without the necessity of giving their names in writing.

From Susa Alexander turned his attention again to

affairs in Greece. Since the defeat of Agis and the inflic-
tion of punishment on the Spartans he had had neither
time nor cause to occupy himself with Hellas. Though after
the ending of the Panhellenic war of vengeance he still
was *Hegemon* of the Corinthian League, yet through the
colossal successes of the last years and through the extension of his empire to India the relation of power between
the *Hegemon* and the Greek allies had altered very much
to their disadvantage. Conscious of these superhuman
and extraordinary achievements, Alexander now issued
from Susa the request that he should be recognised as a
god by the Greek allies.

To understand this step we must first remove certain
misinterpretations which it has received. It is a widespread
error that Alexander, in the interest of the unity of his
world-empire, demanded worship as a divinity from all his
subjects. There is no indication to point to his having issued
this request to the Asiatics as well. The request is attested
in the case of the Greeks, and, as we may assume, only in
the case of the Greeks of the Corinthian League. This
makes it clear also that his request was not addressed to the
Macedonians; for Macedonia was outside the league.
The idea of a general official cult for the empire was
quite alien to Alexander, though his successors after his
death put his portrait on coins instead of the types of the
gods.

Equally erroneous is the conception, formerly widespread but held by some people even to-day, that the idea
of apotheosis was Oriental; and this is why they see in the
act a sign of the king's growing Orientalism. We may here
exclude from consideration the unique divine kingship of
Egypt, the effect of which even on Alexander was, as we
saw, quite local in its limitations. In the third millennium a
worship of the ruler as divine had been developed along
with the notion of world-empire in Mesopotamia; but from
Hammurabi (about 2000) onwards it had disappeared,
and thus—this is the important point—the Achaemenids

had never been worshipped as gods by their subjects. In Alexander's day the idea was quite unknown to the Asiatic East and cannot have been borrowed thence.

Modern scholarship has recognised that it is rather a purely Greek idea, which was called into life again by Alexander. With the Greeks the dividing line between gods and men, as their legends and myths bear out, had always been fluid. As Heracles had earned a place among the Olympians by his deeds, so in the bright light of history the mortal who had performed superhuman tasks in the eyes of his contemporaries, had in his lifetime been the recipient of divine honours. Lysander, for instance, when he was at the summit of his power, had been worshipped as a god with altars and paeans by the Samian oligarchs. Clearchus, tyrant of Heracleia, a pupil of Isocrates, had caused himself to be worshipped by his subjects as son of Zeus. Moreover Philip's partisans at Ephesus had set up his statue in the Temple of Artemis, and had thus paid him divine honours. When Philip himself at the marriage feast at Aegae (336) had his own image carried in a procession as the thirteenth along with the twelve chief gods of Macedonia, which made him appear, if not a god, at least as enthroned with the gods, one may conjecture in this the influence of Greek ideas upon the Macedonian court. Nor was it only practice that gave Alexander precedent; theory also played its part. His teacher Aristotle said in his *Politics*, that if there is a man who in ability and political capacity is incomparably superior to all others, such a man is 'as a god among men', and added that against such there is no law; 'for they are a law to themselves'. And had not Isocrates written to his father Philip in his latest letter that, if he forced the Great King to submission, nothing remained for him but to become a god? Had not Alexander now accomplished infinitely more than Philip?

*

It was in harmony with purely Greek ideas that after his victorious return from India he claimed divine honours from the Greeks. The idea was all the more familiar to him, because, seven years before, the priest of Ammon had greeted him as son of Zeus. If then he had not committed himself to proclaiming officially in the Greek world this divine sonship,[1] the announcement of which he had accepted with faith, in the sense of the Greek conception, as a divine revelation and a recognition of his superhuman divine force, yet this consciousness of a divine sonship had always remained in his mind. Possessed by it, elevated by his fabulous successes and in expectation of his plans for world-sovereignty, he now took the decisive step of going further than these special revelations, and of requiring divine honours from the Greeks of the Corinthian League. It is a mistaken view of Alexander's character to bar out this inner religious experience and to assume that the demand was a purely political move, the only object of which was to lift him as a god above the stipulations of the Corinthian League and to subject the autonomous Greek cities and their lands to his divine will.[2] Certainly his apotheosis, if accepted, meant a great increase of his personal prestige with the cities of the league, a consummation which could not but be desirable to him; and on the theory of Aristotle his will would then have been raised above the laws. But on the one hand, Alexander had already, as we saw, previously set himself above the provisions of the league treaty, without needing a divine authority, merely on the ground of his growing predominance, and he could continue to do the same. On the other hand the Greeks, though they admitted the apotheosis, did not on that account recognise his will as divine law, but—at any rate in the case of the Athenians—refused him obedience and were determined to resist him to the uttermost even by violence. In the practice of political life they made a distinction between the god whom they worshipped with a cult, and the earthly *Hegemon*, whose rights and duties were fixed in their eyes afterwards as before by the Covenant of the league. It must be mentioned that even later the Hellenistic cult of kings,

[1] Cp. p. 128.   [2] [So Tarn and E. Meyer think.]

though as imperial cult it meant more in the several Greek states than Alexander's apotheosis, was never an obstacle to disobedience, and had no influence whatever on the practice of political life.

This distinction between the political and religious spheres, along with the Greek character of the apotheosis, explains to us the fact that the Greeks complied with Alexander's wish without serious scruples. Naturally the members of the anti-Macedonian factions argued against it, but if those political consequences had really been bound up with the apotheosis, the opposition would have been of a different kind, and the speeches in the popular assemblies would not have been as harmless or as ironical in their tone as those that have been handed down to us; nor would a champion of freedom like Demosthenes, after an original protest, have finally advised the Athenian people to recognise the king 'as son of Zeus or as Poseidon too if he wished'. The indifference, which treated the question almost as a bagatelle, demonstrates that it was a question not of high politics but of religion, which in the opinion of the *illuminati* to whom the old polytheism was no longer possessed of any meaning, had no exciting importance.

We are ill-informed how the affair was managed. That the initiative proceeded from Alexander is certain; but we do not hear in what shape it reached the Greeks. It can scarcely have been a command, but more probably a desire which he either expressed or caused to be expressed to the *Synhedrion*, and which, however formulated, was indubitably equivalent to a demand. The *Synhedrion* may then have communicated the desire to the several members of the league; for actually no uniform league cult was created, but the individual states by popular decree received the king among the gods of their community. What form they chose, whether as god or as son of a god (see Demosthenes), was obviously entirely left to them. The prevailing assumption that at Athens, on the proposal of

Demades, Alexander received his cult as the 'new Dionysus' has recently been proved erroneous.[1]

In the spring of the next year (323) ambassadors from
Hellas reached Alexander at Babylon to honour him with
golden crowns. They appeared not as envoys to an earthly
king, but with wreaths on their heads as 'festal ambassadors' (*Theoroi*) who come to a god, as Arrian states.
Hellas had complied with his desire.

The effort to rearrange affairs in Greece called forth as
well new orders of Alexander, issued from Susa in the
spring of 324. This time they were commands, and he sent
them to the *Synhedrion* by Nicanor of Stagira. The one
which concerned the local leagues of the Achaeans, Arcadians and Boeotians, is obscure to us, because we have
it only in a mutilated form. The other edict was very important. By it Alexander ordered that in the territory of the
league all exiles—with the exception of temple-robbers and
murderers, usually omitted from amnesties—should return
to their homes and be entirely or partially reinstated in
their previous properties. The sanction was added, that in
case any city refused to receive its exiles back Antipater,
the representative of Alexander, was to compel them by
force. Politically one must regard this decree as an act of
wise statesmanship. Alexander attacked one of the worst
cancers of the Greek system of small states and endeavoured to remove it; and one will esteem the decree all the
more highly, because under existing political conditions
many of the exiles to be restored must have been his political opponents, whom he might hope to reconcile by this
act. On the other hand it is obvious that this order, issued
by Alexander alone, without any co-operation of the *Synhedrion*, was a glaring violation of the Covenant of the
league. Though the paragraph in question is not preserved to us, yet according to the spirit of the Covenant it
cannot be doubtful that an arrangement like this could

[1] A. D. Nock, *Journal of Hellenic Studies*, xlviii. p. 21; *ib.*, W. W. Tarn,
p. 217.

only be made by the co-operation of *Hegemon* and *Syn-hedrion*.

We may emphasise the fact that in the tedious discussions of this edict no trace is anywhere to be found of any reference to the religious importance that Alexander obtained by apotheosis in the league cities. This last stage of the way to the ignoring of the *Synhedrion* and the forming of an autocratic position is rather to be explained exclusively by Alexander's vastly increased consciousness of power. The decree is not a result of the claim to apotheosis, which, as we have shown, had no political object; on the contrary, both have their roots in the same psychological fact. In the decree speaks the man who was aiming at world-sovereignty and was determined to shake off the inconvenient fetters of the Covenant of the league. To the *Synhedrion*, to which Nicanor handed the original edict, fell merely, it appears, the task of communicating copies of it to all the members of the league. In this last stage of his development Alexander used the *Synhedrion* simply as the place of publication for the expression of his absolute and omnipotent will. It was probably under the impression of the news thus heard from Susa—the mass marriages with Persian women and this edict—that Aristotle sent to Alexander the well-known warning to treat the Hellenes as a *Hegemon* and the barbarians as a despot.[1] Teacher and pupil could no longer understand each other.

Among the exiles this decree naturally evoked the greatest enthusiasm. When Nicanor at the Olympic Games of 324 in the festival assembly, to which the exiles had collected at the news of what was impending, caused a letter of Alexander to be read by the herald, in which the king communicated to the exiles the contents of his edict, there was a loud shout of joy in the *Altis*. It may be an exaggeration to put the number of the exiles who had gathered together as high as 20,000; yet the number gives us an

---

[1] [This date (324) is independently given by the author and Wilamowitz, *Aristoteles und Athen*, i. 339, note 39.]

approximate conception of the extent of the revolutions in political life and the tenure of property in the Greek states that must have been brought about by the execution of the edict. How difficult the process was, is shown by an inscription from Tegea.[1]

It is conceivable therefore that when Nicanor appeared in Hellas with this edict in the spring of 324, and the object of his mission became notorious, great excitement and unrest seized the cities. Athens was hardest hit; it had to return to the Samian exiles the island of Samos, which it had occupied a generation before and distributed among Athenian cleruchs. The Aetolians too became restive, for they had to receive exiles into the Acarnanian town of Oeniadae, which they had occupied. It was consequently into an atmosphere of great tension that Harpalus arrived, the unfaithful treasurer of Alexander, who, as we saw (p. 207), had run away with his stolen treasures, and, to save himself, speculated on raising Athens to revolt against Alexander by means of his ill-gotten gains. Since previously he had supported Athens with grain, on the occasions of great scarcity which befell Hellas between 330 and 326, and in reward had been granted Attic citizenship, he now hoped to be admitted into the Piraeus. By the advice of Demosthenes he was denied entrance, and a correct attitude was adopted. But when he had left at Taenarum his army and fleet and the bulk of his treasure, and came again with only two triremes, craving admission as a 'suppliant', he was admitted into the Piraeus by Philocles, *strategos* for 325–4 (and consequently before the change of officials in 324). The question what was to be done with Harpalus was all the more delicate, for messengers had already appeared in Athens demanding his surrender, sent by Philoxenus, Alexander's director of finance for Asia Minor. As no direct commands from Alexander had arrived, it was possible to adopt the expedient suggested by Demosthenes of arresting him for the time being

[1] [Dittenberger, *Sylloge*³, 306.]

and depositing his stolen moneys on the Acropolis for Alexander.

After an interval, however, Harpalus escaped from Athens, and the people received with surprise the information that only half the money he had brought with him, which by his statement amounted to 700 talents, had been deposited on the Acropolis. What had become of the other half? It is significant of the low moral standard of political life at Athens, that it was assumed as a matter of course that the missing sum had been employed by Harpalus in the bribery of leading politicians. Then began the notorious 'Harpalus trial', which vividly exhibits the absolute rottenness of Attic democracy at the time. It is not the place here to relate in detail how the investigation of the case was committed to the Areopagus on the proposal of Demosthenes, how the Areopagus, early in 323, after six months' delay published a report on the guilty persons with the amount of the bribes they had taken, and how the popular tribunal inflicted heavy fines on those whom the Areopagus had declared guilty. Among the condemned, who belonged to different political parties, was Demosthenes, who, as he could not pay the fine of 50 talents, was imprisoned,[1] but soon afterwards escaped to Troezen.

This affair of Harpalus, in which it was a question of moneys, which, though Alexander's property, had disappeared into the pockets of political leaders at Athens, was not exactly calculated to improve the relations between Athens and the king, which had already been severely strained by the decree concerning the exiles; on the contrary, Athens was deeply compromised in the eyes of Alexander. The tension grew into an increasing opposition to him, as the people were determined not to obey the royal command concerning the surrender of Samos. Alexander did not intend to give way, and soon wild rumours

[1] [Plutarch, *Demosthenes* 26, uses the same phrase as Demosthenes, *On the Trierarchic Crown*, LI, 8, which implies the special executive action of the Council.]

circulated about an impending collision in arms. That such thoughts were also expressed by the retinue of Alexander is revealed by the statement, that at a great feast in Ecbatana in the autumn of 324 a certain Gorgus of Iasus, one of Alexander's body-guard, known to us by documents as a patron of the Samians, had a proclamation made by a herald that should Alexander besiege Athens, he would present to him 10,000 equipments and as many catapults and all other artillery in sufficient quantity. In spite of this heated state of feeling the contemporary negotiations about the apotheosis of Alexander led to the acceptance of the demand; as we saw, this question was not conceived as a political one, and the Athenians like the rest of the Greeks felt themselves in no way bound by their recognition of Alexander's divinity to obey his earthly commands. Perhaps by this concession they thought to make him more inclined to yield on the greater political question.

In the beginning of the summer of 324 Alexander had left Susa to visit Ecbatana, the splendid Median capital of the Achaemenids. He despatched the major part of the army to the Tigris under Hephaestion, while he himself with the hypaspists and some chosen corps used the opportunity to sail down the Eulaeus into the Persian Gulf with Nearchus' fleet; since his return to Persepolis the 'longing' had seized him to sail on the Persian Gulf, as previously on the Indian Ocean, and to make himself acquainted with the mouths of the Tigris and the Euphrates. When he had satisfied the longing, he went back up the Tigris and rejoined Hephaestion. After removing, in his progress, the dams constructed by the Persians to foil attacks from the sea, he came with his army to Opis.

Here, at the nearest point to Babylon and the line of communication with the West, he wanted to dismiss his veterans to their homes. This led to a terrible scene. When Alexander made known to the assembly of the Macedonian army his well-meant decision, to send home with rich presents those veterans who from age or wounds were no longer fit to fight, there was an outburst of anger against the king for his attitude to Persians and Persian ways, and especially against the military reforms at Susa, which seemed to indicate a preference for the Persians and so annoyed them most deeply. Behind his resolution they suspiciously scented the intention of separating himself altogether from the Macedonians as people unfit for war; and so in open mutiny the assembly shouted at him that they would all go home, and scornfully added, he might take the field with his 'father'. From this allusion to Ammon one must not conclude that Alexander had in any way demanded of the Macedonians recognition of his sonship to Ammon. Just because the idea of divine sonship was something quite foreign to them, they mistook its real meaning, and saw in it merely a reflection on their revered king Philip. Now, in a moment of mad passion, it was their one object to wound the king personally as deeply as possible. In that they succeeded. Scarcely had Alexander heard these words, with which the most sacred experience of his inner life was publicly ridiculed, when he jumped down from the tribune with his officers among the mutineers, caused the hypaspists to arrest the ringleaders, thirteen in number, whom he pointed out with his hand, and lead them off to execution.

He was now master of the situation. Silence fell on the tumultuous assembly, and no one dared to say a word. Amid a complete hush Alexander ascended the tribune. In tacit rejection of the distorted view of his relation to his divine father, which had been expressed in that scornful cry, he began his speech with an acknowledgment of his earthly father, whom as a matter of fact he had never disowned. With burning words he reproached the soldiers for their ingratitude, and recalled to them how much they owed to his father Philip, who found them at the beginning of his reign wretched herdsmen, dressed in sheepskins and feeding their cattle on the mountains, and made them the ruling people in Greece. Then he reminded them of all he himself had done for them, how he had made them lords of the East, and with them shared all dangers and fatigues. But he would not detain them; they should all return to Macedonia and tell the people there that they had left their king to the protection of the vanquished barbarians. With the word of command 'Dismiss' he jumped down from the tribune and shut himself up in the royal castle, refusing to see anyone.

Nor could anyone get speech with him the next day. The Macedonians were at their wits' end; they had not seriously intended, what they had cried out in the heat of passion, that they would all leave him, but he had taken them at their word. They were all dismissed and felt the disgrace deeply. What were they to do? On the third day Alexander sent for the noble Persians and distributed among them appointments in the army, and gave the non-Macedonian formations, especially the *Epigoni*, the proud names 'Persian *Agema*', 'Persian *Pezhetairoi*' and so on. Moreover he appointed several of the Persian nobles as his 'kinsmen', who alone by Persian custom had the right to salute the king with a kiss. When the Macedonians heard of this counter-measure their last resistance was broken. They rushed to the castle, threw their arms down before the gate, cried out and begged for pardon. Then Alexander came out of the gate, and when he saw his old comrades in arms repentant before him, his anger was dissipated, and tears burst from his eyes. When emotion made him speechless and an old Macedonian officer stepped up and respectfully said to him that the appointment of Persians as 'kinsmen' gave them especial pain, he cried out 'I make you all my kinsmen', and the old Macedonian was the first to be allowed to kiss him.

Thus peace was restored between the king and his Macedonians. Alexander had won a complete victory by the overpowering forcefulness of his nature. He had brought the mutinous troops back to obedience, and even attached them more closely to himself without making any conces-

sion. But there was still lacking the reconciliation between
Macedonians and Persians, which in the interest of his
empire was the darling wish of his heart. With this in view,
he now instituted a great feast of reconciliation. At the
table the Macedonians sat next to the king, after them the
Persians and some leading men of other nationalities, in all,
we are told, 9000 persons. The feast began with the liba-
tions which Alexander and his guests poured to the gods
out of the same mixing bowl, the conduct of the ceremony
being in the hands of Greek soothsayers and Persian
Magians. In the sacrificial prayers Alexander uttered the
wish that besides all other good things concord and partnership in rule might be granted to Macedonians and Persians.
He could not have revealed his political aims more clearly:
the two nations, conquerors and conquered, were to live in
harmony with one another and rule conjointly. In this he
saw the strongest possible prop for the future of his Asiatic
empire; this alone is the natural reference of the words.
Nor were the different religions of the two nations to be
any obstacle to their political and cultural amalgamation,
and so, as if to set the pattern, he caused Greek soothsayers
and Persian Magians to function side by side. This moment is a very great one in the life of Alexander; thoughts
which had long occupied him, suddenly came to the light
of day, clearly defined. Recently,[1] however, out of this
'prayer of Opis' has been read a confession of the brotherhood of humanity and through Stoic doctrine it has been
connected with Christianity. These ideas ascribed to Alexander were quite strange to him. The actual prayer makes
it most plain that the ideal which was before him was
simply the fraternisation of Macedonians and Persians.
There is no trace whatever of Alexander's treating all mankind as one brotherhood.

The festivals were followed by the dismissal, as previously
designed by Alexander, of about 10,000 veterans. The consequence was that the old Macedonian elements in the

[1] W. W. Tarn, *Cambridge Ancient History*, vi. 437.

army who were most hostile to his new idea, were lessened, and this must have been welcome to him. To each man on discharge he gave not only his pay up to his arrival home, but a talent besides. He retained the children whom Asiatic wives had borne to them, in order to prevent family dissensions at home, and promised to educate them in Macedonian fashion, to train them as soldiers, and later, when young men, himself to take them to their fathers in Macedonia. He committed to Craterus, who stood next to him after Hephaestion, and was very popular with the Macedonians, the task of leading the veterans back. Craterus was also ordered to replace Antipater as imperial viceroy in Europe, while Antipater was to come out to the camp with fresh troops. The reason for this exchange was partly because the relations between Antipater and the imperious Olympias had constantly led to quarrels and complaints on both sides, which were painful to Alexander as a son. There was the further reason that the policy of Antipater towards Hellas, on account of its oligarchic colouring, did not harmonise with Alexander's views. And so Craterus, the new viceroy, was instructed to see to 'the freedom of the Greeks', a phrase which doubtless refers to the clauses about freedom in the Covenant of the league. Thus while the decree about the exiles was causing commotion in Greece, Alexander as *Hegemon* took his stand on the maintenance of the Covenant.

From Opis Alexander and his army went over Mt. Zagros to Ecbatana. The authorities tell us nothing about any measures of government taken during this residence of several months in the Median capital. Compared with the feverish activity which Alexander manifested immediately after his arrival at Babylon in the spring of 323, these months at Ecbatana are like the calm before a storm. Certainly his program of action was fixed and ready when he appeared at Babylon. We may therefore assume that his future plans took definite shape at Ecbatana at the latest, and, as was always the case before new undertakings, were carefully worked out, if indeed he did not begin them in the equally long and quiet stay at Susa.

What was the nature of these plans? With his return to Susa Alexander could regard the conquest of Asia as essentially complete, though certain regions in northern Asia Minor had not yet been subjugated. His Indian campaign showed us that he could not remain content with the occupation of the Achaemenid Empire, but was impelled, not merely by the desire of conquest but also by the joy of scientific discovery, to reach out beyond its limits, to the furthest confines of the inhabited world. Though he was obliged to stop at the Hyphasis, and was unable to reach his goal, the Ocean, yet the voyage down the Indus had led him into the Indian Ocean, and had caused him to establish by means of Nearchus the connexion between the delta of the Indus and the mouths of the Euphrates and the Tigris, thereby fixing the southern limit of Asia. This result was now to be exploited for the trade of the empire by the settlement of these coasts, especially those of the Persian Gulf, a notion which had been before his mind already, as the instructions to Nearchus showed.

But new problems had in the meantime come up in Alexander's restless brain. The opposite coast of Arabia was still unexplored, and the shape of the country unknown. Might it not be possible to find a way round Arabia to Egypt, and institute a connexion by sea between Babylon and Alexandria? Magnificent prospects for the intercommunication and commerce of the empire opened before him. Great advances were to be expected in the geographical views of the ocean and of the world. Immediately after returning to Babylon Alexander ordered an expedition to circumnavigate Arabia; the limits of the Achaemenid Empire were again to be transcended.

At that time he was much absorbed by oceanographical problems, as we may observe from his intense interest in the old problem of the Caspian Sea, which had occupied him when he stayed on its southern shore (330). 'He was

seized by the longing', run the words again. He sent a *
certain Heraclides with orders to build ships there, sail
across the Caspian and so establish whether it was really
an inland sea, as Aristotle had taught him, and not rather
a bay of the ocean, as the old Ionians had assumed, and as
had appeared debatable to him himself after the discovery
of the Indian Ocean. At the same time, it is possible that
considerations of commercial policy may have contributed
to the mission. Owing to Alexander's death neither this
undertaking nor the Arabian expedition was carried out.

These are the expeditions which Alexander actually set
on foot in the few months of life yet granted him. Scarcely
was he dead, than there were found in the royal archives
memoranda, which disclosed that the Arabian expedition
was only the prelude to still vaster plans. These official
memoranda (*Hypomnemata*) contained probably the working out and calculations as to the technical accomplishment of his last plans, and the military and financial resources required for them.[1] We possess only a brief table
of contents, from which it appears that 1000 warships
of larger type than triremes were to be built in Phoenicia,
Syria, Cilicia and Cyprus for a campaign against the Carthaginians and the other coast peoples who lived in Africa,
Spain, and the coasts adjoining up to Sicily. It is mentioned also that a road was to be made along the African
coast to the Pillars of Heracles, and that in correspondence
with the requirements of so great a naval enterprise harbours and docks were to be constructed at suitable places.

These accounts of the *Hypomnemata* indicate nothing less
than that Alexander, after becoming lord of Asia, actually
thought of a conquest of the whole world. He is probably
the only man in history who conceived this gigantic plan
of becoming 'world ruler' in the proper sense of the word. *
His empire now reached westwards—in the north to the
Adriatic, in the south to Cyrene, which was a friendly

[1] [Tarn holds that the *Hypomnemata* were a compilation not earlier
than 200 B.C. and perhaps later; *Journal of Hellenic Studies*, 1921, p. 1.]

ally; in these last plans it was a question of winning the coasts of the western Mediterranean. Obviously the first stroke was to be aimed at Carthage, which was then the most important naval and commercial power in the West. Whether he would have succeeded in carrying out his plans, is a question, the answer to which is beyond the competence of the historian; but one can scarcely deny the possibility in the case of Alexander, who accomplished so much that was apparently impossible.[1] Another question is whether he would have succeeded in forming out of the then-known world an empire which would have had any prospect of continuance. The question is probably to be answered in the negative. Created simply by his unique personality, this empire would have lost its vitality with his death. That later on the Roman world-empire maintained itself vigorously for centuries, is no argument to the contrary; in this case for generation on generation stone was laid on stone, till the colossal building stood firmly compacted, borne by the iron will to power of a strong nation. Alexander, on the other hand, would have at most created an ephemeral episode, since for such ideas he had neither the Macedonians nor the Greeks behind him— he stood quite alone.

We should assume *a priori*, on the analogy of the careful preliminary preparation of Alexander's other enterprises, that in these plans he was not indulging merely in baseless fancies, but had endeavoured beforehand as much as possible to obtain information about the strength of the various states of the West and their political relation to one another. We happen to know that, when he was in the Far East, he sent for the 'Sicilian History' of the expert Philistus, the statesman of Dionysius I, through which he could certainly obtain a deep insight into the wars of the Western Greeks with the Carthaginians and their Italian neighbours. Another thing gave him a personal interest in the

---

[1] [The author does not deign to confute Livy (IX, 17-18). The comparison of Alexander to Papirius Cursor is certainly ludicrous.]

problems of the Western Greeks and to some extent information about them: his brother-in-law, Alexander the Molossian, at the time when he himself crossed into Asia, entered the service of the Tarentines to fight for them against the Lucanians and Bruttians of Lower Italy, and lost his life in the war. Certainly nothing now was further from Alexander's thoughts than a Panhellenic policy like that of his early years, but it is more than possible that in a conquest of the West it would have been his concern to rescue the Greek element there, and to make Greek culture dominant in the region of the Western Mediterranean. That he had actually begun already to think and work out the necessary military preparations for this campaign, is evident in the scanty extracts from the *Hypomnemata*, together with his notes on the building of a fleet and the construction of a road in stages.

Some modern writers have rejected as a later legend these notes from the *Hypomnemata*.[1] But the notes go back to a first-class source, Hieronymus of Cardia, and we have no right to strike them out of Alexander's history. Psychologically it is quite intelligible that he should have formed these plans of ruling the world. In ten years he had subjected all Asia up to India; no nation and no fortress had been able to resist him. He was a young man of thirty-two, and humanly speaking could count on a long life. Did it correspond to his perpetual delight in the onset of battle and his constant 'longing' for the limits of the world, now to lay aside the sword and to devote the rest of his life to building up peacefully what he had won? That would be a new Alexander, and would have little in common with the historical figure. We have no right to reject this well-attested and credible statement of the *Hypomnemata*. Without these latest plans of world-conquest we should draw an incomplete and incorrect picture of Alexander.

We may take it that he kept these plans secret, and only

---

[1] [W. W. Tarn, *Journal of Hellenic Studies*, xli. 1921, pp. 1 ff. The author replies in *Berl. Akad. Abh.* 1928, xxx. p. 593.]

discussed and worked them out in a narrow circle of inti-
mates. There were very few who were ready to follow him
on these dizzy paths. The only man in his suite who completely understood him was the friend of his youth,
Hephaestion. All the more terrible was his loss, when at
Ecbatana during an orgiastic festival of Dionysus this friend
was carried off by a fatal fever. In passionate sorrow Alexander gave himself up to mourning. For three days he lay
by his friend's corpse without taking food or drink. Achilles
mourned for his Patroclus. Many stories circulated afterwards regarding the forms in which his pain expressed itself. How much is true, it is difficult to decide. It is certain
that he wished at once to see his dead friend elevated to
the divine sphere. He sent messengers to the oasis of Siwah
to ask his father Ammon whether he might sacrifice to
Hephaestion as hero or as god. He ordered Perdiccas to
take the corpse to Babylon, where a monument of unheard-
of magnificence and costliness was to be erected to him.
To immortalise the name of the deceased in the army, the
hipparchy of the *Hetairoi*, which he had commanded as
Chiliarch, was called 'Hephaestion's chiliarchy'. On the
other hand, the office of Grand Vizier, which Hephaestion
had held with the title of Chiliarch, was not filled at all.
The place next to the king remained empty.

At last Alexander roused himself from mourning and began the march back to Babylon. On the way he took the
field against the Cossaeans, a warlike and predatory tribe
in Mt. Zagros, who, relying on their lurking-places in the
lofty mountains, had maintained their independence of the
Great Kings. Being now attacked in winter, they could not
retire to their snow-covered mountain heights, but had to
oppose Alexander in the valleys. In forty days their subjection was completed.

As he continued his march to Babylon, he was met on the
way by embassies from the most different peoples of the
earth, ready to do homage to the new lord of the East.
From Africa came Libyans and possibly Ethiopians, and

above all Carthaginians. From Italy came Lucanians and Bruttians, Etruscans and Romans, from the far West perhaps also Iberians and Celts. The sending of these embassies was an echo of the news that he had returned as victor from India. By the variety of these envoys we get an idea of the deep impression made on the peoples of the West by the erection of the powerful empire of Alexander, and of the majesty with which his personality was surrounded in the eyes of the whole world. Though these peoples certainly knew nothing yet of those latest plans of world-conquest, nevertheless from the Carthaginians at least, who had already suffered a severe loss of prestige in the conquest of Tyre, their metropolis, and in the foundation of Egyptian Alexandria, the fear was not distant that Alexander, who by alliance with Cyrene had advanced to their flank, would one day threaten their land or damage it by his trade policy. At any rate, by the union of the whole East in the hand of one who had never been conquered, a new factor of power was created, which was bound to put the politicians of the West on their guard—all the more so, the less they could for the moment see through Alexander's future plans—and to make them endeavour to cultivate good relations with this new power. Apart from the general situation, special occasions for the sending of embassies may be conjectured for the Italian peoples: for the Lucanians and Bruttians, on account of their war with Alexander's brother-in-law, Alexander the Molossian; and for the Etruscans because of their piracies which had endangered members of the Corinthian League. As to the Romans, it is in itself not easy to believe that then, in the middle of the Samnite War, they sent an embassy to Babylon. Yet one will not, like the ex-consul of Rome, Arrian, reject this statement, when one hears from another source that Alexander had once already sent a severe reprimand to the Romans on account of the share of the Antiates in the piracies of the Etruscans. If one reflects that Alexander, when he received all these envoys, was already secretly

planning a war of conquest against the West, one can imagine with what keen interest he will have regarded these
people and talked to them, in order, if possible, to get more
exact information about their countries.

When he crossed the Tigris to approach Babylon, he
was encountered by envoys of the 'Chaldaeans', who
warned him against entering Babylon; for according to an
oracle given by Marduk this would be bad for him. Alexander had some reason to scent behind this a lie of the
crafty priests; he had learned that they had only carelessly
obeyed and soon ignored the command which he had
given them in 331 to rebuild the temple of Marduk destroyed by Xerxes, because by the completion of the work
they would lose the rich temple revenues, which now
flowed into their pockets. He therefore rejected their warning. But when they begged him at least to enter the city
from the west and not from the east, he was willing to meet
them in this, but soon saw that the marshes in the west
made this impossible. So in spite of the warnings of the
priests he entered the city from the east. Naturally the
oracle was regarded as fulfilled in his death soon afterwards.

The first thing he did in Babylon was to throw himself
with fiery zeal into the preparations for his Arabian expedition. He did not intend a conquest of the Arabian
mainland; but at most some spots on the coast or adjacent
islands, which offered good harbours or were suitable for
stations, were to be occupied, in order to serve as support
for the future voyages of trading ships. The grand object-
ive was the circumnavigation of Arabia, the discovery of
the way into the Red Sea and up it to Heroonpolis (near
Suez), and the establishment of a connexion by sea between Babylon and Alexandria. For this expedition a fleet
had to be collected at Babylon. The ocean fleet of Nearchus, which had sailed up the Euphrates to Babylon,
awaited the king there, and was to be increased by ships
built with the cypresses of Babylonia. Orders too were
given for warships to be built in the reliable dockyards of

the Phoenician cities; divided into sections, they were to be transported overland to Thapsacus, put together again there, and brought down the Euphrates to Babylon.

At the same time Alexander caused a beginning to be made with the excavation of a great harbour at Babylon, so big that it could hold, Arrian says, 1000 warships with their ship-houses. This is only a figure, which does not warrant the conclusion that Alexander then or later wanted to collect 1000 warships there. The gigantic harbour was rather intended not only for the Asiatic war fleet, which was much smaller, but as a station for merchant ships as well; in the future Alexander counted on a great development of trade by sea between India, the Persian Gulf and Egypt, and Babylon was to be the chief place of exchange for this eastern trade. In general, Babylon, in accordance with its ancient tradition, was made by Alexander once more the centre of the Asiatic world. The prevailing view that he made Babylon the permanent capital of his whole empire is erroneous. That is true only of his Asiatic empire. If his western plans materialised, he could not rule his world-empire from Babylon. By its positoin Alexandria in Egypt was excellently adapted for the purpose, at least as capital for the western part of his world-empire.

In the first instance, before the voyage with the fleet began, the coast of Arabia had to be explored as far as possible. Alexander had previously despatched in a thirty-oared vessel Archias of Pella, who had already approved himself in a high position during Nearchus' voyage. But Archias did not venture further than the island of Tylos (Bahrein) in the Persian Gulf. After he had given in his report, Androsthenes of Thasos was despatched with the same object in a like craft. He also does not seem to have got beyond Tylos, but he brought back valuable observations on the flora of the island. As by his description it has been calculated that he saw it in winter (Dec.-Jan.), it follows that these voyages of exploration were ordered from Ecbatana (324-5). The third to be sent was Hieron

of Soloi, who received positive orders to go round Arabia
to Heroonpolis. He got at least as far as the promontory of Maketa, which Nearchus had seen from Ormuz.
But when he saw how endlessly far the coast stretched
beyond that promontory, he returned and announced to
Alexander that Arabia was astonishingly large, not much
smaller than India. As barren of result was the synchronous
expedition of Anaxicrates, whom Alexander ordered to
take the reverse direction and go from Heroonpolis round
Arabia into the Persian Gulf. He passed through the
strait of Bab-el-Mandeb, but returned for lack of water.

All these accounts show that Alexander and his contemporaries had no idea of the shape and size of Arabia; but
they also show how passionately in spite of these failures
he pressed forward the preparations for his great sea expedition. He caused the fleet to carry out manœuvres on
the Euphrates, and offered wreaths as prizes for the best
rowers and steersmen. This time he himself intended to
accompany the fleet, which not only shows his personal
interest in this voyage of discovery, but perhaps permits
the inference that he meant by this route to appear again
in the Mediterranean at Alexandria, and then to address
himself to his great plans for the West.

Meanwhile he also took steps to put in hand his plan of
settlement of the north coast of the Persian Gulf. From the
reports of Nearchus he had become convinced that by
regular settlement of the coast and adjacent islands a
'second Phoenicia' could be created. He now sent Miccalus
of Clazomenae with 500 talents to Phoenicia and Syria,
in order to enlist suitable people there out of the seafaring
population, and also to buy slaves who might be settled in
those parts.

To promote this eastern trade, on the gulf between the
mouths of the Eulaeus and Tigris an 'Alexandria-Charax'
was founded (perhaps in 324, when he visited this region),
a town which was suited by its position to become the
chief export harbour for Babylon, while, to promote navi-

gation, he had already in 324 removed the Persian dams on the Tigris. Above all Alexander was anxious to enhance the prosperity of the whole of Babylonia by an improved regulation of the network of canals. That had been always, since the days of Hammurabi, the chief task prescribed by nature to the rulers of Babylon—a task which to-day once more is occupying modern engineering—so to regulate the annual inundations of the Euphrates and Tigris by canals and dikes that they might become a blessing instead of a curse to the land. With complete understanding of what was required Alexander devoted himself to the work in person. From Babylon he undertook a voyage of inspection through the canal area, and examined and repaired the bunds on the canal of Pallacottas, which was intended to win a great part of the desert for cultivation. He also travelled on this canal into the lakes bounding the Arabian desert, and, probably for protection against Bedouin Arabs, founded an Alexandria, in which he settled Greek mercenaries, volunteers, and veterans.

When he returned from this voyage to Babylon, he found Peucestas, the satrap of Persis, there, who had brought 20,000 Persians trained for the army, Cossaeans, Tapurians, and other efficient troops from the neighbouring peoples. From Caria and Lydia too came new troops, as well as reinforcements of cavalry from Macedonia. The arrival of these new military units, especially of the 20,000 Persians, caused Alexander again to undertake a reorganisation of the army. It was the last he executed or at least began. Instead of placing Macedonian and Persian units side by side (the arrangement introduced at Opis, rather in the heat of conflict than after calm consideration) he resolved on bringing about in the military units a real amalgamation of the two peoples, which would correspond most nearly with his political intentions. This meant the complete abandonment of the old Macedonian phalanx. For each of its smallest units, the decads, was in future to consist of four Macedonians, armed in Macedonian fashion, and twelve Persians, who were armed either with bows or javelins, the command being entrusted to a Macedonian. Apart from the close connexion of the two peoples, it was an attempt at an organic combination of different arms within the same cadre. In judging this peculiar experiment we must not, as is usually done, overlook the fact that it was certainly intended solely for the Asiatic empire, since it can be explained only by Alexander's Asiatic policy; in Macedonia of course the old phalanx was to continue in being. The death of Alexander soon afterwards prevented the complete execution of this novel idea. This Macedonian-Persian army never came into action; after Alexander's death the whole policy of amalgamation was abandoned, and its military product with it. At any rate we may be sure that if this new army failed to approve itself in practice, Alexander would not have hesitated to replace it by another organisation, just as he removed the Persian satraps, when they did not approve themselves.

This spring many embassies from Greece reached Babylon. They had been sent there with the most varied petitions. Many of them approached the king with golden crowns, themselves garlanded, 'like Theoroi, who came to honour a god', and thus testified that their native city had introduced his apotheosis (p. 213). Those ambassadors who had to make representations against the decree for the recall of the exiles had to return home unsuccessful; Alexander never dreamed of concession.

About May his envoys returned from the oasis of Siwah, and announced that Ammon had declared that Hephaestion should be reverenced as a hero. Though the idea of a divine cult was thereby rejected, Alexander was highly delighted that the oracle sanctioned the middle course, and forthwith gave orders that Hephaestion should receive heroic honours. In particular he sent orders to Cleomenes of Naucratis to erect two *heroa* of great size and extraordinary splendour to Hephaestion in Alexandria, one in the city itself, the other on the island of Pharos. This was

so near to his heart that we are told he promised to Cleomenes a general pardon for all past and future official
lapses, if he did justice to the commission. But the death of
the king soon after stopped its execution; Ptolemy, the
new satrap, to whom Cleomenes was subordinate, had no
idea of erecting the *heroa*. That Alexander intended these
monuments to be erected in Egyptian Alexandria, is another indication that according to his plans at the time
this city was to play a special part in his world-empire.

After the arrival of the message from Ammon, the actual
funeral of Hephaestion took place at Babylon. With this
the general mourning, ordered by Alexander for the whole
country, came to an end. Hephaestion was no longer the
dead man but the hero, and Alexander was the first to
offer to him the sacrifice appropriate to a hero (*Enagisma*).

A very difficult problem is raised by the great monument which after Hephaestion's death Alexander ordered
in his honour at Babylon. The description Diodorus gives
us of it sounds quite fantastic, and yet it might be based on
the actual design. The work was entrusted to the architect
Deinocrates, who had drawn the plans for Egyptian Alexandria. On a surface one stadion square, the monument
was to rise to a height of over 130 cubits, in five stories becoming smaller, as they rose higher. The outer walls of these
stories were to be decorated with unheard-of magnificence.
On the lowest exterior were to be placed 240 gilded beaks
of *Pentereis* (quinqueremes, the largest type of vessel), and
on their *hérissons* were to be set kneeling archers and other
figures of 4-5 cubits in height. On the second story gigantic
torches (15 cubits high) were to be fastened, decorated with
golden crowns and eagles flying upwards, to which snakes
looked up from below. Round the third story was to run
a hunting scene; round the fourth a gilded Centauro-
machy; round the fifth lions and bulls alternately. Above
that the structure was to be finished off with Macedonian
and 'barbarian' weapons—certainly not, as Diodorus
thinks, to signify victory and defeat, but to symbolise the

amalgamation of the Macedonians and Persians in one army, which the king was then trying to carry out; for no doubt the 'barbarian' weapons were Persian. At the apex of the whole were to stand gigantic sirens, hollow inside to contain the singers, who, themselves unseen, were to sing their songs from within. The expenses of this fabulously wonderful structure were calculated at 10,000-12,000 talents. It is very interesting to see how in this last artistic design of Alexander's epoch the ideas of Greek and of Oriental art were blended; that the Babylonian ziggurats—though not stepped buildings like this, but inclined planes—influenced the shape of this structure, is beyond all doubt.

As most of our authorities, including Arrian, call this building a pyre, it is generally assumed that it was burned together with the corpse of Hephaestion. This cannot however be correct, nor is it stated by Diodorus, to whom we owe the above description. In reality the building, as we learn from the above-mentioned *Hypomnemata*, was still unfinished when Alexander died. How could it be conceivable that the gigantic structure with its wealth of varied works of art could be made in the few months between the deaths of Hephaestion and Alexander? It was never completed; by order of the assembly of the army it was stopped for ever after Alexander's death. The authorities, Justin and Plutarch, who call this monument not a pyre but a tomb (*tumulus, tymbos*) are probably right. Alexander's idea probably was to found a stately *heroon* to his favourite friend, which in size and costliness was to be a worthy peer of the colossal buildings of Babylon, and in the heart of Asia was to proclaim for ever the fame of Hephaestion, as the *heroa* of Alexandria would do to the western world. In the ornamentation of the exterior it is tempting to look for special reference to Hephaestion's relation to Alexander. In the hunting scene obviously there is an allusion to the king's companion of the chase. The ship-beaks and the Macedonian and Persian arms might point to Hephaestion having been Alexander's faithful helper in his maritime plans and in his policy of amalgamation. It was precisely these ideas which were then most profoundly occupying the king.

The conclusion of the period of mourning and the solemnities in honour of the new hero were immediately succeeded by the last preparations for the start of the Arabian expedition, which was to follow in a few days. In the meantime Alexander offered the usual sacrifices for a successful issue, and other sacrifices by direction of the seers, and then celebrated with his friends a feast, which lasted the whole night. Greek actors appeared, and he himself took part in the competition by reciting a scene from the *Andromeda* of Euripides. He also gave a merry-making to his army and distributed sacrificial flesh and wine among the regiments. When in the morning—it was the 17th of Daisios by the Macedonian calendar (2 June 323) —he was about to go to bed, his friend Medios invited him to a smaller merry party, in which he participated. After having had his sleep out, on the evening of the same day he went again to Medios, and again the party lasted till dawn. This night, between the 17th and 18th of Daisios, the first symptoms of a fever showed themselves in him. It was the malarial fever which so easily comes on during summer in the marshy district of Babylon. Though Alexander drank little at the symposia, as credible authorities assure us in contradiction to the exaggeration and inventions of the hostile tradition,[1] but only kept them going long in order to talk to his friends, yet the succession of so many festivities, coupled with the extraordinary exertions to which he had subjected himself since his arrival in Babylon, may have weakened his strength to resist the disease.

It is touching to follow his struggle with the fatal malady by the journals of these last days, which were drawn up later, probably to refute by an official document the lie that he was poisoned. We see how daily, as long as his strength lasted, he offered the usual sacrifices to the gods. We see above all how his whole thoughts were devoted to the impending

[1] [See W. W. Tarn, *Cambridge Ancient History*, vi. 396.]

expedition to Arabia. On the 18th of Daisios, though he had been feverish since night, he sent from his sick-bed an order to the generals that the infantry should be ready to start on the 22nd and those sailing with him on the 23rd. On the evening of the 18th he was carried on a litter from the royal palace, in which he was residing on the west bank, over the Euphrates to the royal gardens, where it was hoped that the fresher air would promote his recovery; and as a result he seems to have been better on the next day, the 19th. He talked to his friend Medios and played dice with him. He sent orders to the generals to appear next morning. After a feverish night, on the morning of the 20th he received a report from Nearchus on the state of the preparations for the departure of the fleet and of his experiences on the ocean, and repeated to him and the other generals his order that the fleet should start on the 23rd. Though from the 21st the fever never left him, he sent for the generals again, and ordered that everything should be kept ready for his reception on the fleet and for the start; for he constantly hoped to get better of the disease and to be able to start with the others.

But on the 22nd he felt very ill. In spite of that he spoke to some generals about appointments, and again gave orders about the sea-voyage. After he had been so ill on the 23rd that he could no longer give his orders about the voyage to the generals in person—it was the day on which he had hoped to be able to start—on the 24th he ordered the generals to assemble overnight in the court, and the other officers outside in front of the gates. Evidently a disquieting change for the worse had set in. Next day, the 25th, as he was getting worse, he had himself conveyed back over the Euphrates to the palace. When the generals came in to him there, he could recognise them but was not able to utter a word to them. In the night, and the next day the 26th, the fever became more virulent. As the king this day had seen no one, his troops, especially his Macedonians, became greatly excited. The rumour spread that he was dead, and that there was an attempt to keep the news from them. So by threats they forced the aides-de-camp on the 27th to open the doors, and now his old companions in arms filed past his couch in a long procession, silent and in deep emotion. He could now only with difficulty nod slightly to individuals and silently greet them with his eyes. It was a touching moment, in which everything was forgotten that had ever come between the king and his people.

The friends of Alexander were in despair. Human art could do no more; only the gods could help. They did not turn to a Greek god, but to the principal god of Babylon, Marduk-Bēl, who had been from time immemorial venerated as a god of healing. On the evening of the 27th Daisios six of his friends went to Marduk, to receive in Greek fashion by sleeping in the temple an answer to the question, whether it would be better for Alexander to be brought into his temple, to be healed by the god as his suppliant. After the end of their sleep, on the morning of the 28th (13th June) they received the god's answer, that Alexander should not be brought into the temple, but it would be better for him to stay where he was. Towards the evening of that day Alexander closed his eyes for ever. *

CHAPTER IX

RETROSPECT

When Alexander died, he was not yet thirty-three. He was carried off at the very height of his youthful vigour, like his ancestor and model Achilles. He had not completed the thirteenth year of his reign. A retrospect of his gigantic life work brings before us a personality of quite unique genius, a marvellous mixture of demonic passion, and sober clearness of judgment. In this iron-willed man of action, who was a realist in policy if anyone ever was, beneath the surface lay a non-rational element: for example, his 'longing' for the undiscovered and the mysterious, which, coupled with his will to conquer and his delight in scientific discovery, sent him to the limits of the known world. Among these elusive factors also which are without rational basis was his lively faith in his descent from Heracles and Achilles, which supplied him with much impetus and vigour. In his simple piety, which was in no way undermined by philosophical scepticism, he was firmly persuaded that he was under the special protection of the gods, and therefore believed in his mission. In a recent brilliant essay on 'Ancient Generalship'[1] it was said, 'This sense of divine possession is characteristic of the conduct of the great men of antiquity'; that is true of no one more than Alexander. Consequently, he saw in the prophet's salutation of himself as son of Ammon only a confirmation of the divine energy which he felt within him, and that is why later he demanded divine honours from the Greeks and required from them the recognition of his apotheosis. This firm belief in his mission gave him an absolute confidence in victory,

[1] Generaloberst Hans von Seeckt, *Antikes Feldherrstum*, Weidmann 1929, p. 11.

without which his will and actions would be unintelligible. The supernatural in his temperament gave him also his control over men.

The general and the statesman are indissolubly bound up in Alexander; as general he was the executor of his political will. The general is easier to comprehend, since we have finished performances to survey, whereas the tasks of the statesman were still in process of evolution when he died. Alexander is the type of the royal general, who has unlimited control over the military material and apparatus of his country and is responsible to himself alone. He had no trials for conduct in the field to fear, such as the Athenian democracy loved, and no need to whitewash himself. Moreover as *Hegemon* of the Corinthian League, he was outside any military criticism of the *Synhedrion*. He had further the good fortune to inherit the best army in the world at the time, together with a tried body of officers, and to have been initiated into the art of war by his father, who was himself a great general. These fortunate conditions made it easier for him fully to develop his military genius, but the important point was that this genius was born in him. It is quite unnecessary to recur to the modern attempt to transfer the credit for his military achievements to Parmenio and to contest his own strategic glory. Military experts in ancient as in modern times agree that Alexander as a general was as great a genius as any in history.

As a tactician we saw him fight and win the three great pitched battles, the Granicus, Issus and Gaugamela, by the 'oblique battle formation' developed by his father. But only the tactical idea was common to them. Its execution in detail Alexander varied according to the peculiarities of the ground and of the enemy, most elaborately in the dangerous situation at Gaugamela, which led him to the idea of a second battle-line with a possible square formation. Completely different was the set of problems he had to solve in the terribly difficult guerilla war in Eastern Iran. Here we have a still more brilliant exhibition of his

independence of his father's tradition in his operations with
flying corps and his adaptation to the different mode of
warfare of the new enemy. The severe fighting in the
mountainous region north of Kabul, and especially the
capture of Aornos, display Alexander in all his greatness.
Perhaps the most signal stroke of genius is to be seen in his
last great field battle on the Hydaspes, when he had to
deal with the totally new problem presented by the huge
elephant host of Porus.

His strategic genius we saw from the beginning in his
plan for the Asiatic campaign, according to which, on
account of the difficult situation in Greece, he resolved
first to win the Mediterranean coasts of the Persian empire
with his land army in order to eliminate the superior
Persian fleet. We saw with what tenacity and how in spite
of all temptations he pursued this plan, up to the conquest
of Egypt, and how thus he actually became master of the
sea. When he led his army into the interior of Asia, he
faced new problems. Up to the Euphrates the march of
the Ten Thousand had made all clear, and Xenophon
had familiarised the Greek world with their route. What
lay beyond the Euphrates, was completely unknown
country. So it was into mysterious distances that Alexander
led his army, overcoming all natural obstacles, over the
snowy Hindu-Kush and over broad rivers, and finally
through the Punjab to the Hyphasis, where the morale of
his troops gave out and he turned round.

Yet there is nothing adventurous in his march. On the
one hand, always and from the beginning he tried to get
advance information about the foreign country which he
wished to conquer, took care, as far as was possible, to be
enlightened by his spies about political military and local
conditions, and as a result entered into alliances with
individual rulers by clever diplomacy, as before his Indian
campaign, or sent out voyages of exploration, as before
the Arabian expedition. On the other hand, he never
advanced without having covered his rear. The Danube

campaign and the punitive treatment of Thebes are to be regarded as precautions taken to cover his rear for the Asiatic campaign. When afterwards he made his first conquests in Asia, he began at once to secure the conquered territories from the military point of view, and to ensure peace and order by administrative arrangements. Later when he penetrated into the heart of Asia, and went ever to more remote countries, he followed the same principle, and thus in spite of the tremendous distances, which finally he put between himself and home, he succeeded in never losing connexion with it. Only once, at Issus, was he, by an unusual chain of events, cut off from his base of operations, yet in a few hours he carved his way out of the dangerous situation. What proves his systematic method is that even in the Far East the drafts for his army from Macedonia and Greece always reached him according to his directions. This was only possible because he deliberately and most carefully built up a system of rest stages. Without such measures his successes and his triumph over distances, which our military experts often admire more than his battles, would not be conceivable.

Unfortunately our information about his system of stages is extremely scanty, since the ancient authorities apparently knew nothing of the idea; so we must postulate rather than describe the army roads. But of many of the military and administrative measures which he took in the conquered territories, it may be assumed that they were meant in part or in the first instance to serve the temporary needs of the army, even if they were also to be permanent. From 330 onwards Ecbatana may be regarded as the central point of this system; it was there that he left Parmenio with a strong force and there that he concentrated the imperial treasure. Naturally he also saw to food supply depots; magazines on the military roads are sometimes mentioned. His numerous city foundations in Eastern Iran, by which the land, conquered with so much difficulty, was secured from the military standpoint, served in the first place to maintain communications in view of the Indian campaign, though the main object of these city-foundations lay in the future.

Among Alexander's great qualities as a general is the tenacity with which, when he once regarded anything as essential, he carried it out to the bitter end. He lay seven months before Tyre, till he had got hold of it. On this account alone, one should not, as both ancients and moderns have done, compare Pyrrhus with him, that will-of-the-wisp, who after two months abandoned the siege of Lilybaeum, though it meant the collapse of his whole Sicilian expedition.

He showed himself, too, a great leader of men, by participating in all the dangers and fatigues of his troops; in this way he carried them along with him. In battle he set them an example of supreme personal bravery; on the march there were no toils he did not share. If in sieges causeways or anything of the kind had to be constructed, he himself took a hand in the task, praised those who succeeded, and punished those who failed. When outstanding successes had been gained, he liked to reward his troops, by holding games and all sorts of festivities for them. His extensive money gifts to his army were a compensation for the prohibition of plundering the conquered districts, which for political reasons he thought necessary. This presupposes strict discipline. By the humanity with which after battles he cared for the wounded, he won the hearts of his soldiers. To his Macedonian officers he preserved to the end the attitude of a comrade. Though not imposing in figure, for he scarcely reached middle height, he dominated everybody by his wonderfully bright eyes. The towering nature of his personality is most clearly exhibited in the fact that the men nearest to him, who after his death in many cases showed themselves to be strong rulers, blindly obeyed him during his lifetime.[1] Nearchus says once, with reference to the beginning of his ocean voyage,

[1] [Cassander, when king himself, shuddered at the sight of a statue of Alexander at Delphi. Plutarch, *Alexander* 74, 4.]

that the army believed in Alexander's wonderful luck, and was of opinion that there was nothing he could not dare and do. It was that mystical faith of an army in its leader, which Caesar also and later Napoleon were able to evoke.

It is more difficult to understand or even to judge the statesman in Alexander than the general; for his views as a statesman were in a state of flux, when he was called away by an early death. None of his political creations had as yet taken definitive shape, and new plans were constantly emerging from his restless brain. It is impossible to conceive how different the world would have looked, if he had lived only ten or twenty years longer. How differently then should we be able to judge the youthful work which he did up to 323. We must never forget that we have only beginnings before us. In no single instance had the last word been spoken.

Looked at externally, his evolution seems to show a continuous development from King of Macedonia and *Hegemon* of the Corinthian League to Great King of the Persian empire and finally to world-ruler, and thus it has generally been represented in antiquity and to-day. But if from the standpoint of law one examines his relation to these different complexes of government, one finds instead of succession the continuance side by side of these different positions. Here, as generally, the historian cannot be content to work out the legal aspect; the true historical problem for him is to consider how the practice of political life stood to these forms.

Let us first consider the legal forms. By acclamation of the army Alexander became lawful king of Macedonia, and immediately afterwards by resolution of the *Synhedrion Hegemon* of the Corinthian League, which Philip had united as a free and sovereign league of states by union in his person with the kingdom of Macedonia. To this double position corresponded the duality of his war aims on crossing the Hellespont: as *Hegemon* he wished to conduct the Panhellenic campaign of vengeance, as King of Macedonia he wanted to conquer territory. But he did not incorporate in Macedonia what he conquered, as Philip had done as far as possible with his conquests; by immediately organising as satrapies the earliest conquests on the soil of Asia Minor he expressed the fact that these territories were to remain outside of Macedonia; then, as *Hegemon*, he incorporated in the Corinthian League the liberated Greek cities of Asia Minor, which were not included in the satrapies. As king he continually conquered more territories, till after the final victory over Darius he caused himself to be acclaimed by his Macedonians as King of Asia at Arbela. Yet in spite of this sanction from the assembly of the Macedonian army, this Asiatic empire, as was said above, was not incorporated in the kingdom of Macedonia, but simply united with it by personal union. The acclamation of the army rather expressed the fact that it was the King of Macedonia to whom now belonged the rule over Asia. The foundation of Alexander's power was and remained his monarchy over Macedonia. To whatever boundless size this Asiatic empire might grow, in political law it remained, just like the Corinthian League, an annex joined by personal union to Macedonia.

The result of this was the quite different legal position which Alexander held in these three parts of his whole empire. In Macedonia he was and remained like Philip and his predecessors the king of the people and army, beside whom the nation in arms preserved its old rights in the assembly of the army. To the Greeks of the Corinthian League he was their *Hegemon* with the rights and duties laid down by the Covenant of the League. As King of Asia he was to the Asiatics an absolute ruler in the sense of the Achaemenids, as whose legal successor he regarded himself after the death of Darius. But this Asiatic absolutism was not uniform, since under the Achaemenids it had developed in various forms in different parts of the empire, and as far as possible Alexander allowed these forms to continue unchanged. In Egypt, for instance—if we may count it as belonging to the monarchy of Asia on the ground that it was an early part of the Achaemenid empire—he was Pharaoh and also divine; in Babylon, like Cyrus and Darius of old, king of the city but not a god; in the Phoenician and Cypriot cities he kept their kings as his vassals, just as he retained Porus and Abisares in India. On the other hand, his absolutism did not hold good in Asia with regard to the Macedonians and Greeks of the army that attended him or to the Greek cities which he founded. From the legal standpoint this triple division of the whole empire remained unchanged till his death, for he created no new legal formula for the control of the whole area. He remained the King of Macedonia, to which the Corinthian League and the monarchy of Asia were bound by personal union. The unity of the whole world empire rested on his personality.

We have now to ask whether in the actual practice of political life Alexander adhered to these legal forms as regards his different status in the three parts of his empire. In particular the question arises whether the enormous authority which he acquired as King of Asia influenced his position with reference to Macedonia and the Corinthian League. The first point to be established is that Alexander was fully conscious of the legal distinction between his position in Asia and in Europe, that is, in Macedonia and the Corinthian League. This follows from the statement that from the death of Darius he sealed letters destined for Europe with his old Macedonian seal, but on the other hand those intended for Asia with the seal of Darius. An attempt has been made to interpret this as expressing the change from Macedonian sovereignty to the position of successor to the Achaemenids. The essence of the statement is rather that it testifies to the parallelism of the two legal positions. It is of the utmost moment that Alexander showed himself conscious in principle that his legal position in Asia did not also hold good for Europe. To Europe he remained up to the end of his life King of Macedonia, and as such also *Hegemon* of the Corinthian League. Even when he was in Asia, he acted as King of Macedonia, when he had to send to Europe a communication affecting Macedonia or the League. The seal of Darius was used only for the kingdom of Asia.

On the other hand, in the externals of Alexander's life his Asiatic monarchy appears ever more obtrusively as time goes on. We must not, however, overlook the fact that in tradition, especially that hostile to him, this 'Orientalisation' of the king is treated with special jealousy and great prejudice. Let us first examine his behaviour as King of Asia. The use of Darius' seal confirms the view that after the death of Darius Alexander felt himself to be his legitimate successor; henceforth on principle he regarded the Asiatics no longer as his enemies but as his subjects. Starting from this, he reached the thoroughly statesmanlike conviction that he must enlist the vigour contained in these nations for the great problems that Asia presented to him. This course commended itself the more as it was to be hoped that it would have a reconciling and calming influence on the subjected peoples. In Caria and Egypt he had already committed the civil administration to natives; and so now that he had been proclaimed King of Asia at Arbela, he began to appoint Persian nobles as satraps. But they received only the civil power; each had a Macedonian officer at his side as commander of the troops. The ultimate control was thus in Macedonian hands. A still more urgent necessity was the recruiting of his army with the élite troops of Asia, for his European troops were insufficient for the colossal plans he was revolving in his brain. The filling up of gaps with Asiatic forces was absolutely imperative from the military point of view. Here, as in the administrative posts, he chose Iranians, especially Persians, and after the conquest of Eastern Iran its inhabitants too. Of the Semitic peoples he utilised for the fleet the seafaring Phoenicians and Syrians, but did not put them into the land forces. We have seen how in the various reorganisations he connected these Iranians ever more closely with his army. Yet even in the last innovation at Babylon (323), when he actually drafted Persians into the decads, the command remained in Macedonian hands.

He did not, however, stop at the use of Iranians in the administration and the army, a use which will be recognised as politically right and required by circumstances, but went beyond it to the idea of a race-fusion of his Macedonians with these Iranians, an idea which dominated him more and more, as we saw, in his last years. He himself set the example by his marriage with Roxane (327), and later by the mass-marriage of Susa (324) he expressed most plainly his political intentions. Obviously he regarded this fusion as a means to an end; his aim was to build a bridge between the Macedonians, who were increasingly dissatisfied with the military employment of the Persians, and these same Persians, and to restore concord and agreement between the two peoples, so that hand in hand they might afford a sufficient guarantee against possible hostile reactions on the part of other nations of the empire. Thus conceived, the policy of fusion may be regarded as a statesmanlike idea, however surprising the thought of race-breeding promoted by government may appear, and however doubtful it is whether such a fusion as Alexander desired was at all feasible, and finally, whether it would have had the effect for which he hoped.

The notion of world sovereignty,[1] which laid hold of him ever more strongly in his last years, must have contributed largely to the birth of such a thought in his mind. Only a world ruler, before whose eyes peoples lose their national significance, is capable of conceiving such a scheme. When in the memoranda about Alexander's latest plans it is stated that he intended to transfer Asiatics to Europe and *vice versa*, in order that by mixed marriages concord between the two continents might be brought about, the scanty extract leaves too many questions open for any certain inferences as to his last thoughts on the matter. In any

[1] [For the view of W. W. Tarn which denies this, see *Journal of Hellenic Studies*, xli. 1921, p. 1. It was first developed by J. Kaerst.]

case the information neither compels nor justifies us in thinking that fusion was contemplated with any other race than the Iranian.

In the 'Prayer at Opis' Alexander expressed very clearly the conception he held of his monarchy over Asia and his policy of reconciliation, when at the great feast of union he prayed to the gods that concord and partnership of rule might be granted to the Macedonians and Persians (p. 221). As the Macedonians alone were insufficient for the ruling of Asia, the previously dominant Persians, who already under the Achaemenids had taken up a privileged position before the other nations of the world empire, were to be called to the leadership along with them. Alexander's Asiatic empire—for only to this can his words refer—was thus to become a Macedonian-Persian empire. In this ideal, only to be brought about by concord, he seems to have seen the best guarantee for the security and permanence of his Asiatic empire, and his civilising policy.

His wish to be King of Asia in the form of ruler of a Macedonian-Persian empire, Alexander also expressed in his attire.[1] The statements concerning his royal dress, as it was after Darius' death, are very contradictory, since probably he only gradually adopted a definite use, and, especially at first, dressed differently, according as he had to appear before Macedonians and Greeks or before Persians. But one thing seems established, that he never adopted the entire costume of a Persian king; all are unanimous that he never wore the Persian trousers, which the Greeks regarded as especially barbaric and ridiculous. Nor does he ever seem to have worn the tiara, though this is disputed. The costume which is described to us as that which he wore every day, was a mixture of Macedonian and Persian garments. He wore the Macedonian *chlamys*, a mantle and a purple one like that worn by the Macedonian nobility, and the purple *causia*, the specially Macedonian head-covering, a round flat cap. From Persia he took the purple chiton

[1] Eduard Neuffer, *Das Kostüm Alexanders*, Diss. Giessen, 1929.

with the white stripe inserted in the middle, and the diadem, the ribbon, which the Persian king bound round his
tiara, and Alexander round his *causia*. It seems certain
that his purpose was to wear this or similar attire only in
Asia as King of Asia, and if he had returned to Macedonia
or Hellas, he would assuredly have appeared in purely
Macedonian garb, just as he sealed the documents he sent
there with the royal seal of Macedonia.

Though the idea of Macedonians and Persians sharing
the rule of Asia was before his mind, he practised Asiatic
absolutism solely towards Asiatics, and not towards the
Macedonians of the army who accompanied him in Asia.
These he continued to regard as citizens of his kingdom of
Macedonia. While Bessus was punished according to Persian laws, Philotas and other Macedonians suspected of
high treason were brought before the assembly of the
Macedonian army, and we never hear that this assembly
lost its old rights in Asia. It is stated that when Alexander
had to sit in judgment on Macedonians or Greeks he did
so in simple form in a plain judgment hall, but on the other
hand, when it was a question of Orientals, he delivered
judgment in a magnificent tent of audience on a golden
throne, like the Great King, and with a great display of military pomp. We have already observed that even as King of
Asia he preserved an attitude of comradeship with the Macedonian officers, and to the Macedonian rank and file on the
march and in battle he was always the old army king. At
the feast of reconciliation at Opis, though it was there that
he proclaimed the common rule of Macedonians and Persians, nevertheless the Macedonians had the place of
honour by Alexander above the Persians. In spite of the
employment of Persians in administration and in the army,
the command, as we saw, was reserved to the Macedonians.
They were to take their place before the Persians in this
joint rule.

In spite of all this the Macedonians were dissatisfied
that Iranians were brigaded with them in the army, and

especially that their king partially adopted Persian dress and also many details of the ceremonial of the Persian court. These are the things which are again and again adduced as stumbling-blocks, when the Macedonians take up a hostile attitude, as in the catastrophe of Cleitus and at the mutiny of Opis. They felt that they were the victors, and they looked down with contempt on the vanquished Orientals, whose masters they intended to be. It is the profound tragedy of the life of Alexander that he could not convince the Macedonians of the necessity of his Iranian policy—apart from the idea of the fusion of races it must be regarded as necessary—and that thus a widening gulf opened to divide the king ever more and more from his people.

To be sure, they had once to face the unpleasant fact that Alexander in his endeavour to impose on them the obligation of the Persian *proskynesis*, contemplated lowering them to the level of Persians. If like the Persians they were to throw themselves on the ground before him, this made him their absolute monarch. In this experiment Alexander abandoned the different treatment of Macedonians and Asiatics, and sought to introduce in personal intercourse an equality between the two nations, in which the Persian—not the Macedonian—pattern would set the tone. We saw how, influenced by the passive resistance of his Macedonians, Alexander gave up the attempt, and never returned to it.

We here return to the question alluded to above, whether the immense preponderance of power which Alexander acquired in Asia, affected his relation to the Macedonians and Greeks. In his attempt to introduce *proskynesis*, we get our first example. The attempt concerned only those Macedonians and Greeks who were with him in Asia—for, as a matter of course, the innovation was only to hold good for his Asiatic court—and one will hardly find a similar example in his relation to his Macedonian kingdom; but in his dealings with the

Corinthian League there are contrary indications. Certain instances of neglect of the rights possessed by the league were to be observed in his earlier years, as in the condemnation of the Chiot traitors in Egypt. Still more damning is the condemnation and execution of Callisthenes, which was brought about by a private hearing before the king, though Callisthenes as a Greek should have been brought before the *Synhedrion*, which Alexander had at first thought of doing. There was a much more glaring case of interference in 324, when Alexander issued his decree about the exiles. Here he completely overrode the *Synhedrion*, and by his own authority issued decrees to the states of the League, which most deeply concerned their interests. One must consequently admit that his position as *Hegemon* was not uninfluenced by habituation to his Asiatic absolutism.

If from the development of Alexander's own political attitude we turn to the organisation of his Asiatic kingdom, we shall find it true that, as in generalship, so in administration he was free from any uniformity of treatment. According to differing territorial circumstances he chose very different forms of government, and in accordance with the change in his ideas attempted new experiments, yet he had no hesitation in cancelling what did not stand the test of practice. This especially applies to the administrative forms of the satrapy, which from the first, along with the name, he took over from the Achaemenids as the basis of his organisation. In the early years, in the western part of his later empire, he gave the office as a rule to Macedonians. In the case of the first satrapy, that of Lesser Phrygia, he conferred on the satrap the full authority of the previous Persian satraps. But in the case of the second, that of Lydia, he introduced an important innovation, which he usually adopted later in this western area: while he entrusted this satrap with the military and civil power, he made a separate office for finance and taxation, which he bestowed on a special officer, not subordinate to the satrap. This meant a very considerable limitation of the powers of the satraps. Besides, he placed a special commandant over the fortress of Sardis, just as he did later over the great fortresses of Pelusium, Memphis, Babylon, Susa and Persepolis; the commandants of these imperial fortresses, it appears, were directly responsible to him.

Even in the western area he sometimes from policy gave the civil power to natives, as in Caria and Egypt, but in those cases he committed the military power to Macedonian officers. In the eastern area—first of all in Babylonia—he regularly adopted this arrangement for several years, placing beside the Persian satraps, whom he appointed with civil powers only, Macedonian officers with the title of *Strategos* or overseer (*Episkopos*). This measure corresponded, as we saw, to his idea of giving the Persians a share of authority, but of reserving the real power to the Macedonians. Of special finance officers we hear nothing in the eastern satrapies, possibly because the economy of these regions was based not on currency but on kind. But this arrangement, anyhow, never became a fixed scheme. In the difficult years of the war in Eastern Iran he sometimes had unfortunate experiences with his Persian satraps. So from 328 onwards, with one exception, he made no more Oriental satraps, and when after his return from India he learned that in his absence many of the Oriental satraps had behaved badly, he punished and deposed them with iron severity. At the time of his death only three satrapies were occupied by Iranians, and all the rest were in Macedonian hands. This disappointment did not shake him in his idea of the fusion of the nations, but as a practical statesman and in the interest of the security of his empire he drew the necessary consequences and did not shrink from thus admitting that the experiment had been a failure. The political conditions of India suggested to him other combinations; there he generally left the small Rajahs in their principalities under his Macedonian satraps, but more powerful rulers, like Porus and Abisares, he placed outside the satrapies as independent vassal princes.

The separate treatment of finance and taxation, an absolutely original idea of Alexander's, showed that he had a special interest in the financial arrangements of his new empire.[1] In this department later on he introduced important innovations, which led gradually to a centralisation. At first, in Egypt he put the financial administration of the whole country and its dependencies in the hands of the Greek Cleomenes; and soon afterwards he combined several satrapies into large financial districts under the guidance of financial directors. Asia Minor west of the Taurus formed such a district under Philoxerus, and Cilicia, Syria and Phoenicia a second under Coeranus. In 330 when he had become master of the huge Persian treasure houses, he resolved to separate the military chest and the imperial chest, which had hitherto followed the movements of the army, and to centralise the latter under his friend Harpalus as imperial treasurer by concentrating all the treasures at Ecbatana. Thus Harpalus, who soon removed to Babylon, was the sole head of the whole financial administration, of the taxes and treasures of the Asiatic empire.

Harpalus had not merely to guard the treasure, but to set to work to turn it into coined money. Alexander, as we saw, on principle abandoned the hoarding policy of the Persian kings, and by a currency began to put the idle bullion into circulation. Through the ever-increasing generosity, with which he distributed the money in grants to officers, soldiers and friends, and through the growing expenses of his court, the new treasures were soon passing from hand to hand. At his death the state-treasure is said to have been no more than 50,000 talents.

Alexander's effort to unify the financial organisation is very plainly seen in his measures for the coining of money. While in Persian days the Great King had reserved to him-

[1] See H. Berve, *op. cit.* i. 302.

self the coinage of gold, but had allowed the satraps to coin silver, which they did in very different types and values, Alexander reserved to himself the coinage of silver too, so that in the satrapies—with one passing exception in the case of Mazaeus—there was only a royal currency, which was probably provided by the financial directors in the name of the king. Above all, he introduced a uniform standard, and probably for political reasons chose the Attic standard. In a short time the new tetradrachm of Alexander was to have the highest value in the currency of the world. This creation of a uniform imperial currency is a remarkable instance of the insight of Alexander's economic policy. In the region of finance and currency he carried out a centralisation, which raises his system high above the confusion of the Achaemenid empire.

We see Alexander too as an economist who knew what he was aiming at, when we recall what has been already related in detail about his development of trade and intercourse. He founded numerous cities, which were able and were intended to be the props of this distant traffic. His most magnificent foundation, Alexandria in Egypt, was from the first designed to be an emporium. Even among the new cities in the Far East were many, whose position on the old trade routes, shows that they were designed to serve trading purposes; and so some of them are prosperous at the present day, like Herat, Kandahar and Khojend. He opened new sea routes for trade: the voyage of Nearchus connected his new colonial territory in India with Babylon; he himself intended shortly before his death to connect Babylon with Egypt by an expedition by sea round Arabia; he rendered the Tigris navigable, and a 'new Phoenicia' was designed on the coast of the Persian gulf; great harbour works were begun in Pattala and Babylon for the promotion of navigation and trade. All these are achievements and designs of colossal dimensions, which display a genius at work, who intended to divert into the paths he regarded as right the world commerce of his world-empire.

It was indicated above, of what extraordinary importance were Alexander's coining of the Persian hoarded treasures and his creation of an imperial currency for the economic life of these lands. It meant a quite new basis for the extension of money dealings. What efforts he made to raise the prosperity of the population and the fruitfulness of the countries has been shown us in his exertions to improve the network of Babylonian canals. He aimed at something of the sort in his design for the draining of Lake Copais in Boeotia, which was never carried out. From the activity of Gorgus in India (p. 193) we may see that Alexander was eager to exploit the mineral wealth of the new world. Even when far away he did not forget the economic interests of his home; after the conquest of the Aspasians north of Kabul he picked out the finest and biggest of the great herds of cattle he had obtained in booty and sent them to Macedonia to improve the home breed. These are but scattered and accidentally preserved pieces of information, which give us however some idea how manifold were his economic interests.

Finally we come to his civilising policy. Alexander marched out as the enthusiastic admirer of Greek culture who was to open up the East to its influence. Did he remain faithful to this object after he had become acquainted with the old cultures of the East, which could not fail to impress his susceptible nature? Was he still faithful after the idea of a fusion of the nations had laid hold upon him in his last years with ever-increasing force? One thing is undeniable: in spite of all Iranian policy he was personally to the last an enthusiastic admirer of Greek culture. The pupil of Aristotle never abandoned the idea of making his triumphal march also a journey of discovery, and of causing it to serve Greek science through the examination of lands hitherto unknown by the staff of experts who accompanied him. Out of the later years we need only call to mind the zealous work of investigation in India, Nearchus' voyage of exploration, and finally the mission of Heraclides to the Caspian Sea. Moreover, the attempt which Harpalus made to acclimatise European plants in the gardens of Babylon may unquestionably be set down to Alexander's initiative.

His love of Greek literature remained unchanged to the end. He started out with Homer, and later he sent from the Far East for other works of literature, classical and modern. He had especial veneration for the three great tragedians, above all for Euripides, whom he knew so well that at times he could recite scenes out of him from memory (p. 236). If the poets who accompanied his travelling court were not of the first rank, that was not the fault of his taste but of the low level of Greek poetry at the time. Beside the poets there were also in his camp philosophers and philosophically educated men of the most different schools, Cynics like Onesicritus and Anaximenes, a Democritean like Anaxarchus, and his pupil Pyrrho the sceptic.

The intellectual life at the court of Alexander, which we picture as very animated, was thoroughly Greek. So far as we know, he had no acquaintance with the literatures of the Oriental peoples. This is probably not to be explained simply by the lack of knowledge of the languages, as the deficiency might have been removed by the use of interpreters. The literatures of Egypt, Babylon, Persia and India apparently remained unknown to him. He seems to have had a certain interest in the Indian Gymnosophists, and at his invitation the Indian Calanus was a guest at his court for several years up to the time of his self-immolation (p. 180); but we hear nothing of any deep intellectual intercourse. If Alexander, as we saw, sacrificed to the Oriental gods, he was behaving thereby as a true Greek. But it is noteworthy that, though for political reasons he caused the Persian Magians to officiate along with the Greek soothsayers at the feast of reconciliation at Opis, he never sought any acquaintance with the sacred books of the Persian religion. From the literary point of view he remained exclusively Greek.

Greek art too remained for him *the* art. In Egypt he

ordered the execution of extensions to the temples of Ammon at Karnak and Luxor, and in Babylon he arranged the rebuilding of the temple of Marduk, but these acts were dictated by political reasons. In both cases the buildings were of course executed in the native style; yet it has recently been observed that the reliefs in those sanctuaries at Karnak and Luxor exhibit the influence of Greek art.[1] We never hear that he caused Oriental artists to work for him; on the contrary he exclusively employed Greeks. He preferred to have his portraits made by Apelles and Lysippus, which witnesses to his understanding of the art of the time. His architects also were Greeks, but in the buildings which he commissioned them to erect, a certain approximation to Oriental art is observable in the gradually growing tendency towards colossal dimensions. We recognised a direct influence of the gigantic Babylonian ziggurats in the design for the mausoleum of Hephaestion at Babylon, and even in its forms as well (p. 235). The tent of audience at Susa also was modelled on the Persian *Apādana*. The six temples which according to his latest memoranda he planned for Greece and Macedonia, at Delos, Delphi and Dodona, and at Dion, Amphipolis and Cyrrhus—they were never executed—were to be colossal buildings, though in pure Greek forms; the gigantic sum of 1500 talents was to be spent on each of them. At the same cost a huge temple to Athena was to be erected at Ilium. It is also stated that he intended to build a monument to his father Philip of the size of the Pyramid of Cheops—a plain proof with what reverence he clung to his earthly father to the end; in this too there is clear evidence of rivalry with the East.

If thus, at least in architecture, an Eastern influence is unmistakeable, on the other hand Alexander appears as the representative of pure Hellenism in his cult of competitive games, and in their introduction into the Orient. He liked to arrange gymnastic and musical competitions, when after a victorious issue he wished to give his troops refresh-

[1] This is stated on the authority of G. Rodenwaldt.

ment and distraction, and to render his gratitude to the gods. Competition for a prize of victory was a specific element of Greek culture, and it was quite unknown to the East. So when Alexander exhibited such games after sacrificing to Apis at Memphis, he meant in this way to proclaim that henceforth Greek culture should have a footing in Egypt alongside of Egyptian (p. 117). In the East, especially in Hither Asia, where the requisite Greek performers were more easily procured, he instituted such games with special magnificence after his return from India, and gave proof thereby of his wish to extend Greek art in the Oriental world.

But nothing actually had so strong an effect on the Hellenisation of the East (so far as one can speak of anything of the kind) as Alexander's foundation of cities[1]—particularly those new foundations, which are expressly designated as *Poleis*, that is, as Greek cities, such as were founded in great numbers after the first model of Alexandria in Egypt, pre-eminently in Eastern Iran and India. The colonists settled in these cities were chiefly Greek mercenaries, many thousands of whom were left behind in these spots, along with a lesser number of Macedonians, probably veterans for the most part. As these mercenaries to a great extent came from that uprooted proletariat, whose settlement in Asia Minor Isocrates had recommended to Philip (p. 35), one may from this point of view regard Alexander's city-foundations as a solution on a grand scale of a social and economic problem. Often in practice if there was not much time available, only the city walls were built by the army under Alexander's orders, and the rest of the building left to the colonists. These cities received from him a Greek constitution: a council, popular assembly and city magistrates. In spite of this they seem not to have possessed complete autonomy, and in all likelihood were directly under the king.

[1] V. Tscherikower, 'Die hellenistischen Städtegründungen von Alexander d. Gr. bis auf die Römerzeit,' *Philologus*. Suppl. xix. Heft 1, 1927.

For obvious practical reasons Alexander always founded his cities in connexion with already existing townships—Alexandria in Egypt, for instance, was close to Rhacotis—and the old inhabitants continued to live in these townships. The natives however did not belong to the citizen body of the new *polis*; only Greeks and Macedonians received citizenship. In this way there came into existence Greek communities, where Greek law, Greek worship and Greek habits of life prevailed, in immediate connexion with older native settlements. Even if at first the colonists held aloof from the natives, in the course of time approximation was bound to take place, and ultimately a mixture ensued. For want of Greek women Greeks and Macedonians were compelled to take Oriental wives, and it was inevitable that through them Oriental customs and views of life entered Greek families. On the other hand the juxtaposition created the possibility of elements of Greek culture being appropriated by the natives.

At the time of the foundation of the cities in Eastern Iran Alexander had already conceived the idea of bringing the Iranians into closer relation with the Macedonians and Greeks, and soon afterwards he was busy with the fusion of these peoples. The prospect therefore of a gradual mixture of cultures in the settlements cannot have run counter to the views which he then held. Was he thus unfaithful to his original object of spreading Greek culture in the East? Personally, in spite of all the political concessions which he made to the Iranians, he remained to the last, as we saw, a thorough admirer of Greek culture, and it must accordingly still have been his ambition to make Greek culture prevail as far as possible. But just as he had learned as a politician that he could not rule his Asiatic Empire with Macedonians alone, so in active contact with Oriental cultures it must have become clear to him that neither could he make Greek culture exclusively dominant. The chief requisite was that centres should at first be created from which the spread of Greek culture could take its start—and that is what he accomplished by the cities which he founded. Though mixtures of culture might be expected later, yet in his attitude to Greek culture he must have had the desire and confident expectation that it would be the leading factor. The great question of the future in fact was, which of the two cultures would prove itself the stronger. For many centuries this was the chief problem of the history of civilisation. The first condition was created by the city-foundations of Alexander. *

PART III

APPENDIX

CHAPTER X

PROSPECT

WE see the greatness of Alexander as a whole, only when we contemplate the effects of his life-work on successive periods of history. In the few years of his reign he actually put the ancient world on a new basis. The whole subsequent course of history, the political, economic and cultural life of after times, cannot be understood apart from the career of Alexander. John Gustav Droysen, who was the first clearly to recognise the importance of Alexander in the history of the world, began his talented youthful work upon him with the striking words: 'The name of Alexander betokens the end of one world epoch, and the beginning of another'.   *

It is not my task to relate the history of the following centuries. I shall do no more than briefly trace the exercise of Alexander's influence and the fate of his ideas through the course of antiquity. It will be possible merely to indicate with a few strokes the historical background, so far at least as is necessary for our understanding. Politics, economics and culture are at every moment of history most closely bound together, and only when they are regarded in their reciprocal relations does one obtain a complete historical picture. The results produced by Alexander in these three directions will perhaps come out more clearly if, as in our retrospect, we examine in succession these three factors of historical life.

Through the unexpected early death of Alexander the leaders of the army present at Babylon were suddenly faced by extremely difficult problems. The conduct of the deliberations fell to Perdiccas, to whom the dying king had handed his signet ring. As the unity of the empire had to be maintained and therefore a new king elected, the assembly of the Macedonian army came once more to the front. But the wishes of the infantry, in whom the old Macedonian spirit was strongly intrenched, and of the cavalry, who had become more accessible to Alexander's modern ideas (p. 77), could not be reconciled. After a vehement conflict, which well nigh led to fighting and bloodshed, an unlucky compromise was effected: Arrhidaeus, the candidate of the infantry, an epileptic but a son of Philip, and the still unborn son of the Bactrian Roxane —he was born a few weeks later—favoured by the cavalry, were to rule conjointly. Thus two minors, neither capable of ruling, were to take the place of the irreplaceable. The weaker this phantom monarchy was, the stronger burned the ambition of the generals who aimed at power. At first they went off to their satrapies according to the new distribution decided upon at Babylon, Ptolemy son of Lagus to Egypt, Lysimachus to Thrace, Antigonus to Greater Phrygia, while Perdiccas stayed with the kings at Babylon.

Before they left Babylon, the question was decided, on what principles the government was to be carried on. To remove the responsibility from himself, Perdiccas laid before the assembly of the army the above-mentioned memoranda (*Hypomnemata*) on the latest plans of Alexander, and it was unanimously resolved to cancel them[1]— which was natural enough, as these plans served precisely those ideas of Alexander to which the Macedonians had for years presented a fruitless opposition. This decision affected alike the policy of fusion and the policy of world empire, which was to lead to the conquest of the West. The two favourite ideas of Alexander, which stirred him in his later years with more and more passionate intensity, were thus rendered inoperative by the resolution of the army. Yet they did not disappear from history. Certainly, his successors in the next generation strove to hinder the

[1] [For a different view, see W. W. Tarn, *Journal of Hellenic Studies*, 1921, p. 1.]

fusion of Macedonians and Greeks with Orientals by the principle of a national Macedonian government; yet in the end the mere fact of living side by side led to much mixture of races, and though the idea of world conquest never again became a question at issue for Macedonians and Greeks, yet the pattern of Alexander was not without its effect in bringing about the world dominance of the Roman Empire.

The news of the sudden death of the king, which startled the whole world, did not produce disturbances anywhere among the Oriental peoples. It is a powerful testimony to Alexander's organising genius that they made no attempt to recover their independence. He had known how to reconcile them to their new conditions. The disturbances which broke out in Bactria did not proceed from the native population. It was the Greek colonists who were to blame; they had risen even before his death, and longing for Greek life, endeavoured to win their way back to their native land. The attempt was suppressed with bloodshed by order of Perdiccas.

On the other hand, on the news of Alexander's death a storm broke out in Greece, which completely swept away the Corinthian League. Under the leadership of Demosthenes, who was received back with great honour, Athens rose and summoned the Greeks to fight for freedom against Macedonia. In the place of the 'Corinthian' there was to be a 'Hellenic' League, the hegemony of which was undertaken by Athens. No legal objection could be made to the abolition of the Corinthian League; the members had pledged themselves in the Covenant to Alexander's posterity as well as to himself, but at the moment of the rising there was as yet no legal offspring. But this formal point of law, though mentioned by our best authority, was scarcely decisive: what really caused the outbreak was the excitement occasioned in Athens and also in Aetolia by Alexander's decree about the exiles. This state of feeling had reached its highest tension. So the so-called 'Lamian

War' followed, in which Antipater was victorious. Athens, whose position as a sea-power was lost for ever by the defeat of her fleet at Amorgos (July 322), received a Macedonian garrison and had to alter her democratic constitution in an oligarchic sense and restore Samos to the Samians. Antipater, who concluded peace with each of the insurgent states individually, dissolved the Hellenic League, but he did not restore the old League of Corinth. Yet this creation of Philip's genius did not cease to play its part in history. Hellenistic rulers, who aimed at the protectorate of Greece, attempted several times with more or less success to revive Philip's League of Corinth.[1]

Soon afterwards began the conflict of the ambitious satraps, who in constantly shifting coalitions strove with each other for the mastery. Such a wealth of forceful personalities as were found in the circle of the Diadochi (successors) was never repeated till the epoch of the *condottieri* and tyrants of the Italian Renaissance. The most powerful of the Diadochi was Antigonus, who gradually acquired a great part of Asia and aimed at sole sovereignty over Alexander's empire. Against him and his son Demetrius in long years of fighting was arrayed a coalition of Ptolemy of Egypt, Seleucus of Babylon, Lysimachus of Thrace, and Cassander, son of Antipater of Macedonia. The monarchy, by which the unity of the empire could still be formally maintained, soon disappeared; King Philip Arrhidaeus was murdered by the vindictive Olympias (317); Olympias herself was soon afterwards vanquished and executed by Cassander; and the little Alexander with his unhappy mother Roxane was murdered by Cassander, too. The house of Alexander ended in a horrible massacre. No longer was there a king, but only satraps fighting, and fighting each other for power. In 306, after his victory at Salamis, Antigonus assumed the title of king, thus laying claim to the whole empire of Alexander. But his rivals

[1] An inscription of 302 B.C. from Epidaurus is discussed in *Berliner Akademische Abhandlungen*, xxvi. 1927.

parried the blow, by calling themselves kings as well, in a different sense to Antigonus, however; for they only meant they were kings of their territorial possessions. In this way the unity of Alexander's empire was lost. After Antigonus had been conquered and killed at Ipsus in 301, his son Demetrius with his astonishing elasticity kept his antagonists at bay for many years. These conflicts of the Diadochi ended only in 281 at the battle of Corupedium. With Lysimachus, who at the age of eighty here fell fighting bravely to the last, and with his victor Seleucus, who was soon afterwards murdered, the last of Alexander's companions in arms passed away.

As the result of over forty years of fighting, out of the empire of Alexander three great monarchies came into being: Egypt under the Ptolemies, Asia under the Seleucids, and Macedonia under the Antigonids. Beside them was Greece, partially controlled by Macedonia, at times also wooed by Egypt, but in spite of the great new leagues, the Aetolian and the Achaean, a prey to internal dissensions, and therefore a shuttlecock in the conflict of the great powers. Similarly about thirty years after the death of Charlemagne (843), through the quarrelling of his grandchildren, his world-empire was broken up into three separate states. Thus the European and Oriental parts of Alexander's empire became detached, and, within the East, Asia and Egypt became separate as of old. But Alexander's unwearying struggles had not been in vain; for centuries more the East remained under Macedonian rule, and could thereby in his sense be made still more accessible to Greek culture and economic ideas.

The kingdom of the Ptolemies was small in extent in comparison with that of the Seleucids, but it was consolidated by strict centralisation; nature had made Egypt, its centre, almost unassailable, and it had enormous natural wealth. With this support the first Ptolemies extended their sway, conquering Cyrene and Cyprus as well as southern Syria, and establishing themselves on the south and west coasts of Asia Minor as far up as Thrace. The chief aim of their policy was to control the sea in the eastern basin of the Mediterranean, and thus to play the leading part in international politics and with their trade to dominate the commerce of the world. In the realm of the Seleucids no such centralisation of government was possible as in Egypt, where there was only one foreign people, the Egyptians; the Seleucids ruled peoples of very different races, Semites, Anatolians and Iranians. Even Alexander had treated very differently the different parts of the country, out of regard for their peculiarities and traditions, and probably the Seleucids did the same. But they were not strong enough to keep their great empire together. Very soon parts of it fell off: in the first place, India was taken from them by Chandragupta, the founder of the Maurya dynasty, who united the basins of the Indus and Ganges into one great state; then, in the third century, Bactria, Parthia, Galatia, and the kingdom of Pergamum broke away, and later the Jewish kingdom of the Hasmonaeans.

Neither the state of the Ptolemies nor that of the Seleucids was a national state. They were territorial states, in which a Macedonian dynasty, supported on a thin upper crust of Macedonians and Greeks, ruled over millions of Orientals. There was no right of imperial citizenship. Only the third great power, Macedonia, can be described as a national state; for there a Macedonian dynasty ruled over a predominantly Macedonian people. In this point we see lay a special strength, when we compare Macedonia with the other two powers, a strength which was also demonstrated in its more uniform military system. That is why the Romans found Macedonia their most dangerous opponent among the powers of the East.

The effort to maintain a succession to Alexander is particularly clear in the case of Ptolemy I. He insisted on the transference of the body of the great king to Egypt, but he did not place it in the oasis of Ammon, as had been Alexander's own desire, but in Memphis, whence it was subsequently transferred to the magnificent tomb which had been erected for it in the royal quarter of Alexandria. Ptolemy, whose special reverence for Alexander is evidenced to us in his Memoirs, sought to obtain for his realm exclusively the éclat and blessing that proceeded from the name of Alexander. In Alexandria, where according to Greek ideas heroic honours were due to the great king, as founder of the city as well as for other reasons, he set up a cult of Alexander, whose annual priest was eponymous for the entire kingdom. During the whole of the Ptolemaic period the Greek and the demotic documents were dated not merely by the year of the king, as was usual in Egypt, but also by the year of this priest of Alexander.

From the first the Seleucids and Ptolemies aimed at attracting as many Macedonian and Greek settlers as possible into their kingdoms; only in this way could they obtain a counterpoise to the masses of Orientals. The Seleucids secured their objectives by founding, after the model of Alexander, numerous cities with a Greek organisation. Seleucus I and his son Antiochus I are among the greatest colonisers of history. Not only in Asia Minor, where Antigonus had been their predecessor in this respect, but especially in northern Syria, they carried through a great program of city-foundations, with the result that a 'New Macedonia' arose in these parts. Further eastwards their foundations are also to be found; they were very numerous in Mesopotamia, and above all in Eastern Iran, where Alexander had shown the way. From military considerations, besides, they initiated many military colonies, which as country communities had no city organisation. The Ptolemies followed a different policy. In their foreign possessions, as in southern Syria and elsewhere, they founded Greek cities, but in Egypt itself, Ptolemais in Upper Egypt, the foundation of Ptolemy I, is the sole Greek city that they added to Alexandria and Naucratis. Conversely they pursued an intensive interior colonisation by settling their

Macedonian and Greek army in the country villages and by assigning to them lands in fief.

The rule of the Seleucids and Ptolemies was absolute, as Alexander's had been in his capacity of King of Asia. He in fact was their pattern. According to the precedent he set, for them as for the Hellenistic kings generally, the usual emblem of the royal power was the diadem, originally a Persian symbol. In the case of the Ptolemies there was a special difference, due to the fact that in the eyes of their Egyptian subjects they were their Pharaohs. Accordingly immediately after becoming king (305) Ptolemy I, again following the example of Alexander, assumed the Egyptian royal titles offered him by the priests, in which was expressed the Egyptian cult of the king (as Horus, as son of Ra, and so on); and similarly all the Ptolemies to the end of the dynasty were represented on Egyptian monuments as divine Pharaohs. Seleucus I—and his successors—like Alexander was regarded by the Babylonians as their special king, though in this instance there was no divine cult connected with the monarchy.

This absolutism was limited in respect to the Macedonians by the fact that the Seleucids and Ptolemies, again following the example of Alexander, preserved unimpaired the rights of the assembly of the Macedonian army. In later days, as the Macedonians changed under eastern influence, this institution became less and less important. Naturally it was preserved more effectively in Macedonia. On the other hand, absolutism, at all events nominally, was not enforced upon the Greeks, many of whom had been granted freedom and autonomy. But in fact the royal authority in varied forms and degrees did interfere in the government of these cities.

Apart from such partial limitations, this Hellenistic absolutism towards all its subjects wore the colour of the so-called 'enlightened absolutism', which regards beneficence to the people as its royal duty. Recent writers are in the habit of assigning the credit to these Hellenistic monarchs;

but when we remember what pains Alexander took, from his first entry into Asia, to reconcile the conquered peoples to the new régime as his subjects, leaving as far as possible their old arrangements in force, and sparing their traditional racial peculiarities, one is at liberty to say that it was he who took the lead in this fundamental conception of government. While he however had been in this respect in opposition to his tutor Aristotle, his successors were led by philosophical doctrines to the 'enlightened' conception of the royal office. Propositions of the sort were then much discussed in treatises on 'Monarchy'. The philosophical influence can be traced most clearly in Antigonus Gonatas, the son of Demetrius, who founded the Antigonid line in Macedonia. He studied in Athens under Zeno, the founder of the Stoic school, and during his long reign put Stoic ideas into practice. His theory of a king's duties is mirrored in the famous dictum that monarchy is a 'glorious service', a phrase which is exactly analogous to the saying of Frederick the Great that 'the king is the first servant of the state'. The relations of the Ptolemies and Seleucids to the philosophy of their period were much less substantial, and yet Cynic and Stoic ideas seem also to have influenced their conception of the duties of a king.

The first great kings of these dynasties took very seriously the performance of their duties. In the case of the Ptolemies we can follow in detail the way in which by daily hard work they sought to do justice to the great task imposed on a king by an absolute monarchy. The burden of audiences must have been colossal; everyone, even the fellah, could appeal personally to the king over the heads of all intervening courts of justice. On account of this conscientious labour Mommsen once compared the monarchy of the Lagids to that of Frederick, from which, he said, it was not distant in its fundamental features. In the interests of an orderly administration, the daily official business of the kings had to be embodied in documents. Again it was Alexander who set the example; it was on the pattern of his

Ephemerides that the Ptolemies and other Hellenistic rulers had their daily actions recorded in official journals.

To complete our characterisation of the Hellenistic monarchy we have another very important point to bring out, the cult of the Hellenistic king. It has nothing to do with the above-mentioned Egyptian cult of the Ptolemy as Pharaoh. Nor are other Oriental ideas and traditions relevant, as is occasionally assumed. Rather it arose out of those Greek ideas which led to the apotheosis of Alexander —though it is not to be derived from the pattern of Alexander. The mere fact that it developed gradually in the second generation after Alexander forbids this direct connexion. In its full development it was something quite different from the apotheosis of Alexander: the cult of the Hellenistic king became an official cult of the state, which was binding on Macedonians and Greeks as well as Orientals, whereas Alexander never introduced a state cult of his person, and his apotheosis affected only the cities of the Corinthian League. We can therefore with reference to these Hellenistic kings speak of a divine monarchy of the kingdom, but not, as often is held, with reference to Alexander. Yet it is unmistakeable that the apotheosis of Alexander was a historical presupposition for this different sort of cult of the Hellenistic king, and exercised an indirect influence on its origin. The Greek idea of the veneration of men of superhuman achievements as divine was revived by Alexander more strongly and unmistakeably than ever before. The consequence was that in the next generation after his death Greeks were more than ever inclined to show divine honours in different forms and degrees to men who had done great things for them, in particular to those who had emancipated them or merely proclaimed their emancipation. The examples known to us show how potent these ideas became in the Greek world after Alexander's death and in consequence of his action. None however of his direct successors, neither Ptolemy I nor Seleucus I, claimed divine honours for himself.

The first step to the cult of the Hellenistic king was taken by Ptolemy II Philadelphus. Probably more to promote the prestige of his dynasty than from religious requirements, he instituted after the death of his father a state cult of him as 'Divine Saviour' (*Soter*) and also founded a great festival, which was to be held every four years and celebrated throughout the Greek world. Later when his mother Berenice died, he combined both his parents in the cult as 'Divine Saviours' (*Theoi Soteres*). Likewise when his sister and consort Arsinoe II died in 270, he founded a state cult of her as the 'Divine Philadelphos' (she who loves her brother). Up to then only deceased members of the dynasty had been deified, and on the ground that a deity had 'removed' the deceased—whereupon the king arranged the cult. Now Philadelphus took the decisive step in advance; he created a state cult of himself the survivor and his dead sister in common, under the title of the 'Divine Brother and Sister'. Thus the door was opened to the further development of the Ptolemaic cult of the king. From the third Ptolemy onwards the king and his consort in their lifetime, as soon as he had accomplished any considerable feat, received worship as divine.

The very cult epithets of these Ptolemies, which the Egyptians had difficulty in reproducing in their language, show us that this cult of the Hellenistic king was of purely Greek origin; Soter (the Saviour), Euergetes (the Benefactor), Epiphanes (the self-manifestor) are ideas of Greek religion. The cult, however, was meant, as was said above, not only for Macedonians and Greeks but also for Egyptians. These apotheosised Ptolemies, as associated gods, were combined not only with Greek gods, like the Alexander of Alexandria, but also with the principal divinities of the Egyptian country districts. Thus the Isis priests of the island of Philae were priests of Isis and of the apotheosised Ptolemies as well. A cult was created in which all subjects, no matter of which race, were united. One can already discern a religious policy at work in the creation by Ptolemy I of the cult of Sarapis for both Greeks and Egyptians.

The example of Philadelphus was soon followed by the Seleucids, but the forms of the apotheosis were different in character. To begin with, while no doubt the cult was paid only to the dead, the first kings were assimilated to definite gods; thus Seleucus I, as a god, was described as 'Seleucus Zeus Nikator' (the Conqueror), and his son Antiochus I as 'Antiochus Apollo Soter' (the Saviour). Nor was the cult of the king so uniformly organised in the Seleucid domains as in the highly centralised kingdom of the Ptolemies. The Greek cities seem to have had their own eponymous priests, while in the satrapies arch-priests (*Archiereis*) were at the head of the cult. It is impossible to go into further detail about the different forms of the royal cult in the different kingdoms, but it is necessary to insist that in Macedonia the cult was never admitted. This was probably due to the simple and unostentatious character of Antigonus Gonatas, but above all to the temper of the Macedonian people, which, as we perceived in the case of Alexander, was quite hostile to these Greek ideas. In the Eastern realms the royal cult threw round king and people a firm bond, which, though it could not compensate for the lack of national sentiment, nevertheless joined all subjects in veneration of the king as divine, and created a spiritual unity, in the centre of which stood the royal house.

These Hellenistic kingdoms, whose juxtaposition produced a certain equipoise in the political situation of the Eastern Mediterranean world, might have offered successful resistance to the Romans, if they had kept together their considerable military strength, and given attention in time to the world power that was taking shape in the West. Instead, by continual rivalry, frequently by open warfare, they tried to weaken each other, and so were successively swallowed by the Roman world-empire. But these great monarchies did not fail to influence the development of the Roman empire, and the ideas which went back to Alexander were realised again in Roman history.

After the middle of the third century B.C., when Hellenism obtained an entry into Rome and extended rapidly in the educated circles there, the brilliant picture of the world-conqueror Alexander affected Roman society too. It was the Romans who first gave Alexander the title of 'The Great' (*Magnus*). It was left to Greek historians to draw a parallel between Alexander and the great Scipio Africanus, the conqueror of Hannibal, and the founder of the Roman world-empire; they made Scipio the son of Jupiter Capitolinus, and transferred to him the legend about Alexander that he was the offspring of a sacred snake; but these ideas were keenly discussed in Roman society also. It was only later that the bright image of Alexander was clouded over in Roman literature by hostile depreciation.

A still more important point is that the world-empire of Alexander and the kingdoms of the Diadochi influenced the final plans of the dictator Caesar. By the conquest of Gaul Caesar had extended the frontiers of the Roman empire to the Atlantic Ocean and the North Sea. When the defeat of Pompey and his partisans left him master of the empire, he planned a great campaign, calculated to last three years, first against the realm of the Getae and Dacians on the Danube, and then against the Parthians, who at that time ruled from the Euphrates to the frontier of Bactria, where the Indo-Scythians held sway. The annexation of this empire to the Roman *Imperium* would have created a world-empire, similar to that which was the ultimate goal of Alexander's last designs. That Caesar was not merely contemplating vengeance for the defeat of Crassus, but that this war, which was to be waged with sixteen legions, was really intended to complete the conquest of the world, is shown by the statements as to Caesar's plans of campaign. After the subjection of the Getae and Dacians his purpose was to invade the Parthian empire by way of Lesser

Armenia, and evidently to conquer the whole empire; for, as Plutarch states, he meant after subjecting the Parthians to return through Hyrcania, which adjoined the Indo-Scythian empire. Further, he intended to march along the Caspian Sea, which was then supposed to be a gulf of the Ocean, and after crossing the Caucasus to proceed along the Black Sea, invade the country of the European Scythians, take the Germans in the rear, overrun their land, and re-enter Italy by way of Gaul. Thus, as our authority states, he would compass the Roman globe 'since the *Imperium* would be bounded by Ocean on all sides'.

If, as is not improbable, these words correctly reproduce Caesar's ideas,[1] we find him in the footsteps of Alexander, who so passionately sought for the Ocean in the East as the boundary of his world-empire. There can be no doubt that these Parthian plans of Caesar's exhibit no fortuitous co-incidence with the plans of Alexander, but that Caesar, who from his youth upwards had been a fervent admirer of Alexander, had him and his world-empire consciously before his eyes. Fundamentally different as were these two gifted natures, and however much the elderly dictator lacked the impetus of the youthful conqueror, they came remarkably near to each other in their final plans. But Caesar's were not destined to be fulfilled any more than Alexander's. Three days before he proposed to set out to join his army, he was murdered by the conspirators.

The Roman world-empire could not permanently be ruled according to the forms of the Roman republic. This had been made manifest by the history of the previous de-cades, in which the republican constitution had proved itself the more inadequate to the needs of the world-empire, the greater that empire grew. Caesar's monarchical aspira-tions can thus be explained by the conditions of Rome at the time. But he could not found his monarchy on Roman

[1] Plutarch, *Caesar*, 58. E. Meyer says, 'Caesars Gedanken gibt dieser Bericht gewiss richtig wieder'.

traditions. Even the powerful position which had been given him shortly before his death as dictator for life—and this in reality abolished the republic—failed to satisfy him. What title he would have chosen instead, had he lived longer, is a much disputed question. But we may assume as certain that in the shaping of his monarchic position he had before him as pattern the absolute sovereignty of Alexander, as further developed in the Hellenistic monarchies of the Diadochi. Had Caesar returned home victorious from Parthia, he would certainly have taken over the diadem of Alexander and the Diadochi as the external symbol of this royal power.

Indeed, he had already introduced the Hellenistic divine monarchy. The idea of deification had been spontaneously offered to him by the Hellenistic East. Probably in these parts divine honours had long been paid to Roman governors, but it was an extraordinary step forward, when, after the victory of Pharsalia (48), which decided the rivalry of Caesar and Pompey, all the Greek cities of the province of Asia celebrated Caesar in an Ephesian inscription as the 'god descended from Ares and Aphrodite who had revealed himself' (*Theos Epiphanes*) and 'the common saviour of the human race' (*Sotēr*).[1] It was with intention that at the outset they emphasised the descent of the Julian family from Aphrodite, on which Caesar laid as much weight as Alexander on his descent from Achilles or Heracles. The 'Theos Epiphanes' was certainly a stale title, but the 'common saviour of the human race' was a new idea, expressing a recognition of the victor of Pharsalia as the monarch of the world-empire. What was voluntarily offered by the Hellenistic East, had to be clothed in other forms for Rome and Italy, where Caesar regarded it as highly important to introduce the divine monarchy. The divine honours, decreed to him by the subservient Senate, had to be connected with Roman ideas. Consequently, at Rome he was raised to the number of the state gods as *Jupiter Julius*, and

[1] Dittenberger, *Sylloge Inscriptionum Graecarum*, p. 347.

a priest for his cult, a *flamen Julianus*, was appointed, on the model of the *flamen* of Jupiter, Mars and Quirinus; Fundamentally, this was nothing but the Hellenistic conception of the divine king in a Roman form. Moreover, many other honours, which he caused to be conferred on him, betray their Hellenistic origin, such as the right of portraiture, which permitted him to put his head on the coinage, the Hellenistic oath to the king, which was introduced into the Roman oath in the shape of an oath by the 'Genius of Caesar', the celebration of his birthday as a public holiday to be observed with state sacrifices and so on.[1]

Shortly before his death there were persistent rumours that he intended to leave Rome and transfer his capital to the East, whether to Ilium, which at his visit in 48 he had honoured in the same way as Alexander, or to Alexandria. In fact these ideas naturally suggested themselves on the assumption that he returned victorious from the Parthian war, since in that case the centre of gravity of the empire was bound to be shifted further East. Alexandria would have been extremely well suited for the centre of such a world-empire, and probably Alexander too would have chosen this city for his capital, if he had carried out his latest plans (p. 230). There was this additional point to appeal to Caesar; he could have carried out his imperial policy far more easily on the soil of Alexandria, soaked with Hellenism, than in Rome, where republican traditions were ingrained, for his policy did not aim at a national Roman *Imperium* but at an international world-empire which was to embrace the whole world of Hellenistic-Roman culture.

After Caesar's death these Hellenistic ideas found a champion in Mark Antony, who, though a Roman triumvir, in Alexandria, as consort of Cleopatra, demeaned himself like a Hellenistic king and dreamed of a conquest of the Eastern empire of Alexander. To his son born to him by Cleopatra, whom he significantly named Alexander,

[1] See the author's *Bonner Kaiserrede*, 27 Jan. 1915.

he promised dominion over all Asia from the Euphrates to India. If Antony had been victorious, Alexandria would certainly have been the capital of the world. But the victor in the struggle of claimants was not he but Caesar's adopted son Octavian, the later Augustus, who represented a national Roman policy in contrast to an Hellenistic-Oriental one. His victory was of momentous bearing on the world's history; for it was by this victory alone that Rome for the next centuries retained its commanding position as capital of the world, until finally Constantine removed the seat of government to the East. In opposition to Caesar's plan of a cosmopolitan world-empire, Augustus, who was a thorough Roman, founded an *Imperium Romanum*, in which the Romans were the lords of the other nations.

This is not the place to set forth how Augustus with extraordinary insight and wisdom succeeded in clothing his actual monarchy with republican forms. Mommsen was the first to teach us this in his great work *Römisches Staatsrecht*. But it is relevant to emphasise the fact that this 'first of the citizens', as Augustus liked to describe himself, did not disdain some externals of Hellenistic rule: he too claimed the Hellenistic prerogatives, which Caesar had taken over, his likeness on coins, the oath by his genius, and the public celebration of his birthday. On the other hand, in contrast to Caesar, he admitted the Hellenistic divine monarchy only with great limitations. In Rome he altogether forbade divine honours, though he did not interfere with the Italian communities in this matter; in the provinces he allowed his cult only along with that of the goddess Rome. Naturally no bounds were set to private veneration. It deserves mention too that in the province of Egypt, which was excluded from control by the Senate and subject to him alone, he assumed as successor to the Ptolemies, an openly royal and special position. Here he and his successors, like Alexander and the Ptolemies, received from the natives the old Pharaoh worship. But as with Alexander, so with Augustus, it had a purely local significance.

This is not the place either to relate how in the course of centuries individual emperors effaced the Roman foundations of Augustus in favour of a Caesarian and Hellenistic view of the state, till Caesarian absolutism finally triumphed. The see-saw of Roman and Hellenistic tendencies or of Augustan and Caesarian ideas gives movement and tension to the internal history of the Imperial age. In foreign policy too Caesar's ideas of extending and rounding off the world-empire actuated many emperors after Augustus, who though officially the peace emperor, did a great deal by so-called frontier wars. Here we can but refer to Trajan, because he had constantly in his mind not only Caesar but Alexander, the latter certainly as an unattainable ideal. He most brilliantly fulfilled the first part of Caesar's program by the Dacian wars, and then undertook also the second part, war with Parthia, personally taking command, and faithfully keeping the image of Alexander before him. After the occupation of Ctesiphon, the Parthian capital, he like Alexander was seized by a longing to sail down the Tigris to the Ocean—the Persian Gulf—and when he went out on the sea and saw a ship starting for India, we are told he exclaimed that he too would have gone to India, had he been still young, and that he esteemed Alexander happy. On the strength of this, later authorities speak erroneously of Indian wars contemplated by Trajan; but these words betray only the sorrowful resignation of the elderly monarch, who would gladly have rivalled the youthful hero. Afterwards at Babylon Trajan showed his veneration for Alexander in symbolic fashion, by sacrificing to him as a hero in the room of the old palace, in which he died. Later emperors too did homage to the memory of Alexander, especially at the beginning of the third century, and in some cases in a very tasteless way—and also in the fourth century Julian the Apostate, who in his Persian campaign felt himself on the tracks of Alexander—but no homage is so impressive as this which Trajan, one of the best of the Roman emperors, paid to him.

Now that we have returned to Alexander's death-bed, it is time to conclude this sketch of the after-effects of his policy, and in conclusion to emphasise the fact that while the foundations of the Roman empire find their explanation in Roman history, its extension was strongly influenced by Alexander's idea of world dominion. Thus in the last instance one must go back to Alexander, when one takes a historical view of the reawakening of the Roman empire in the Middle Ages.

We turn now to the question, what effects had Alexander's life-work on the economic development of the world? If one is to understand the phenomenal revolution which he brought about in the economic life of the time, one must picture what was the economic position of the world that preceded him. In economic matters the East and the West down to Alexander had stood side by side, as two circles which were in contact and mutual relation, but on the whole formed two individual entities. Probably in the second millennium the non-Greek Cretans and the East had trade dealings with one another, and through the medium of Crete Oriental products from time to time reached Greece. Then at the beginning of the first millennium Phoenician merchants came to the Greeks, and disposed of their Oriental wares to them, as also along the coasts as far as Spain. Probably too the Greek colonists on the western fringe of Asia Minor, where the two circles intersected, carried on trade with their hinterland, though under Persian rule to a much less extent than previously under the Lydians. Moreover, the foundation of Naucratis in the Nile Delta under the protection of the Pharaohs of the Saitic dynasty, who favoured foreign trade, made possible direct commercial relations with Egypt; but it was quite the exception for Greek traders and artisans to penetrate far into Asia. On the Syrian coast there was not a single Greek colony; the coastal cities of Asia Minor were the only ends of the trade routes coming from the Far East which were in Greek hands.

At a stroke this was all altered, when Alexander conquered all Hither Asia up to the Indus delta, and Egypt up to the First Cataract. Vast areas were thrown open to Greek enterprise, regions of raw material and markets of boundless range. This was not due to conquest alone; the vital point was that Alexander deliberately took in hand the opening up of his conquests to Greek economy, and no less that his successors followed his example and, equally with full intention, took up his economic policy and vigorously carried it forward. In Alexander's wars the previous barriers between East and West were removed, and in the next generation thousands of Greek traders and artisans entered the new world, to seek their fortunes in the new Greek cities, which shot up out of the ground like mushrooms. In this way the two previously detached circles came more and more to coincide and form a single economic circle; and when the Western Mediterranean was attracted into the orbit of the great revolution that occurred in the East, there was finally created a world commerce, which embraced the whole inhabited world, and extended from Spain to India, and beyond through Central Asia to China. This development was completed only under the Roman Empire, but its basis was the conquest of Asia by Alexander. The parallel that was recently drawn between the economic consequences of this feat and of the discovery of America is a sound one.

If we attempt to paint in somewhat more vivid colours this short sketch of the general course of development, we are constantly hampered by the fragmentary character of our authorities, except in the case of Egypt. For the Seleucids our tradition is particularly scanty. It was stated above, that they were colonisers on a grand scale, who followed the example of Alexander and even surpassed him. There the motive of their policy was represented as the desire to attract as many Macedonians and Greeks as possible into the country, but here we must point out that many of the new cities were intended also to serve the purposes of trade. They were accordingly founded by deliberate choice on the great trade routes, which from of old crossed Asia, as is very clear in the case of Seleucia on the Tigris, the first capital of Seleucus I and the meeting-place of the trade routes from the West and from the distant East. This city, which Mommsen called the successor of Babylon and the precursor of Bagdad, soon became one of the first mercantile cities of the world. When for political reasons Seleucus afterwards removed his capital farther west to Antioch, which he built on the Orontes in northern Syria, his chief care was to connect Antioch and its Mediterranean harbour at the mouth of the Orontes, Seleucia in Pieria, with the great network of roads to the East, and so to link it up with Seleucia on the Tigris. This was attained by the construction of new roads. In the same way the Seleucids improved the old Persian roads, which led from the Far East through Asia Minor to the Aegean coast, and flanked them with numerous new cities. In so doing they greatly promoted the trade of the coastal cities of Asia Minor.

Though India was soon lost to the Seleucids by the foundation of Chandragupta's empire (p. 270), yet traffic with India remained an important item in their foreign trade. For intercourse with India they had at their disposal not only the old trade routes by land, but the sea route recently discovered by Nearchus. Both were used, but the sea route more often, when complications with the Parthians interfered with communications by land. The promotion of trade relations was served by the diplomatic intercourse which the Seleucids kept up with Chandragupta and his successors. Megasthenes[1] went frequently as

[1] [Megasthenes' work on India is reconstituted by B. C. S. Timmer, *Megasthenes en de indische Maatschappij*, Amsterdam, 1931.]

ambassador of Seleucus I to Palimbothra (Pataliputra) on the Ganges, and afterwards wrote for the Greeks the best book yet written on India. A certain Daïmachus of Plataea also went as ambassador to India, this time to Amitrochates, the son and successor of Chandragupta. There were also constant diplomatic relations with his son, Asoka, who introduced Buddhism into Western India. Quite in the temper of Alexander, the Seleucids extended their eastern trade beyond India. We have already said that in Alexander's day Chinese silk had reached India. In the next centuries China exported more and more silk, and the silk route led into and through the Seleucid empire. Thus by way of barter Hellenistic products reached Central Asia and China, even in later days, when the Parthian empire rose to power. Recently in Northern Mongolia have been found remains of fabrics from Syria, which are to be ascribed to the first century B.C.[1] It is assumed not without reason that the Han dynasty in particular had close relations with Hellenistic Hither Asia.

The mission also of Patrocles to the Caspian Sea by order of Seleucus I and his son Antiochus is connected with the trade interests of the Seleucids. He was entrusted with the scientific commission of investigating whether the Caspian is an inland sea or an arm of the Ocean, a question which formerly Alexander had wanted Heraclides to solve; but like Alexander the Seleucids too had motives of trade policy, since Patrocles was also to explore the route of the Indian caravans, which ran along the south edge of the Caspian, as far as the Black Sea. He was certainly very unfortunate in his treatment of the geographical problem; he did not go far enough north and so got the impression that the Caspian is an arm of the Ocean, an error which Eratosthenes then introduced into geography. But he wrote a valuable work on the trade routes from India to the Caspian and farther to the Black Sea. In this expedition of Patrocles the Seleucids carried out one of Alexander's

[1] See L. Curtius, *Die Antike*, vi. (1930), p. 95.

last plans, but they omitted to attempt his final great undertaking, which he was preparing for when he died, the
circumnavigation of Arabia. No doubt they said to themselves that their chief commercial rivals, the Ptolemies,
would derive the greater benefit from a connexion by sea
between Babylonia and Egypt. Notwithstanding, they
were unwilling to give up altogether the valuable spices
from the lands of the Sabaeans and Minaeans in Southern
Arabia. They compelled the Gerrhaeans, who lived on the
east coast of Arabia on the Persian Gulf, to send to Babylonia at least part of the wares they got from Southern
Arabia, but could not prevent them from taking another
part across Arabia to Petra, south of the Dead Sea, and
thus into the kingdom of the Ptolemies.

On Ptolemaic economy we are far better informed than
on that of the Seleucids. For about a hundred years, and
especially during the last fifty years, we have been accumu-
lating a vast and increasing material of thousands of Greek
papyrus documents, which not only on all other branches
of public and private life but also on the economic life of
the Ptolemaic age give us such rich information as we
possess for no other country of the ancient world. If our
knowledge is still patchwork, since, apart from some royal
decrees, it is chiefly details of daily life which those documents reveal to us, yet gradually many general questions
are being cleared up.

The Ptolemies did not frame a policy of foreign conquest
any more than the Seleucids, but they did aim at extending their foreign connexions; and in possession of Egypt,
naturally the richest country in the world, supported by a
fleet and army, they strove to play the leading part in the
Eastern Mediterranean. This strong international position
they based on their economic and commercial policy, and
in the above-mentioned extensions of their territory considerations of commerce played a great if not decisive part.
When Ptolemy I occupied Cyprus, he was certainly influenced by the fact that this island possessed in abundance

the two raw materials not supplied by Egypt, timber and copper. In the several wars which the Ptolemies waged with the Seleucids for Syria, occupying Coele-Syria with Palestine and Phoenicia, and for a long time even the port of Antioch, Seleucia in Pieria, reasons connected with trade policy were doubtless their motives. Syria was an extremely important trading region, which had always been of great significance for the trade between East and West. Here was the terminus of the caravan route which led from Dura on the Euphrates by way of Palmyra and Damascus to Tyre. Here also ended the route which led from Southern Arabia northwards along the west coast of Arabia to the important Nabataean centre of Petra, and thence to Gaza, so that, merely by the occupation of Southern Syria, the Ptolemies diverted into their dominions a considerable part of the valuable spices of Southern Arabia. They had also trade in view in their occupation of the coast of Asia Minor and their acquisition of the Cyrenaica, which in *silphion* produced an extremely valuable article of export, which they accordingly, as it appears, monopolised. The Mediterranean trade was notably affected by the coming of the league of the Aegean islands under their protection, until on the fall of their sea-power Rhodes took their place. While in command of the sea the Ptolemies also suppressed piracy, following in this the example of Alexander, who likewise had taken measures against pirates, as soon as he was master of the sea.

Not content with controlling the Mediterranean, the Ptolemies were determined to make the Red Sea as well available for their commerce. Here again they followed Alexander's example in opening up new routes by sea and in extending the knowledge of the world, though what they did was only a partial realisation of his latest design of circumnavigating Arabia. Probably without knowing it, they were also following in the steps of the old Pharaohs, who at the zenith of Egyptian history in the 3rd and also in the 2nd millennium sent their ships to the coast of Somaliland

(Punt), the land of incense and myrrh. Philadelphus, who had keen interest in economic matters, was the pioneer. He restored the canal of Necho, which led from the Pelusian arm of the Nile through the Bitter Lakes into the Red Sea, and thus established a connexion by ship between the Red Sea and the Mediterranean. Moreover, starting from Coptos in Upper Egypt he constructed the caravan road through the desert to Berenice on the Red Sea, in the latitude of Assouan. He too like his successors made a series of settlements on the African coast of the Red Sea, which at first were chiefly designed as stations for elephant-hunting —for they required African elephants to oppose the Indian elephants of the Seleucids—but at the same time naturally served as stations for merchant vessels. When in the second century elephants were no longer used in warfare, the settlements continued to be useful as ports and emporia for trading ships. From the time of Euergetes I ships also ventured through the dreaded strait of Bab-el-Mandeb out to the coast of Somaliland, to fetch for the king incense and myrrh for his spice-monopoly.

This unclosing of the Red Sea to traffic led also to trade relations with the Arabian coast, on which Philadelphus himself set foot.[1] But the Ptolemies did not confine their aims to the coast of Africa and Arabia; they endeavoured furthermore to divert part of the Indian trade by sea to their country and thus withdraw it from the rival Seleucids, though at first with no great success. Philadelphus entered into diplomatic relations with India; he sent a certain Dionysius there as ambassador, and the famous Asoka knew the Ptolemies as well as other Hellenistic kings. But at first trade could not be carried on directly with India, as the Egyptian merchants did not venture beyond Aden or the island of Socotra off the south of Arabia. So the Indian merchants came there and exchanged their goods with them. This system did not change, till about 100 B.C. a bold Greek captain called Hippalus trusted himself to

[1] W. W. Tarn, *Journal of Egyptian Archaeology*, xv. 9.

the monsoons and was driven by them overseas to the Indus delta. From that time intercourse with India by sea increased gradually, but only grew important under Augustus, when Alexandria became the intermediary of Indian trade westwards.

The Ptolemies also opened up trade with the interior of Africa. Here again they trod in the footsteps of Alexander, who had once sent to the Upper Nile an expedition which was to solve a scientific problem, but doubtless entered as well into practical relations with the Ethiopians. The first Ptolemies too despatched emissaries into the Soudan, who in some cases got beyond Meroe, and Philadelphus advanced the Egyptian frontier to Nubia, chiefly no doubt to occupy the great gold mines in Wādi-Alāki, which were afterwards exploited for the Ptolemies. And so the products of the interior of Africa—ebony, ivory, animal skins—were brought down the Nile to Egypt.

All the goods of the whole world that were imported into Egypt from the north and west of the Mediterranean as well as from the east and south were concentrated in Alexandria, which the great king had the genius to found, and which Ptolemy I in the early days of his governorship made the seat of government. To make this city by severe centralisation the centre both of Egyptian trade and of international commerce was one of the chief aims of the Ptolemies, and it was realised. For centuries, until it was thrown into the shade by Rome, Alexandria was the greatest and most flourishing commercial city of the world. From it the agricultural and industrial products of Egypt, the imported goods of Africa, Arabia, and India—except what was used in the country—and the raw materials made up into manufactured goods went forth into the wide world, to Massalia (Marseilles) and Carthage, with which there were close trade relations, to Italy and Sicily, to Greece, Syria and Asia Minor, and further north to the coasts of South Russia. Alexandria soon became a great centre of international trade, where the merchants and freighters of the

whole world mingled with the natives. From the middle of
the second century B.C. Roman merchants too settled there.

We would gladly learn whether the forms of Ptolemaic
economy went back in detail to those of Alexander, but we
know too little of the latter to be able to answer this question. However, there seem to have been certain connexions
between the economic tendencies of the Ptolemies and of
that Cleomenes of Naucratis whom Alexander in 331 set
at the head of the finance administration. In any case,
during Alexander's lifetime Cleomenes collected a huge
amount of money (8000 talents) by speculations in corn
and similar commodities. It was characteristic of the
Ptolemies too to endeavour to bring as much money as
possible into the royal treasury. One may compare them
in this respect with the Mercantilists of the seventeenth and
eighteenth centuries, who likewise regarded the procuring
of money as the chief problem of the ruler's state-craft. In
other ways too these offer many analogies. Just as the
development of mercantilism presupposed the arrival in
Europe of great stores of precious metals through the discovery of America and the sea route to India, and just
as the transition was thereby facilitated from mediaeval
economy based on kind to an economy based on money
and thus to capitalism, so the fact that Alexander by coinage brought into circulation the hoards of precious metal
amassed by the Achaemenids, had as its consequence a
development of monetary economy in the world market.
An old writer said:[1] 'When Alexander carried off the
treasures of Asia, there arose the mighty power of wealth
of which Pindar sang'. The gradual growth of monetary
economy after Alexander can be traced in Egypt in the
royal economy as well as in the economy of temples and
private individuals. Moreover, the Ptolemies—following
Cleomenes, it appears—gave Egypt a currency of its own.

The same applies to the means employed by the Ptolemies in the interest of this tendency to procure money,

[1] [Athenaeus, vi. p. 321 e.]

and many parallels with the modern mercantilists may again be drawn. Thus we have the great predominance, which is plainly recognisable in the documents, of taxes in money over taxes in kind (only the land-tax was levied in kind), and also the system of state enterprise. On the one hand, the king was the largest land-owner in the country; like the Pharaohs of old, he claimed a superior ownership of the whole soil, so that a great part of the country was royal domain, while the other part was made over to temples or to settled soldiers (as fiefs) or to great magnates (as a gift). Consequently, the economy of the whole country was under royal control. The provisioning of the country and the capital was one of the chief tasks of the king, for the performance of which he took over the ancient Egyptian system of depots. The foreign export of grain too was entirely in his hands. On the other hand, the king was the greatest large-scale manufacturer in the country. As such he monopolised entirely or partially the most important industries, for example, the manufacture of papyrus, the conversion of spices (*aromata*) into perfumes and unguents, the native oil manufacture, the brewing of beer, the manufacture of textiles in part and so on. It was from the Pharaohs that the Ptolemies adopted the monopoly of minerals (the natural monopolies), and moreover greatly developed the monopoly system in comparison with the economy of Greek cities. It is true in general of the Ptolemaic economy that it represented a mixture of Pharaonic traditions and Greek ideas, with the qualification that the latter suffered a great change under the influence of absolutism. The great money treasures which thus accumulated, the Ptolemies increased by banking; for they introduced into Egypt the Greek banking system, but completely altered it by monopolising the whole of the banking business. Through their central bank at Alexandria they also transacted business in money with foreign countries. We can infer this from the statement that in the First Punic War the Carthaginians asked Philadelphus for a loan of 2000 talents, which however he refused, in order to preserve his neutrality towards Rome.

In spite of this considerable absorption of functions by the state the Ptolemies furthered as far as possible the economic development of Greeks in country and city, while leaving as a rule the Egyptians in their former oppressed condition. One of the principal aims of the Ptolemies, as of Alexander—and also, as we saw, of the Seleucids—was to attract Greeks into their country, and so, notwithstanding all royal monopolies, opportunity had to be afforded to them to attain greater prosperity and wealth than in their native land. So far we have only isolated bits of information to show how this was carried out in practice. For instance, it was left to Greek initiative to fetch from the Somali coast the raw-materials, incense and myrrh, for the king's monopoly of spices—a dangerous business, but a lucrative one, as is probable on account of the great variety of the circles of Alexandria who took part in the case known to us. Similarly in other ways Greek enterprise must have been given opportunity to get gain. Of course, in view of the system prevailing, this private activity of the Greeks could only be one that was privileged and regulated by the king. This again corresponds to modern mercantilism. Useful as the parallel is, in so far as it helps us to arrange the details of the documents in one general conception, we must not overlook a great difference: in contrast to modern mercantilism, which has served the interests of national states, Ptolemaic mercantilism had a fiscal character, since the very idea of a national state was absent. This short sketch of Ptolemaic economy must here suffice; our object is not to give an account of the Hellenistic age, but merely to consider the after-effects of Alexander's work.

The economic revolutions which have been described as brought about by Alexander's conquest of Asia and Egypt, and which confronted the Greek merchant and industrialist in the East, in process of time increasingly influenced the economic development of Greece itself; the whole foundation indeed of Greek trade in the Mediterranean was changed. Down to Alexander, Athens, supported by its central position among the Greek colonies, with its first-rate harbour of the Piraeus, had been the natural centre of Greek trade since the days of the first Athenian sea-league. At first it seemed as if the new prospects which these revolutions opened out for a revival of trade and industry would favourably affect the economic development of Greece. Even in the years (317–307) in which Athens was ruled by Demetrius of Phalerum, it enjoyed great economic prosperity. But in time the East, opened up by Alexander, was sure increasingly to draw off from the business life of the mother country its efficient elements; and when the new trading towns in the East, Alexandria, Antioch, Seleucia on the Tigris, grew enormously and became gigantic cities which finally surpassed the largest cities of early days with their several hundred thousand inhabitants, the centre of gravity of economic life shifted ever further from the West. Naturally enough those towns of the mother country, which were in a very favourable geographical position in relation to this new world, prospered, while the others decayed. One can point to the parallel of what happened after the discovery of America; the European states which turned their faces to the new world made a great advance, and Lisbon, Antwerp and London took the leading position in the world's markets, which had previously been held by Venice and Genoa. Thus Athens, which no longer lay in the centre of Greek traffic, was deprived of its dominant position by Corinth, which became the first mercantile town of Greece and remained so up to its brutal destruction by the Romans (146). This predominance Corinth owed to its favourable position on the Isthmus, which, for seafarers who wished to avoid the dreaded Cape Malea, was the natural half-way house between the East and Italy. To avoid the inconvenience of the transport of goods over the

Isthmus, Demetrius, the son of Antigonus, thought of piercing it; the project was often considered and in part attempted in antiquity, but its execution was left to modern engineering (1893).

A favourable situation was also the chief reason of the great rise of Rhodes. It was situated exactly where the trade routes intersected, which led from Alexandria over the sea northwards, and from Antioch and Tyre westwards, and was thus marked out to be the go-between for the ancient and modern worlds. It is pertinent to observe that ship-building became perfected there, with the result that the sailing-ships exclusively employed in commerce ventured to break away from the coast and steer across the open sea. With a favourable wind one could sail from Alexandria to Rhodes in four days, and from there it took ten more days to the Crimea. As the whole of the Alexandrian trade to Greece went by way of Rhodes, there were very close relations between the island and the Ptolemies. Rhodes, which was not governed by a radical democracy but was a republic of well-to-do merchants, soon developed into a prominent trading power, and at times like any old Hansa city used the war fleet, with which it kept the sea clear of pirates, to protect its trade policy.

For the Greek cities on the west coast of Asia Minor a period of growing prosperity set in, owing to their liberation by Alexander from the Persian yoke. The Diadochi promoted this development; Antigonus by the rebuilding of Smyrna, and Lysimachus by doing the same for Ephesus. Then came the effects of the vigorous Hellenisation of Asia Minor by the Seleucids, by which trade in the hinterland was greatly developed. The magnificent buildings of this age, even in their ruins, witness to the wealth of these Greek cities of Asia Minor. For a time their prosperity was endangered by the inroads of the predatory Gauls. Still greater ravages were committed later by the Roman tax-farmers (*publicani*) after the province of Asia had been delivered over to them by Gaius Gracchus. But

Caesar lent the cities a helping hand, and with Augustus once more a period of prosperity set in.

The impetus which Alexander gave to trade generally benefited also his native country of Macedonia. The two seaports founded by Cassander, Cassandreia (Potidaea) and Thessalonice (Salonica), grew into important centres of trade. During the long and wise reign of Antigonus Gonatas (277–239) Macedonia also made great economic strides. A vital consideration was that Macedonia, after becoming once more an independent kingdom, no longer remained a recruiting ground for the other rulers. On the other hand, the Hellenistic kings continued to draw from Greece the man-power for their fleets and armies. From this cause and from emigration into the new world it came about that, while before the time of Alexander, as we saw, Greece suffered from over-population with the result that the landless craved for expansion, now in the course of the third century, after the superfluous elements were all settled in the East, there set in a pause in the movement of population. In the second century began a fatal falling off of numbers, not in consequence of emigration—which had long ceased—but in consequence of an economic social and even moral decline, aggravated by the misery of Roman rule, which was expressed, Polybius says, in a deliberate limitation of the family to one or two children.

The effects of the economic revolution produced by Alexander soon made themselves felt in the west of the Mediterranean basin. The Greek cities of Sicily and Lower Italy, which had always been in trade relations with the eastern Greeks, could not but re-act to the change that had taken place in the East, particularly as the Ptolemies from their side began early to seek trade relations with the West. Agathocles apparently was the first to put himself into association with the East; he not only, after the example of the Diadochi, assumed the title of king, though not the diadem, but also by marrying a daughter of Ptolemy I sought to ally himself with the new Egyptian dynasty. In the economic sphere he expressed this connexion by adapting his silver coinage to the Ptolemaic (Phoenician) standard, which was also adopted by Massalia. King Hieron of Syracuse too (third century) cultivated these relations with the Ptolemies. He presented King Ptolemy with a gigantic ship, the *Syrakosia* or *Alexandris*, which he had built for the transport of corn and passenger traffic between the East and West. It is still more important to observe that in his taxation system he was influenced by the Hellenistic East. At any rate his taxation-law, known to us from Cicero's *Verrines* as the *Lex Hieronica*, shows surprising affinities to a law of his contemporary Philadelphus, which regulated the farming of taxes, and is known to us from a papyrus.

Even outside the Greek world the mercantile states of the West took up intercourse with the Hellenistic East. We have the case of Carthage, the greatest city of the West, which, as is shown by the request for a loan from Philadelphus mentioned above, was in friendly relations with the Ptolemaic kingdom. Trade with Alexandria is proved by the finds from Carthaginian graves, in which we may observe a gradual substitution of Hellenistic imports from Alexandria for purely Egyptian articles.

The entry of Rome herself into the Hellenistic trade system was more momentous still. Soon after the departure of Pyrrhus from Italy, Philadelphus, who then had by his side his clever sister and consort Arsinoe II, sent an embassy to Rome, to offer congratulations on this victory (*c.* 273), and a Roman embassy to Alexandria returned thanks for the civility, thus laying the foundation of the traditional friendship between Egypt and Rome. A few years later, Rome, which had with the mastery of the Greek cities of Lower Italy taken over new objects and new opportunities of trading, proclaimed in unmistakeable fashion its determination to enter into competition with other mercantile states. It was the period when Roman capitalist circles began to be active, and when a breach with the agrarian policy, exclusively pursued up to that time, was imminent, a breach which led to the first Punic War (264). Four years before this turning point (268) the Senate, rightly seeing that Rome could not get on among modern commercial states with its awkward copper currency, resolved, after having previously experimented with the Campanian currency, to introduce a silver coin, the *denarius*, on the model of the *drachma* of Alexander. To provide the new coin with a favourable circulation, the *denarius* was then given a slightly superior weight to the *drachma* of Alexander. One can but highly admire the accuracy with which the Senate drew this conclusion from the altered state of the world. The circle was thus closed, which united the whole world in a uniform system of trade.[1] Alexander's seed had sprung up indeed.

In the domain of culture the after-effects of Alexander's career are deeper and more durable than in the region of politics and economics. But they are more difficult to sketch briefly, as we have before us a vast quantity of isolated phenomena stretching over the world from Spain to China. One can do no more here than draw the broad lines of development and illustrate by individual examples the victorious advance of Hellenism at first in the East and later under the leadership of Rome in the West, then the awakening and strengthening of the Oriental reactions which finally led to the Orientalisation of the East and partly also of the West.

Alexander's leading principle of extending in the East Greek culture, which even before his time had begun to pass the frontiers of the Greek world, was adopted and carried out by his successors consciously and with vigour. The Seleucids especially, who both from the political and economic points of view had the greatest interest in attracting as many Greeks and Macedonians as possible into their kingdom, supplied the facilities for a large-scale development of Greek life in the numerous cities which, after

[1] See W. Otto, *Kulturgeschichte des Altertums*, 1925, p. 79 ff.

Alexander's example, they founded. Thus in the middle of the Oriental world rose Greek *Poleis*, whose citizens had brought with them and continued to use Greek language and religion, law and social customs. These cities decorated themselves with market places and public buildings for their councils and assemblies to meet in, and with temples of Greek gods. Everywhere gymnasia were constructed with palaestrae and baths; for the Greeks were well aware that their national gymnastic training, which was thoroughly foreign to the Orientals, was the best means of preserving their special character—and that was their aim, at any rate in the first generation, when they still felt themselves to be the victorious and dominant race, the superiors of the Oriental native. In the second book of the *Maccabees* (iv. 13) the gymnasial system is well described as 'the extreme of Hellenism'. Naturally the concentration of Greek population was greatest in the capitals of the Seleucids, Seleucia on the Tigris, and Antioch, both of which played a great part also in intellectual life. Though in Antioch there was too a large conflux of Syrians, Jews and other foreigners, yet the Seleucids endeavoured, not without success, to preserve for the city its Greek character.

The Ptolemies, however, succeeded in far greater measure in making their capital a centre of Hellenistic culture. It is true that many foreigners settled in Alexandria side by side with the Macedonians and the citizens of the Greek *Polis*; Rhacotis also remained as before an Egyptian quarter, and at an early date foreigners from every part of the world collected there, just as there gathered too an ever-increasing Jewish Dispersion (*Diaspora*), which was granted special community rights, outside the body of citizens, a so-called *Politeuma*. In spite of the international character which Alexandria soon acquired, it became a centre of Greek intellectual life, thanks to the first two Ptolemies, who deliberately aimed at making their capital, as far as possible, the intellectual and artistic focus of the whole civilised world. They succeeded to such a degree that once it was customary to call this period of the history of civilisation the 'Alexandrian'.

This description has been given up by modern writers as going too far, but Alexandria was certainly one of the greatest centres of culture of that period, and afterwards for centuries played a prominent part. It was the principal seat of the study of the various branches of science. After the death of Aristotle, who had embraced all human knowledge, these departments of science were severed from philosophy, and constituted independent subjects of research; in Alexandria this new science reached its zenith in the third century. But, as before so later, Athens remained the centre for philosophy, which could flourish more profitably in its quiet surroundings than in the bustle and noise of the royal court. At Athens not only the old schools, the Academy and the Peripatetics, continued to exist, but the founders of new schools, like Zeno, the founder of the Stoic school, and Epicurus, though not Athenians, yet as a matter of course founded their schools there. Ptolemy I, who intended to cultivate philosophy too, attempted to attract Theophrastus, the head of the Peripatetic school, to Alexandria, but Theophrastus declined the invitation, as did Menander the comedian, and Athens remained the home of the New Comedy.

It was due to Ptolemy I that the new departments of science found their home in Alexandria, and his creation of the Museum was of the greatest import in this respect. Probably in organising it he was advised by Demetrius of Phalerum, the pupil of Theophrastus, who had gone to his court, after his political career in Greece was at an end; but if Ptolemy listened to his suggestions, it must be assumed that he himself had a personal interest in these studies. As one of the oldest friends of Alexander's youth, who as 'body-guard' had been in the closest contact with him during the Asiatic campaign and had witnessed his passionate absorption in science, he doubtless owed this interest to his association with him. As Ptolemy left an affectionate memorial of his royal friend in his *Memoirs*, no doubt in his magnificent liberality to the sciences he believed he was acting as Alexander would have done. To this extent we may see in Alexander the primal source of the cultivation of science in Alexandria. The Museum, named after the cult of the Muses connected with it, was on the model of the Lyceum, the school of Aristotle, but was not intended to serve teaching so much as research. We might describe it in modern terms as a 'Royal Academy'. The king summoned thither the most distinguished scholars in the various branches of learning, and gave them maintenance and a salary, so that they might continue their researches without material anxieties. There had been nothing of the kind in the *Poleis* overseas.

As in the Lyceum Aristotle had provided the means of scientific research, so for the scholars of the Museum the necessary apparatus was supplied on a grand scale. The most important foundation was the Library, founded by Ptolemy I on the advice and with the help of Demetrius, and completed by his son Philadelphus. For the first time in the Greek world arose a library, where the whole treasures of Greek literature were collected in several hundred thousand papyrus rolls. In the Serapeum Philadelphus added another smaller library. Later, in rivalry with the Ptolemies, the Attalids created a library in Pergamum, of whose arrangements our excavations have given us some idea. But there is nothing to compare with Ptolemy's creation, save the great cuneiform library, founded in the seventh century by Assurbanipal king of Assyria, to the remains of which we chiefly owe our knowledge of Old Babylonian literature. However much we admire this act of Assurbanipal, it is significant of the difference between Oriental despotism and the 'enlightened absolutism' of the Ptolemies, that the cuneiform library of the king was stored up in his palace at Nineveh 'for the object of his own reading', while the library of Alexandria was to serve the general aims of science. From the textual criticism and exegesis of these literary treasures 'Philology' developed as a new science.

It is out of place to describe how subjects of Natural Science were promoted and flourished here. It will suffice to mention that for astronomical study an observatory was erected, and that a new impetus was given to medicine by permission for the dissection of human bodies, whereby scientific anatomy became possible. Zoological studies too were served by the zoological garden, in which Philadelphus out of personal interest collected rare examples of exotic animals. The first scholars of the day worked in Alexandria: Euclid the mathematician, Herophilus the doctor, the many-sided Eratosthenes, and many others. Foreign scholars also were in the closest relations to their Alexandrian colleagues, like Archimedes of Syracuse, the most talented of mathematicians and mechanical inventors, the astronomer Aristarchus of Samos—unless he was himself an Alexandrian—who grasped the heliocentric idea of Copernicus, that the earth turns on its axis round the sun, an idea which to be sure he was not yet able to prove.

Though this origin and development of the various branches of science can only be indicated, it must be emphasised that by the investigations and descriptions which Alexander caused his staff of scholars to make, he supplied much valuable material and the necessary stimulus to many sciences. It has often been pointed out how much Theophrastus' work *On Plants* owes to him. The extension of the geographical horizon and the correction of earlier maps by Alexander was of vast importance for geography. The new facts that he and his successors disclosed were worked up by Eratosthenes in his new picture of the earth in the third century.

It was not only science that was promoted in Alexandria, but also poetry and art. The Ptolemies endeavoured to attract to their capital and keep there the most famous poets and artists of their day. Of the Alexandrian poets let us single out the greatest of them, Callimachus of Cyrene,

who was occupied with the drawing up of the learned
catalogue of the Library. At times also Theocritus of
Syracuse stayed there and wrote some of his most beautiful
idylls. The liberality with which the Ptolemies rewarded
the victors in the musical competitions and the splendour
of their festivals attracted poets, musicians and artists of the
most varied kinds to Alexandria. It was from Alexander
that the Diadochi took over the idea of making the Games
(*Agones*) an instrument of propaganda for Greek culture in
the East (p. 258). The special circumstances of Alexander's
moving court and camp were the reasons why in some cases
the actors and musicians whom he fetched for his competitions formed themselves into unions under the direction of
prominent artists. It is easy to conjecture that this led to the
formation of the permanent bodies of '*Dionysiac Technitae*'
(artists), who in the Hellenistic Age took over the furnish-
ing of the musical *Agones*; out of their organisation and for
payment they supplied the necessary personnel, the writer,
the actors (tragic and comic), the musicians (lyre players,
flutists and so on.) This arrangement which was so important for the artistic life of the future, and gradually
covered the whole area of Greek culture, owed its origin,
it appears, to Alexander. Plastic artists also obtained from
the Ptolemies much opportunity of practising their art.
The attraction which the city had exercised on artists at
its formation was sure to increase, when it was decorated
by degrees with the most magnificent buildings, palaces
and temples. Here one might mention the wonderful
Pharos or lighthouse, the work of Sostratus of Cnidus.

With these extraordinarily successful efforts of the Ptolemies to make Alexandria the centre of Greek culture it is
at the first glance difficult to reconcile the fact that in the
Nile valley, apart from the single exception already mentioned, Ptolemais in Upper Egypt (p. 271), they founded
no Greek cities; and many think that they had no intention
of Hellenising the country. In reality—obviously from political or economical reasons, as to which we can only con-

jecture—they employed only different means to extend Greek population and therewith Greek culture in their country. They actually did much for Hellenisation in settling their troops, chiefly Macedonians and Greeks,— the Egyptians were at first excluded from service in the army—as cleruchs on fiefs held directly from the king. No close colonies arose in this way; according to the position of their lands the cleruchs belonged to the county towns or villages. These Macedonians and Greeks were widely dispersed over the country, sometimes in more compact bodies, as on the soil of the Fayum which was recovered by draining. But the soldiers were not the only Greek inhabitants of the country. Greek merchants and artisans also, for whom, as we saw, a lucrative employment was made possible in a different way from the Egyptians, settled in the country in increasing numbers, especially in the principal towns of the districts. Thus in these towns which had been from the earliest times the centres of Egyptian life, Greek quarters were gradually formed, in which soon arose all the outward signs of Greek culture, gymnasia, theatres and temples of Greek gods. Even in villages, which were very frequently occupied by Greek soldiery, gymnasia are occasionally found. The best evidence of the spread of Greek culture in the land is afforded by the finds of literary papyri scattered over the whole country up to the First Cataract. If Greek papyrus documents give us an idea of this spread of the Greek language, the remains of literary papyrus rolls are more notable from the standpoint of culture; they show us not only what authors were popular, but also that Greek literature was read not merely in the metropolis but to a large extent in the villages. Of course, there were also numerous villages, in which Egyptian life continued completely unchanged.

This settling together of Macedonians and Greeks, who had come from the most different places in the Greek world to live permanently side by side in the cities of Alexander and the Seleucids and in the settlements of Egypt, naturally exercised a great levelling effect. The differences of race, which in the mother country came out strongly in language and law, religion and custom, were sure to be smoothed away in this chance mixture of Greek society. The process is most noticeable in the matter of language. Local dialects gradually disappeared and the ground was prepared for a common language. In the only papyrus document we possess of Alexander's age there are Dorisms as well as Atticisms throughout the predominantly Ionic text, while in the numerous documents from the third century onwards such mixtures of dialect or dialectic forms do not occur. There we find nothing but the so-called 'common speech' (*Koine*). As the result of the progress of culture in the fifth and fourth centuries, the Attic language, Ionised in vocabulary and idiom, could alone claim to be the universal language of the world. The spread of this language was greatly influenced by Philip's adoption, which we have noticed, of Attic for his chancery and by Alexander's following suit after him. Soon a *Koine* was formed for literature too, and prevailed through the Hellenistic age, until at the beginning of the empire it was driven out by Atticism.

Like the dialects, the different views of law which were held by the mixed society disappeared in the new settlements. People could not any longer maintain the rights they had possessed in their *Poleis*. The laws were binding for all citizens, from whatever district they might have come. It appears that in the legislation of the Hellenistic age Attic law, already widely diffused by the Delian League, enjoyed the principal consideration. At any rate, the laws of Alexandria, as a valuable papyrus has informed us, went back to the laws of Solon. Moreover, the grants of privileges to certain cities, as well as the approved rights of other cities, granted from time to time by kings, contributed to a certain balance in this respect. Gradually in spite of local differences, in law as in language a certain unity began; and it is intelligible how under the emperors

Greek law often held its own against Roman, and to some extent succeeded in influencing the latter.

Equally in religion a levelling of local peculiarities came about through the intercourse of the different Greek settlers. A decisive point was that the royal founders of a city as a rule determined to what gods temples should be built, as is recorded in the case of Alexander, for instance, at the founding of Alexandria in Egypt. Equally the laws of the cities appointed by what gods the citizens should take the loyal oath.

Through all these influences the local differences of the settlers were more and more toned down, and the contrast between Macedonians and Greeks, which had still been strong under Alexander and his immediate successors, was softened, though it probably never disappeared,[1] partly because of the special military privileges, which the Macedonians possessed down to the Roman age. Nevertheless, if this unification of the Greek element, in place of its previous subdivision, lent force to efforts in the direction of Hellenisation, there were influences on the side of the Orientals, which strengthened their position in the conflict of cultures. First and foremost comes their numerical superiority. No exact figures can be given, but there is no doubt that in spite of all the Greek settlements there was a vast majority of Orientals. At the highest point of development in Egypt, in face of perhaps seven million Egyptians, there was not nearly a million of Macedonians and Greeks. In Asia, even after the large-scale colonisation by the Seleucids, there were extensive areas in which either no Greek cities existed or only a few in isolation. It was merely a quite thin upper-layer of Macedonians and Greeks that was spread over Egypt and Asia; apart from the above-mentioned more thickly settled regions, their cities and settlements were like islands rising out of a great sea.

Another obstacle was the extraordinary tenacity with

[1] [See Plutarch, *Aratus*, c. 38, for the feeling of Greeks towards Macedonians.]

which the Orientals generally clung to their own standards
of civilisation; whether these were high or low, it was with
difficulty that they could be induced to part with them.
This statement applies to their languages, which, in spite
of the spread of Greek they preserved, with the exception
of the Jews of the *Diaspora*. It applies more strikingly still
to their religion, and here we come to a point which
touches the ultimate cause of the final failure of Hellenisation. While the Greeks, as we said before, were always
ready to recognise in foreign gods their own, and were
willing to substitute their familiar names for the foreign
ones, the Oriental peoples invariably refused to take over
Greek gods and cults. When Ptolemy I wanted to create a
common cult for Greeks and Egyptians, he could not think
of suggesting a Greek god to the Egyptians; the Osiris-
Apis of Memphis was raised to be this common god under
the name of Sarapis. He was readily accepted by the
Greeks, who saw in him now Pluto, now other of their gods,
but the Egyptians called him in their native texts Osiris-
Apis as before. One may see in the behaviour of the Greeks
a profound recognition that the gods who reveal themselves
in nature are everywhere the same, though they may be
addressed by different names; one may praise them for their
toleration: but in the history of civilisation this attitude
spelt weakness as against the Orientals, who would make
no compromise or bargain. Official polytheism had long
been unable to satisfy the Greeks themselves, and the
educated had long sought a substitute in philosophy. The
inclination to proselytism was consequently all the weaker
on the Greek side. Indeed the thought had previously been
quite alien to them, and in their search for religious satisfaction they were more prone to seek an answer in foreign
cults. According to a dictum of Wilamowitz, the rule of the
Hellenes over the East was bound to fail, 'because they
could not conquer its soul'.   *

In spite of these contrasts of principle and the great
numerical preponderance of the Orientals, within the limits

thus imposed Alexander's idea of spreading Greek culture in the East was realised with great success by his immediate successors in Asia and Europe. The brilliance with which Greek life developed in their capitals has been already shown. In other ways too the cities founded by Alexander and his successors maintained themselves as centres of Greek culture, and in the differently conceived settlements of the Ptolemies Greek language and life grew and expanded. But, apart from religion, always an exception, the Hellenisation of the Orientals in the cities, which as a rule were founded in connexion with Oriental settlements already in existence, was gradually limited to the Oriental population that lived side by side with the new-comers; in the country, where no Greeks lived, Oriental life pursued the even tenor of its way.

The extension of the Greek language among the educated upper classes of Orientals from the new foundations to other cities of the East was probably influenced by the fact that Greek became the official language of the empire, the language which magistrates used in their proclamations. Only exceptionally, when in the state interest all subjects had to be made cognisant of the contents of a document, was a translation into the native language published alongside of the Greek text, as we have it recorded for Egypt. Accordingly, the upper circles of Orientals, who were in close intercourse with Greek officials, or were ambitious to carve out a career for themselves, soon learned Greek in addition to their mother tongue, without giving up the latter; for instance, in Egypt the priests at an early date used Greek in intercourse with the officials, since this was prescribed. No doubt Oriental traders and artisans quickly began to do the like for trade reasons. The Jews of the *Diaspora* adopted the world language very soon, and so intensively that in the third century in Egypt it became necessary to translate the Scriptures into Greek, because in public worship the congregations could no longer understand them sufficiently in the original Hebrew. Thus arose the

Septuagint, the Greek translation of the Old Testament, in the third and second centuries; and a Hellenistic Jewish literature as well. But this Hellenism was only an outward veneer; in reality the Jews remained Jews, who adhered faithfully to their Law, and confronted the Gentiles with an exclusiveness that the Maccabaean movement only heightened. Later on there were conflicts in many places between Jews and Greeks.

Even in the second generation after Alexander we find some prominent Orientals, who were so completely Hellenised that they contributed to Greek literature books written in Greek. One is Berosus, a priest of Marduk in Babylon, who dedicated to Antiochus I a book on old Babylonian history, which he had written in Greek, using the cuneiform traditions. The other is Manetho, an Egyptian priest, who under Philadelphus wrote an Egyptian history in Greek, using the traditions of the Egyptian temples. These books are the more interesting evidence of the victory of Hellenism, in that before their time neither Babylonians nor Egyptians, though they left valuable annals and the like, ever thought of writing a history of their country in the sense of Greek historiography, as Berosus and Manetho now did. Another Semite before them entered much more deeply into Greek intellectual life than they. This was Zeno, of Phoenician descent, from Citium in Cyprus, who at the end of the fourth century, after studying philosophy at Athens, founded there the Stoic school, which for centuries played a leading part in the intellectual life first of the Greeks and then of the Romans. Hellenised Semites appeared also later in Greek philosophy, like the Carthaginian Cleitomachus, originally called Hasdrubal, who in the second century became the head of the Academy at Athens.

We may observe at an early date the influence of Greek art, or the co-operation of Greek artists in Oriental works, as in the above-mentioned reliefs of Alexander's age at Karnak and Luxor (p. 258), or in the tomb of Petosiris in

Hermopolis, of the age of Ptolemy I. On the other hand, we pointed above (p. 258) to Oriental influence on Greek art in Alexander's day. Thus early there began in the East a blend of cultures, very typical of the Hellenistic period, and creative of much new life by the reciprocal fertilisation and penetration of Greek and Oriental.

Outside the sphere of Oriental culture Greek art went on developing pure and undefiled, in Hellas and the islands, especially Rhodes, and also in the Greek cities on the coast of Asia Minor, like Miletus, Priene and Magnesia. This, particularly holds good of Pergamum, with the monuments commemorating the victories of Attalus, and the Great Altar. In Pergamum the struggle with the Galatians was conceived as a fight with the 'barbarians', and thus there was preserved as a source of vigour the old healthy national idea of a contrast between Greeks and barbarians, which elsewhere, as we shall see, had disappeared. In connexion with this we find very early at Pergamum the beginnings of a style of art which revived the classical and from the second century onwards spread throughout the Greek world. *

In the East, however, there were not only blends of culture, but mixtures of race, which assumed great dimensions in course of time. The assembly of the Macedonian army at Babylon after Alexander's death rejected his policy of fusion, and his successors therefore in Asia and Egypt did not think of promoting it, but pursued a national Macedonian policy instead. Nevertheless, the permanent settlement of Macedonians and Greeks side by side with Orientals had as its final consequence—without the action of governments—a relaxation of this proud standpoint of superiority and a readiness to contract marriages with the Oriental neighbour. From the middle of the third century we find in Egypt the first proofs of such mixed marriages. In the second century there is a Greco-Egyptian mixed population, definitely formed, and constantly growing. Thus the natural conditions of life, though only here and there and in the lower classes, led to a mixture of races. The historical result was different from that at which Alexander had aimed; while he had thought exclusively of a fusion with the Iranians, the actual mixtures took place with those peoples whom he had not contemplated, Egyptians and Semites (p. 208).

Still, the basic idea, which had dominated Alexander in his latest years, was so far realised that the old contrast of 'Greek and Barbarian' was by these mixtures entirely abolished; even Alexander by his Iranian policy and by its culmination, the policy of fusion, had broken away from this national principle, though it was he who in his youth had made it stronger than ever by the adoption of the Panhellenic idea.

What was accomplished in actual historical development during these generations was plainly not without influence on the theory of the philosophers. No doubt theory went ahead of practice; the Cynics had maintained cosmopolitan views before Alexander (p. 13). If, however, these ideas were deepened by the Stoic school and made the basis of their new view of the world, the motive power was certainly supplied by the fact that Alexander had thrown down the barriers between Greek and barbarian; the development of the next generations, which removed the barriers for all barbarians, only brought theory and practice more closely together; and thus Hellenism both in theory and practice received its cosmopolitan character. About a century after Alexander the great scholar Eratosthenes spoke as the representative of the modern Hellenistic man, when he blamed those, who, like Aristotle in contrast with Alexander, had divided men into Greeks and barbarians, the former to be treated as friends, the latter as enemies, and demanded that they should rather be divided by their moral and intellectual qualities into good and bad; for there were many bad Greeks, and among the barbarians many very highly educated, like the Indians and Iranians, and also the Romans and Carthaginians, who were politically worthy of admiration. This saying of Eratosthenes, in which he coolly and clearly draws out the result of the experiences of this revolutionary century, stands like a landmark in the history of the Greeks; the old epoch in which there had been a strong Greek national sentiment was over, and its place was taken by the idea of an international citizenship of the world. We shall have to return again to the consequences of this change which had gradually matured since the time of Alexander.

The influence of Alexander in the spread of Greek cul-ture is not limited to the East; the victorious march of Hellenism westwards is not to be understood apart from his life's work. If he could not carry out his latest plans, which were directed to the West, yet by laying the founda-tions for a world-wide spread of Greek culture in his eastern empire, he created the necessary conditions for its expansion westwards, beyond the political frontiers of his realm. Even before his day Greek culture had exhibited a need of expansion, and no doubt without him it might have extended farther in the West; but the conquest of Rome by Hellenism—and that is what counted in the history of the world—would never have taken place, as it did, without the conditions created by him. Since the days of the kings Rome had taken over from the Greek cities of Lower Italy many elements of Greek culture, first the alphabet, then the cults of gods, art and some legal ideas —yet these were but drops compared to the broad stream, with which in increasing measure from the middle of the third century B.C. Greek culture saturated Roman society. The beginning of this process has rightly been dated at 240 —a year after the victorious end of the first Punic War— when the Greek freedman Livius Andronicus of Tarentum produced for the first time a Latin translation of a Greek play for the Roman games. There are two things charac-teristic of Rome in this affair. In the first place it was the Senate by whose orders the performance was given. It is extremely noteworthy that this step came officially from the government. When we remember that it was also the

Senate which had twenty-eight years earlier initiated a silver coinage, to introduce Roman trade into the Hellenistic trade area, it is very significant that the same Senate now ordered this production of a Greek play. This justifies us in speaking of a program of culture, parallel to the economic program; connexion with the Hellenistic world was now to be sought in the intellectual sphere. For this reason it seems legitimate to say that the Hellenising of Rome presupposes the life-work of Alexander; if Greek culture had not already attained a world-wide position, the Senate would have seen no occasion to introduce it into Rome.

Secondly it was of the highest import that that Greek play was produced in a Latin rendering. For the future history of Europe it was of the greatest moment that the Romans, when they took over Greek literature, adhered to Latin, their mother tongue. This independence which the Romans retained against foreign culture distinguishes them from Oriental peoples, and corresponds to their strong proud national self-consciousness, in which at the last resort lies the secret of their wonderful strength. But while from the beginning Greek poetry was rendered in Latin, Latin prose had not yet then developed, and the first imitations of Greek prose literature at Rome were in the Greek language. The first Roman who attempted to write a Roman History, Q. Fabius Pictor—the Roman counterpart to Berosus and Manetho—about the end of the third century wrote his *Annals* in Greek, and so did his immediate successors. Cato the Elder in the second century was the first to produce a Latin history in his *Origines*. From that time onwards Romans wrote their prose works only in Latin.

It is not the place to describe here how this Hellenisation, inaugurated by the Senate, the representative of the ruling aristocracy, expanded steadily during the following centuries in Roman society, especially in the circle of the Scipios in the second century. It should only be noted that in language, as in other matters and principally in art, the Romans, notwithstanding all Hellenisation, constantly asserted their own peculiar character, so that the result was a Greco-Roman mixture whose quality, though determined by the Greek ingredient, yet possessed a specifically Roman note. In Cicero and the poetic circle of Augustus this Greco-Roman mixed culture attains a height which lifts it far above the decadent Greek culture of the period. For the whole course of later European history down to the present day it was of cardinal significance that the Romans were permanently successful in diffusing this Greco-Roman culture over the west of the continent, particularly over Spain and Gaul. They laid the foundations of the Romance nations and their culture, and decided that Latin should be the language of the West, as Greek was of the East. Be it also noticed that this Greco-Roman culture, which developed a Greco-Roman art at the beginning of the Imperial age, had a second effect on the East now under the Roman rule, especially in Syria, where the Romans erected great buildings at Baalbek and Palmyra. The essential independence and importance of this Greco-Roman mixed culture compels us to make the Hellenistic period cease with Augustus, and with him to begin a new era of ancient history, that of the Roman empire.

While the Romanisation of western Europe shows its effects to the present day, the Hellenisation of the East had finally to give way to Orientalism. This difference is explained not only by the advantages of the Roman method of colonisation and by the strong protection which the Roman empire afforded to the colonies of the West, but chiefly because in the West it was a question of bringing culture to barbaric peoples who were on an inferior level, while in the East the task was to extend Greek culture to peoples of a high-level primaeval civilisation. In the East alone could there be a real warfare of cultures. To be sure, when Alexander reached these Oriental peoples, the zenith of their development was past by centuries or even millennia; their creative power seemed to have died out, and their condition was generally one of stagnation. But the Greek culture offered them by Alexander and his successors woke them out of their lethargy. No matter whether they allowed this Greek culture to affect them or felt themselves impelled to oppose it, their intellectual powers were strengthened, and their life began to pulse more vigorously.

The struggle was bound to end in the triumph of the East; the rise of the Orientals corresponded with a gradual relaxation of Greek vitality. There were divers causes which contributed to this. First we may point to the disintegrating effects of the mixture of the colonists with varied Orientals, which in time altered the aspect of the Greek world in the East. Power and will to resist the Oriental ways disappeared; the Oriental wives brought their customs and above all their religion into Greek families. Then there was the very considerable influence of the different climate, which suggested the assumption of Oriental habits that had themselves largely grown up under the influence of this climate. When Livy makes a speaker in 189 say that the Macedonians living in Alexandria, Seleucia, Babylonia and other colonies had degenerated into Egyptians, Syrians and Parthians, there is, for that time, some rhetorical exaggeration, but also some truth. The most fatal thing, however, was that the Greeks lost, as we saw, their proud national self-consciousness, which had been formerly expressed in the antithesis of Greeks and barbarians, and thereby lost as well a strong impulse to develop their national energies. It is no accident that the great works of Greek culture which possess eternal value for us were created not in the days of cosmopolitanism, but in those earlier centuries when the Greeks, proudly conscious of their vigour and superiority, chose that formula in which to express their national feeling. Certainly the Hellenisation of the East, as far as it succeeded, was a great feat on the part of the Greeks, but the chief benefit was derived by the Orientals: they as a rule were the receivers, the Greeks the givers; and finally, with the loss of their national feelings, the Greeks gave themselves up.

A further important consideration which led to the decay of Greek power was the foreign rule of the Romans, which in the second century paralysed the Greek world, and pre-eminently Greece itself. Worse than the economic results was the intellectual oppression that was thus exercised. No nation can prosper which has not its complete freedom, but is under foreign rule; and the situation is desperate, when as in this case there is no prospect of the recovery of freedom. A nation which can no longer believe in itself and its mission is lost.

These reasons enable us to understand how from the second century decay becomes more and more evident in all the performances of Greek culture. The issue of the great struggle with the rising Orientals could not be doubtful. The course of this conflict can be sketched only in brief outline. Previously the Seleucids had been the protectors and promoters of Hellenism throughout the whole of Hither Asia, but this protection became limited to a very confined area, when by the defeat of 129 they were obliged to resign to the Parthians all territory beyond the Euphrates, and were reduced to ruling over Syria and Cilicia only. The Parthian kings, the Arsacids, not only tolerated Hellenism in their kingdom, for they needed Greek trade, but often, officially as Philhellenes, coquetted with Hellenism, with the object of promoting it and giving a Hellenistic veneer to their court at Ctesiphon, opposite Seleucia on the Tigris, where they had fixed their capital. In Parthian art too Greek influences are unmistakeable; but this Philhellenism was confined to the court, and among the Parthian people, especially the magnates and the army, was definitely looked on with disfavour. These circles tenaciously adhered to Oriental ways, and a reaction against Hellenism began. In Egypt too from the beginning of the third century there set in a nationalistic movement, which for a time resulted in the loss of Upper Egypt, and, under the weak government of the later Ptolemies, led to a strengthening of the Egyptian element against the Greeks.

This reaction of the East against Hellenism, waking up here and there at first, and later becoming general, is of extraordinary interest for the present day, which is witnessing a re-awakening of the East and a recoil against the European. Just as in this century it is the efforts to make Asia European which brings about this phenomenon, so then it was the efforts of Alexander and his successors to Hellenise Asia which produced a like revulsion.

If one surveys the whole course of the progressive advance of Orientalism, one sees that the development—apart from local differences—was not accomplished at the same rate in the different regions of culture and did not end in the same way. Earliest and most sweeping was the victory of the East in religion; its victory was complete also in language; but Greek art and science were never conquered, they repeatedly fertilised the East down to the coming of Islam. The religious victory of the East is explained by the tolerant spirit of the Greeks, confronted by the obstinacy of the Oriental in adhering to his religion. There was also the fact that the Oriental religions had certain qualities which exerted a growing power of attraction on Greeks dissatisfied with their own religion, so that they entered more and more into the different Eastern world of thought and feeling, just as to-day many Europeans take refuge in Buddhism. The greatest charm was exercised by the great Oriental religions of the future life which promised bliss hereafter to the believer, that is to each individual, quite apart from his nationality. From early days the Greeks had been familiarised with such ideas by the Orphic teaching and the Eleusinian mysteries, but now the Oriental religions tempted and won them by a vigorous propaganda, which was all the more decisive, as a longing for this comfortable assurance of a future life ran through the lower classes, who could find no solace in philosophy.

This strong Oriental movement was not limited to the Hellenistic East, but passed triumphantly through Greece and laid hold of Rome and the West. The Divine Mother of Asia Minor led the way—Cybele, whose orgiastic cult was introduced into Rome in obedience to a Sibylline oracle during the Hannibalic War (204). If there was an external occasion for this, later cults came westwards in the course of the general expansion which was promoted by Oriental traders, who more and more sought the West, and everywhere practised their native cults in religious groups. Thus Egyptian gods reached the West, Isis, Osiris, and the new god Sarapis, who was compared with various gods and in the second century A.D. embraced them all as 'Pantheos': under the cry of 'Sarapis is One' his worship was very extensively diffused in the empire. The 'Syrian gods' too, Hadad and Atargatis, became widely known, as Syrian merchants grew prominent in trade. With the gods came astrology, originally a part of old Babylonian religion, but now erected into a spurious science which pretended to fix beforehand the fate of each individual by the constellation at the hour of his birth or conception. Berosus, whom we have above mentioned as historian, had tried to impart this Babylonian teaching to the Greeks; and after the canonical hand-book had been written in Egypt in the second century, astrology victoriously proceeded westwards. Cato the Elder warned his countrymen against the Chaldaeans, as its heralds were called, and in 139 they were banished from Rome. But they returned—in the same way the cult of Isis was several times but fruitlessly forbidden in Rome; and finally the disastrous fatalistic superstition reached the highest circles, even the imperial throne, and for many centuries was busy in Europe. It is a sign of the disintegration of society to-day that this superstition has again crept in. Later came the Persian Mithras with his mysteries, after he had undergone some changes in Asia Minor, and with him the dualistic doctrine of Zarathustra. This Mithras cult, particularly through the Roman army, spread as far as Germany and Britain.

All these Oriental cults not only were rivals of the Roman state gods but also carried on an embittered warfare with one another. At last they were all defeated, along with the gods of the Roman state, by the new Christian religion, which surpassed them all in the depth of its ideas. It found the struggle more difficult and carried it on more vigorously with its Oriental competitors than with the gods of the Roman state, whose authority had been weakened by the others. By origin Christianity was an Oriental religion. Its victory led to a great increase of Oriental influence in the world; but in the history of its expansion and inner development Hellenism once more played a part of importance. It is a strong proof of the vigour still possessed by Hellenism that this new Oriental religion required the Greek language for its propaganda. In this Greek *Koine* we have the confessional books of Christianity. By the spread of Hellenism in Asia Minor, where Christian propaganda first began, the way was made smooth for it. Moreover, the inner development of Christian doctrine was affected by the fact that it gradually entered into close connexion with the spirit of Greek science, so that one can speak of a Hellenisation of Christian doctrine. Here we may point to the great Fathers of the Church, Clement and Origen of Alexandria (second and third centuries A.D.), who in conflict with the foes of Christianity borrowed the intellectual weapons of Greek science and laid the foundation of an alliance with Greek philosophy. Thus in the history of Christianity the old city of Alexander again played a leading part. The centre of this work was the Christian Catechetical school, whose arrangements were influenced by the pattern of the pagan Museum, the creation of Ptolemy I.

The age of Origen was followed by a political revolution which was to be fatal to the existence of Hellenism in the East. In 226 the rule of the Parthian Arsacids was overthrown by Ardashir I (Artaxerxes), who founded the dynasty of the Sassanids. He was related to a family of Persian dynasts, who at Istakhr, not far from Persepolis, had preserved their independence under the Seleucids and the Arsacids, and had cultivated the old Persian tradition, and especially the religion of Zarathustra. In the new Persian empire of the Sassanids, which aimed at being a renewal of the Achaemenid empire, this Persian religion was elevated into a state church, and the Persian national feeling thus aroused led—in contrast with the Arsacid policy—to a consciously hostile reaction against Hellenism. For centuries first Rome and then Byzantium, as representing Greco-Roman and Byzantine culture, had to fight with this Persian empire, till in the middle of the seventh century it succumbed to the advance of the Moslems and became a part of the empire of the Caliphs. In spite of antagonism of principle, the high culture of the Sassanids could not quite escape Greek influences, just as in its turn it affected Byzantium also.

Even before the national reaction of the Sassanids against Hellenism, the Romans had dealt a death-blow to Eastern Hellenism by the shameful destruction of the Greek city of Seleucia on the Tigris, which they burnt down in 164 during the war of Verus with the Parthians. Through this disaster the Greeks lost their bulwark beyond the Euphrates. The Greek language tended to disappear, and Aramaic, which had already had the widest circulation under the Achaemenids, spread more and more.

Elsewhere also the Oriental languages, which never ceased to exist in the country outside the Greek cities, finally drove out Greek altogether. In Syria Aramaic was so vigorous during the whole Seleucid period that under the empire as the 'Syrian language' it became an important literary language, which we find in particular in the service of the Christian Church, and which has also left us secular works like the Syro-Roman law-book, from which we can see that in Syria beside Roman law Greek

law also had its place. The extinction of Hellenism is witnessed by the further fact that Macedonian names of cities
disappear and give way to the old native names; thus
Aleppo and Acco bear again their old names, their Hellenistic names Beroea and Ptolemais being forgotten.

Equally in Egypt the native language was finally victorious over the Greek. The last Greek papyrus texts—
Arabic-Greek bilingual—belong to the tenth century. As
the oldest papyrus is of the age of Alexander, it is a vast
period—about 1300 years—during which we can follow
the effects of Alexander's life-work in the continuance of
the Greek language in the Nile valley. The Egyptian
language prevailed. In spite of all the success of Hellenisation, the old tongue had always survived amongst the
masses of the people, and after they became Christian, as
the so-called 'Coptic', it developed a literature which like
the Syrian was predominantly Christian, but also included
a secular literature, in connexion with which we may mention a Coptic version of the romance of Alexander. We may
regard it as a last triumph of Hellenism that from the third
century A.D. the Egyptians transcribed this Coptic language, which is nothing but the latest development of the
old Egyptian, in the Greek alphabet, with a few additional
demotic signs, and soon gave up hieroglyphs and the
demotic script. Coptic, in spite of the Arabic of the new
conquerors, continued till the eighteenth century, and
in a few cases into the nineteenth century; and the Coptic
Bible is still read, though not understood, in the Coptic
Liturgy. But as in Hither Asia Arabic was the real
conqueror.

Lastly if we turn to the development of art in the East,
we cannot here fully show how in course of centuries that
mixture of Greek with Oriental art, the beginnings of
which we described above, went through various complicated changes. The external and internal reasons which
in general led to the weakening of the Hellenic factor were
bound to tell in the artistic sphere, and in the process of

time the Oriental elements in the combination became more prominent. Yet in many departments Hellenistic art showed itself a creative and vigorous factor of culture. It should be noticed that even in the art of the Sassanids, in spite of the nationalistic attitude of their rulers, Hellenistic influences are unmistakeable. The arched building, which in domes and vaulting was greatly developed in Sassanid art—for example, in the palace of the founder of the dynasty, Ardashir I, at Firusabad—is based on the previous development of these forms in Syrian Hellenistic art, though the arch was not unknown to the ancient East.

Thanks to the latest surprising results of exploration, the evolution of Hellenistic art in Bactria, and its influence eastwards, deserve our special interest. In this country, for which Alexander had to fight hard, and in which about the middle of the third century Diodotus set up an independent Greek kingdom, Greek culture seems to have reached a high level. For the most part we know only the coins of the Bactrian kings, but with their fine portraits and their divine types they show such an extraordinary beauty and maturity of artistic power that we may draw conclusions from them as to the general cultivation of art in the country. Separated from the western world by the growth of Parthia, the expansive force of state and culture turned eastwards, and at the beginning of the second century, when these rulers succeeded in occupying the valley of the Kabul and the Punjab, and later for a time the southern valley of the Indus, Bactrian art won an increasingly important influence in Indian life. Bactrian artists hellenised the Indian gods, and after the analogy of the types of Greek gods represented Buddhist subjects in the language of Greek art; they even, as the latest investigation has made probable, first created for the Indians the meditative type of Buddha, by borrowing from Greek divine types. Though this Greco-Indian art is exhibited in numerous works of art, first during the early empire in the art of Gandhāra, the district of Peshawar, yet probably these types go back to an earlier date. The extraordinary finds of the Prussian Turfan expeditions, which we now see in Le Coq's splendid arrangement in the Berlin Ethnological Museum, have recently given us the startling information that Greco-Buddhist art reached Eastern Turkestan, where it meets us in numerous monuments from the fourth to the ninth century. Even so the distant harvest of Hellenistic art is not yet exhausted; for this art of Eastern Turkestan exercised a strong influence on the art of China and even of Japan in painting and sculpture. Thus the perspective point of view entered the art of East Asia by this mediation from Greek art, which had adopted it in the fifth century. The Persian poet Nisami (twelfth century) relates in his book on Alexander that Iskander reached China from India by way of Tibet, and that a competition arose between Greek and Chinese painters, in which finally the Greeks won. According to our present knowledge we may find in this poetic fancy a deeper meaning: Greek art would never have carried its effects as far as China, if Alexander had not conquered the East up to India and spread Greek culture so far.

Recent research has likewise recognised more clearly that the art of Islam and Islamic culture in general were strongly influenced by Hellenism. While Mommsen called Islam 'the executioner of Hellenism', present Islamic scholars see in Hellenism one of the components of Islamic culture, and actually one of the foundations upon which it was built. It was always known that the Arabs took over Greek philosophy, medicine and other sciences, and gave back Aristotle to Mediaeval Europe. The special part which Alexandria, where there were still learned scholars at the time of the Arab conquest of Egypt, played in the transmission of Greek sciences to the Arabs, has just lately been proved. Moreover, it is only recent research which has shown that beside the Sassanid and Byzantine arts Hellenistic art was one of the sources of the Islamic art which was gradually evolved. The new view-point could be formulated authoritatively in the phrase: 'without Alexander no Islamic civilisation'.[1]

The book of Nisami on Alexander that we have just mentioned is one of the last phases of the Alexander romance,[2] which in its oldest constituents took its origin in Alexandria at an early date, and later, from the beginning of the Middle Ages, spread over the whole world, East and West alike. Though the Greek version of Pseudo-Callisthenes, which is the basis of all these Oriental and western works, is not a popular book, as was previously supposed, but has a semi-learned kernel, cognate with the historians of Alexander and particularly with Cleitarchus, yet the unprecedented circulation of this strange literary product demonstrates what a huge impression the heroic figure of Alexander made upon succeeding generations. By the Latin translations of Julius Valerius (fourth century) and of the Archpresbyter Leo (tenth century) the Alexander romance of Pseudo-Callisthenes became known to the civilised peoples of Europe, and was reproduced in different languages as far as Iceland. Even the German poem on Alexander by the priest Lamprecht (about 1130) through the medium of the French poem by Alberich of Besançon (eleventh century) goes back to the same source. Similarly the Oriental peoples took over this half prosaic, half fabulous book of Pseudo-Callisthenes, translated it and incorporated into it many features of the legend about Alexander which had grown up in the East. While the Christian Orientals preserved the feature of the legend that arose out of Egyptian local patriotism, whereby Alexander was son of the last Egyptian Pharaoh, Nectanebo II (p. 131), Firdausi and Nisami from Persian national pride made him a scion of the Achaemenid house and thus their own

---

[1] C. H. Becker, *Der Islam als Problem* (*Der Islam*, i. 1910), p. 15; E. Herzfeld, *Die Genesis der islamischen Kunst* (*ib.* p. 27).

[2] A. Ausfeld, *Der griechische Alexanderroman*, 1907. W. Kroll, *Historia Alexandri Magni*, i. 1926.

national hero. In the Moslem poets Alexander himself is a Moslem, who, as in Nisami, goes to Mecca and prays in the Kaaba. In the Koran Alexander lives on; for the Dhulkarnain ('he with the two horns'), mentioned in the 18th *Sure*, is interpreted as Iskander, probably a reminiscence of the son of Ammon decorated with the two horns of Ammon. Even in Jewish eschatological literature Alexander plays a part. So each race in its own way tried to appropriate Alexander.

The most astonishing thing of all is that according to the reports of modern travellers even in our own day the memory of Alexander is green in many places. Thus Franz von Schwarz,[1] who at the end of last century lived long in Turkestan, states that the headmen of the Eastern mountainous districts of Badakhshan maintain that they are directly descended from Alexander, while the other inhabitants of this country regard themselves as descendants of his generals and warriors; in Marghelan, the capital of Ferghana, men even to-day venerate a red silk banner believed to have been used by Alexander in his campaigns, and his supposed tomb is held sacred. Sven Hedin has reported something of the same kind. As Alexander never reached these eastern regions, von Schwarz conjectures that perhaps the old population of Bactria and Sogdiana were driven by the Mongols into these regions and took with them recollections of Alexander to their new home. Thus the name of Alexander was not wiped out even by the devastating marches of Jenghiz Khan and Tamerlane.

But in the West throughout the Middle Ages at least to the Renaissance he survived in men's minds purely as the fabulous hero of romance, and his true history was forgotten. Only gradually has the real Alexander been roused to life again. It will soon be a century since Droysen wrote his talented pioneer work. Since then each generation has tried to form its ideas of this unique personality, and that

[1] F. von Schwarz, *Alexanders des Grossen Feldzüge in Turkestan*, 1906, p. 95.

will be so, as long as we have a culture which does not re-
pudiate its connexion with the ancient world.[1]

[1] The English reader is referred also to E. R. Bevan, article
Alexander in *Encyclopaedia Britannica*, 1910; D. G. Hogarth, *Philip
and Alexander of Macedon*, 1897; B. I. Wheeler, *Alexander the Great*, 1900;
Sir P. M. Sykes, *Ten Thousand Miles in Persia*, 1902; *Cambridge History
of India*, vol. i. chaps. xv.-xvi., E. R. Bevan. To the German author-
ities should be added the following articles in Pauly-Wissowa's
Lexikon: *Kallisthenes*, i. (F. Jacoby), ii. (W. Kroll); *Kleitarchus* (F.
Jacoby); ἑταῖροι (Plaumann); *Reiterei* and *Sarisse* (E. Lammert);
Schlachtordnung (Makedoner) and *Kriegskunst* (E. and F. Lammert).

NOTES

THE ABBREVIATIONS for the most commonly cited ancient sources and modern works follow:

ANCIENT SOURCES
Arr.: Arrian
Curt.: Quintus Curtius Rufus
Diod.: Diodorus Siculus
Just.: Justin
Plut. *Alex.*: Plutarch, *Alexander*

MODERN WORKS
Badian, "Harpalus,": E. Badian, "Harpalus," *Journal of Hellenic Studies*, LXXXI (1961), 16–43.
Burn, *Alex.*: A. R. Burn, *Alexander the Great and the Hellenistic World*. New York, 1962.
Fuller, *Generalship:* J. F. C. Fuller, *The Generalship of Alexander the Great*. New Brunswick, N. J., 1960.
Jacoby, *FGrH:* F. Jacoby, *Die Fragmente der griechischen Historiker*, Vols. IIB and IID. Berlin, 1927–30.
Pearson, *Lost Histories:* Lionel Pearson, *The Lost Histories of Alexander the Great*. New York, 1960.
Robinson, *Alex.*: C. A. Robinson, Jr., *Alexander the Great. Meeting of East and West in World Government and Brotherhood.* New York, 1947.
Robinson, *Hist. of Alex.*: *The History of Alexander the Great.* Vols. I and II. Providence, 1953–63.
Tarn, *Alex.*: W. W. Tarn, *Alexander the Great*. Vols. I and II. Cambridge, 1948.

NOTES TO THE TEXT

Page
xxix. For bibliography on Cleitarchus see Pearson, *Lost Histories*, pp. 212–42, and J. R. Hamilton, "Cleitarchus and Aristobulus," *Historia*, X (1961), 448–58. Wilcken appears to have followed the usual German tradition on an early date for Cleitarchus. Both Tarn and Pearson have argued for a later date in the opening decades of the third century B.C.

3. Alexander was born in the summer of 356 (Plut. *Alex.* 3. 3–5), though we remain uncertain of the date. He died in June, 323. Thus he was thirty-two at the time of his death, and, contrary to Wilcken's statement, well into his thirty-third year, having nearly reached his thirty-fourth.

30. On Greek and Macedonian warfare in general the reader will find useful F. E. Adcock's *The Greek and Macedonian Art of War* (Berkeley and Los Angeles, 1957; paperback edition, 1962). On Alexander in particular one must now refer to Major-General J. F. C. Fuller, *The Generalship of Alexander the Great* (New Brunswick, N. J., 1960), especially pp. 39–54 on the organization of the Macedonian army.

34. The essence of Isocrates' argument can be seen in the *Panegyricus,* 133–34 and 170–89. In addition to his oration, *Philip,* one should read Isocrates' third epistle, *To Philip,* although its authenticity has been questioned. See J. P. V. D. Balsdon, "The 'Divinity' of Alexander the Great," *Historia,* I (1950), 367, n. 24.

45. Unfortunately our literary sources are nearly silent on the formation of the League of Corinth; see two slight passages in Diodorus (16. 89. 1–3) and Justin (9. 5). The most complete account of the settlement at Corinth is found in the fragments of an inscription which states the terms of the treaty. Text and commentary (with bibliography) is in M. Tod, *Greek Historical Inscriptions,* II (Oxford, 1948), No. 177. The Hellenic League was apparently revived in 302 B.C. Portions of the inscription noting this renewal have survived (*Inscriptiones Graecae,* IV². 68), and lend some inferences about Philip's settlement. Also see M. Cary, "A Constitution of the United States of Greece," *Classical Quarterly,* XVII 1923), 137–48, and Carl Roebuck, "The Settlements of Philip II with the Greek States in 338 B.C.," *Classical Philology,* XLIII (1948), 73–92. Also J. A. O. Larsen, *Representative Government in Greek and Roman History* (Berkeley, 1955).

48. Diodorus (16. 89. 3) relates that at Corinth Philip was made commander-in-chief (*strategos autokrator*) of the Greeks. Some scholars have used this and other evidence to suggest that in effect Philip was the military ruler of the Greek cities, and that the Corinthian League was a military alliance (*symmachia*), not a general peace designed to provide for the internal good order of Greece, as the inscription (see note above) seems to indicate. Moreover, Arrian (7. 9. 5) only adds to the confusion: ". . . and Philip having been appointed *hegemon autokrator* of all the Greeks together for the campaign against the Persians . . ."

Wilcken has offered a reasonable solution. It would appear that Philip, and Alexander after him, held two positions. The first was that of *hegemon* of the League, a civil and military post which enabled him to provide for the security of Greece. Either concurrently, or shortly afterward, Philip was also appointed *strategos autokrator,* enabling him to command a Greek and Macedonian allied army to campaign against Persia. Thus while the League was used as a vehicle for Philip's overseas command, his generalship probably should be kept separate from his executive authority as *hegemon* of the League.

49. Diodorus (16. 95. 2–4) ends his account of Philip by suggesting that his success in establishing such a powerful kingdom was due more to his skill in diplomacy than to the force of arms, and that Philip himself took more pride in his diplomatic successes than in his prowess on the field of battle.

53. There is a general paucity of evidence on Alexander's boyhood and training. Philip's career is covered in some detail by Diodorus in his sixteenth book, but even in his account of Philip's later years, Alexander is not a prominent figure. Arrian's account commences with the invasion of Asia by Alexander; the first two books of Curtius, which undoubtedly contained a number of stories about Alexander's youth, are lost, and Diodorous' Book 17 opens with Alexander's accession to the throne. Justin barely mentions Alexander before Philip's death. Our single account of this early period is found in Plutarch (*Alex.* 1–10), who fills us in on some of the details of Alexander's youth as well as the court intrigue at Pella. Of interest is an essay by J. R. Hamilton, "Alexander's Early Life," *Greece and Rome,* 2nd ser., XII (1965), 117–24.

54. Alexander's attitude toward sex has been of some concern mainly because the accounts of it may reflect later traditions hostile to him. Tarn (*Alex.,* II, 319) regrets having to write on the subject as "it might suggest the worst kind of popular historiography; but it is very necessary to straighten the matter out." In brief, a number of passages in ancient authors suggest that Alexander had several homosexual attachments; see Athenaeus, *Deipnosophists* 13. 603a-b; Plut. *Alex.* 67. 4; Curt. 6. 5. 23; 10. 1, 25–26 ff; 7. 9. 19. Tarn regards such stories as a part of the Peripatetic tradition designed to discredit Alexander's character, and he argues vigorously against their basis in fact (*Alex.,* II, 319–26). E. Badian, in a closely reasoned paper, "The Eunuch Bagoas" (*Classical Quarterly,* N.S. VIII [1958], 144–57), uses Tarn's defense of Alexander's character in this instance as a vehicle for attacking the whole theory of a hostile Peripatetic tradition. Badian's article and Tarn's sec-

tion on Alexander's sex life are excellent examples of the method and style of these two modern scholars.

While a number of other tales of Alexander's involvement with women (e.g., his liason with Thalestria, Queen of the Amazons) existed in antiquity, Wilcken's argument here seems quite reasonable. Whatever the nature of Alexander's sex life, the evidence indicates that it was not a consuming interest of his, and is really a subject deserving little attention.

60. For the events leading up to and including Philip's death see Diod. 16. 91–95; Arr. 2. 14. 5; Plut. *Alex.* 9. 3–10. 4; Just. 9. 6–7, 11. 2; Athenaeus 13. 557b-e. Wilcken's view that Alexander was not involved in the conspiracy against his father generally is in accord with Tarn and others.

63. Tarn went to some length to show that Alexander was not responsible for the deaths of possible rivals for the throne; see *Alex.*, II, 260–62. Probably the best recent discussion of the whole mystery is E. Badian, "The Death of Philip II," *Phoenix*, XVII (1963), 244–50. While Badian is unwilling, on the basis of the meager and confused evidence, to assign direct blame for Philip's murder, he does point up rather well the alignment of factions in the Macedonian court. That a conspiracy existed is almost certain, and it does seem that Alexander stood above all to benefit most. It cannot be proved that Alexander was directly implicated, but Wilcken's blanket rejection of his involvement must be viewed in the more realistic framework of court intrigue at Pella.

66. Of course, this is a highly subjective interpretation. There are those who would argue with equal force that Alexander's motives were different. Perhaps Alexander viewed his Asian expedition in part as an opportunity to seek a firmer kingship in his own right and relieve himself of the shackles placed on him by the Macedonian nobility. Tarn (*Alex.*, I, 8) argued simply that he went to Asia because he never thought of not doing it; it was his inheritance. Another compelling reason for the Asian adventure was that Alexander needed money, the Macedonian kingdom being on the verge of bankruptcy. In order to maintain the professional (and expensive) Macedonian army, and to pay debts incurred in the development of that force, added monies were needed, as Macedon was unable, through its own meager resources, to secure its new position in a hostile world. See Burn, *Alex.*, p. 64, E. Badian, "Alexander the Great and the Creation of an Empire," *History Today*, VIII (1958), 372, and, most recently on this subject, P. A. Brunt, "The Aims of Alexander," *Greece and Rome*, 2nd ser., XII (1965), 205–15.

67. Antipater never was to go to Asia, but remained behind as Alexander's regent in Greece. Parmenio accompanied Alexander as far as Ecbatana and thus was present at the major battles and sieges at the Granicus, Issus, Tyre, Gaza, and Gaugamela. The middle Asian and Indian campaigns, however, were fought without the benefit of Parmenio's "advice," and Alexander proved equally successful there. See E. Badian, "The Death of Parmenio," *Transactions of the American Philological Association*, XCI (1960), 328–29; Burn, *Alex.*, pp. 70, 77–78; and Burn, "The Generalship of Alexander," *Greece and Rome*, 2nd ser., XII (1965), 140–43.

68, l. 9. This incident is described in Arrian (1. 1. 8–10). It is easy to be sceptical of such a maneuver; to use it successfully would require discipline of the highest order and instant obedience to command under the most difficult and chaotic conditions of combat. Yet, a similar maneuver apparently was employed later at Gaugamela. There the phalanx opened gaps in the line, and a number of Darius' terrible scythed chariots passed through the aisles thus formed. See Diod. 17. 58. 1–4; Arr. 3. 13. 5–6; Curt. 4. 13. 33.

68, l. 35. Arr. 1. 3. 5–6. This "longing" is Alexander's *pothos*. See V. Ehrenberg, *Alexander and the Greeks* (Oxford, 1938), pp. 52–61. Ehrenberg's chapter on *pothos* is now reprinted in G. T. Griffith (ed.), *Alexander the Great: The Main Problems* (Cambridge, 1966), pp. 74–83. Ehrenberg argues that this *pothos*, or longing for "things not yet within reach, for the unknown, far distant, unattained," became Alexander's primary motive force.

75. The ancient evidence for the Theban episode is in Arr. 1. 7. 1–9. 10; Diod. 17. 8. 2–14. 4; Plut. *Alex.* 11. 4–13. 3. Not much has been added to Wilcken's argument on the destruction of Thebes. It is evident that Alexander acted in his capacity as *hegemon* of the League, that the Greek cities with outstanding grievances against Thebes were most hostile and vigorously urged her destruction, and that Alexander found the Theban rebellion a convenient excuse to warn the rest of Greece. In any case, the destruction of Thebes may have served its purpose. Except for the revolt led by King Agis of Sparta in 331 (and, of course, the continuing anti-Macedonian intrigue in Athens), no other mainland city ever openly raised the standard of revolt against Alexander's rule. Greece was now secure.

78. To the extent that Alexander was faced twice with serious mutinies from his troops, in India (in 326) and at Opis (in 324), Wilcken's view is correct. Yet it must be pointed out that the earliest serious opposition to Alexander came from his own staff, most of whom were members of the Macedonian nobility.

It was only after the Court had been purged of dissidents that the infantry rebelled. See E. Badian, "Harpalus," *Journal of Hellenic Studies*, LXXXI (1961), 16–43, esp. 20.

79, l. 5. These are the figures given by Arrian (7. 9. 6).

79, l. 16. On Callisthenes see Pearson, *Lost Histories*, pp. 22–49. Also see the testimonia, fragments, and commentary in F. Jacoby, *Die Fragmente der griechischen Historiker*, IIB and IID (Berlin, 1927–30), No. 124, translated in Robinson, *Hist. of Alex.*, I, 45–77.

80. Wilcken had maintained this view, that Ptolemy had used the *Ephemerides* as a source, as early as 1894, and he repeated it here. Tarn (*Alex.*, I, 13, and II, 1, 23, 263), among others, shared in this belief. C. A. Robinson, Jr., *The Ephemerides of Alexander's Expedition* (Providence, 1932), pp. 70–73, suggested that the *Ephemerides* were genuine and accurate journals of the campaign. L. Pearson, "The Diary and Letters of Alexander the Great," *Historia*, III (1955), 435–39, argued, however, that the Diary is late and not genuine, a literary composition based, in fact, on the work of Ptolemy and his contemporaries. Recently, Alan Samuel, "Alexander's Royal Journals," *Historia*, XIV (1965), 1–12, has shown that, while the *Ephemerides* were contemporaneous with Alexander, they were not an official Macedonian journal. They derive rather from Babylonian sources which may have kept a detailed account of Alexander's last days. Indeed the only ancient references to the *Ephemerides* are to Alexander's final illness and death; there is nothing to suggest that an official Royal Journal was kept earlier. If it ever existed, all trace has been lost.

83. Wilcken took this story literally from Diodorus (17. 17. 1–2) and Justin (11. 5. 10). Badian rejects this implication that the spear plunged into Asian soil represented a claim to all of Asia itself, and regards the story as absurd and *ex post facto*. He does, however, suggest a possible parallel with Roman fetial procedure, during which the priests of the fetial college hurl a spear into the enemy's territory as a part of a formal declaration of war. See E. Badian, "The Administration of the Empire," *Greece and Rome*, 2nd ser., XII (1965), 166, n. 1.

87. On the engagement at the Granicus see Fuller, *Generalship*, pp. 147–54.

89. There now begins what Badian describes as the myth of the Hellenic Crusade, the war of revenge of the Greeks against the ancient and common enemy. Alexander may have found this myth useful in rallying his forces behind him in his role as *strategos* of the Hellenic League. See Badian, *History Today*,

VIII (1958), 373–76.

91. The whole question of Alexander's relationship with the Greek states of Asia Minor is too complex to deal with here. Basic reading includes Ehrenberg, *Alexander and the Greeks*, pp. 1–51; E. Badian, "Alexander the Great and the Greeks of Asia," in *Ancient Society and Institutions. Studies Presented to Victor Ehrenberg* (Oxford, 1966), pp. 37–69; and Tarn, *Alex.*, II, 199–232. On Alexander's imperial administration in general see G. Glotz and R. Cohen, *Histoire Grecque*, IV (Part I, *Alexandre et le démembrement de son Empire* [Paris, 1938]), 222–43.

96, l. 5. A translation of the Callisthenes fragment (Jacoby, No. 124, F. 31) can be found in Robinson (*Hist. of Alex.*, I, 69). Arrian (1. 26. 1) and Plutarch (*Alex.* 17. 3–4) both tell versions of the story.

96, l. 23. Sources for Gordium: Arr. 2. 3. 1–8; Plut. *Alex.* 18. 1–2; Curt. 3. 1. 14–18; Just. 11. 7. 3–16. While Wilcken accepts the story of cutting the knot with a sword, Tarn (*Alex.*, II, 262–65) suggests that to cut the knot would "be cheating"; further, this "would have been utterly out of character" for Alexander, who would presumably follow the oracle literally and *untie* the knot. No analysis, however, will change popular opinion of this little story—the world prefers to believe that Alexander *cut* the knot. Moreover, a number of modern scholars regard the whole Gordian knot episode as a piece of fiction.

102. Although see Polybius' (12. 17. 1–22. 7) biting criticism of Callisthenes as a military writer in general and of his account of Issus in particular. Callisthenes may well have not participated in the battle, as Wilcken points out, but unless he had some extraordinary vantage point on high ground overlooking the field of operations, it is unlikely that his account was based on personal observation. Other accounts of the battle are Arr. 2. 7. 1–11. 10; Diod. 17. 33. 1–34. 9; Plut. *Alex.* 20. 1–6; Curt. 3. 9. 1–11. 27; Just. 11. 9. Also see Fuller, *Generalship*, pp. 154–62.

104. On the Pompeian mosaic see M. Bieber, *Alexander the Great in Greek and Roman Art* (Chicago, 1964), pp. 46–48 (with bibliography).

105. The ancient writers were unanimous in their praise of Alexander for the generous and courteous treatment accorded the captives from Issus and particularly the family of Darius. See Arr. 2. 12. 1–8; Diod. 17. 35. 1–38. 7; Plut. *Alex.* 21. 1–5; Just. 11. 9; Curt. 3. 12. 18–26.

106. Arr. 2. 14. 4–9. On the letters which appear in the ancient sources, see Pearson, *Historia*, III (1955), 443–50. Pearson ac-

cepts Arrian's dependence on Ptolemy for this correspondence, but is reluctant to commit himself on its authenticity. C. B. Welles, in a note in his translation of Diodorus' Book 17 in the Loeb Classical Library (pp. 228–29, n. 1), discusses the exchange of messages between Alexander and Darius (with ancient sources cited), and suggests that much of the correspondence was fictional.

109. In his account of Tyre, Wilcken does not put enough emphasis on the strategic importance of that ancient city. At least as old as the early twelfth century B.C., Tyre had long been the most prosperous and powerful of the Phoenician cities. Producing manufactured goods and ships on their own, and serving as transshippers for goods moving between Asia and the Mediterranean, the Tyrians had also sent their sailors and traders far and wide. Tyre had become the mother of new cities and colonies, not the least of which was Carthage, in Alexander's time the most powerful state in the western Mediterranean. The Persians had been utilizing Tyrian ships and the city itself as a base for their fleet for at least a century. To Alexander, whose campaign thus far has been marked by cautious generalship, the seizure of this last remaining Persian naval station was vital to the maintenance of unhindered communications and security in the eastern Mediterranean. On the incredible siege itself see Arr. 2. 16. 1–24. 6; Diod. 17. 40. 2–46. 6; Curt. 4. 2. 1–4. 21. Also Fuller, *Generalship*, pp. 206–16.

111. Arr. 2. 25. 1–3. Diodorus (17. 54. 1–5) places this letter and the exchange with Parmenio in the spring or summer of 331, a year after the siege of Tyre, while both armies were marching toward their fateful encounter at Gaugamela. Like Diodorus, Plutarch (*Alex.* 29. 4) puts this story in 331. The confusion in the ancient sources may arise from Alexander's having been in Phoenicia *twice*, once on the way to Egypt in 332 when Tyre was besieged, and again in the following year en route to Mesopotamia. Curtius gives both versions, a letter after Tyre (4. 5. 1–9) and an embassy a year later (4. 11. 1–22), although the Parmenio-Alexander dialogue is given only in the second (331) account. For a review of the problem of sorting out this diplomatic correspondence, see Welles, Loeb Diodorus, VIII, 228–29, n. 1.

113. Tarn (*Alex.*, II, 348–50) clearly disagrees with Wilcken's position on the early syncretism between Greek and foreign deities. Tarn maintains that virtually no such meaningful identification of Hellenic with Egyptian gods was known before Alexander's time.

119. The bibliography on Alexander's religious policy in Egypt, and, especially, on the foundation of Alexandria is large. On the founding of the city and matters related to it, the evidence is collected in Aristide Calderini, *Dizionario dei nomi geografici e topografici dell'Egitto greco-romano*, I (Cairo, 1935), *s. v. "Alexandreia"*. I now believe that the correct view on the foundation is that of C. B. Welles, "The Discovery of Sarapis and Foundation of Alexandria," *Historia*, XI (1962), 271–98 (with full bibliography). In brief, Welles suggests that Alexandria was founded not before Alexander journeyed to the oracle of Ammon at Siwah, as most modern historians (including Wilcken) following Ptolemy believe, but on the *return* from the oracle. Also see my note "Alexander and the Return from Siwah," *Historia*, XVI (1967), 369, in support of Welles' view.

123. Diodorus 17. 49. 2–3. Curtius (4. 7. 9) places the meeting at Lake Mareotis. Cyrene is 350–400 miles from Paraetonium. Did Alexander request such a meeting? Had the Cyreneans known that Alexander would be traveling the coastal track toward Paraetonium? Or were the envoys actually on the way to Egypt to learn something about the new king when, by chance, they met Alexander's caravan on the way? Why was the meeting not set up for Paraetonium? The edge of the Sahara is no place for a casual rendezvous. The answers to such questions must be largely conjectural, since the story as related by the ancient writers makes little sense. True, it is characteristic of the careful Alexander to secure his frontiers. He did so in Macedon (the Danube), in Asia Minor (the Aegean and Phrygia), in the Levant (the eastern Mediterranean), and now the Libyan and Sudanese borders of Egypt. If this incident is not a later interpolation, its original significance had been lost by the time the later writers, Diodorus and Curtius, got hold of it. It is also interesting that Arrian does not mention the envoys as he is normally most careful about relating such incidents. See Robinson, *Hist. of Alex.*, II, 55–56.

129. The sources for the journey to Siwah are Arr. 3. 3. 1–4. 5; Diod. 17. 49. 2–51. 4; Plut. *Alex.* 26. 6–27. 6; Curt. 4. 7. 5–32; Just. 11. 11; Callisthenes fragment 14a (Jacoby, No. 124) in Strabo 17. 1. 43. There are numerous modern interpretations of what happened at the oracle, representing a wide range of opinion, E.g., C.A. Robinson, Jr., *Alexander the Great. Meeting of East and West in World Government and Brotherhood* (New York, 1947), pp. 113–16, and Arthur Weigall, *Alexander the Great* (New York, 1933), pp. 199–207. Tarn (*Alex.*, II, 347–59) sup-

ports Wilcken's view that Alexander's divine sonship came from the priest's greeting and not from the oracle itself, that Alexander went to Siwah to consult the oracle about the future, not to be called the son of God, and that no one knows what the oracular response really was. The conclusions of both Wilcken and Tarn were accepted by J. P. V. D. Balsdon, "The 'Divinity' of Alexander," *Historia*, I (1950), 371. The modification of this "standard" version is that of Welles (*Historia*, XI [1962], 281–82), who has accepted the testimony in the romance of Pseudo-Callisthenes (1. 30. 5) that one of Alexander's main reasons for consulting the oracle was to receive advice about the conditions under which he should found a city bearing his name. Alexander then returned to Egypt by way of the coast (*contra* Ptolemy in Arr. 3. 4. 5, but following most ancient writers and Ptolemy in Arr. 3. 3. 5) to found Alexandria. It may be suggested (following Welles only in part) that Alexander was initially attracted by the strip of land between Lake Mareotis and the island of Pharos, journeyed to Siwah in part to consult the oracle to confirm his judgment and receive its blessing (the founding of a city was a religious act, as Welles points out), and only then returned to the site to found Alexandria.

135. On the dating of the battle of Gaugamela, as well as other matters related to this crucial engagement, see A. R. Burn. "Notes on Alexander's Campaigns," *Journal of Hellenic Studies*, LXXII (1952), 84–91, and G. T. Griffith, "Alexander's Generalship at Gaugamela," *ibid.*, LXVII (1947), 77–89. Tarn deals with the battle in *Alex.*, II, 182–90, and Fuller, *Generalship*, pp. 163–80 (sources cited), does much to clear up the confusion between the versions of Arrian and Diodorus. See Arr. 3. 11. 1–15. 7; Diod. 17. 57. 1–61. 3; Plut. *Alex.* 31. 3–33. 7; Curt. 4. 13. 26–16. 30.

139. On Alexander in Babylon see Arr. 3. 16. 3–5; Diod. 17. 64. 3–6; Plut. *Alex.* 35. 1–8; Curt. 5. 1. 17–45.

141. On Alexander's administration of his oriental satrapies see Glotz and Cohen, *Alexandre et le démembrement de son Empire*, pp. 239–43, and Badian, *Greece and Rome*, 2nd ser., XII (1965), 169–82.

142. Arr. 3. 16. 6–11; Diod. 17. 65. 1–67. 1; Plut. *Alex.* 36. 1–2; Curt. 5. 2. 8–17.

145. Arr. 3. 18. 10–12; Diod. 17. 70. 1–72. 6; Curt. 5. 6. 1–7. 12; Plut. *Alex.* 37. 1–38. 4. Arrian alone in his brief account fails to mention Thais. Neither Pearson (*Lost Histories*, pp. 218–19) nor Tarn (*Alex.*, II, 47–48) believes the Thais story. Burn (*Alex.*, p. 122) is not certain that the story should be dis-

missed as fantasy, while G. Radet (*Alexandre le Grand* [6], [Paris, 1950], pp. 188–99) believes the story to be genuine, the incident a restaging of the *Bacchae*.

Tarn (*Alex.*, II, 48) suggests that Alexander burnt the palace deliberately as a "political manifesto to Asia." Badian (*History Today*, VIII [1958], 376) maintains that Alexander fired the palace as a sign to the Greeks, now in revolt under King Agis of Sparta, that he was fulfilling his role as the leader of the Hellenic Crusade. Badian's suggestion, however, assumes that Alexander had not yet received word of Agis' defeat at Megalopolis. Curtius (6. 1. 21) tells us that Agis was vanquished (a little) before Gaugamela, that is, probably sometime in September, 331. (Diodorus' chronology [17. 62. 1–63. 4] of the rebellion is nonsense. A close reading of 17. 62. 1–3 will show that the reasons given for the revolt make no sense, as all hope of Persian assistance would be gone *after* the disaster at Gaugamela.) If Alexander reached Persepolis in late January, 330 B.C., he was almost certainly in possession of news from Greece. It is unlikely that a message of such importance as the defeat of Agis would have taken longer than a month to travel from the Peloponnesus to wherever Alexander was in Mesopotamia or Persis. Indeed, given the conditions of travel by swift ship across the Aegean (even in September or October) and the secure communications link of the Persian Royal Highway, Alexander probably knew of Agis' defeat while he was still in Babylon or Susa. One awkward statement remains, that of Arrian (3. 16. 10), who relates that while at Susa, Alexander sent silver home to Antipater for use in the war against the Lacedaemonians. It would appear that Alexander still believed the war to be on, yet in the next sentence, Arrian informs us of the arrival of fresh cavalry and infantry from Macedon. Faced with serious rebellion in Greece, is it likely that Antipater or Alexander would permit a force to be sent to Asia? There is reason, therefore, to question the reliability of Arrian here. It may be that such a contingent did reach Alexander at Susa, released by Antipater now that the rebellion had been put down and Greece was secure, and that money was sent back to Antipater for whatever military or diplomatic uses were necessary. In any event, it seems likely that whatever motivated Alexander to burn Persepolis, he did so in full knowledge of the defeat of Agis.

That Persepolis was deliberately looted and fired is certain. See Erich F. Schmidt, *The Treasury of Persepolis and Other Discoveries in the Homeland of the Achaemenians*, The Oriental Institute of the University of Chicago, Oriental Institute

Communications, No. 21 (Chicago, 1939), pp. 16–78, *passim.* Also A. T. Olmstead, *History of the Persian Empire* (Chicago, 1948), pp. 519–22.

154. Badian (*History Today*, VIII [1958], 497) suggests that the destruction of the palace at Persepolis was one of the few miscalculations of Alexander's career. In choosing to fire the palace for the sake of a Greek revolt (already suppressed), he nullified his own legitimacy as the Achaemenid successor and raised an Iranian national war against him. See Arr. 3. 18. 11–12.

156. On military organization, especially in Asia, Tarn's work (*Alex.*, II, 135–69) is good. Valuable discussions have been added by P. A. Brunt, "Alexander's Macedonian Cavalry," *Journal of Hellenic Studies*, LXXXIII (1963), 27–45, and G. T. Griffith, "A Note on the Hipparchies of Alexander," *Ibid.*, pp. 68–74.

159. This is based on Arrian (4. 6. 3–4), who says that Alexander marched 1500 stades in three days and arrived at dawn on the fourth. His forces consisted of half the Companion cavalry, some archers, and light-armed troops from the phalanx. Arrian's distance is correct; the modern way, largely through open country from Alexandreschate (modern Leninabad) to Maracanda (Samarkand) measures about 160 miles. There are no major barriers, the route lying along the Jaxartes, across the barren Golod'naya Steppe and into the valley of the Zeravshan. Yet it is difficult to believe that such a force, whose speed would have been determined by the slowest contingents (here the light-armed infantry), could have moved so quickly with the intent of lifting a siege. If true, it must have been one of the great forced marches of history.

162. Both Tarn (*Alex.*, II, 326) and Badian (*History Today*, VIII [1958], 499) view the marriage purely as one of political convenience, for the purpose of ending the struggle with the Iranian barons.

165. The sources for this sad affair are Arr. 3. 26. 1–4; Plut. *Alex.* 48. 1–49. 7; Diod. 17. 79. 1–80. 4; Curt. 6. 7. 1–7. 2. 34 (highly rhetorical); Just. 12. 5. 1–3. Tarn (*Alex.*, I, 62–64, and II, 270–72) claims that Philotas' death was perfectly judicial, while Parmenio's was plain murder. Badian, *Transactions of the American Philological Association*, XCI (1960), 324–38, in a major discussion, views Philotas' execution as "judicial murder" and Parmenio's as "undisguised assassination," and both as a part of the continuing struggle waged by Alexander against the old-line Macedonian families. See Badian, "Alexander the Great and the Loneliness of Power," *Studies in Greek and Roman History* (New York, 1964), pp. 193–97.

167. This tragedy is related by Arr. 4. 8. 1–9. 6; Plut. *Alex.* 50. 1–51. 6; Curt. 8. 1. 19–2. 13; Just. 12. 6. 1–7.

169. Tarn .(*Alex.*, II, 359–69) rejects Wilcken here, and argues that Alexander did indeed intend becoming a god. Having taken from Aristotle (*Politics* 1284a) the idea that any man of surpassing excellence is like a god among men, and Isocrates' comment (*Epistle* 3) that if Philip should conquer Persia nothing would be left for him except to become a god, Alexander attempted to promulgate his divinity here at Bactra in the interest of his policy of fusion. Thus for Tarn, Alexander's motives are political, not religious. Tarn is followed by Robinson (*Alex. the Great*, pp. 165–67), who argues that Alexander's political reason for deification was to set up a means of dealing with the Greek world. Apparently Alexander had insured his position in Egypt and in Asia, but only now would solve the problem of his relationship to the Hellenic world by becoming a god of *all* the men over whom he ruled. Balsdon (*Historia*, I [1950], 363–82) has laid the theories of both Tarn and Robinson to rest, returning substantially to Wilcken's view, that *proskynesis* was introduced only as an attempt to provide a court ceremony to be shared in common by Greeks, Macedonians, and Asians. E. G. Hogarth argued in a similar fashion in the nineteenth century; see "The Deification of Alexander the Great," *English Historical Review*, II (1887), 317-29, esp. 319–21.

The sources on the incident at Bactra are Arr. 4. 9. 9–12. 5; Plut. *Alex.* 54. 1–55. 1; Curt. 8. 5. 5–24. There is a lacuna in Diodorus' text, and Justin (12. 7. 1–3) is of little value.

171. The sources on Callisthenes in general and his demise in particular are collected in Jacoby, *FGrH*, IIB, No. 124, T. 1–21; trans. in Robinson, *Hist. of Alex.*, I, 45–54. See the narrative accounts in Arr. 4. 12. 6–14. 4; Plut. *Alex.* 55. 1–5; Curt. 8. 6. 1–8. 23. The whole incident is discussed in full by T. S. Brown, "Callisthenes and Alexander," *American Journal of Philology*, LXX (1949), 225–48. An analysis of Callisthenes' role as a historian of Alexander can be found in Pearson, *Lost Histories*, pp. 22–49. Agreeing with Wilcken about the deleterious effect that Callisthenes' death had on the Alexander tradition is Tarn, *Alex.*, II, 130–31; Brown, *loc. cit.*, pp. 225–26; and Badian, *History Today*, VIII (1958), 500; but also see Badian, *Classical Quarterly*, N.S. VIII (1958), 154–56, where he casts real doubt on the existence of a hostile "Peripatetic tradition" as it applied to Alexander historiography.

174. On Alexander's ambitions in the East, see most recently A. K. Narain, "Alexander and India," *Greece and Rome*, 2nd ser.,

XII (1965), 155–56; also Tarn, *Alex.*, I, 86–87. It is also worth noting that "India" is here used in its larger geographical context. In fact, Alexander only touched a corner of what is now the modern Indian nation.

176. See Narain, *Greece and Rome*, 2nd ser., XII (1965), 155–65, for a brief review of Alexander's Indian campaign. For the extent and nature of Greek influences in the eastern marches and the subsequent history of that region, see W. W. Tarn's masterful *The Greeks in Bactria and India* (2nd ed., Cambridge, 1951), and the survey by George Woodcock, "The Indian Greeks," *History Today*, XII (1962), 558–67.

179, l. 9. On the Aornos campaign see Fuller, *Generalship*, pp. 245–54. The sources are Arr. 4. 28. 1–30. 4; Curt. 8. 11. 1–25; Diod. 17. 85. 1–86. 1; Just. 12. 7. 12–13. One must reemphasize the importance of Sir Aurel Stein's work, *On Alexander's Track to the Indus* (London, 1929), pp. 120–59.

179, l. 33. The identification of Alexander's success in taking the citadel of Aornos with Heracles' failure to do so occurs in Diod. 17. 85. 2; Curt. 8. 11. 2; Just. 12. 7. 12; Arr. 4. 30. 4. Arr. 4. 28. 1–4 discusses the whole legend of Heracles in India. Ptolemy figures prominently in Arrian's account of the siege of Aornos and may be the source. Wilcken's view that Cleitarchus is the source for the Heracles story is purely subjective and is not based on any evidence in the ancient authors.

181. Accounts of Alexander and the Gymnosophists can be read in Diod. 17. 107. 1–5; Arr. 7. 2. 4–3. 6; Plut. *Alex.* 69. 3–4. Moses Hadas (*Hellenistic Culture* [New York, 1959]) points out that the Stoics had a keen interest in virtuous men who met death in some memorable way. Calanus apparently was a favorite example; no less than eight different ancient authors mention him (see Hadas, p. 306, n. 1).

183. See Fuller, *Generalship*, pp. 180–99. The sources are Arr. 5. 8. 1–19. 3; Curt. 8. 13. 1–14. 46; Diod. 17. 87. 1–89. 6; Plut. *Alex.* 60. 1–8; Just. 12. 8. 1–7.

186. The incident on the banks of the Hyphasis is told by Arr. 5. 25. 1–28. 4; Diod. 17. 93. 1–94. 5; Curt. 9. 1. 35–3. 19; Plut. *Alex.* 62. 1–4 (although note Plutarch's error in placing the event on the banks of the *Ganges*). The versions of Arrian and Curtius are marked by interesting speeches from Alexander and Coenus, the latter representing the Macedonians who were pressing for an end to the campaign.

204, l. 7, As Wilcken thanks Nearchus for bringing out the human side of Alexander, we in turn may appreciate Wilcken's efforts in choosing to present this aspect of Alexander's personality. While one may inveigh against any attempt to get at Alexander's personal feelings or private motives because of the poor state of our sources, it is nonetheless refreshing to witness some humanity in a character who is usually portrayed as superhuman.

204, l. 32. Wilcken's observation here needs some comment. As a matter of fact, parts of India had been organized under Achaemenid control and incorporated into the satrapy of Hindush. The eastern boundary of the satrapy is not known, although it is likely that it was a river. The Hydaspes, however, is nowhere mentioned in the Persian sources (Olmstead, *History of the Persian Empire*, pp. 144-45), although there is no reason to rule it out. Achaemenid rule never penetrated into the south of the great Indian subcontinent, and was limited to the Indus valley. Thus to the extent that Alexander moved into the Punjab across the Indus and the Hydaspes (either of which might have been the Achaemenid frontier), he was in territory never under Persian rule.

The northern frontier of the Persian empire had been the Jaxartes, so defined by Cyrus the Great (Olmstead, *loc. cit.*, pp. 47-48. Both Bactria and Sogdiana are mentioned in the Behistun inscription.) Alexander had crossed the Jaxartes, but barely, and his northernmost foundation, Alexandreschate, was apparently on the near side of the river itself. Thus Alexander only twice stepped beyond the frontiers of an area which at one time or another had been under Achaemenid control, at the Jaxartes and in the Punjab. Can it be argued that two such slight penetrations beyond the Persian empire transformed Alexander from the Achaemenid successor to the Great King of Asia? Or are the two concepts synonomous? Moreover, there were parts of the Persian empire which never fell to Alexander, Cappadocia and Armenia in particular. See Tarn, *Greeks in Bactria and India*, pp. 153-54.

206. On the punishment of the miscreant satraps see especially Badian, "Harpalus," pp. 16-25. It is Badian's view that the deposition of so many officials represents a "reign of terror" by which Alexander rid himself of all those who might have threatened his station, and thus fully asserted his own authority.

207. For the evidence on Harpalus see Berve, *Alexanderreich*, II, No. 143. Some of the narrative can be found in Arr. 3. 19. 7; Diod. 17. 108. 1-8; Just. 13. 5. 9; Curt. 10. 2. 2-3; Plut. *Demosthenes* 25. 1-6. The most extensive recent critical treatment of the Harpalus affair is Badian, "Harpalus," pp. 16-43.

211. Aristotle *Politics* 1284a; the letter from Isocrates to Philip (*Epistle* 3) is thought by many modern scholars to be spurious.

See Balsdon, *Historia*, I (1950), 363–71.

213. This famous remark is attributed to Demosthenes by Hyperides (*Against Demosthenes* 31), one of the famous orator's accusers in the trial over the Harpalus affair. The translation should be: "[let] Alexander be the son of Zeus and of Poseidon too if he wishes."

214. Arr. 7. 23. 2. Balsdon (*Historia*, I [1950], 385) quite rightly points out that the passage in Arrian might just as well mean that the envoys arrived *as if* they had come on a sacred embassy to honor a god, and that the offering of the golden crown is not necessarily an indication of divinity. Balsdon deals with the "deification decree" in some detail (pp. 383-88), citing the evidence, and concluding that Alexander himself played no part in the attempt at apotheosis, but that this was a scheme of his Greek supporters to "ingratiate themselves to him," and to compromise their opponents. Tarn (*Alex.*, II, 372-73) argued specifically against Wilcken's thesis that Alexander was religiously motivated, and proposed that his intentions were purely political (see my note below).

216. The text of the inscription now appears in Tod, *Greek Historical Inscriptions*, II, No. 202, with full commentary. The literary evidence for the exiles decree occurs in Diod. 17. 109. 1-2; 18. 8. 1-7; Curt. 10. 2. 4-7; Hyperides *Against Demosthenes* 18; Dinarchus *Against Demosthenes* 81, 103. It was Tarn's view that Alexander, as the leader of the League of Corinth, had no constitutional right to force the cities to take back their exiles. Thus Alexander, in addition, issued a deification request, for, in Tarn's words, "The Covenant [of the League] bound Alexander the King but did not, and would not, bind Alexander the god . . ." In this way the Macedonian king circumvented the League constitution and settled the question of the exiles, but became a god in order to accomplish these ends. Probably the best discussion of the whole matter is Badian ("Harpalus," pp. 25-31), who dissociates the request for deification from the exiles decree and views the latter as a means of solving a serious military and political problem created in part by Alexander's own Asian policies.

217. For the accusations against Demosthenes and others charged with being implicated with Harpalus see the three extant speeches of Dinarchus, *Against Demosthenes, Against Aristogiton*, and *Against Philocles*, and Hyperides, *Against Demosthenes*. Also Plut. *Demosthenes* 25. 1-26. 5.

220. The story of the mutiny at Opis is told by Diod. 17. 108. 1-3, 109. 2-3; Arr. 7. 8. 1-11. 7; Curt. 10. 2. 12-4. 3; Plut. *Alex.* 71. 1-5.

221. The attribution to Alexander of the concept of the "Brother-hood of Mankind" has found its chief exponent in W. W. Tarn. The main evidence is Alexander's prayer at the banquet at Opis celebrating the reconciliation with his troops (Arr. 7. 11. 8–9). Wilcken's interpretation of the prayer is virtually a translation of Arrian's text. Tarn (*Alex.*, I, 116-17) read far more into the prayer than the text allows. The whole question is too complex to deal with in a single note. Tarn's view can be read in "Alexander the Great and the Unity of Mankind," *Proceedings of the British Academy*, XIX (1933), 123–66, and in *Alex.*, II, 399–449 (esp. pp. 434–49, dealing with the banquet at Opis). Tarn was followed by Robinson in his *Alexander the Great*, pp. 224–25, and in *Alexander the Great, Conqueror and Creator of a New World* (New York, 1963), pp. 143, 150. The idea of universal brotherhood has been rejected by Burn, *Alexander the Great*, p. 175. Badian wrote a devastating attack on the thesis in "Alexander the Great and the Unity of Mankind," *Historia*, VII (1958), 425–44 (see pp. 428-32 on the Opis banquet). Thus with the recent criticisms of the Tarn thesis, we have returned to what is substantially Wilcken's position.

224, l. 1. Again, this is Alexander's *pothos*, according to Arrian (7. 16. 2). See Ehrenberg, *Alexander and the Greeks*, pp. 52–61, for a full discussion.

224, l. 33. Tarn (*Alex.*, II, 398) rejects the idea of world conquest with the statement ". . . such a belief is only a speculation from the land of dreams and has nothing to do with history."

226. The plans are given in Diodorus (18. 4. 1–6). Wilcken later refined his views in a major article, "Die letzten Pläne Alexanders des Grossen" (*Sitzungsberichte der preussischen Akademie der Wissenschaften*, Philosophisch-historische Klasse [Berlin, 1937], pp. 192–207), in which he continued to defend the validity of most of the plans. The problem has aroused keen interest among several modern scholars, and there is a large periodical literature on the subject. Some writers have followed Tarn, who argued in a series of papers that the plans are a forgery and quite late. Tarn's full position was last stated in *Alex.*, II, 378–98; he is followed by Pearson, *Lost Histories*, pp. 261–62. C. A. Robinson, Jr. ("Alexander's Plans," *American Journal of Philology*, LXI [1940], 402–12) generally supported Tarn's view that Wilcken's position was untenable, but did not reject the idea of further plans. Basing his argument on Arrian (4. 15. 5–6; 5. 25. 1–2), Robinson suggested that Alexander's plans consisted mainly of ocean exploration around Asia-Africa (the continents were not yet

clearly defined in the fourth century B.C.) and through the
Pillars of Heracles, and a military expedition to the Black
Sea. Wilcken's side was supported by what Tarn called the
"German belief" in Alexander's world-kingdom (see Tarn,
et al., for bibliography). Two more recent articles of interest
(with full bibliographies) are F. Hampl, "Alexanders des
Grossen *Hypomnemata* und letzte Pläne," *Studies Presented to
D. M. Robinson*, II (St. Louis, 1953), 816–29, and F. Schachermeyr, "Die letzten Pläne Alexanders des Grossen," *Jahreshefte
des österreichischen archaeologischen Institutes*, XLI (1954),
118–40.

229, l. 4. The sources for the story of the embassies are Arr. 7. 15.
4–6; Diod. 17. 113. 1–4; Just. 12. 13. 1. Curtius' text here is lost.
Of special interest has been Arrian's statement about the
embassy from Rome. Tarn discussed the embassies in detail
(*Alex.*, II, 374–78) and suggested (p. 376) that the story of
their arrival dates from the first century B.C.

229, l. 21. Wilcken has made an attempt to rationalize the story of
the Chaldean warning told in Arr. 7. 16. 5–18. 6. Also see
Diod. 17. 112. 1–6; Plut. *Alex.* 73. 1–2; Just. 12. 13. 3–5.

233. See the note to p. 214.

236, l. 30. One might also add that Alexander's strength may have
been generally spent by the arduous military campaigns and
wearying marches that lay behind him. In order to have
accomplished what he did, he probably expended an extraordinary amount of energy.

236, l. 34. On the question of the sources for Alexander's last days
see Pearson, *Historia*, III (1955), 429–39, and *Lost Histories*,
pp. 185–86; also Samuel, *Historia*, XIV (1965), 1–12. The main
narrative accounts are Arr. 7. 25. 1–28. 1; Plut. *Alex.* 75. 2–77.
3; Diod. 17. 117. 1–5; Curt. 10. 5. 1–6, 10. 14–20; Just. 12. 13.
10. All the ancient writers mention the rumor that Alexander
had been poisoned, the main tradition being that Antipater
was the instigator of a plot which sent the potion to the king
at Babylon. The poison is said to have been highly corrosive;
in Curtius' version it was so powerful as to melt iron. The
poison tradition is at obvious variance with the account of
Alexander's final illness since the victim who had been given
such a devastating ingredient could hardly have lingered in
life for about ten more days.

238, l. 23. Samuel (*Historia*, XIV [1965], 8) has revised the date of
Alexander's death from June 13 to June 10.

239. Here Wilcken corrects a slip made earlier. See p. 3 (with note).

243. Of interest here may be the review of Alexander's qualities
both as a statesman and a general made by a modern general;

see Fuller, *Generalship*, pp. 264–314.

255. On currency see A. R. Bellinger, *Essays on the Coinage of Alexander the Great*, American Numismatic Society, *Numismatic Studies*, No. 11 (New York, 1963), and Gerhard Kleiner, *Alexanders Reichsmünzen*, in *Abhandlungen der deutschen Akademie der Wissenschaften zu Berlin*, Philosophisch-historische Klasse, Jahrgang, 1947, Nr. 5 (Berlin, 1949).

256. While it is true that Alexander's expedition opened up new trade routes, redirected the flow of money in the eastern Mediterranean, and broke up the Persian gold hoard, it is difficult to know whether he was motivated by some great economic plan or whether his new cities and centralized currency were only means of enforcing political unity.

261. It is not unusual that the pattern of settlement should be within the framework of urban foundations. The city was the traditional Greek means of settlement and political association. Indeed, it might be suggested that what Alexander's expedition really marked was the revival of Greek expansion into the East after having been blocked by the Persian empire for over two centuries. The extent and survival of Hellenism in the East, however, has been a subject of debate; e.g., see Burn, *Alex.*, pp. 188–210.

265. It is only rather recently that some historians have begun to withdraw from the "standard" view of Alexander's importance advocated by Wilcken here. Burn (*Alex.*, pp. 203–10) suggests that Alexander's impact was ephemeral. C. B. Welles ("Alexander's Historical Achievement," *Greece and Rome*, 2nd ser., XII [1965], 216–218) recognizes that while Alexander opened up the East to Greek civilization he brought no new political system or new philosophy. Moreover, the changes in the world of Hellenism are attributed more to internal developments than to Alexander himself. Alexander's achievement rather was to conquer the Persian empire; he was "his own greatest accomplishment." In short, the more recent view is that the force of Alexander's personality as it affected popular tradition and historiography was far more profound than the historical accomplishments which he actually wrought.

268, l. 12. We have some information about the attempt to revive the Hellenic League in 302 B.C. by Kings Antigonus and Demetrius Poliorcetes. See *Inscriptiones Graecae*, IV². 68, with discussions by Tod, *Greek Historical Inscriptions*, II, 228–31 (bibliography cited), and Cary, *Classical Quarterly*, XVII (1923), 137–48.

268, l. 30. Diod. 19. 11. 4–9. Diodorus makes a moral issue of Olympias' demise, suggesting that such a woman deserved a death worthy of her cruelty. Both Philip and Alexander were objects of Diodorus' praise for their ability to bear their good fortune with moderation. Of that fascinating Macedonian royal family it appears that only Olympias failed to learn the lesson.

270. The extent to which strength is a virtue in international politics is a dubious point. Certainly Macedon was a formidable foe, as Rome discovered in the third and second centuries. Yet its very power soon brought it into conflict with the ascending star in the West. Egypt, however, remained an independent state until the death of Cleopatra in 30 B.C. One wonders if the careful defensive diplomacy of the Ptolemies did not in the long run have a more meaningful kind of merit than the superb military organization of Macedon.

274. The problem of the origin and early practice of Hellenistic kingship is very complicated. For bibliography on the question see Balsdon, *Historia,* I (1950), 375, n. 66.

277. Now see F. Pfister, "Alexander der Grosse. Die Geschichte seines Ruhms," *Historia,* XIII (1964), 37–79.

280. Is it possible that Caesar was so naive (or daring!) as not to recognize what a furor would be created in Rome at the suggestion of moving the capital to the East? One need only recall the dramatic impact on the Roman people created by Octavian's later charge that Antony intended to move the capital to Alexandria. Wilcken's identification of Caesar with Alexander and with the Hellenistic ideals that grew out of Alexander's life makes stimulating reading, but one must be cautioned against pressing these points too closely. This is highly interpretative.

284. Wilcken introduces here a fascinating problem, and a complex one. Perhaps one general observation may be permitted. It is certainly true that Alexander's conquest opened up the East to Mediterranean, especially Greek, trade. Yet it is problematic how many Greek or Roman traders ever got beyond Alexander's, or even Augustus', empire. Greek and Roman commerce was still largely confined to the Mediterranean and the lands immediately adjacent. Trade with India and East Asia apparently was carried on through middlemen, primarily local people. The analogy with the opening of the New World should not be forced. New World commerce was at first controlled by European interests, but then by a combination of European and American interests. Except for the Near East, there never occurred the extensive conjunction of Mediterranean and Oriental interests akin to those of Europe and the New World. The unity of the economic

sphere of the ancient Mediterranean stretched roughly from the Atlantic to the Persian Gulf. India, East Asia, and inner Africa, while supplying special items, cannot be considered a part of that sphere. See M. Rostovtzeff, *The Social and Economic History of the Hellenistic World*, II (Oxford, 1941), 1238–48. Also see Donald F. Lach, *Asia in the Making of Europe*, I (Chicago, 1965), 11–19, for an overview of East-West contacts in the Hellenistic and Roman periods. Lach's notes include bibliography on detailed works dealing specifically with trade between the Mediterranean and India and China.

307. Burn (*Alex.*, p. 207), in an only slightly different context, suggests that one of the reasons why Alexander's plans for an international commonwealth failed was that there simply were not enough Macedonians and Greeks to crush local particularism.

309. On the nature of the diffusion of Hellenism among the peoples of the eastern Mediterranean, see Hadas, *Hellenistic Culture,* chapters II–VIII, *passim,* which contain materials on the Jews' response to Greek influences.

310. On the portraits of Alexander himself see Bieber, *Alexander the Great in Greek and Roman Art.*

319. It might be observed that Paul of Tarsus was among the best representatives of the age which Alexander, his successors, and Rome produced. Paul was a Hellenized Jew and a Roman citizen. He was, therefore, superbly suited by ethnic origin and religious background, by education, and by citizenship, to act as the articulator of the new belief. It was Paul, the embodiment of the *oikoumene* (personified in a way that perhaps Alexander might never have imagined), who combined elements of Hebrew theology, the teachings of Jesus, and oriental mysticism with the universally intelligible vehicle of the Greek language and systematic thought, and spread the faith throughout a world made secure for him through the medium of his Roman citizenship.

322. On the Greek influences in the development of Buddha in human form see Tarn, *Greeks in Bactria and India*, pp. 396–408.

324. On the early versions of Pseudo-Callisthenes see the valuable account of F. P. Magoun, *The Gests of King Alexander of Macedon* (Cambridge, Mass., 1929). An important recent study of the sources and transmission of the Romance is by Reinhold Merkelbach, *Die Quellen des griechischen Alexanderroman* (Munich, 1954). On the tradition of Alexander in the Middle Ages see George Cary, *The Medieval Alexander* (Cambridge, 1956).

BIBLIOGRAPHY

The following bibliography represents a collection of materials of some importance or interest, concentrating mainly on works published since the appearance of Wilcken's *Alexander*. No attempt has been made to make it complete, although all the works mentioned in the new notes for this edition are cited for reference purposes. On the earlier period of modern scholarship one should check Tarn's bibliography at the end of the sixth volume of the *Cambridge Ancient History*. Also see G. Walser, "Zur neueren Forschung über Alexander den Grossen," *Schweizer Beiträge zur allgemeinen Geschichte*, XIV (1956), 156–89, for a number of recent studies, as well as a fine summary of the progress of modern Alexander scholarship. Walser's article has been reprinted in G. T. Griffith (ed.), *Alexander the Great. The Main Problems* (Cambridge, 1966), with some additional bibliographical notations by Griffith (hereinafter cited "Griffith: *Main Problems*"). The topical arrangement of works in Walser seems to me to be well-suited to bibliographical purposes, and I have depended in part on it in the organization of my own listings.

GENERAL WORKS ON ALEXANDER

Benoist-Méchin, Jacques. *Alexander the Great. The Meeting of East and West.* Trans. from the French by M. Ilford. New York, 1966.

Burn, A. R. *Alexander the Great and the Hellenistic World.* New York, 1962.

Glotz, G., and Cohen, R. *Histoire Grecque.* Vol. IV, Part 1. *Alexandre et le démembrement de son Empire.* Paris, 1938.

Radet, Georges. *Alexandre le Grand.* 6th ed., Paris, 1950.

Robinson, C. A., Jr. *Alexander the Great. Conqueror and Creator of a New World.* New York, 1963.

Robinson, C. A., Jr. *Alexander the Great. Meeting of East and West in World Government and Brotherhood.* New York, 1947.

Savill, Agnes. *Alexander the Great and His Time.* 3rd ed., London, 1959.

Schachermeyr, Fritz. *Alexander der Grosse. Ingenium und Macht.* Graz, 1949.

Snyder, John W. *Alexander the Great.* New York, 1966.

Tarn. W. W. *Alexander the Great.* Vols. I and II. Cambridge, 1948.

Weigall, Arthur. *Alexander the Great.* New York, 1933.

HISTORIOGRAPHY AND METHODOLOGY

Badian, E. "The Eunuch Bagoas," *Classical Quarterly*, N.S. VIII (1958), 144–57.

Brown, Truesdell S. "Clitarchus," *American Journal of Philology*, LXX (1950), 134–55.

Brown, Truesdell S. *Onesicritus. A Study in Hellenistic Historiography*. Berkeley and Los Angeles, 1949.

Hamilton, J. R. "Cleitarchus and Aristobulus," *Historia*, X (1961), 448–58.

Jacoby, F. *Die Fragmente der griechischen Historiker*. Vols. IIB and IID. Berlin, 1927–30.

Kornemann, Ernst. *Die Alexandergeschichte des Königs Ptolemaios I von Aegypten*. Berlin, 1935.

Pearson, Lionel. "The Diary and Letters of Alexander the Great," *Historia*, III (1955), 429–55 (reprinted in Griffith: *Main Problems*).

Pearson, Lionel. *The Lost Histories of Alexander the Great*. New York, 1960.

Robinson, C. A., Jr. *The Ephemerides of Alexander's Expedition*. Providence, 1932.

Robinson, C. A., Jr. *The History of Alexander the Great*. Vols. I and II. Providence, 1953–63.

Samuel, Alan. "Alexander's Royal Journals," *Historia*, XIV (1965), 1–12.

Tod, M. *A Selection of Greek Historical Inscriptions*. Vol. II. Oxford, 1948.

Todd, Richard. "W. W. Tarn and the Alexander Ideal," *The Historian*, XXVII (1964), 48–55.

ADMINISTRATION AND FINANCES

Altheim, Franz. *Alexander und Asiens. Geschichte eines geistigen Erbes*. Tübingen, 1953.

Badian, E. "The Administration of the Empire," *Greece and Rome*, 2nd ser., XII (1965), 166–82.

Badian, E. "Alexander the Great and the Greeks of Asia," *Ancient Society and Institutions. Studies Presented to Victor Ehrenberg*, pp. 37–69. Oxford, 1966.

Badian, E. "Harpalus," *Journal of Hellenic Studies*, LXXXI (1961), 16–43 (reprinted in Griffith: *Main Problems*).

Bellinger, A. R. *Essays on the Coinage of Alexander the Great*. American Numismatic Society, *Numismatic Studies*, No. 11. New York, 1963.

Berve, Helmut. *Das Alexanderreich auf prosopographischer Grund-*

lage. Vols. I and II. Munich, 1926.

Cary, M. "A Constitution of the United States of Greece," *Classical Quarterly,* XVII (1923), 137–48.

Ehrenberg, Victor. *Alexander and the Greeks.* Oxford, 1938 (Ehrenberg's chapter on *pothos* reprinted in Griffith: *Main Problems*).

Kleiner, Gerhard. *Alexanders Reichsmünzen. Abhandlungen der deutschen Akademie der Wissenschaften zu Berlin.* Philosophisch-historische Klasse. Jahrgang, 1947, Nr. 5. Berlin, 1949.

Larsen, J. A. O. *Representative Government in Greek and Roman History.* Berkeley, 1955.

Roebuck, Carl. "The Settlements of Philip II with the Greek States in 338 B.C.," *Classical Philology,* XLIII (1948), 73–92.

MILITARY AFFAIRS

Adcock, F. E. *The Greek and Macedonian Art of War.* Berkeley and Los Angeles, 1957.

Brunt, P. A. "Alexander's Macedonian Cavalry," *Journal of Hellenic Studies,* LXXXIII (1963), 27–45.

Burn, A. R. "The Generalship of Alexander," *Greece and Rome,* 2nd ser., XII (1965), 140–54.

Burn, A. R. "Notes on Alexander's Campaigns," *Journal of Hellenic Studies,* LXXII (1952), 84–91.

Fuller, J. F. C. *The Generalship of Alexander the Great.* New Brunswick, N. J., 1960.

Griffith, G. T. "Alexander's Generalship at Gaugamela," *Journal of Hellenic Studies,* LXVII (1947), 77–89.

Griffith, G. T. "A Note on the Hipparchies of Alexander," *Journal of Hellenic Studies,* LXXXIII (1963), 68–74.

Marsden, E. W. *The Campaigns of Gaugamela.* Liverpool, 1964.

Narain, A. K. "Alexander and India," *Greece and Rome,* 2nd ser., XII (1965), 155–65.

RELIGION AND IDEAS

Badian, E. "Alexander the Great and the Creation of an Empire," *History Today,* VIII (1958), 369–76, 494–502.

Badian, E. "Alexander the Great and the Loneliness of Power," *Studies in Greek and Roman History,* pp. 192–205. New York, 1964.

Badian, E. "Alexander the Great and the Unity of Mankind," *Historia,* VII (1958), 425–44 (reprinted in Griffith: *Main Problems*).

Balsdon, J. P. V. D. "The 'Divinity' of Alexander," *Historia,* I (1950), 363–88 (reprinted in Griffith: *Main Problems*).

Brunt, P. A. "The Aims of Alexander," *Greece and Rome,* 2nd ser., XII (1965), 205–15.

Hampl, F. "Alexanders des Grossen *Hypomnemata* und letzte Pläne," *Studies Presented to D. M. Robinson*, pp. 816–29. St. Louis, 1953.

Hogarth, E. G. "The Deification of Alexander the Great," *English Historical Review*, II (1887), 317–29.

Robinson, C. A., Jr. "Alexander's Plans," *American Journal of Philology*, LXI (1940), 402–12.

Robinson, C. A., Jr. "The Extraordinary Ideas of Alexander the Great," *American Historical Review*, LXII (1957), 326–44 (reprinted in Griffith: *Main Problems*).

Schachermeyr, Fritz. "Die letzten Pläne Alexanders des Grossen," *Jahreshefte des österreichischen archaeologischen Institutes*, XLI (1954), 118–40 (reprinted in Griffith: *Main Problems*).

Tarn, W. W. "Alexander's Plans," *Journal of Hellenic Studies*, LIX (1939), 124–35.

Tarn, W. W. "Alexander the Great and the Unity of Mankind," *Proceedings of the British Academy*, XIX (1933), 123–66 (reprinted in Griffith: *Main Problems*).

Welles, C. B. "Alexander's Historical Achievement," *Greece and Rome*, 2nd ser., XII (1965), 216–28.

Wilcken, Ulrich. "Die letzten Pläne Alexanders des Grossen," *Sitzungsberichte des preussischen Akademie der Wissenschaften.* Philosophisch-historische Klasse, pp. 192–207. Berlin, 1937.

SPECIAL PROBLEMS

Badian, E. "The Death of Parmenio," *Transactions of the American Philological Association*, XCI (1960), 324–38.

Badian, E. "The Death of Philip," *Phoenix*, XVII (1963), 244–50.

Brown, Truesdell S. "Callisthenes and Alexander," *American Journal of Philology*, LXX (1949), 225–48 (reprinted in Griffith: *Main Problems*).

Calderini, Aristide. *Dizionario dei nomi geografici e topografici dell'Egitto greco-romano.* Vol. I. Cairo, 1935.

Griffith, G. T. "The Macedonian Background," *Greece and Rome*, 2nd ser., XII (1965), 125–39.

Hamilton, J. R. "Alexander and His So-called Father," *Classical Quarterly*, N.S. III (1953), 151–57 (reprinted in Griffith: *Main Problems*).

Hamilton, J. R. "Alexander's Early Life," *Greece and Rome*, 2nd ser., XII (1965), 117–24.

Schmidt, Erich F. *The Treasury of Persepolis and Other Discoveries in the Homeland of the Achaemenians.* The Oriental Institute of the University of Chicago, Oriental Institute Communications, No. 21. Chicago, 1939.

Stark, Freya. *Alexander's Path from Caria to Cilicia.* London, 1958.

Stein, Sir Aurel. *On Alexander's Track to the Indus*. London, 1929.
Welles, C. B. "The Discovery of Sarapis and the Foundation of Alexandria," *Historia*, XI (1962), 271–98.

LATER REFLECTIONS

Bieber, Margaret. *Alexander the Great in Greek and Roman Art*. Chicago, 1964.
Cary, George. *The Mediaeval Alexander*. Cambridge, 1956.
Magoun, F. P. *The Gests of King Alexander of Macedon*. Cambridge, Mass., 1929.
Merkelbach, Reinhold. *Die Quellen des griechischen Alexanderroman*. Munich, 1954.
Pfister, F. "Alexander der Grosse. Die Geschichte seines Ruhms," *Historia*, XIII (1964), 37–79.
Woodcock, George. "The Indian Greeks," *History Today*, XII (1962), 558–67.

GENERAL BACKGROUND

Hadas, Moses. *Hellenistic Culture*. New York, 1959.
Lach, Donald F. *Asia in the Making of Europe*. Vol. I. Chicago, 1965.
Olmstead, A. T. *History of the Persian Empire*. Chicago, 1948.
Rostovtzeff, M. *The Social and Economic History of the Hellenistic World*. Vols. I–III. Oxford, 1941.
Tarn, W. W. *The Greeks in Bactria and India*. 2nd ed., Cambridge, 1951.
Tarn, W. W., and Griffith, G. T. *Hellenistic Civilization*, 3rd ed., London, 1952.

INDEX